D1568303

NATHANIEL HAWTHORNE:

A REFERENCE BIBLIOGRAPHY

1900-1971

With Selected Nineteenth Century Materials

Compiled by

Beatrice Ricks

Joseph D. Adams

Jack O. Hazlerig

Central Missouri State University
Warrensburg, Missouri

G. K. HALL & CO., 70 LINCOLN STREET, BOSTON, MASS.

1972

Library of Congress Cataloging in Publication Data

Ricks, Beatrice
    Nathaniel Hawthorne.

    1. Hawthorne, Nathaniel, 1804-1864--Bibliography.
I. Adams, Joseph D., joint author. II. Hazlerig,
Jack O., joint author. III. Title.
Z8393.R53   016.813'3   72-6535
ISBN 0-8161-1021-2

This publication is printed on permanent/durable acid-free paper.

ISBN 0-8161-1021-2

PREFACE

The bibliography is comprised mainly of two parts: a master-list of bibliographic items, alphabetically arranged, the items consecutively numbered; and an index where references are numerically listed under works and various topics.

The format is designed to (a) provide information about individual books and articles by and about Nathaniel Hawthorne, (b) reflect the history and development of interest in Hawthorne and his work, and (c) give direction to the use of this bibliography.

A few brief annotations have been inserted to indicate the area of study. Explication or critiques have not been offered; the aim is to bring together the bulk of scholarship directed toward Hawthorne study. Works whose titles reveal their subject matter, and works which have earned reputations as standard critical texts in Hawthorne scholarship are entered without comment.

The bibliography centers upon the period from 1900 to 1971, offering as nearly as possible a comprehensive coverage for this period. Some nineteenth century critical items have been included for scholarly and biographical interest.

Hawthorne's own writings, chronologically arranged, are divided into representative *Complete Collections*; representative *Par-*

tial Collections; Diaries, Letters, Notebooks; Romances, Collected Stories, Biography.

While renowned bibliographers have provided such compendia, the critical attention devoted to Hawthorne's work indicates a continuing fascination with his thought.

We wish to thank Mrs. Eloise P. Kibbie, Dr. Wasyl Huculak, and other members of the library staff of Central Missouri State University for their assistance.

Beatrice Ricks
Joseph D. Adams
Jack O. Hazlerig

TABLE OF CONTENTS

v

Masterlist of Bibliographic Entries

MASTERLIST OF BIBLIOGRAPHIC ENTRIES

1
Abcarian, Richard. "The Ending of 'Young Goodman Brown,'"
SSF, 3 (1966), 343-45.

2
Abel, Darrel. "Black Glove and Pink Ribbon: Hawthorne's
Metonymic Symbols," NEQ, 42 (1969), 163-80.

3 Abel, Darrel. "The Devil in Boston," PQ, 32 (1953), 366-81.

4
Abel, Darrel. "Giving Lustre to Gray Shadows: Hawthorne's
Potent Art," AL, 41 (1969), 373-88.

5
Abel, Darrel. "Hawthorne's Dimmesdale: Fugitive from Wrath,"
NCF, 11 (1956), 81-105.

6
Abel, Darrel. "Hawthorne's Hester," CE, 13 (1952), 303-09.

Hester typifies Romantic individualism which Hawthorne
opposes.

See Frederic I. Carpenter, "Scarlet A. Minus," CE, 5
(1944), 7-14; also reply of Frederic I. Carpenter, CE, 13
(1952), 457-58; and rejoinder of Darrel Abel, CE, 14
(1953), 54. See also "Hester the Romantic," in THE
SCARLET LETTER HANDBOOK by Seymour L. Gross, pp. 49-56.

7 Abel, Darrel. "Hawthorne's House of Tradition," SAQ, 52
(1953), 561-78.

8 Abel, Darrel. "Hawthorne's Pearl: Symbol and Character,"
ELH, 18 (1951), 50-66.

9 Abel, Darrel. "Hawthorne's SCARLET LETTER," NAR, 71 (1950),
135-48.

9.1 Abel, Darrel. "Hawthorne's THE SCARLET LETTER," Expl, 29
(1971), Item 62.

10 Abel, Darrel. "Hawthorne's Skepticism about Social Reform:
With Special Reference to THE BLITHEDALE ROMANCE,"
UKCR, 19 (1953), 181-93.

11   Abel, Darrel. THE IMMORTAL PILGRIM: AN ETHICAL INTERPRETATION
          OF HAWTHORNE'S FICTION. Diss. Mich.: 1949.

12
      Abel, Darrel. "Immortality vs. Mortality in SEPTIMIUS FELTON:
          Some Possible Sources," AL, 27 (1956), 566-70.

13
      Abel, Darrel. "Le Sage's Limping Devil and 'Mrs. Bullfrog,'"
          N&Q, 198 (1953), 165-66.

          A passage in Chapter III of Le Sage's THE DEVIL UPON
          TWO STICKS a possible source for Hawthorne's "Mrs.
          Bullfrog."

14   Abel, Darrel. "Literary Consummations I: Massachusetts and
          Virginia," in AMERICAN LITERATURE. Vol. II: LITERATURE
          OF THE ATLANTIC CULTURE. Greak Neck, New York:
          Barron's Educ. Ser., 1963, pp. 186-208.

          Rev. by Gay Wilson Allen, AL, 36 (1965), 545-56.

15   Abel, Darrel. "A Masque of Love and Death," UTQ, 23 (1953),
          9-25.

16   Abel, Darrel. "Modes of Ethical Sensibility in Hawthorne,"
          MLN, 68 (1953), 80-86.

16.1 Abel, Darrel. "'A More Imaginative Pleasure': Hawthorne on
          the Play of Imagination," ESQ, 55 (1969), 63-71.

17   Abel, Darrel. "The Theme of Isolation in Hawthorne,"
          Person, 32 (January,1951), 42-59; (April, 1951), 182-90.

          Moral existence depends upon maintaining a balance
          between the real and the ideal, self and society.

18   Abel, Darrel. "'This Troublesome Mortality': Hawthorne's
          Marbles and Bubbles," SIR, 8 (1969), 193-97.

18.1 Abel, Darrel. "'A Vast Deal of Human Sympathy': Idea and
          Device in Hawthorne's 'The Snow-Image,'" Criticism, 4
          (1970), 316.32.

19   Abel, Darrel. "Who Wrote Hawthorne's Autobiography?"
          AL, 28 (1956), 73-77.

20   An Account of the First Reunion of the Descendents of
          Major William, and John Hathorne Held at Salem, Mass.,
          June 23, 1904, EIHC, 41 (1905), 77-92.

21 Adams, Charles Francis. "Hawthorne," NAR, 71 (July, 1850), 135-48.

An early opinion of Hawthorne.

22 Adams, Charles Francis. "Hawthorne's Place in Literature." In Hawthorne Centenary Celebration at the Wayside, 1905, pp. 42-76.

23 Adams, James Truslow. THE EPIC OF AMERICA. Garden City, N. Y.: Blue Ribbon Bks., 1941, pp. 197, 325.

Hawthorne left us "a classic of the Puritan heart."

24 Adams, John F. "Hawthorne's Symbolic Gardens," TSLL, 5 (1963), 242-54.

24.1 Adams, Joseph D. INITIATION RITUAL IN THE SHORT FICTION OF NATHANIEL HAWTHORNE. Diss.: Lehigh, 1972.

Division of initiations (1) into society, (2) into religious communities, and (3) into love.

25 Adams, Raymond. "Hawthorne and a Glimpse of Walden," EIHC, 94 (1958), 191-93.

26 Adams, Richard P. "American Renaissance: An Epistemological Problem," ESQ, 35 (1964), 2-7.

27 Adams, Richard P. "The Apprenticeship of William Faulkner," TSE, 12 (1962), 113-56.

Faulkner influenced by his early reading of Hawthorne.

28 Adams, Richard P. "Hawthorne: THE OLD MANSE Period," TSE, 8 (1958), 115-51.

29 Adams, Richard P. "Hawthorne: A Study of His Literary Development," DA, 11 (Columbia: 1951), 3.

30 Adams, Richard P. "Hawthorne's PROVINCIAL TALES," NEQ, 30 (1957), 39-57.

31 Adams, Richard P. "Romanticism and the American Renaissance," AL, 23 (1951-52), 419-32.

Thinks the greatest works of early American Romanticism are not those of Emerson and Hawthorne.

32 Aderman, Ralph M. "The Case of James Cook: A Study of
   Political Influence in 1840," EIHC, 92 (1956), 59-67.

   An account of pressure brought by Hawthorne, et al, on
   Paulding to release Cook from the navy.

33 Aderman, Ralph M. NATHANIEL HAWTHORNE'S ENGLISH REPUTATION
   TO 1904. Diss. Wis.: 1951.

34 Aderman, Ralph M. "Newly Located Hawthorne Letters,"
   EIHC, 88 (1952), 163-65.

   Three letters of 1855 in the John Rylands Library.

35 Adkins, Nelson F. "The Early Projected Works of Nathaniel
   Hawthorne," PBSA, 39 (1945), 119-55.

   Discussion of various aspects of "The Story Teller."

36 Adkins, Nelson F. "Hawthorne's Democratic New England
   Puritans," ESQ, 44 (1966), 66-72.

37 Adkins, Nelson F. "Notes on the Hawthorne Canon," PBSA, 60
   (1966), 364-67.

38 Adkins, Nelson F. "Hawthorne's 'Snow Image,'" Colophon, 1
   (1936), 611-12.

39 [Alcott, Bronson] THE JOURNALS OF BRONSON ALCOTT. Sel. and ed.
   by Odell Shepard. Boston: Little Brown & Co., 1938.

40 Alden, John. "Hawthorne and William Henry Smith: An Essay
   in Anglo-American Bibliography," BookC, 5 (1956),
   370-74.

41 Allen, John D. "Behind 'The Minister's Black Veil,'" in
   ESSAYS IN MEMORY OF CHRISTINE BURLESON IN LANGUAGE AND
   LITERATURE BY FORMER COLLEAGUES AND STUDENTS.
   Thomas G. Burton, ed. Johnson City: Res. Advisory
   Council, East Tennessee State U., 1969.

42 Allen, M. L. "The Black Veil: Three Versions of a Symbol,"
   ES, 47 (1966), 286-289.

   Symbol of the black veil used in UDOLPHO and in
   stories by Dickens and Hawthorne.

43 Allen, M. L. "Hawthorne's Art in His Short Stories," SA, 7
     (1961), 9-41.

43.1 Allen, Margaret V. "Imagination and History in Hawthorne's
     'Legends of the Province House,'" AL, 43 (1971), 432-37.

44 Allen, Walter. THE URGENT WEST: THE AMERICAN DREAM AND
     MODERN MAN. New York: Dutton, 1969.

     Hawthorne's characters in a realm where moral law
     prevails.

     Rev. by Richard Lehan, NCF, 24 (1969), 123-26.

45 Allison, Alexander W. "The Literary Contexts of 'My
     Kinsman, Major Molineux,'" NCF, 23 (1968), 304-11.

45.1 Alsen, Eberhard. "The Ambitious Experiment of Dr. Rappaccini,"
     AL, 43 (1971), 430-31.

46 Alsen, Eberhard. "Hawthorne: A Puritan Tieck: A Compara-
     tive Analysis of the Tales of Hawthorne and the
     Märchen of Tieck," DA, 28 (Ind.: 1967), 2199A.

47 Altick, Richard D. THE ART OF LITERARY RESEARCH. New York:
     W. W. Norton & Co., 1963, pp. 52, 120-21, 157, 164.

48 Altick, Richard D. THE SCHOLAR ADVENTURERS. New York:
     The Free Press, 1950.

49 AMERICAN LITERARY MANUSCRIPTS: A CHECKLIST OF HOLDINGS IN
     ACADEMIC, HISTORICAL, AND PUBLIC LIBRARIES IN THE UNITED
     STATES. Comp. by Committee on Manuscript Holdings,
     Amer. Lit. Group, Mod. Lang. Assn. of Amer. Austin:
     Tex. U. P., 1960.

     Rev. by Albrecht, Robert C., NEQ, 35 (1962), 266-68.

50 American Literature Group of the Modern Language Association.
     REPORT OF THE COMMITTEE ON TRENDS IN RESEARCH IN AMERICAN
     LITERATURE, 1940-1950. Baton Rouge, La.: Louisiana St.
     U., [1951]

     See rev. by Jay B. Hubbell, AL, 23 (1951-52), 390-91.

51 Anderson, Charles R. "Person, Place, and Thing in James's THE
     PORTRAIT OF A LADY," in ESSAYS ON AMERICAN LITERATURE IN
     HONOR OF JAY B. HUBBELL. Clarence Gohdes, ed. Durham,
     N. C.: Duke U. P., 1967, pp. 179-80.

     Hawthorne compared with James.

52 Anderson, D. K., Jr.   "Hawthorne's Crowds," NCF, 7 (1952),
39-50.

To think Hawthorne indifferent to society is to overlook
his use of crowds.

53 Anderson, George K.   THE LEGEND OF THE WANDERING JEW.
Providence: Brown U. P., 1965.

The "Wandering Jew" motif in "A Virtuoso's Collection,"
"A Select Party," and "Ethan Brand," shows Hawthorne's
variation of theme.

54 Anderson, Norman A.   "'Rappaccini's Daughter': A Keatsian
Analogue?" PMLA, 83 (1968), 271-283.

Story has textual and allegorical parallels to
Keats's "Lamia."

54.1 Anderson, Quentin.   "Hawthorne's Boston," THE IMPERIAL SELF:
AN ESSAY IN AMERICAN LITERARY AND CULTURAL HISTORY.
New York: Knopf, 1971, pp. 59-87.

55 Anderson, Quentin.   "Henry James and the New Jerusalem,"
KR, 8 (1946), 515-66.

56 Anderson, Quentin.   THE AMERICAN HENRY JAMES. New Brunswick,
N. J.: Rutgers U. P., 1957.

Comparison of Hawthorne and James. Notes that
PROFESSOR FARGO is reminiscent of THE BLITHEDALE ROMANCE.

57 Anderson, Quentin. gen. ed.   HISTORY OF AMERICAN LITERATURE.
New York: Collier Bks., 1962.

58 Anderson, Quentin.   "Introduction," TWICE-TOLD TALES AND
OTHER SHORT STORIES. New York: Washington Square P.,
1960.

59 Angoff, Charles.   "Introduction," THE HOUSE OF THE SEVEN
GABLES. Charles Angoff, ed. Fine Editions Club,
1956.

60 Angoff, Charles.   A LITERARY HISTORY OF THE AMERICAN PEOPLE.
New York: Knopf, 1931, I, 391.

61 Anna, Sister, S. H.   "Eldorado in Salem," EJ, 35 (1946), 153-5.

62 Anon. "Catalog of Portraits in the Essex Institute," EIHC, 71 (1935), 150-51.

No. 123 a portrait of Hawthorne.

63 Anon. "A Century of THE SCARLET LETTER," PubW, 157 (1950), 1203, 1691.

64 Anon. "Contemporary Literature," NBR, 53 (1870), 149-50.

64.1 Anon. "Exquisite Beauty of Finish," HarpNMM, 2 (1851), 854-55. Excerpted in STUDIES IN THE HOUSE OF THE SEVEN GABLES. Roger LAsselineau, Comp. Columbus, Ohio: Charles E. Merrill Studies, 1970, pp. 7-8.

65 Anon. "Hawthorne and Thoreau," TPWk, 6 (1905), 369.

66 Anon. "The Hawthorne Statue," Atl, 94 (1904), 140-41.

67 Anon. "The Light and the Dark," TLS (September 29, 1961), 637-38.

68 Anon. "The Literary Artist in America," TLS (August 17, 1956), xx-xxi.

69 Anon. "Nathaniel Hawthorne," N&Q, 8 (1961), 203.

70 Anon. NYT, September 13, 1948, p. 16.

News story of discovery by Samuel T. Sukel of Pittsfield, Mass., of fourteen hitherto unknown stories by Hawthorne.

71 Anon. "Puritan Romancer," TLS, 2495 (1949), 770.

72 Arader, Harry F. "American Novelists in Italy: Hawthorne, Howells, James, and Crawford," DA, 13 (Pa.: 1953), 791-92.

73 Archer, Susan M. "Hawthorne's Use of Spenser," DA, 28 (Pa.: 1967), 1424A.

74 Arden, Eugene. "Hawthorne's 'Case of Arthur D,'" AI, 18 (1961), 45-55.

75 Armes, William D. "Hawthorne, Cilley, and Fancy's Show-Box," **Nation.** 88 (1909), 356-57.

75.1 Armour, Richard. "Nathaniel Hawthorne," and "THE SCARLET LETTER - An A for Effort," in THE CLASSICS RECLASSIFIED. Illustrated by Campbell Grant. New York: Bantam Books, Pathfinder Editions. 1960, pp. 59-62, 63-75.

An "irreverent retelling" of Hawthorne's classic.

76 Arnavon, Cyrille. HISTOIRE LITTÉRAIRE DES ETAS-UNIS. Paris: Librairie Hachette, 1953.

77 Arner, Robert D. "Hawthorne and Jones Very: Two Dimensions of Satire in 'Egotism; or, the Bosom Serpent,'" NEQ. 42 (1969), 267-75.

77.1 Arner, Robert D. "Of Snakes and Those Who Swallow Them: Some Folk Analogues for Hawthorne's 'Egotism; or The Bosom Serpent,'" SFQ. 35 (1971), 336-46.

78 Arnold, Armin. D. H. LAWRENCE AND AMERICA. London: Linden P., 1958; New York: Philosophical Library, 1959, pp. 66-74.

79 Arnold, Armin, ed. THE SYMBOLIC MEANING: THE UNCOLLECTED VERSIONS OF "STUDIES IN CLASSIC AMERICAN LITERATURE." Fontwell, Arundel, England: Centaur P., 1962; New York: Viking, 1964.

80 Arnold, Armin. "The Transcendental Element in American Literature: A Study of Some Unpublished D. H. Lawrence Manuscripts," MP, 60 (1962), 41-46.

81 Arnold, William Harris. "First Editions of Hawthorne," in FIRST EDITIONS OF BRYANT, EMERSON, HAWTHORNE,.... Jamaica, New York: Marion Press, 1901, pp. 21-29.

82 Arnold, William Harris. VENTURES IN BOOK COLLECTING. New York: Charles Scribner's Sons, 1923), 3, 5ff.

83 Arthos, John. "Hawthorne in Florence," MALQ, 59 (1953), 118-29.

84 Arthos, John. "THE SCARLET LETTER Once More," BSTCF, 5 (1964), 31-38.

A study of the dual forces of Enlightenment and Puritanism.

[85]Arvin, Newton. HAWTHORNE. Boston: 1929; New York: Russell & Russell, 1961.

85.1
Arvin, Newton. "Nathaniel Hawthorne," AMERICAN PANTHEON. Daniel Aaron and Sylvan Schendler, eds. New York: Delacorte P., A Seymour Lawrence Book, 1966, pp. 60-105.

"The Relevance of Hawthorne," pp. 60-69;
"New Pigment for an Old Canvas," pp. 69-73;
"Hawthorne's Journals," pp. 73-81;
"Hawthorne's Tales," pp. 82-96;
"The Unfinished Window," pp. 97-105.

[86] Arvin, Newton, ed. HAWTHORNE'S SHORT STORIES. New York: Knopf, 1946; Vintage, 1955.

Selections, with an Introduction on Hawthorne's themes and art.

[87]Arvin, Newton, ed. THE HEART OF HAWTHORNE'S JOURNALS. Boston and New York: Houghton Mifflin Co., 1929; repr., Barnes & Noble, Inc., 1967.

Rev. by Stanley T. Williams, AL, 1 (1929-30), 219-21.

[88]Arvin, Newton. "Introduction," THE SCARLET LETTER. New York: Harper's Modern Classics, 1950.

[89]Arvin, Newton. "The Relevance of Hawthorne," NSt, 7 (1928), 3-5.

A study suggested by the "new nationalists," especially Mumford's THE GOLDEN DAY.

[90]Ashton, Leonora Sill. "The Man Who Loved the Fall," Instr, 45 (1936), 61, 69.

[91]Askew, Melvin W. "Hawthorne, the Fall, and the Psychology of Maturity," AL, 34 (1962), 335-43.

Hawthorne treats fall of man from an Adamic existence not in theological but in psychological terms. The psychological process carries with it the theological correlatives of felix culpa and the disintegration of Eden. Some stories deal with the fall accompanied by failure to achieve maturity.

[92] Askew, Melvin W. "The Pseudonymic American Hero," BuR, 10 (1962), 224-31.

On name-changing in Hawthorne and others.

93 Askew, Melvin W. "The Wounded Artist and His Work,"
    KM (1961), 73-77.

> Artists eternalize psychological problems and thus
> control them. Hawthorne, thus, deals with his own
> schizoid tendencies in "Wakefield."

94 Asselineau, Roger. "Hawthorne Abroad," in HAWTHORNE
    CENTENARY ESSAYS. Roy Harvey Pearce, ed. Columbus,
    Ohio: Ohio St. U. P., 1964, pp. 367-85.

95 Asselineau, Roger. "Hawthorne Abroad," LanM, 59 (1965), 156-63.

95.1 Asselineau, Roger, Compiler. STUDIES IN THE HOUSE OF THE
    SEVEN GABLES. Columbus, Ohio: Charles E. Merrill
    Studies. Charles E. Merrill Publishing Co., 1972.

96 Astrov, Vladmir. "Hawthorne and Dostoievski as Explorers of
    the Human Conscience," NEQ, 15 (1942), 296-319.

> Hawthorne as critic of conventional morality.

97 Atkins, Lois. "Psychological Symbolism of Guilt and
    Isolation in Hawthorne," AI, 11 (1954), 417-25.

98 Austin, Allen. "Distortion in 'THE (Complete) SCARLET LETTER,'"
    CE, 23 (1961), 61.

> See: Sam S. Baskett, "Reply," CE, 23 (1961), 62;
> and "THE (Complete) SCARLET LETTER," CE, 22 (1961),
> 321-88; W. R. Moses, "A Further Note on 'The Custom
> House,'" CE, 23 (1962), 396.

99 Austin, Allen. "Hester Prynne's Plan of Escape: The Moral
    Problem," UKCR, 28 (1962), 317-18.

100 Austin, Allen. "Satire and Theme in THE SCARLET LETTER,"
    PQ, 41 (1962), 508-11.

> Hawthorne ridicules hardheartedness of Puritan rulers
> in order to point up necessity of compassion.

101 Austin, Gabriel C. A DESCRIPTIVE GUIDE TO THE EXHIBITION
    COMMEMORATING THE DEATH OF NATHANIEL HAWTHORNE. New York:
    Grolier Club, 1964.

102 Austin, James C. FIELDS OF THE ATLANTIC MONTHLY: LETTERS TO AN EDITOR, 1861-1870. San Marino, Calif.: Huntington Lib., 1953.

103 Austin, James C. "The Hawthorne and Browning Acquaintance: Including an Unpublished Browning Letter," VN, 20 (1961), 13-18.

See Lionel Stevenson, "The Hawthorne and Browning Acquaintance: An Addendum," VN, 21 (1962), 16.

104 /List of/ Autograph Letters and Manuscripts of /Nathaniel Hawthorne/, EIHC, 41 (1905), 99-110.

105 Bacon, Edwin Monroe. "Hawthorne at 'The Wayside,'" LITERARY PILGRIMAGES IN NEW ENGLAND. Boston, Chicago: Silver, Burdect & Co., 1902, pp. 402-14.

106 Bacon, Edwin Monroe. "Hawthorne's Salem," LITERARY PILGRIMAGES IN NEW ENGLAND. Boston, Chicago: Silver, Burdett & Co., 1902, pp. 200-18.

107 Bacon, Edwin Monroe. "In Maine's Chief College Town," LITERARY PILGRIMAGES IN NEW ENGLAND. Silver: 1902, pp. 163-66.

108 Bader, Arno L. "Those Mesmeric Victorians," Colophon, n. s. 3 (1938), 335-53.

Hawthorne, the "most inclined to mesmerism."

109 Baker, Paul R. THE FORTUNATE PILGRIMS: AMERICANS IN ITALY, 1800-1860. Cambridge: Harvard U. P., 1964.

Rev. by E. P. Richardson, NEQ, 37 (1964), 546-48.

110 Baldensperger, Fernand. "A Propos de 'Nathaniel Hawthorne en France,'" MLN, 56 (1941), 343-45.

111 Bales, Allen. "A Study of Point of View in the Novels of Nathaniel Hawthorne," DA, 20 (Northwestern: 1960), 3724.

112 Bales, Kent R. "Nathaniel Hawthorne's Use of the Sublime," DA, 28 (Calif., Berkeley: 1968), 4162A-63A.

113 Ballowe, James. "Mythic Vision in American Literature," Discourse, 10 (1967), 324-32.

114 Bank, Stanley. "Nathaniel Hawthorne's BLITHEDALE ROMANCE:
A Pivotal Work for Studying American Literature,"
DA, 28 (Columbia: 1967), 663A-64A.

114.1 Bank, Stanley, ed. "Nathaniel Hawthorne: The Truth of the
Human Heart," in his AMERICAN ROMANTICISM: A SHAPE
FOR FICTION. New York: Putnam's, 1969, pp. 244-88.

114.2 Barnes, Daniel R. "'Physical Fact' and Folklore: Hawthorne's
'Egotism; or The Bosom Serpent,'" AL, 43 (1971), 117-21.

115 Barnett, Gene A. "Art as Setting in THE MARBLE FAUN,"
TWA, 54 (1965), 231-47.

116 Barnett, Gene A. "Hawthorne's Italian Calendar," ESQ, 43
(1966), 68-70.

117 Barnett, Gene A. "Hawthorne's Italian Towers," SIR, 3 (1964),
252-56.

118 Barnett, Gene A. "Hawthorne's Use of Setting in His Major
Novels," DA, 22 (Wis.: 1961), 1991-92.

119 Barrett, C. Waller. "Gleanings in a Field of Stubble,"
AuCJ, 4 (1952), 5-11.

120 Barrett, C. Waller. ITALIAN INFLUENCE ON AMERICAN LITERATURE.
New York: Grolier Club, 1962,

121 Barrie, James M. Letter from James M. Barrie, dated
December 5, 1903, stating that Hawthorne is America's
greatest man of letters. EIHC, 41 (1905), 68.

122 Barrows, Herbert. SUGGESTIONS FOR TEACHING "15" STORIES.
Boston: Heath, 1950, pp. 17-19.

123 Barth, J. Robert. "Faulkner and the Calvinist Tradition,"
Thought, 39 (1964), 100-20.

124 Bartlett, I. H. "The Democratic Imagination," in THE
AMERICAN MIND IN THE MID-NINETEENTH CENTURY. New York:
Thomas Y. Crowell Co., 1967, pp. 94-113.

See particularly "Nathaniel Hawthorne: The Democrat
as Puritan," pp. 105-109.

125 Bashore, James Robert, Jr. "The Villains in the Major Works of Nathaniel Hawthorne and Henry James," DA, 19 (Wis.: 1959), 2939.

126 Baskett, Sam S. "THE (Complete) SCARLET LETTER," CE, 22 (1961), 321-28.

The importance of "The Custom House."

127 Baskett, Sam S. "Reply," CE, 23 (1961), 62.

Reply to Allen Austin's "Distortion in 'THE (Complete) SCARLET LETTER," CE, 23 (1961), 61.

128 Baskett, Sam S., and Theodore B. Strandness. "The Skeptical Vein," THE AMERICAN IDENTITY: A COLLEGE READER. Boston: D. C. Heath, 1962.

Contains short biographical sketch and story "Young Goodman Brown."

128.1 Bassan, Maurice. "Nathaniel Hawthorne and His Son," HAWTHORNE'S SON: THE LIFE AND LITERARY CAREER OF JULIAN HAWTHORNE. Columbus, Ohio: Ohio St. U. P., 1970, pp. 3-35.

Rev. by Terence Martin, AL, 42 (1971), 585-86.
Rev. art., Barbara M. Tyson, "Father and Son: Julian Hawthorne as Heir and Interpreter," CEA, 33 (1971), 19.

129 Bassan, Maurice. "A New Account of Hawthorne's Last Days, Death and Funeral," AL, 27 (1956), 561-65.

Source is a letter from Sophia Hawthorne, September 4, 1864, to a former servant then resident in California.

130 Bassan, Maurice. "Julian Hawthorne Edits Aunt Ebe," EIHC, Special Hawthorne Issue, 100 (1964), 274-78.

131 Bassan, Maurice. "Papers of Julian Hawthorne at Yale," YULG, 39 (1964), 84-89.

132 Batchelor, Rev. Dr. George. "The Salem of Hawthorne's Time," EIHC, 84 (1948), 64-74.

133 Battaglia, Francis J. "THE HOUSE OF THE SEVEN GABLES: New Light on Old Problems," PMLA, 82 (1967), 579-90.

133.1 Battaglia, Frank. "THE (Unmeretricious) HOUSE OF THE SEVEN GABLES," SNNTS, 2 (1970), 468-73.

[134] Bates, K. L.   OUR OLD HOME.   New York: Crowell, 1912.

[135] Baughman, Ernest W.   "Public Confession and THE SCARLET
LETTER,"   NEQ, 40 (1967), 532-50.

[136] Baxter, Annette K.   "Independence vs. Isolation: Hawthorne
and James on the Problem of the Artist,"   NCF, 10 (1955),
225-31.

[137] Baym, Nina.   "THE BLITHEDALE ROMANCE: A Radical Reading,"
JEGP, 67 (1968), 545-69.

THE BLITHEDALE ROMANCE consistent with Hawthorne's
moral humanism but incoherent as a fictional structure.

[137.1] Baym, Nina.   "Hawthorne's Holgrave: The Failure of the
Artist-Hero,"   JEGP, 69 (1970), 584-98.

[137.2] Baym, Nina.   "Hawthorne's Women: The Tyranny of Social
Myths,"   CentR, 15 (1971), 250-72.

[138] Baym, Nina.   "The Head, the Heart, and the Unpardonable Sin,"
NEQ, 40 (1967), 31-47.

Critics mistake Hawthorne's sinners as acting through
"cold intellect."   Selfish passions motivate the
sinners, and they are described in hellfire imagery.

[138.1] Baym, Nina.   "THE MARBLE FAUN: Hawthorne's Elegy for Art,"
NEQ, 44 (1971), 355-76.

[139] Baym, Nina.   "Passion and Authority in THE SCARLET LETTER,"
NEQ, 43 (1970), 209-30.

[139.1] Beard, James Franklin.   "Introduction," THE HOUSE OF THE SEVEN
GABLES.   Barre, Mass.:   Imprint Society, 1970.

[140] Beatty, Lillian.   "Typee and Blithedale: Rejected Ideal
Communities,"   Person, 37 (1956), 367-78.

[141] Beatty, Richmond Croom, with Sculley Bradley, and E. Hudson
Long, co-eds.   THE SCARLET LETTER BY NATHANIEL HAWTHORNE:
AN ANNOTATED TEXT, BACKGROUNDS AND SOURCES, ESSAYS IN
CRITICISM.   New York: W. W. Norton & Co., 1961.

[142] Beaver, Harold.   "Introduction," in AMERICAN CRITICAL ESSAYS:
TWENTIETH CENTURY.   Harold Beaver, ed.   London: Oxford
U. P., 1959.

143 Becker, John E., S. J. "Hawthorne's Historical Allegory," DA, 30 (Yale: 1969), 715A.

143.1 Becker, John E. HAWTHORNE'S HISTORICAL ALLEGORY. New York: Kennikat Press, 1971.

144 Beebe, Maurice. "The Fall of the House of Pyncheon," NCF, 11 (1956), 1-17.

145 Beebe, Maurice. LITERARY SYMBOLISM. San Francisco: Wadsworth, 1960.

145.1 Beebe, Maurice, and Jack Hardie. "Criticism of Nathaniel Hawthorne: A Selected Checklist," SNNTS, 2 (1970), 519-87.

Excludes many pieces before 1930, foreign works, transient reviews, and "routine" discussion in reference books and histories of American literature.

146 Beers, Henry A. "Fifty Years of Hawthorne," YR, 4 (1915), 300-15.

147 Beers, Henry A. "Fifty Years of Hawthorne," in FOUR AMERICANS. New Haven: Yale U. P., 1920, pp. 33-57.

148 Beidler, Peter G. "Theme of the Fortunate Fall in THE MARBLE FAUN," ESQ, 47 (1967), 56-62.

149 "Belated Honors to Hawthorne in Salem," LitD, 46 (1913), 18-19.

Sketch given of the statue of Hawthorne by Bela L. Pratt which Salem proposed to erect.

150 "Belated Monument to Nathaniel Hawthorne," CurOp, 54 (1913), 140.

151 Belden, Henry Marvin. "Poe's Criticism of Hawthorne," Anglia, 23 (1901), 376-404.

152 Bell, John M. "Hawthorne's THE SCARLET LETTER: An Artist's Intuitive Understanding of Plague, Armor and Health," JOrg, 3 (1969), 102-15.

152.1 Bell, Michael Davitt. HAWTHORNE AND THE HISTORICAL ROMANCE OF NEW ENGLAND. Princeton: Princeton U. P., 1971.

Rev. by John McElroy, AL, 43 (1972), 658-59.

153 Bell, Millicent. "Hawthorne's 'Fire-Worship': Interpretation and Source," AL, 24 (1952), 31-39.

Domestic fire is a "half-conscious symbol of the old Puritan belief."

See Roy R. Male, "Criticism of Bell's 'Hawthorne's 'Fire-Worship':....'" AL, 25 (1953), 85-87.

154 Bell, Millicent. HAWTHORNE'S VIEW OF THE ARTIST. New York: New York St. U. P., 1962.

Revs. by Harry Hayden Clark, NEQ, 37 (1964), 108-10; Richard Coanda, Criticism, 6 (1964), 97-98; Richard Harter Fogle, AL, 35 (1963), 92-93; Sidney P. Moss, ABC, 3 (1963), 3; James Schroeder, CE, 24 (1963), 490; Arlin Turner, NCF, 17 (1963), 399-400.

155 Bell, Millicent. "Melville and Hawthorne at the Grave of St. John (A Debt to Pierre Bayle)," MLN, 67 (1952), 116-18.

156 Benét, William Rose, and Norman Holmes Pearson. "Nathaniel Hawthorne, 1804-1864," in THE OXFORD ANTHOLOGY OF AMERICAN LITERATURE. New York: Oxford U. P., 1941, pp. 400-42.

157 Bennett, James O'Donnell. "Hawthorne's THE SCARLET LETTER" in MUCH LOVED BOOKS: BEST SELLERS OF THE AGES. Liveright: 1927, pp. 103-08.

158 Benson, Adolph B. "Hawthorne's Sketch of Queen Christina: A Note," ScSt, 31 (1959), 166-67.

158.1 Benson, Eugene. "Poe and Hawthorne," Galaxy, 6 (1868), 742-48. Repr. in HAWTHORNE AMONG HIS CONTEMPORARIES. Kenneth W. Cameron, ed. Hartford, Conn.: Transcendental Books, 1968, pp. 120-23.

159 Bercovitch, Sacvan. "Diabolus in Salem," ELN, 6 (1969), 280-85.

Influence of Bunyan's THE HOLY WAR on Hawthorne's portrait of John Endicott.

160 Bercovitch, Sacvan. "Endicott's Breastplate: Symbolism and Typology in 'Endicott and the Red Cross,'" SSF, 4 (1967), 289-99.

By his use of typology, Hawthorne makes of the breastplate a metaphor that opens into a consumate "symbol of Puritanism."

161 Bercovitch, Sacvan. "The Frontier Fable of Hawthorne's MARBLE FAUN," SDR, 4 (1966), 44-50.

162 Bercovitch, Sacvan. "Hilda's 'Seven-Branched Allegory,'
an Echo from Cotton Mather in THE MARBLE FAUN,"
EALN, 1 (1966), 5-6.

163 Bercovitch, Sacvan. "Miriam as Shylock: An Echo from
Shakespeare in Hawthorne's MARBLE FAUN," FMLS, 5
(1969), 385-87.

164 Bercovitch, Sacvan. "Of Wise and Foolish Virgins: Hilda vs.
Miriam in Hawthorne's MARBLE FAUN," NEQ, 41 (1968),
281-86.

165 Berek, Peter. THE TRANSFORMATION OF ALLEGORY FROM SPENSER TO
HAWTHORNE. Amherst: Amherst Coll.P., 1962.

166 Bergeron, David M. "Arthur Miller's THE CRUCIBLE and
Nathaniel Hawthorne: Some Parallels," EJ, 58 (1969),
47-55.

Analogues between Miller's play and Hawthorne's work--
particularly THE SCARLET LETTER--appear in settings,
characters, themes.

166.1 Bergman, Herbert. "'The Interior of a Heart,' THE CRUCIBLE
and THE SCARLET LETTER," UCQ, 15 (1970), 27-32.

166.2 Berthold, Dennis A. HAWTHORNE AND THE AESTHETICS OF
IMPERFECTION. Diss. (Wis.: /1972/.

166.3 Betsky, Seymour. HAWTHORNE'S THE SCARLET LETTER: AN EXERCISE
IN EVALUATION. Utrecht /?/, 196? /?/

167 Bewley, Marius. THE COMPLEX FATE: HAWTHORNE, HENRY JAMES
AND SOME OTHER AMERICAN WRITERS, with Introduction and
Two Interpolations by F. R. Leavis. New York and
London: Chatto & Windus, 1952, 1954.

Rev. by Randall Stewart, AL, 26 (1955), 580-83.

168 Bewley, Marius. "Hawthorne and 'The Deeper Psychology,'"
Mandrake, 2 (1956), 366-73.

169 Bewley, Marius. "Hawthorne's Novels," THE ECCENTRIC DESIGN:
FORM IN THE CLASSIC AMERICAN NOVEL. New York: Columbia
U. P., 1959, pp. 147-86.

Rev. by Benjamin T. Spencer, AL, 31 (1959-60), 505-07.

[170] Bewley, Marius. "Hawthorne's Short Stories," THE ECCENTRIC DESIGN: FORM IN THE CLASSIC AMERICAN NOVEL. New York: Columbia U. P., 1950, pp. 113-86.

[171] Bewley, Marius. "James's Debt to Hawthorne," Scrutiny, 16 (Sept., 1949), 178-95; 16 (Winter, 1949), 301-17; 17 (Spring, 1950), 14-31.

Repr. in THE COMPLEX FATE. London: Chatto and Windus, 1952.

[172] Bewley, Marius. "Revaluations XVI: James Fenimore Cooper," Scrutiny, 19 (1952), 98-125.

[173] Bezanson, Walter E. "The Hawthorne Game: 'Graves and Goblins,'" ESQ, 54 (1969), 73-77.

[174] Bickford, Gail H. "Lovewell's Fight, 1725-1958," AQ, 10 (1958), 358-66.

A record of ballads, poems, historical accounts, and sermons that have memorialized Lovewell's legend.

[175] Bicknell, John W. "THE MARBLE FAUN Reconsidered," UKCK, 20 (1954), 193-99.

[176] Bier, Jesse. "Hawthorne and the Romance: His Prefaces Related and Examined," MP, 53 (1955), 17-24.

[177] Bier, Jesse. "Lapsarians on THE PRAIRIE: Cooper's Novel," TSLL, 4 (1962), 49-57.

In THE PRAIRIE Cooper closest to artistry of Hawthorne and Melville.

[178] Bier, Jesse. THE RISE AND FALL OF AMERICAN HUMOR. New York: Holt, Rinehart and Winston, 1968.

Rev. by Walter Blair, AL, 40 (1969), 551-53.

[179] Binder, Sister M. Claudia. STUDIEN ZUR CHARAKTERISIERUNGS-STECHNIK IN KURZGESCHICHTEN W. IRVING, E. A. POE, AND NATHANIEL HAWTHORNE. Diss. Graz.: 1950.

[180] Birdsall, Richard D. BERKSHIRE COUNTY: A CULTURAL HISTORY. New Haven: Yale U. P., 1959.

Berkshire was for a time a second home for many of the literary figures, including Hawthorne.

Rev. by Luther S. Mansfield, NEQ, 32 (1959), 279-81.

[181] Birdsall, Richard D. "Berkshire's Golden Age," AQ, 8 (1956), 328-55.

[182] Birdsall, Richard D. "The First Century of Berkshire County." BPLQ, 9 (1957), 20-39.

[183] Birdsall, Virginia Ogden. "Hawthorne's Fair-Haired Maidens: The Fading Light," PMLA, 75 (1960), 250-56.

Women like Phoebe, Priscilla, and Hilda represent not just innocuous females, but key elements of human relationships reflecting Hawthorne's view of human nature and of good and evil.

[184] Birdsall, Virginia Ogden. "Hawthorne's Oak Tree Image," NCF, 15 (1960), 181-85.

[185] Birkhead, Edith. THE TALE OF TERROR: A STUDY OF THE GOTHIC ROMANCE. London: Constable & Co., Ltd., 1921, pp. 203-13, passim.

[186] Birrell, Augustine. "Nathaniel Hawthorne," ET CETERA: A COLLECTION, &C. London: Chatto & Windus, 1930, pp. 199-222.

[187] Black, Stephen A. "THE SCARLET LETTER: Death by Symbols," Paunch, 24 (1965), 51-74.

[188] Blackmur, Richard Palmer. "American Literary Expatriate," THE LION AND THE HONEYCOMB: ESSAYS IN SOLITUDE AND CRITIQUE. New York: Harcourt, 1955, pp. 61-78.

[189] Blackmur, Richard Palmer. THE CELESTIAL RAILROAD AND OTHER STORIES: NATHANIEL HAWTHORNE. With Afterword by R. P. Blackmur. New York: New Amer. Lib. of World Lit., Inc., 1963.

[190] Blackstock, Walter. "Hawthorne's Cool, Switched-on Media of Communication in THE MARBLE FAUN," LangQ, 7, iii-iv (1969), 41-42.

[191] Blair, Walter. "Color, Light, and Shadow in Hawthorne's Fiction," NEQ, 15 (1942), 74-94.

[192] Blair, Walter. "Dashiell Hammett: Themes and Techniques," in ESSAYS ON AMERICAN LITERATURE IN HONOR OF JAY B. HUBBELL. Clarence Gohdes, ed. Durham, N. C.: Duke U. P., 1967, p. 306.

Hawthorne compared with Hammett.

[193] Blair, Walter. "Hawthorne," in EIGHT AMERICAN AUTHORS: A REVIEW OF RESEARCH AND CRITICISM. Floyd Stovall, ed. New York: Norton, 1956, pp. 100-152. 1963 edition has "Bibliographical Supplement: A Selective Check List, 1955-1962" by J. Chesley Matthews, pp. 428-434.

194 Blanck, Jacob. BIBLIOGRAPHY OF AMERICAN LITERATURE. IV: NATHANIEL HAWTHORNE TO JOSEPH HOLT INGRAHAM. New Haven: Yale U. P., 1963, pp. 1-36.

194.1 Blanck, Jacob, ed. "Nathaniel Hawthorne," MERLE JOHNSON'S AMERICAN FIRST EDITIONS, 4th ed. Revised and Enlarged. Waltham, Mass.: Mark Press, 1965, pp. 222-26.

194.2 Blanck, Jacob. BIBLIOGRAPHY OF AMERICAN LITERATURE. V: WASHINGTON IRVING TO LONGFELLOW. New Haven and London: Yale U. P., 1969.

Rev. by James D. Hart, AL, 41 (1970), 619-20.

195 Blankenship, Russell. "Hathaniel Hawthorne, 1804-1864" in AMERICAN LITERATURE AS AN EXPRESSION OF THE NATIONAL MIND. New York: Henry Holt & Co., 1931; rev. 1949, pp. 371-77.

Rev. by Reed Smith, AL, 4 (1932), 78-82.

196 Blodgett, Harold. "Hawthorne as Poetry Critic: Six Unpublished Letters to Lewis Mansfield," AL, 12 (1940), 173-84.

Hawthorne's letters containing criticism of Mansfield's poem "The Morning Watch."

197 Bloemker, Vernon L. "Allegiance as a Recurring Theme in the Writings of Nathaniel Hawthorne," DA, 27 (Nebr.: 1967), 3419A-20A.

198 Bloom, Edward A. THE ORDER OF FICTION. New York: Odyssey, 1964.

198.1 Blow, Suzanne. "Pre-Raphaelite Allegory in THE MARBLE FAUN," AL, 44 (1972), 122-27.

199 Blyth, Marion Dalrymple. "The Paganism of Nathaniel Hawthorne," DA, 23 (So. Calif.: 1962), 1015-1016.

200 Boas, George, ed. ROMANTICISM IN AMERICA. New York: Russell & Russell, 1961.

201 Bochner, Jay. "Life in a Picture Gallery: Things in THE PORTRAIT OF A LADY and THE MARBLE FAUN," TSLL, 11 (1969), 761-77.

202 Bode, Carl. "Hawthorne's FANSHAWE: The Promising of Greatness," NEQ, 23 (1950), 235-42.

203 Boewe, Charles Ernest. HEREDITY IN THE WRITINGS OF HAWTHORNE, HOLMES AND HOWELLS. Diss. Wis.: 1955.

204 Boewe, Charles Ernest. "Rappaccini's Garden," AL, 30 (1958), 37-49.

205 Boewe, Charles Ernest. "Romanticism Bracketed," ESQ, 35 (1964), 7-10.

206 Boewe, Charles Ernest, and Murray G. Murphey. "Hester Prynne in History," AL, 32 (1960), 202-04.

207 Bogan, Louise. "Foreword," THE SCARLET LETTER. New York: Barnes & Noble, 1960.

208 Bohner, Lina. BROOK FARM AND HAWTHORNE'S BLITHEDALE ROMANCE. Diss. Berlin: 1936.

209 Bolton, Sarah Knowles. FAMOUS AMERICAN AUTHORS. New York: Crowell, 1954.

Juvenile literature.

210 Bonham, Sister M. Hilda, IHM. "Hawthorne's Symbols SOTTO VOCE," CE, 20 (1959), 184-86.

On THE SCARLET LETTER.

211 "Books Read by Hawthorne, 1828-1850. From the 'Charge Books' of the Salem Athenaeum," EIHC, 68 (1932), 65-87.

Hawthorne's reading and list of books which Hawthorne drew from the Salem Athenaeum.

212 Booth, Edward Townsend. "New Adam and Eve in an Old Manse," GOD MADE THE COUNTRY. New York: Knopf, 1946, pp. 202-219.

Biographical account of Hawthorne and his wife at the Old Manse.

213 Booth, Philip. "Off Hawthorne's Salem," Poetry, 97 (1960), 46-49.

Rev. art. THE MIDDLE PASSAGE, Louis O. Coxe.

214 Borges, Jorge Luis. "Nathaniel Hawthorne," in OTHER INQUISITIONS, 1937-1952. Tr. Ruth L. C. Simms. Austin: Texas U. P., pp. 47-65.

214.1
Borges, Jorge Luis. "Nathaniel Hawthorne," LetN (Sept.-Oct., 1970), 69-90.

215 Bouvé, Pauline Carrington. "Is It the Grave of Hester Prynne?" Mentor, 16 (1928), 32-35.

Describes a tombstone in a Boston graveyard: "Here Lyes ye body of Elizabeth Pain."

216 Bowden, Edwin T. THE DUNGEON OF THE HEART: HUMAN ISOLATION AND THE AMERICAN NOVEL. New York: Macmillan Co., 1961.

Rev. by Robert H. Knox, NEQ, 34 (1961), 558-61.

216.1 Bowen, James Keith. "More on Hawthorne and Keats," ATQ, 1 (1969), 12.

217
Bowers, Fredson. "Hawthorne's Text," in HAWTHORNE CENTENARY ESSAYS. Roy Harvey Pearce, ed. Columbus: Ohio State U. P., 1964, pp. 401-25.

218 Bowers, Fredson. "Practical Texts and Definitive Editing," in TWO LECTURES ON EDITING: SHAKESPEARE AND HAWTHORNE. By Charleton Hinman and Fredson Bowers. Columbus, Ohio: Ohio St. U. P., 1969, pp. 21-70.

219 Bowers, Fredson. "A Preface to the Text," in THE CENTENARY EDITION OF THE WORKS OF NATHANIEL HAWTHORNE. Vol. I, THE SCARLET LETTER. William Charvat, et al., eds. Columbus: Ohio St. U. P., 1962, pp. xxix-xlvii.

220 Bowers, Fredson. "Some Principles for Scholarly Editions of Nineteenth Century American Authors," SB, 17 (1964), 223-28.

221 Bowers, Fredson. "Textual Introduction: THE BLITHEDALE ROMANCE," in THE CENTENARY EDITION OF THE WORKS OF NATHANIEL HAWTHORNE. Vol. III. THE BLITHEDALE ROMANCE AND FANSHAWE. William Charvat, et al., eds. Columbus: Ohio St. U. P., 1964, pp. xxvii-lv.

222 Bowers, Fredson. "Textual Introduction: FANSHAWE," in THE CENTENARY WORKS OF NATHANIEL HAWTHORNE. Vol. III. THE BLITHEDALE ROMANCE AND FANSHAWE. William Charvat, et al., eds. Columbus: Ohio St. U. P., 1964, pp. 317-330.

223 Bowers, Fredson. "Textual Introduction: THE HOUSE OF THE SEVEN GABLES," in THE CENTENARY EDITION OF THE WORKS OF NATHANIEL HAWTHORNE. Vol. II. William Charvat, et al., eds. Columbus: Ohio St. U. P., 1965, pp. xxix-lx.

224 Bowers, Fredson. "Textual Introduction," THE MARBLE FAUN:
OR, THE ROMANCE OF MONTE BENI, in THE CENTENARY WORKS
OF NATHANIEL HAWTHORNE. William Charvat, et al., eds.
Columbus, Ohio: Ohio St. U. P., 1968.

224.1 Bowers, Fredson. "Textual Introduction," OUR OLD HOME: A
SERIES OF ENGLISH SKETCHES in THE CENTENARY WORKS OF
NATHANIEL HAWTHORNE. Vol. V. William Charvat, et al,
eds. Columbus, Ohio: Ohio St. U. P., 1970, pp. xliii-
cxv.

225 Bowers, Fredson. "Textual Introduction," THE SCARLET LETTER,
in THE CENTENARY WORKS OF NATHANIEL HAWTHORNE. Vol. I.
William Charvat, et al, eds. Columbus, Ohio: Ohio St.
U. P., 1962, pp. xlix-lxv.

226 Bowman, George William. "Hawthorne and Religion," DA, 14
(Ind.: 1954), 2063-64.

227 Boyle, Thomas E. "The Tenor in the Organic Movement: A View
of American Romanticism," Discourse, 11 (1968), 240-51.

228 Boynton, Percy H. A HISTORY OF AMERICAN LITERATURE. New York:
Ginn & Co., 1919, pp. 236-51.

229 Boynton, Percy H. "Nathaniel Hawthorne," LITERATURE AND
AMERICAN LIFE. New York: Ginn & Co., 1936, pp. 518-37.

230 Bradley, Sculley, Richard C. Beatty, E. Hudson Long. "THE
SCARLET LETTER": AN ANNOTATED TEXT, BACKGROUNDS AND
SOURCES, ESSAYS IN CRITICISM. New York: Norton, 1962.

231 Bradley, Sculley, Richard Beatty, and E. Hudson Long.
"Symbolic and Ethical Idealism," THE AMERICAN TRADITION
IN LITERATURE. New York: Rev. ed., W. W. Norton & Co.,
1961.

232 Bragman, Louis J. "The Medical Wisdom of Nathaniel Hawthorne,"
AMH, 2 (1930), 236-42.

233 Brancaccio, Patrick. "The Ramble and the Pilgrimage: A
Critical Reading of Hawthorne's THE MARBLE FAUN,"
DA, 28 (Rutgers: 1968), 4165A.

234 Brand, Howard. "Hawthorne on the Therapeutic Role," JASPsy,
47 (1952), 856.

235 Brant, Robert Louis. "Hawthorne and Marvell," AL, 30 (1958), 366.

Marvell's "The Unfortunate Lover" as source for the final words of THE SCARLET LETTER.

236 Brant, Robert Louis. "Hawthorne's Unfortunate Lovers," DA, 21 (Wash.: 1961), 3778-79.

237 Braswell, William. "The Early Love Scenes in Melville's PIERRE," AL, 22 (1950), 283-89.

238 Brennan, Joseph, and Seymour L. Gross. "The Origin of Hawthorne's Unpardonable Sin," BUSE, 3 (1957), 123-29.

239 Brickell, Herschell. "What Happened to the Short Story?" AtlM, 188 (1951), 74-76.

The contemporary short story owes more to Hawthorne than to any other person.

240 Bricknell, John W. "THE MARBLE FAUN Reconsidered," UKCR, 20 (1954), 193-99.

241 Bridge, Horatio. PERSONAL RECOLLECTIONS OF NATHANIEL HAWTHORNE. New York: Harper, 1893; repr., Haskell House, 1968.

242 Bridgman, Richard. "As Hester Prynne Lay Dying," ELN, 2 (1965), 294-96.

THE SCARLET LETTER as source for AS I LAY DYING.

243 Broderick, John C. "The Concord Club," N&Q, n. s., 2 (1955), 83.

244 Brodtkorb, Paul, Jr. "Art Allegory in THE MARBLE FAUN," PMLA, 77 (1962), 254-67.

245 Broes, Arthur T. "Journey into Moral Darkness: 'My Kinsman, Major Molineux' as Allegory," NCF, 19 (1964), 171-84.

246 Bromfield, Louis. "Hawthorne," AMERICAN WRITERS ON AMERICAN LITERATURE. John Albert Macy, ed. New York: Liveright, 1931, pp. 97-104.

Whitman was "less profoundly American" than Hawthorne.

247 Bronson, Walter C. A SHORT HISTORY OF AMERICAN LITERATURE. Boston: D. C. Heath, 1910.

The Notebooks are windows "through which one may look into the life of the man and the artist."

248 Brooks, Charles Burnell. "Puritanism in New England Fiction,"
DA, 12 (Princeton: 1943).

249 Brooks, Van Wyck. THE AMERICAN ROMANTICS, 1860-1900.
New York: Viking P., 1962.

250 Brooks, Van Wyck. AMERICA'S COMING OF AGE. New York:
B. W. Huebsch, 1915, pp. 64-70.

251 Brooks, Van Wyck. "THE DREAM OF ARCADIA - AMERICAN WRITERS
AND ARTISTS IN ITALY, 1760-1915. New York: E. P.
Dutton & Co., 1958.

Rev. by Warner Berthoff, NEQ, 32 (1959), 251-53.

252 Brooks, Van Wyck. THE FLOWERING OF NEW ENGLAND, 1815-1865.
New York: Dutton, 1936, 1952.

Hawthorne in Salem, pp. 210-27; West of Boston, 374-87;
Romantic Exiles, 460-77.

253 Brooks, Van Wyck. "Hawthorne in Salem," ChilM. New York:
Dutton, 1948, pp. 207-19.

254 Brooks, Van Wyck. "Introduction," THE HOUSE OF THE SEVEN
GABLES. New York: 1950, p. xviii.

255 Brooks, Van Wyck. MAKERS AND FINDERS: A HISTORY OF THE
WRITER IN AMERICA, 1800-1915. New York: 1952. 5 Vols.

256 Brooks, Van Wyck. NEW ENGLAND: INDIAN SUMMER, 1865-1915.
New York: E. P. Dutton & Co., 1940.

257 Brooks, Van Wyck. "Retreat from Utopia," SatR, 13 (1936),
3-4, 14, 16, 18.

Deals especially with Hawthorne. An account of some
Brook Farm idealists after failure of the experiment.

258 Brooks, Van Wyck. "Rome: Hawthorne," in THE DREAM OF
ARCADIA: AMERICAN WRITERS AND ARTISTS IN ITALY,
1760-1915. New York: E. P. Dutton & Co., 1958.

Rev. by Warner Berthoff, NEQ, 32 (1959), 251-53.

259 Brooks, Van Wyck. THE TIMES OF MELVILLE AND WHITMAN.
New York: E. P. Dutton, 1947.

260 Brooks, Van Wyck. THE WRITER IN AMERICA. New York:
       Dutton & Co., 1953.

261 Brooks, Van Wyck, and Otto L. Bettman. "Nathaniel Hawthorne,"
       in OUR LITERARY HERITAGE: A PICTORIAL HISTORY OF THE
       WRITER IN AMERICA. New York: Dutton, 1956, pp. 77-83.

262 Brown, Clarence Arthur. "The Aesthetics of Romanticism," in
       THE ACHIEVEMENT OF AMERICAN CRITICISM: REPRESENTATIVE
       SELECTIONS FROM THREE HUNDRED YEARS OF AMERICAN
       CRITICISM. With foreword by Harry Hayden Clark.
       New York: Ronald, 1954.

263 Brown, Edith Baker. "Hawthorne Centenary," Harpers, 48
       (1904), 986-87.

264
    Brown, E. K. "Hawthorne, Melville, and 'Ethan Brand,'"
       AL, 3 (1931), 72-75.

       Refutes views of Lewis Mumford (HERMAN MELVILLE,
       New York: 1929), and Newton Arvin (HAWTHORNE. Boston
       and New York: 1961) that in Ethan Brand, Hawthorne
       drew a portrait of Melville.

265 Brown, Herbert Ross. THE SENTIMENTAL NOVEL IN AMERICA,
       1789-1860. Durham, N. C.: Duke U. P., 1940.

266 Brown, Merle Elliott. "The Structure and Significance of
       THE MARBLE FAUN," DA, 14 (Mich.: 1954), 1074-75.

267 Brown, Merle Elliott. "The Structure of THE MARBLE FAUN,"
       AL, 28 (1956), 302-13.

268 Brown, Ruth Elizabeth. "A French Interpreter of New England
       Literature, 1846-1865," NEQ, 13 (1940), 305-21.

       Emile Montégut considered Hawthorne the greatest
       writer America had known.

269 [Browne, Benjamin Frederick] "Hawthorne's 'Privateer'
       Revealed at Last," LitD, 83 (1927), 44-49.

270 Browne, Benjamin Frederick. "The True 'Yarn' of a Yankee
       Privateer," ed. by Nathaniel Hawthorne. Excerpts.
       LitD, 89 (1926), 34-40.

270.1 Browne, Nina E. "Best Editions of Nathaniel Hawthorne,"
       BB, 2 (1901), 138-39.

271 Browne, Nina E. A BIBLIOGRAPHY OF NATHANIEL HAWTHORNE.
Boston and New York: Houghton, Mifflin & Co., 1905.

272 Browne, Ray B. "The Oft-Told TWICE-TOLD TALES: Their
Folklore Motifs," SFQ, 22 (1958), 69-85.

Analogues.

273 Browne, Ray B., and Martin Light, eds. CRITICAL APPROACHES
TO AMERICAN LITERATURE, I. New York: Crowell, 1965.

274 Browne, Ray B., and Donald Pizer, eds. THEMES AND DIRECTIONS
IN AMERICAN LITERATURE: ESSAYS IN HONOR OF LEON HOWARD.
Lafayette, Ind.: Purdue Univ. Studies, 1969.

275 Brownell, William C. "Hawthorne," in AMERICAN PROSE MASTERS.
New York: Chas. Scribner's Sons, 1909; Howard Mumford
Jones, ed. Cambridge, Mass.: Belknap P. of Harvard
U. P., 1963.

Excerpt repr. in B. Bernard Cohen's THE RECOGNITION OF
HAWTHORNE. Ann Arbor: Michigan U. P., 1969, pp. 148-53.

276 Browning, Robert B. [See Van Doren, Mark. NATHANIEL
HAWTHORNE, 1949. Browning preferred THE BLITHEDALE
ROMANCE to Hawthorne's other works.]

277 Bruccoli, Matthew J., ed. THE CENTENARY HAWTHORNE NEWS-
SHEET. Occasional Publication of Ohio State University
Center for Textual Studies. Columbus, Ohio: Ohio
University Press.

278 Bruccoli, Matthew J. "Concealed Printings in Hawthorne,"
PBSA, 57 (1963), 42-49.

279 Bruccoli, Matthew J. AN EXHIBITION OF BOOKS, MANUSCRIPTS,
AND LETTERS: 4 July 1804: NATHANIEL HAWTHORNE:
19 May 1864. Columbus, Ohio: Ohio State University,
1964.

279.1 Bruccoli, Matthew J. "Hawthorne," in BIBLIOGRAPHY AND
TEXTUAL CRITICISM: ENGLISH AND AMERICAN LITERATURE.
O. M. Brack, Jr., and Warner Barnes. Chicago:
Chicago U. P., 1969.

280 Bruccoli, Matthew J. "Hawthorne as a Collector's Item,
1885-1924," HAWTHORNE CENTENARY ESSAYS. Roy Harvey
Pearce, ed. Columbus, Ohio: Ohio St. U. P., 1964,
pp. 387-400.

281 Bruccoli, Matthew J. "Nathaniel Hawthorne Stalks Columbus:
An Ohio Ghost?" Serif, 1 (1964), 26-27.

282 Bruccoli, Matthew J. "Negative Evidence about 'The Celestial Railroad,'" PBSA, 58 (1964), 290-92.

Concerns two 1843 pirated imprints.

283 Bruccoli, Matthew J. "Notes on the Destruction of THE SCARLET LETTER Manuscript," SB, 20 (1967), 257-59.

284 Bruccoli, Matthew J. "A Sophisticated Copy of THE HOUSE OF THE SEVEN GABLES," PBSA, 59 (1965), 438-39.

285 Brumbaugh, Thomas B. "Concerning Nathaniel Hawthorne and Art as Magic." AI, 11 (1954), 399-405.

286 Brumbaugh, Thomas B. "On Horatio and Richard Greenough: A Defense of Neoclassicism in America," AQ, 12 (1960), 414-17.

287 Brumm, Ursula. DIE RELIGIOSE TYPOLOGIE IM AMERIKANISCHEN DENKEN. IHRE BEDEUTUNG FUR DIE AMERIKANISCHE LITERATUR UND GEISTESGESCHICHTE. Leiden: E. J. Brill, 1963; New Brunswick, N. J.: Rutgers U. P.

Deals with the influence which typology has had on some American writers, among them Hawthorne.

Rev. by Jesper Rosenmeier, NEQ, 38 (1965), 121-22.

288 Brumm, Ursula. "Thoughts on History and the Novel," CLS, 6 (1969), 317-30.

THE SCARLET LETTER represents both "research and imaginative identification."

289 Bryce, Rt. Hon. James [House of Commons, London] Letter from, dated January 10, 1904, on occasion of Hawthorne Centenary, EIHC, 41 (1905), 46-48.

290 Buchloh, Paul G. "Die Naturdarstellung in Nathaniel Hawthorne's Erzählungen," in AMERIKANISCHE ERZÄHLUNGEN VON HAWTHORNE BIS SALINGER: INTERPRETATIONEN. Paul G. Buchloh, ed. (KBAA 6.) Neumünster, 1968, pp. 89-111.

291 Buckingham, Leroy H. "Hawthorne and the British Income Tax," AL, 11 (1940), 451-53.

Concerns letter describing Hawthorne while consul at Liverpool.

291.1 Budd, Louis J. "W. D. Howells' Defense of the Romance," PMLA, 67 (1952), 32-42.

292
Buitenhuis, Peter. "Henry James on Hawthorne," NEQ, 32
    (1959), 207-25.

293
Burdett, Osbert. "Nathaniel Hawthorne," CRITICAL ESSAYS.
    Faber, 1926, pp. 7-22.

294
Burhans, Clinton S., Jr. "Hawthorne's Mind and Art in
    'The Hollow of the Three Hills,'" JEGP, 60 (1961), 286-95.

295
Burke, W. J., and Will D. Howe. AMERICAN AUTHORS AND BOOKS,
    1640-1940: AN ENCYCLOPEDIA OF AMERICAN BOOKS, AUTHORS,
    PERSONALITIES, PERIODICALS, ORGANIZATIONS, AND OTHER
    PERTINENT INFORMATION COVERING ALL ASPECTS OF THE
    LITERARY WORLD. New York: Gramercy Pub. Co., 1943;
    Crown Pub., 1962.

296
Burnham, Philip E. "Hawthorne's FANSHAWE and Bowdoin College,"
    EIHC, 80 (1944), 131-38.

296.1
Burns, Rex Sehler. "Hawthorne's Romance of Traditional
    Success," TSLL, 12 (1970), 443-54.

297
Burns, Rex Sehler. NATHANIEL HAWTHORNE AND SUCCESS: MIDDLE
    CLASS SUCCESS AND THE INDUSTRIAL REVOLUTION, 1825-1860.
    Diss. Minn.: 1965.

298
Burress, Lee A., Jr. "Hawthorne's Alternate Choice as a
    Fictional Device," WisSL, 4 (1967), 1-17.

    The fictional device of "alternate choice" is a
    reflection of the essentially skeptical quality of
    Hawthorne's mind.

299
Burton, Katherine. "The Rose of All the Hawthornes," CathW,
    142 (1936), 562-66.

300
Burton, Katherine. SORROW BUILT A BRIDGE. New York: Longmans,
    Green, 1937, 1956.

    Rose Hawthorne Lathrop, Mother Alphonsa, O. S. D.

301
Burton, Richard. "American Contribution," in MASTERS OF THE
    ENGLISH NOVEL: A STUDY OF PRINCIPLES AND PERSONALITIES.
    New York: Henry Holt & Co., 1909.

302
Burton, Richard. "Hawthorne," LITERARY LEADERS OF AMERICA.
    New York: 1903, pp. 99-134.

303 Burton, Richard. "Introduction," THE SNOW IMAGE AND OTHER
    TWICE-TOLD TALES BY NATHANIEL HAWTHORNE.
    1899. Reprint, New York: Books for Libraries P., 1970,
    pp. xi-xxi.

304 Buscaroli, Piero. "Hawthorne's Italy," L'It, 205 (1965),
    26-39.

304.1 Bush, Sargent, Jr. "Bosom Serpents before Hawthorne:
      The Origins of a Symbol," AL, 43 (1971), 181-99.

304.2 Bush, Sargent, Jr. "'Peter Goldthwaite's Treasure' and THE
      HOUSE OF THE SEVEN GABLES," ESQ, 62 (1971), 35-38.

305 Bush, Sargent, Jr. "The Relevance of Puritanism to Major
    Themes in Hawthorne's Fiction," DA, 28 (Iowa: 1968),
    2677A.

306 Bystander. "Nathaniel Hawthorne," in THE SHAPERS OF AMERICAN
    FICTION, 1798-1947. George Dixon Snell, ed. New York:
    E. P. Dutton & Co., 1947, pp. 117-29.

307 Cable, Lucy Leffingwell. "Old Salem and 'THE SCARLET
    LETTER,'" Bookman, 26 (1907), 398-403.

308 Cady, Edwin Harrison. THE GENTLEMAN IN AMERICA, A LITERARY
    STUDY IN AMERICAN CULTURE. Syracuse U. P., 1949,
    pp. 31, 56.

    Hawthorne and Melville make use of the concept of the
    Gentleman.

309 Cady, Edwin Harrison. "Introduction," THE SCARLET LETTER.
    Columbus, Ohio: Merrill, 1969, pp. v-xlv.

310 Cady, Edwin Harrison. "W. D. Howells and the Ashtabula
    Sentinel," ArchQ, 53 (1944), 41.

311 Cady, Edwin Harrison. "'The Wizard Hand': Hawthorne, 1864-1900,"
    in HAWTHORNE CENTENARY ESSAYS. Roy Harvey Pearce, ed.
    Columbus, Ohio: Ohio St. U. P., 1964.

312 Cady, Edwin Harrison, Frederick J. Hoffman, and Roy Harvey
    Pearce. "Nathaniel Hawthorne," in THE GROWTH OF
    AMERICAN LITERATURE: A CRITICAL AND HISTORICAL SURVEY.
    New York: American Book Co., 1956, II, 459-521.

313 Caffee, N. M., and T. A. Kirby, eds. STUDIES FOR WILLIAM A.
    READ. Baton Rouge: La. St. U. P., 1940, pp. 301-12.

314 Cahn, Edmond. "Hawthorne's Set of the STATE TRIALS," TLS, (October 7, 1955), 589.

315 Cahoon, Herbert. "Some Manuscripts of Concord Authors," TSB, No. 92 (1965), 2-3.

316 Cairns, William B. A HISTORY OF AMERICAN LITERATURE. New York: Oxford U. P., 1912, 1930, pp. 298-320.

317 Cajoli, Vladimiro. "Ritorno di Hawthorne," FLe, 15 (1960), 3.

317.1 Calhoun, Thomas O. "Hawthorne's Gothic: An Approach to the Four Last Fragments," Genre, 3 (1970), 229-41.

318 Calverton, V. F. THE LIBERATION OF AMERICAN LITERATURE. New York: Scribner's, 1932.

Hawthorne, "almost an alien" in U. S., interested only in its past.

319 Cameron, Kenneth Walter. "Arthur Cleveland Coxe on Hawthorne: An Anglican Estimate in 1851," ESQ, 13 (1958), 51-64.

The portrayal of Hester "might do harm to American morals."

320 Cameron, Kenneth Walter. "Background of Hawthorne's 'The Canterbury Pilgrims,'" ESQ, 13 (1958), 41-45.

Provides Shaker background.

321 Cameron, Kenneth Walter. "Genesis of Hawthorne's 'The Ambitious Guest,'" HEDC, 14 (1955), 2-36.

322 Cameron, Kenneth Walter. THE GENESIS OF HAWTHORNE'S "THE AMBITIOUS GUEST." Hartford, Thistle Press, 1955.

323 Cameron, Kenneth Walter. "Hawthorne in Early Newspapers," ESQ, 13 (1958), 45.

324 Cameron, Kenneth Walter, ed. HAWTHORNE AMONG HIS CONTEMPORARIES: A HARVEST OF ESTIMATES, INSIGHTS, AND ANECDOTES FROM THE VICTORIAN LITERARY WORLD. Hartford, Conn.: Transcendental Books, 1968.

325 Cameron, Kenneth Walter. HAWTHORNE INDEX TO THEMES, MOTIFS, TOPICS, ARCHETYPES, SOURCES, AND KEY WORDS DEALT WITH IN RECENT CRITICISM. Hartford, Conn.: Transcendental Books, 1968.

326 Cameron, Kenneth Walter. "Inventory of Hawthorne's
    Manuscripts: Part One," ESQ, 29 (1962), 5-20.

    Compiled from the holdings of Essex Institute, The
    Houghton Library of Harvard, the Berg Collection and
    the Manuscript Division of New York Public Library,
    the Massachusetts Historical Society, the Boston
    Public Library, the Henry E. Huntington Library,
    and the Pierpont Morgan Library.

327 Cameron, Kenneth Walter. "Melville, Cooper, Irving and John
    Esaias Warren: Travel Literature and Patronage,"
    ESQ, 47 (1967), 114-25.

    Warren, like Hawthorne, acquired a civil service position
    which supported him while he wrote.

328 Cameron, Kenneth Walter. "New Light on Hawthorne's Removal
    from the Customs House," ESQ, 23 (1961), 2-5.

    Letters from the file of the Secretary of the Treasury.

329 Cameron, Kenneth Walter. "Notes on Hawthorne's Manuscripts,"
    in "Symposium on Nathaniel Hawthorne," ESQ, 25 (1961),
    35-37.

330 Cameron, Kenneth Walter. "Prints of American Authors," ESQ,
    28 (1962), 77-106.

    Photo.

331 Cameron, Kenneth Walter. "Privileges at the Boston Athenaeum:
    Hawthorne, Miss Peabody and Sampson Reed," ESQ, 6 (1957),
    21.

331.1 Cameron, Kenneth Walter, ed. MEMORABILIA OF HAWTHORNE, ALCOTT
    AND CONCORD by Frank B. Sanborn. Hartford: Transcendental
    Books, 1970.

332 Cameron, Kenneth Walter, ed. "Twenty Pictures of Hawthorne,"
    ESQ, 39 (1965), 2-12.

    Pictures from 1840 to 1862-1863.

333 Campbell, Donald Allen. A CRITICAL ANALYSIS OF HAWTHORNE'S
    THE BLITHEDALE ROMANCE. Diss. Yale: 1959-60.

333.1 Campbell, Harry M. "Freudianism, American Romanticism, and
    'Young Goodman Brown,'" CEA, 33 (1971), 3-6.

333.2 Canaday, Nicholas, Jr. "Community and Identity at Blithedale,"
    SAQ, 71 (1972), 30-39.

[334]Canaday, Nicholas, Jr. "Hawthorne's Minister and the Veiling Deceptions of Self," SSF, 4 (1967), 135-42.

[335]Canaday, Nicholas, Jr. "Hawthorne's THE SCARLET LETTER," Expl. 28 (1970), Item 39.

[336]Canaday, Nicholas, Jr. "Ironic Humor as Defense in THE SCARLET LETTER," SCB, 21 (1961), 17-18.

[337] Canaday, Nicholas, Jr. "'Some Sweet Moral Blossom': A Note on Hawthorne's Rose," PLL, 3 (1967), 186-87.

Dante as source of prison-door rose in THE SCARLET LETTER.

[338] Canby, Henry Seidel. "The American Tradition," in CONTEMPORARY ESSAYS. William Thomson Hastings, ed. New York: Houghton, Mifflin, 1928, pp. 60-73.

[339] Canby, Henry Seidel. "Hawthorne and Melville," CLASSIC AMERICANS: A STUDY OF EMINENT AMERICAN WRITERS FROM IRVING TO WHITMAN. New York: Harcourt, 1931, 1959, pp. 226-62.

Hawthorne was free from Puritan theology and had a "natural bent" toward realism.

Rev. by Howard M. Jones, AL, 4 (1933), 311-13.

[340] Canby, Henry Seidel. "Nathaniel Hawthorne," THE SHORT STORY IN ENGLISH. New York: Henry Holt & Co., 1909, pp. 246-263.

[341] Cantwell, Robert. FAMOUS AMERICAN MEN OF LETTERS. New York: Dodd, 1956.

[342] Cantwell, Robert. "Hawthorne and Delia Bacon," AQ, 1 (1949), 343-60.

Hawthorne's brief but sympathetic contact with Delia Bacon in England.

[343] Cantwell, Robert. NATHANIEL HAWTHORNE: THE AMERICAN YEARS. New York: Rinehart, 1948. Bibliography by John P. Anderson appended.

Revs. Arlin Turner, AL, 21 (1950), 357-59;
Richard Chase, "The Progressive Hawthorne," PR, 16 (1949), 96-100;
Manning Hawthorne, NEQ, 22 (1949), 105-08;
"Real Man's Life," Time, 52 (1948), 104-08.

[344] Capellán Gonzalo, Angel. "Hawthorne, comp protagonista de sus obras," FMod, (1969), 35-36; 287-95.

[345] Capen, Oliver Bronson. "Country Homes of Famous Americans - Nathaniel Hawthorne," CoLA, 5 (1904), 242-45; 282-83.

[346] "The Cardinal Error of Hawthorne's Career," CrtL, 44 (1908), 162-64.

[347] Cargill, Oscar, gen. ed. AMERICAN LITERATURE: A PERIOD ANTHOLOGY. New York: Macmillan, 1933.

Rev. by Gregory Paine, AL, 6 (1935), 218-20.

[348] Cargill, Oscar. "Nemesis and Nathaniel Hawthorne," PMLA, 52 (1937), 848-62.

See William Peirce Randel, "Hawthorne, Channing, and Margaret Fuller," AL, 10 (1939), 472-76; Austin Warren, "Hawthorne, Margaret Fuller, and 'Nemesis,'" PMLA, 54 (1930), 613-15.

[349] Carleton, William G. "Hawthorne Discovers the English," YR, 53 (1964), 395-414.

[349.1] Carleton, William G. "Hawthorne Discovers the English," in TECHNOLOGY AND HUMANISM: SOME EXPLORATORY ESSAYS FOR OUR TIME. With Foreword by Manning J. Dauer. Nashville, Tenn.: Vanderbilt U. P., 1970, pp. 191-209.

[350] Carlisle, Kathryn. "Wit and Humor in Nathaniel Hawthorne," BardR, 3 (1949), 86-93.

[351] Carleon, Constance H. "Wit and Irony in Hawthorne's HOUSE OF THE SEVEN GABLES," in A HANDFUL OF SPICE: ESSAYS IN MAINE HISTORY AND LITERATURE. Richard S. Sprague, ed. (U. of Maine Studies 88) Orono: Maine U. P., 1968, pp. 159-68.

[352] Carlton, W. N. C. "Hawthorne's First Book - FANSHAWE: A TALE," AmC, 4 (1927), 82-86.

[352.1] Carman, Bliss. NATHANIEL HAWTHORNE. Palo Alto: N. Van Patten, 1929.

[353] Carnochan, W. B. "'The Minister's Black Veil': Symbol, Meaning, and the Context of Hawthorne's Art," NCF, 24 (1969), 182-92.

[354] Carpenter, Frederic I. "'The American Myth': Paradise (To Be) Regained," PMLA, 74 (1959), 599-606.

Discusses the search for myth or hypothesis to explain American character, lists authors who have dealt with this topic, and contrasts Hawthorne with Emerson.

355 Carpenter, Frederic I. AMERICAN LITERATURE AND THE DREAM.
New York: Philosophical Library, 1955.

356 Carpenter, Frederic I. "The Genteel Tradition: A Re-
Interpretation," NEQ, 15 (1942), 427-43.

In THE SCARLET LETTER Hawthorne recognized a certain
heroism in self-reliance, but emphasized its greater
evil.

357 Carpenter, Frederic I. "Hester the Heretic," CE, 13
(1952), 457-58.

See: Darrel Abel, "Hawthorne's Hester," CE, 13
(1952), 303-09; reply of Frederic I. Carpenter,
CE, 13 (1952), 457-58, and rejoinder of Darrel
Abel, CE, 14 (1953), 34.

358 Carpenter, Frederic I. "Puritans Preferred Blondes: The
Heroines of Melville and Hawthorne," NEQ, 9 (1936),
253-72.

In THE BLITHEDALE ROMANCE and THE MARBLE FAUN,
blondness is an ideal virtue and darkness a serious
and sometimes unforgivable sin.

359 Carpenter, Frederic I. "Scarlet A. Minus," CE, 5 (1944),
173-180.

Also in EJ, 33 (1944), 7-14.

The ambiguity of THE SCARLET LETTER illustrates
"a fundamental confusion in modern thought."

360 Carpenter, Nan Cooke. "Louisa May Alcott and 'Thoreau's
Flute': Two Letters," HLQ, 24 (1960), 71-74.

Letters to Mrs. J. T. Fields reveal that Sophia was
instrumental in getting the poem published in the
1863 Atlantic Monthly.

361 Carpenter, Richard C. "Hawthorne's Polar Explorations:
'Young Goodman Brown' and 'My Kinsman, Major Molineux,'"
NCF, 24 (1969), 45-56.

362 Carpenter, Richard C. "Hawthorne's Scarlet Bean Flowers,"
UKCR, 30 (1963), 65-71.

The optimistic denouement of THE HOUSE OF THE SEVEN
GABLES analogous to horticultural symbols which oppose
sterility of the elder Pyncheons with the promise of
the young couple.

363   Cassill, R. V. "That Blue-Eyed Darling Nathaniel,"
      Horizon, 8 (1966), 32-39.

        THE SCARLET LETTER and several stories are essential
        to understanding of our history and our present
        conscience.

364 Casson, Allan. "THE SCARLET LETTER and ADAM BEDE," VN, 20
      (1961), 18-19.

365 Castleman, J. R. "Introduction," THE HOUSE OF THE SEVEN
      GABLES. New York: Charles E. Merrill, 1907.

365.1
     Casty, Alan. Teaching Suggestions and Examples for THE SHAPE
      OF FICTION. Boston, 1967, pp. 1, 16-18.

     "My Kinsman, Major Molineux."

366 A CATALOGUE OF AN EXHIBITION OF FIRST EDITIONS, ASSOCIATION
      BOOKS, AUTOGRAPH LETTERS, AND MANUSCRIPTS OF NATHANIEL
      HAWTHORNE. Buffalo, New York: Lockwood Memorial Library,
      The University of Buffalo, 1937.

367 "Catalogue of Portraits in the Essex Institute, Salem,
      Massachusetts," [Cont. from Vol. 71, p. 80], EIHC,
      71 (1935), 135-66.

     No. 123 is of Nathaniel Hawthorne.

368 Cathcart, Wallace Hugh. BIBLIOGRAPHY OF THE WORKS OF
      NATHANIEL HAWTHORNE. Cleveland: The Rowfant Club,
      1905.

369 Cary, Elizabeth Luther. "Hawthorne and Emerson," Critic
      45 (1904), 25-27.

370 Cecil, L. Moffitt. "Hawthorne's Optical Device," AQ, 15
      (1963), 76-84.

371
     Cecil, L. Moffitt. "THE SCARLET LETTER: A Puritan Love Story,"
      in REALITY AND MYTH: ESSAYS IN AMERICAN LITERATURE IN
      MEMORY OF RICHARD CROOM BEATTY. Nashville, Tenn.:
      Vanderbilt U. P., 1964, 52-59.

372 Cecil, L. Moffitt. "Symbolic Pattern in THE YEMASSEE," AL, 35 (1964), 510-14.

William Gilmore Simms in THE YEMASSEE uses serpent imagery and symbolic method prefiguring Hawthorne.

373 Centenary of THE SCARLET LETTER. PubW, 157 (1950), 1203-1691.

374 Cerf, B. "Trade Winds," SatR, 30 (1947), 6.

374.1 Cervo, Nathan A. "The Gargouille Anti-Hero-Victim of Christian Satire," Ren, 22 (1970), 69-77.

In Hawthorne and others.

375 Chamberlain, Jacob C. FIRST EDITIONS OF NATHANIEL HAWTHORNE, together with Some Manuscripts, Letters, and Portraits, Exhibited at the Grolier Club, December 24, 1904. New York: Grolier Club, 1904.

376 Chandler, Elizabeth Lathrop, ed. "Hawthorne's 'Spectator,'" NEQ, 4 (1931), 288-330.

Repr. HAWTHORNE'S SPECTATOR. Edited by Elizabeth Lathrop Chandler. Portland, Maine: Southworth P., 1931.

A reprint of a manuscript weekly of verse and prose in 1820 which Hawthorne edited in his youth.

377 Chandler, Elizabeth Lathrop. "A Study of the Sources of the Tales and Romances Written by Nathaniel Hawthorne before 1853," SCSML, 7 (1926), 1-64.

Limited to Notebooks and Letters.

378 Chapman, Edward Mortimer. "Masters of Fiction," ENGLISH LITERATURE IN ACCOUNT WITH RELIGION, 1800-1900. New York: Houghton Mifflin, 1910, pp. 268-71.

379 Charney, Maurice. "Hawthorne and the Gothic Style," NEQ, 34 (1961), 36-49.

"Our Old Home," THE ENGLISH NOTEBOOKS, and THE FRENCH AND ITALIAN NOTEBOOKS have perhaps the most significant discussion of style and esthetic theory which Hawthorne has left us.

380 Charney, Maurice. "Hawthorne and Sidney's 'Arcadia,'" N&Q, 7 (1960), 264-65.

380.1 Charteris, Evan. THE LIFE AND LETTERS OF SIR EDMUND GOSS.
        New York: 1931, p. 200.

        Contains letter by Edmund Goss to William Dean Howells.
        See Carl J. Weber, "Lowell's 'Dead Rat in the Wall,'"
        NEQ, 9 (1936), 468-72; 686-88; and George Knox, "The
        Hawthorne-Lowell Affair," NEQ, 29 (1956), 493-502.

381 Charvat, William (1905-1966), Roy Harvey Pearce, Claude M.
        Simpson, Fredson Bowers, Matthew J. Bruccoli, eds.
        THE CENTENARY EDITION OF THE WORKS OF NATHANIEL HAWTHORNE.
        Columbus, Ohio: Ohio St. U. P.

382   Vol. I. THE SCARLET LETTER. Introduction by William
        Charvat; Textual Introduction, Fredson Bowers, 1962.

            Revs., Robert Merideth, MRR, 1 (1964-65), 74-77;
            Rollo G. Silver, AL, 35 (1964), 538-39;
            Willard Thorp, NEQ, 36 (1963), 405-07.

383   Vol. II. THE HOUSE OF THE SEVEN GABLES. Introduction by
        William Charvat; Textual Introduction, Fredson Bowers,
        1965.

384   Vol. III. THE BLITHEDALE ROMANCE and FANSHAWE.
        Introduction by Roy Harvey Pearce; Textual Introduction,
        Fredson Bowers, 1964.

385   Vol. IV. THE MARBLE FAUN: OR, THE ROMANCE OF MONTE BENI.
        With L. Neal Smith, ed. Introduction by Claude M.
        Simpson, Textual Introduction by Fredson Bowers, 1968.

385.1   Vol. V. OUR OLD HOME: A SERIES OF ENGLISH SKETCHES.
        With L. Neal Smith, associate textual ed. Introduction
        by Claude M. Simpson, Textual Introduction by Fredson
        Bowers, 1970.

        Rev. by Buford Jones, AL, 43 (1971), 287.

385.2   Vol. VI. TRUE STORIES FROM HISTORY AND BIOGRAPHY.
        Introduction by Roy Harvey Pearce; Fredson Bowers,
        textual editor. 1971.

385.3   Vol. VII. A WONDER BOOK and TANGLEWOOD TALES. Introduction
        by Roy Harvey Pearce. 1971.

385.4   Vol. VIII. THE AMERICAN NOTEBOOKS. Claude M. Simpson, ed.
        1971.

386 Charvat, William. "James T. Fields and the Beginnings of Book Promotion, 1840-1855," HLQ, 8 (1944), 75-94.

387 Charvat, William. "Note on the Typesetting," in THE CENTENARY EDITION OF THE WORKS OF NATHANIEL HAWTHORNE, VOL. II, THE HOUSE OF THE SEVEN GABLES. William Charvat, et.al., eds. Columbus: Ohio St. U. P., 1965, pp. lxi-lxiii.

388 Charvat, William. THE ORIGINS OF AMERICAN CRITICAL THOUGHT, 1810-1835. New York: A. S. Barnes & Co., Inc., 1936; Perpetua Edition, 1961.

389 Charvat, William. THE PROFESSION OF AUTHORSHIP IN AMERICA, 1800-1870. Matthew J. Bruccoli, ed. Columbus, Ohio: Ohio St. U. P., 1968.

390 Charvat, William. "Introduction," THE SCARLET LETTER. Boston; Houghton, Mifflin, 1963, pp. vii-xvii.

391 Chase, Richard. "The Broken Circuit: Romance and the American Novel," AMERICAN CRITICAL ESSAYS: TWENTIETH century. Sel. with Introduction by Harold Beaver. London: Oxford U. P., 1959.

392 Chase, Richard. "Hawthorne and the Limits of Romance," THE AMERICAN NOVEL AND ITS TRADITION. Garden City, New York: Doubleday, 1957, pp. 67-87.

Rev. by Robert Spiller, AL, 31 (1960), 82-84.
See Earl H. Rovit, "American Literature and 'The American Experience,'" AQ, 13 (1961), 121.

393 Chase, Richard. "The Progressive Hawthorne," PR, 16 (1949), 96-100.

394 Chaudhry, Ghulam Ali. "Dickens and Hawthorne," EIHC, Special Hawthorne Issue, 100 (1964), 256-73.

395 Cherry, Fannye N. "A Note on the Source of Hawthorne's 'Lady Eleanore's Mantle,'" AL, 6 (1935), 437-39.

396 Cherry, Fannye N. "The Sources of Hawthorne's 'Young Goodman Brown,'" AL, 5 (1934), 342-48.

Cervantes thou⌐ . to be the chief source.

396.1 Chisholm, Richard M. "The Use of Gothic Materials in Hawthorne's Mature Romances," DAI, 31 (Columbia: 1970), 382A

397 Choate, Hon. Joseph Hodges. /United States Ambassador at the
    Court of St. James./ Letter from, June 10, 1904, on
    occasion of the Hawthorne Centenary, EIHC, 41 (1905),
    39-45.

398 Chrétien, Louis E. LA PENSÉE MORALE DE NATHANIEL HAWTHORNE,
    SYMBOLISTE NEO-PURITAN. Esquisse d'une Interpretation,
    Paris: 1932.

399 Chu, Limin. AN INTRODUCTION TO AMERICAN LITERATURE, 1607-1860.
    Taipei, Taiwan: Bookmart, 1963. /In Chinese./

    Rev. by Irving Ycheng Lo in AL, 36 (1964), 394-95.

400 Chubb, Edwin Watts. "Curtis and Hawthorne at the Brook
    Farm," in STORIES OF AUTHORS, BRITISH AND AMERICAN.
    New ed. New York: Macmillan, 1926, pp. 266-69.

401 Chubb, Edwin Watts. "Hawthorne and THE SCARLET LETTER," in
    STORIES OF AUTHORS, BRITISH AND AMERICAN. New York:
    Macmillan, 1926, pp. 270-78.

401.1 Cifelli, Edward. "Hawthorne and the Italian," SA, 14
    (1968), 87-96.

402 Clark, C. E. Frazer, Compiler. CHECKLIST OF NATHANIEL HAWTHORNE.
    Columbus, Ohio: Charles E. Merrill Pub. Co., 1970.

402.1 Clark, C. E. Frazer. "Hawthorne's First Appearance in
    England," CEAAN, 3 (1970), 10-11.

403 Clark, C. E. Frazer, ed. LONGFELLOW, HAWTHORNE, AND
    "EVANGELINE": A LETTER FROM HENRY WADSWORTH LONGFELLOW,
    NOVEMBER 29, 1847, TO NATHANIEL HAWTHORNE. Brunswick,
    Maine: Bowdoin College, 1966.

403.1 Clark, C. E. Frazer. "Posthumous Papers of a Decapitated
    Surveyor: THE SCARLET LETTER in the Salem Press,"
    SNNTS, 2 (1970), 395-419.

403.2 Clark, C. E. Frazer, ed. THE NATHANIEL HAWTHORNE JOURNAL.
    Matthew J. Bruccoli, consulting ed. Washington, D. C.:
    Microcard Editions, winter, 1970-71.

    First issue of a projected annual on Nathaniel
    Hawthorne.

404 Clark, Harry Hayden. "Changing Attitudes in Early American Literary Criticism, 1800-1840," in THE DEVELOPMENT OF AMERICAN LITERARY CRITICISM. Floyd Stovall, ed. Chapel Hill: North Carolina U. P., 1955, pp. 15-73.

Hawthorne represents a transition to individualism in criticism. In his review of W. G. Simms, he speaks of the "worn out mould" of Scott's historical pageantry.

405 Clark, Harry Hayden. "Hawthorne: Tradition versus Innovation," in PATTERNS OF COMMITMENT IN AMERICAN LITERATURE. Marston LaFrance, ed. Toronto: Univ. of Toronto P., 1967, pp. 19-37.

Rev. by C. Carroll Hollis, AL, 40 (1969), 580-81.

406 Clark, Harry Hayden. "Hawthorne's Literary and Aesthetic Doctrines as Embodied in His Tales," TWA, 50 (1961), 251-75.

407 Clark, Harry Hayden. "Suggestions Concerning a History of American Literature," AL, 12 (1941), 288-96.

408 Clark, Harry Hayden, ed. TRANSITIONS IN AMERICAN LITERARY CRITICISM. Durham, N. C.: Duke U. P., 1953, p. 187.

"Anti-traditionalism" of Hawthorne.

Rev. by Sherman Paul, NEQ, 27 (1954), 550-53.

409 Clark, Marden J. "The Wages of Sin in Hawthorne," BYUS, 1 (1959), 21-36.

410 Clark, Margaret Tuckerman. "A Hawthorne Letter," YR, 23 (1933), 214-15.
From Sophia Hawthorne to Mr. Tuckerman, dated April 5, 1868.

411 Clark, William H. "Another 'Seven Gables'? /Montpelier, the Knox Mansion at Thomaston, Me.7," CSMM (1944), 12.

412 Clarke, Helen Archibald. HAWTHORNE'S COUNTRY. Garden City, New York: Doubleday, 1913.

Illustrations and typographical descriptions.

413 Clay, Edward M. "The 'Dominating' Symbol in Hawthorne's Last Phase," AL, 39 (1968), 506-16.

No single unifying symbol in Hawthorne's last romances.

414 Clay, Edward M. "Nathaniel Hawthorne's Symbolism as a Synthesis of Permanence and Change," DA, 27 (Mo.: 1966), 1815A-16A.

415 Clendening, Logan. "A Bibliographic Account of the Bacon-Shakespeare Controversy," Colophon, New Graphic Series, 1 (1939), 25-32.

416 Clendenning, John. "Irving and the Gothic Tradition," BuR, 12 (1964), 90-98.

Irving anticipated the later work of Poe and Hawthorne.

417 Cline, John. HAWTHORNE AND THE BIBLE. Diss. Duke: 1948.

418 Coan, Otis W., and Richard G. Lillard. AMERICA IN FICTION: AN ANNOTATED LIST OF NOVELS THAT INTERPRET ASPECTS OF LIFE IN THE UNITED STATES. Stanford, Calif.: Stanford U. P., 1945.

419 Coanda, Richard Joseph. "Hawthorne's Scarlet Alphabet," Ren, 19 (1967), 161-66.

Hawthorne followed Coleridge's chief distinctions of man's faculties of heart, intellect, and imagination in THE SCARLET LETTER.

420 Coanda, Richard Joseph. "Hawthorne on the Imagination," DA, 21 (Wis.: 1960), 1563

421 Cobb, Robert P. SOCIETY VERSUS SOLITUDE: STUDIES IN EMERSON, THOREAU, HAWTHORNE AND WHITMAN. Diss. Michigan: 1955, 1396.

422 Cochran, Robert W. "Hawthorne's Choice: The Veil or the Jaundiced Eye," CE, 23 (1962), 342-46.

423 Cochran, Robert W. "Reply." /To Thomas E. Connolly, "How Young Goodman Brown Became Old Badman Brown,"/ CE, 24 (1962), 153-54.

424 Cohen, B. Bernard. "'The Ambitious Guest': From Fact to Fiction," in WRITING ABOUT LITERATURE. Chicago: Scott, Foresman & Co., 1963, pp. 104-109.

See B. Bernard Cohen's "The Sources of 'The Ambitious Guest,'" BPLQ, 4 (1952), 221-24.

425 Cohen, B. Bernard. "The Composition of Hawthorne's 'The Duston Family,'" NEQ, 21 (1948), 236-41.

426 Cohen, B. Bernard. "Deodat Lawson's CHRIST'S FIDELITY and Hawthorne's 'Young Goodman Brown,'" EIHC, 104 (1968), 349-70.

427 Cohen, B. Bernard. "Edward Everett and Hawthorne's Removal from the Salem Custom House," AL, 27 (1955), 245-49.

428 Cohen, B. Bernard. "Emerson and Hawthorne on England," BPLQ, 9 (1957), 73-85.

Emerson's ENGLISH TRAITS and Hawthorne's OUR OLD HOME reflect the same attitudes toward the British.

429 Cohen, B. Bernard. "Emerson's 'The Young American' and Hawthorne's 'The Intelligence Office,'" AL, 26 (1954), 32-43.

Evidence of greater intellectual rapport between Emerson and Hawthorne than usually thought.

430 Cohen, B. Bernard. ETERNAL TRUTH: A STUDY OF NATHANIEL HAWTHORNE'S PHILOSOPHY. Diss. Ind.: 1950.

431 Cohen, B. Bernard. "The Gray Champion," IUF, 13 (1948), 11-12.

431.1 Cohen, B. Bernard. GUIDE TO NATHANIEL HAWTHORNE. Columbus, Ohio: Charles E. Merrill, 1970.

432 Cohen, B. Bernard. "Hawthorne and Legends," HoosF, 7 (1948), 94-95.

433 Cohen, B. Bernard. "Hawthorne and PARLEY'S UNIVERSAL HISTORY," PBSA, 48 (1954), 77-90.

433.1 Cohen, B. Bernard, and Roy Harvey Pearce. HAWTHORNE'S LIBRARY. (In process.)

434 Cohen, B. Bernard. "Hawthorne's 'Mrs. Bullfrog' and THE RAMBLER," PQ, 32 (1953), 382-87.

Hawthorne's debt to Johnson.

435 Cohen, B. Bernard. "Henry James and the Hawthorne Centennial," EIHC, 92 (1956), 279-83.

436 Cohen, B. Bernard. "A New Critical Approach to the Works of Hawthorne," WayneER, 4 (1950), 43-47.

437 Cohen, B. Bernard. "PARADISE LOST and 'Young Goodman Brown,'" EIHC, 94 (1958), 282-96.

438 Cohen, B. Bernard. "Preface," THE RECOGNITION OF NATHANIEL HAWTHORNE: SELECTED CRITICISM SINCE 1828. B. Bernard Cohen, ed. Ann Arbor: Michigan U. P., 1969, pp. vii-xvii.

439 Cohen, B. Bernard, ed. THE RECOGNITION OF NATHANIEL HAWTHORNE: SELECTED CRITICISM SINCE 1828. Ann Arbor, Michigan: Michigan U. P., 1969.

440 Cohen, B. Bernard. "The Sources of 'The Ambitious Guest,'" BPLQ, 4 (1952), 221-24.

See B. Bernard Cohen's "'The Ambitious Guest': From Fact to Fiction," in WRITING ABOUT LITERATURE. Chicago: Scott Foresman, 1963, pp. 104-09.

441 Cohen, Hennig. "The American as Involved and Dropout: An Afterword," in LANDMARKS IN AMERICAN WRITING. Hennig Cohen, ed. London and New York: Basic Books, Inc., 1969, pp. 379-89.

To call Roderick Usher or Clifford Pyncheon a "dropout" seems a jarring anachronism; however, the situation, if not the term, applies.

442 Colacurcio, Michael Joseph. "The Progress of Piety: Hawthorne's Critique of the Puritan Spirit," DA, 24 (Ill.: 1964), 5405.

443 Colcord, Lincoln. "Notes on MOBY DICK," Freeman, 5 (August 23, 1922), 559-62; (August 30, 1922), 585-87. Reprinted in THE RECOGNITION OF HERMAN MELVILLE. Hershel Parker, ed., and in MELVILLE AND HAWTHORNE IN THE BERKSHIRES. Howard P. Vincent, ed.

An "appreciation" with criticism of Melville for allowing Hawthorne's influence to mar the ending of MOBY DICK.

444 Cole, William I. "Maine in Literature," NEM, n. s., 22 (1900), 730-43.

445 Coleridge, M. E. "The Questionable Shapes of Nathaniel Hawthorne," LittLA, 242 (1904), 348-53.

Also in MR, 16, 1 (1903), 74.

446 Colson, Theodore L. "The Characters of Hawthorne and Faulkner: A Typology of Sinners," DA, 28 (Mich.: 1967), 2204A-05A.

447 Commager, Henry Steele. "Hawthorne as Editor," AHR, 47
(1942), 258-59.

Art.-Rev., of Arlin Turner's HAWTHORNE AS EDITOR.
Baton Rouge: La. St. U. P., 1941.

448 Commager, Henry Steele, and Allan Nevins, eds. HERITAGE OF
AMERICA. Little, 1949, 1951, pp. 650-652.

Nathaniel Hawthorne sees President Lincoln.

449 Condon, Richard A. "The Broken Conduit: A Study of Alienation
in American Literature," PS, 8 (1954), 326-32.

450 Connolly, Thomas E. "Hawthorne's 'Young Goodman Brown':
An Attack on Puritanic Calvinism," AL, 28 (1956),
370-75.

451 Connolly, Thomas E. "How Young Goodman Brown Became Old
Badman Brown," CE, 24 (1962), 153.

Rebuttal to Robert W. Cochran, "Hawthorne's Choice:
The Veil or the Jaundiced Eye," CE, 23 (1962), 342-46,
followed by Robert W. Cochran's reply, CE, 24 (1962),
153-54.

452 Connolly, Thomas E. "Introduction," NATHANIEL HAWTHORNE:
YOUNG GOODMAN BROWN. Thomas E. Connolly, ed. Merrill
Casebooks. Columbus; Ohio: Charles E. Merrill, 1968.

Text plus rptd. criticism.

452.1 Connolly, Thomas E., ed. with Introduction. THE SCARLET
LETTER AND SELECTED TALES. Penguin Books, 1970.

453
Connors, Thomas E. "'My Kinsman, Major Molineux': A Reading,"
MLN, 74 (1959), 299-302.

454
Conway, Moncure D. "Hawthorne, His Uncollected Tales in the
TOKEN Beginning with 1830," NYTSR, June 8, 1901, 397-98.

455
Conway, Moncure D. LIFE OF NATHANIEL HAWTHORNE. E. S.
Robertson, ed. London: Great Writer Series, [1890];
Walter Scott, Ltc., 1895.

Rev. by G. E. Woodberry, Nation, 51 (1890), 216.

456 Conway, Moncure D. "My Hawthorne Experience," Critic,
45 (1904), 21-25.

457 Conway, Moncure D. "The Secret of Hawthorne," <u>Nation</u>, 78 (1904), 509-10.

458 Cook, E. C. "Nathaniel Hawthorne's Growth as an Artist," MS, 2 (1930), 4.

458.1 Cook, Reginald. "The Forest of Goodman Brown's Night: A Reading of Hawthorne's 'Young Goodman Brown,'" NEQ, 43 (1970), 473-81.

459 Cooke, Alice Lovelace. "The Shadow of Martinus Scriblerus in Hawthorne's 'The Prophetic Pictures,'" NEQ, 17 (1944), 597-604.

460 Cooke, Alice Lovelace. "Some Evidences of Hawthorne's Indebtedness to Swift," UTSE, 18 (1938), 140-62.

Believes Hawthorne made a study of GULLIVER'S TRAVELS which gave him the material for at least six narratives.

461 Copeland, Charles Townsend. "Hawthorne's Use of His Materials," <u>Critic</u>, 45 (1904), 56-60.

462 Core, George, ed. REGIONALISM AND BEYOND, ESSAYS OF RANDALL STEWART. Vanderbilt, 1968.

Rev. by Richard Lehan, NCF, 23 (1968), 372-73.

463 Cortissoz, Paul C. THE POLITICAL LIFE OF NATHANIEL HAWTHORNE. Diss. New York: 1955.

464 Cory, Donald Webster, and R. E. L. Masters. VIOLATION OF TABOO: INCEST IN THE GREAT LITERATURE OF THE PAST AND PRESENT. New York: The Julian Press, Inc., 1963, pp. 87-99.

Emphasizes incest in "Alice Doane's Appeal."

465 Cowie, Alexander. "Nathaniel Hawthorne, 1804-1864," THE RISE OF THE AMERICAN NOVEL. New York: Amer. Bks., 1951, 327-62.

466 Cowley, Malcolm. "Five Acts of THE SCARLET LETTER," CE, 19 (1957), 11-16.

Also in TWELVE ORIGINAL ESSAYS ON GREAT AMERICAN NOVELS, Charles Shapiro, ed. Wayne St. U. P., 1958, pp. 23-43.

Rev. by Nevius Blake, NCF, 13 (1958), 170-72.

467 Cowley, Malcolm. "Hawthorne in the Looking Glass," SR, 56 (1948), 545-63.

Mirror images.

468 Cowley, Malcolm. "Hawthorne in Solitude," NR, 109 (1948), 19-23.

Effect of isolation on Hawthorne.

469 Cowley, Malcolm. "The Hawthornes in Paradise," AmH, 10 (1958), 30-35, 112-15.

Also in TREASURY OF AMERICAN HERITAGE. New York: Simon Schuster, 1960, pp. 300-309.

470 Cowley, Malcolm. "Introduction," THE PORTABLE HAWTHORNE. Malcolm Cowley, ed. New York: Viking Press, 1948, 1958. Rev. ed. 1969.

See Richard Chase, "The Progressive Hawthorne," PR, 16 (1949), 96-100.

Rev. by Manning Hawthorne, NEQ, 22 (1949), 105-08.

471 Cowley, Malcolm. THE LITERARY SITUATION. New York: Viking Press, 1954.

471.1 Cowley, Malcolm. A MANY-WINDOWED HOUSE: COLLECTED ESSAYS ON AMERICAN WRITERS AND AMERICAN WRITING. Edited with Introduction by Henry Dan Piper. Carbondale: Southern Ill. U. P., 1970.

Contains interpretations of Hawthorne and others.

Rev. by John Lydenberg, AL, 43 (1972), 673-75.

472 Cowley, Malcolm. "100 Years Ago: Hawthorne Set a Great New Pattern," NYHTBR (August 6, 1950), 1-13.

THE SCARLET LETTER brought Greek tragedy to the American novel.

473 Cox, James M. "Emerson and Hawthorne: Trust and Doubt," VQR, 45 (1969), 88-107.

Contrast between Emerson and Hawthorne not antagonistic.

474 Coxe, Arthur Cleveland. "The Writings of Hawthorne," ChR, 3 (1851), 489-511.

Also in NOTORIOUS LITERARY ATTACKS, Albert Mordell, ed. Boni & Liveright, 1926, pp. 122-37.

475 Coxe, Louis. "Hawthorne," (Poem), <u>Atl.</u> 172 (1943), 87.

476 Coyle, William. "Fearful Confrontations," in THE YOUNG MAN
IN AMERICAN LITERATURE: THE INITIATION THEME. William
Coyle, ed. New York: Odyssey, 1969, pp. 238-40.

Most of Hawthorne's characters are initiates of evil
from birth.

477 Cracroft, Richard H. "Liverpool, 1856: Nathaniel Hawthorne
Meets Orson Pratt," BYUS, 8 (1968), 270-72.

478 Crane, Maurice A. "THE BLITHEDALE ROMANCE as Theatre,"
N&Q, 203 (1958), 84-86.

Experimentation with dramatic forms in THE BLITHEDALE
ROMANCE a prefiguration of the point-of-view technique.

479 Crane, Maurice A. "The Case of the Drunken Goldfish,"
CE, 17 (1956), 309-10.

Hawthorne's use of reverie about the goldfish in a
tavern in THE BLITHEDALE ROMANCE compared with realistic
but less effective treatment of the subject by other
authors.

480 Crane, Maurice A. "A Textual and Critical Edition of
Hawthorne's BLITHEDALE ROMANCE," DA, 14 (Ill.: 1953), 2.

481 Crawford, Bartholow W., et al. AMERICAN LITERATURE. 3rd ed.
New York: 1953, 1957.

An outline history of American literature. Earlier
editions bear title AN OUTLINE-HISTORY OF AMERICAN
LITERATURE.

482 Crawford, Bartholow W., and Alexander C. Kern, Morriss H.
Needleman. AN OUTLINE-HISTORY OF AMERICAN LITERATURE.
New York: 1945.

Rev. by Tremaine McDowell, AL, 28 (1947), 266-67.

483 Crawford, Mary Caroline. "The Old Manse and Some of Its
Mosses," in ROMANCE OF OLD NEW ENGLAND ROOFTREES.
1903, pp. 324-40.

484 Crawford, Mary Caroline. OLD NEW ENGLAND INNS. Boston:
Page & Co., 1924, p. 207. First ed., 1907, under
title: AMONG OLD NEW ENGLAND INNS.

485 Crétien, L. E. LA PENSÉE MORALE DE NATHANIEL HAWTHORNE
(1804-1864), SYMBOLISTE NEO-PURITAN. Diss. Paris:
1932.

486 Crews, Frederick C. "Giovanni's Garden," AQ, 16 (1964), 402-18.

487 Crews, Frederick C. "Introduction," GREAT SHORT WORKS OF NATHANIEL HAWTHORNE. Frederick C. Crews, ed. New York: Harper & Row, 1967, pp. vii-xii.

488 Crews, Frederick C. "The Logic of Compulsion in 'Roger Malvin's Burial,'" PMLA, 79 (1964), 457-65.

Psychological guilt and expiation.

489 Crews, Frederick C. "A New Reading of THE BLITHEDALE ROMANCE," AL, 29 (1957), 147-70.

490 Crews, Frederick C. "The Ruined Wall: Unconscious Motivation in THE SCARLET LETTER," NEQ, 38 (1965), 312-30.

491 Crews, Frederick C. THE SINS OF THE FATHERS: HAWTHORNE'S PSYCHOLOGICAL THEMES. New York: Oxford U. P., 1966.

Revs. by Allan Angoff, LJ, 91 (1966), 12, 14, 16; Choice, 3 (1966), 634; Frederick C. Crews, "The Sins of the Fathers: An Exchange," NCF, 22 (1967), 101-10; R. Diebold, CM, 8 (1967), 92-97; Edward M. Holmes, NEQ, 39 (1966), 537-39; Josipovici, G. D., CritQ, 8 (1966), 351-60; A. N. Kaul, YR, 56 (1966), 148-52; Roy R. Male, NCF, 21 (1966), 193-96; Sidney P. Moss, ABC, 17 (1967), 6; Joel Porte, CSM, 58 (1966), 4; Jacques M. Quen, NCF (1967), 101; Philip Rahv, NYRB, 7 (1966), 21-23; C. T. Samuels, Cw, 84 (1966), 504-06; C. T. Samuels, Cw, 85 (1966), 272; William B. Stein, AL, 38 (1967), 564-65; Lawrance Thompson, BW (1966), 5.

492 Crews, Frederick C. "The Sins of the Fathers: An Exchange," NCF, 22 (1967).

Exchange of views with Jacques M. Quen and Roy R. Male.

493 Crie, Robert D. "The Minister's Black Veil: Mr. Hooper's Symbolic Leaf," L&P, 17 (1967), 211-17.

Hawthorne employs details to hint that the minister uses the veil to escape responsibilities of his manhood.

494 Cronin, Morton. "Hawthorne on Romantic Love and the Status of Woman," PMLA, 69 (1954), 89-98.

Hawthorne is romantic in treatment of legitimate love, but he rejects the romantic ideal of ethical freedom and individual sanctions.

495 Cronkhite, G. Ferris. "The Transcendental Railroad," NEQ, 24 (1951), 306-28.

The railroad as a symbol of the main current of American life.

496 Cross, Wilbur L. THE DEVELOPMENT OF THE ENGLISH NOVEL. New York: Macmillan, 1899, 1927.

Once a standard text. Many references to Hawthorne.

497 Crothers, Samuel M. "Address," [at the Hawthorne Centenary] EIHC, 41 (1905), 9-20.

498 Crothers, Samuel M. "Man under Enchantment," in PARDONER'S WALLET. Houghton, 1905, pp. 249-66.

499 Crowley, J. Donald. "A False Edition of Hawthorne's TWICE-TOLD TALES," PBSA, 59 (1965), 182-88.

500 Crowley, J. Donald, ed. HAWTHORNE: THE CRITICAL HERITAGE. New York: Barnes & Noble, 1971.

501 Crowley, J. Donald. "Nathaniel Hawthorne's TWICE-TOLD TALES: A Textual Study Based on an Analysis of the Tales in the Three Major Collections (Volumes I and III)." DA, 25 (Ohio St. U.: 1964), 7242.

502 Cuff, Roger Penn. A STUDY IN CLASSICAL MYTHOLOGY IN HAWTHORNE'S WRITINGS. Diss. Peabody: 1936.

503 Cummings, Abbott Lowell. "Nathaniel Hawthorne's Birthplace: An Architectural Study," EIHC, 94 (1958), 196-204.

504 Cunliffe, Marcus. "THE HOUSE OF THE SEVEN GABLES," in HAWTHORNE CENTENARY ESSAYS. Columbus: Ohio St. U.P., 1964, pp. 79-101.

505 Cunliffe, Marcus. "New England's Day (Emerson, Thoreau, Hawthorne," in THE LITERATURE OF THE UNITED STATES. London, Baltimore: Penguin Books, 1954, 1959, pp. 75-104.

Hawthorne would have agreed with Emerson that every natural fact is "a symbol of some spiritual fact."

506 Cunliffe, W. Gordon, and John V. Hagopian. "The Minister's
Black Veil," in John V. Hagopian and Martin Dolch, eds.
INSIGHT I: ANALYSES OF AMERICAN LITERATURE. Frankfurt:
Hirschgraben, 1962, pp. 78-81.

507 Curl, Vega. PASTEBOARD MASKS: FACT AS SPIRITUAL SYMBOL IN
THE NOVELS OF HAWTHORNE AND MELVILLE. Cambridge:
Harvard U. P., 1931.

Hawthorne is concerned with the psychological and moral.

507.1 Curran, Ronald T. "Hawthorne as Gothicist," DAI, 30
(Pa.: 1970), 4404A-05A.

508 Curran, Ronald T. "Irony: Another Thematic Dimension to
'The Artist of the Beautiful,'" SIR, 6 (1966), 34-45.

Hawthorne indicates limitations of art and of the
egocentric artist when he directs irony at the
protagonist's personality, his creation, and his
supposed victory over unimaginative humanity.

509 Current-García, Eugene, and Walton R. Patrick. "Hawthorne:
The American Novel in the Nineteenth Century,"
REALISM AND ROMANTICISM IN FICTION. Chicago: Scott,
Foresman, 1962, pp. 1-37; 22-23.

510 Curti, Merle. THE GROWTH OF AMERICAN THOUGHT. New York:
Harper, 1943, pp. 393, 476.

Hawthorne's view of reformers. No churchman presented
man's frailty so engagingly as Hawthorne.

511 Curti, Merle. "Human Nature in American Thought: The Age
of Reason and Morality, 1750-1860," PSQ, 68 (1953),
354-75.

512 Curtis, Edith Roelker. "Mr. Hawthorne Arrives in an April
Snowstorm at Brook Farm," NEG, 2 (1961), 17-25.

Essay also in A SEASON IN UTOPIA: THE STORY OF BROOK
FARM by the same author. New York: Thomas Nelson &
Sons, 1961, 13-19.

512.1 Curtis, George William. "Hawthorne and Brook Farm," in his
FROM THE EASY CHAIR, THIRD SERIES. New York: Harper,
1894, pp. 1-19.

512.2 Curtis, George William. LITERARY AND SOCIAL ESSAYS.
New York: Harper, 1895, pp. 33-93.

513 Curtis, George William. "The Works of Nathaniel Hawthorne,"
    NAR, 99 (1864), 539-57.

514 Curtsinger, Eugene Cleveland. "The Byronic Hero and
    Hawthorne's Seekers: A Comparative Study," DA, 15
    (Notre Dame: 1955).

515 Cushman, Bigelow Paine. "Hawthorne's Moral Ambiguity and
    Bipolarity," DA, 26 (Wis.: 1965), 3298.

516 Daghlian, Philip B., and Horst Frenz. "Evaluations of a
    World Literature Course," CE, 12 (1950), 150-53.

517 Dahl, Curtis. "The American School of Catastrophe," AQ, 11
    (1959), 380.

518 Dahl, Curtis. "The Devil is a Wise One," Cithara, 6 (1967),
    52-58.

        Hawthorne uses the Devil to preach the evil of
        moral isolation.

519 Dahl, Curtis. "When the Deity Returns: THE MARBLE FAUN and
    ROMCLA," in STUDIES IN AMERICAN LITERATURE IN HONOR OF
    ROBERT DUNN FANER, 1906-1967. PLL 5, Supp. (Summer).
    [Charles D. Tenney, "Robert Dunn Faner, 1906-1967: A
    Eulogy," 1-5; "Vita...," 5-6.] Robert Partlow, ed.
    1969, pp.82-100.

520 Dameron, J. Lasley. "Hawthorne and BLACKWOOD'S Review of
    Goethe's FAUST," ESQ, 19 (1960), 25.

        Hawthorne's knowledge of FAUST uncertain but he
        probably knew BLACKWOOD'S review.

521 Dameron, J. Lasley. "Hawthorne's 'THE HOUSE OF THE SEVEN
    GABLES': A Serpent Image," N&Q, 6 (1959), 289-90.

522 Dana, Henry Wadsworth, and Manning Hawthorne. "'The Maiden
    Aunt of the Whole Human Race': Fredrika Bremer's
    Friendship with Longfellow and Hawthorne," AmSR, 37
    (1949), 217-229.

523 Darley, Felix O. C. (Drawings by) "Forgotten Pictures for
    a Famous Book, THE SCARLET LETTER," Century, 108
    (1924), 219-24.

524 Darnell, Donald Gene. "Hawthorne's Emblematic Method,"
    DA, 25 (Tex.: 1965), 5903.

525 Dauner, Louise. "The 'Case' of Tobias Pearson: Hawthorne
     and the Ambiguities," AL, 21 (1950), 464-72.

     Parallels Melville's PIERRE in many respects.

526 Dauphin, Vernon A. "Religious Content in Hawthorne's Works,"
     SoUB, 46 (1959), 115-23.

     Problem of sin eccentric in "Rappaccini's Daughter,"
     superficial in "The Hollow of Three Hills," and
     profound in THE SCARLET LETTER.

527 Davenport, Basil. "Foreword," THE SCARLET LETTER. New
     York: Dodd, Mead, 1948.

528 Davidson, Edward H. "Dimmesdale's Fall," NEQ, 26 (1963),
     358-70.

529 Davidson, Edward H. "Hawthorne and the Pathetic Fallacy,"
     JEGP, 54 (1955), 486-97.

     Above essay also appears in Studies by members of the
     English Department, University of Illinois, in memory
     of John Jay Parry, pp. 26-37.

530 Davidson, Edward H. HAWTHORNE'S LAST PHASE. New Haven:
     Yale U. P., 1949.

     Rev. by Arlin Turner, AL, 21 (1949-50), 360-62;
     Austin Warren, NEQ, 24 (1951), 101-03.

531 Davidson, Edward H. "Introduction and Notes," DR. GRIMSHAWE'S
     SECRET. Edward H. Davidson, ed. Cambridge: Harvard
     U. P., 1954; New York: 1955.

     Rev. by Randall Stewart, AL, 27 (1956), 595-96;
     Carvel Collins, NEQ, 29 (1956), 258-61.

532 Davidson, Edward H. THE LAST PHASE OF HAWTHORNE'S ART. Diss.
     Yale: 1940.

533 Davidson, Edward H. "Nathaniel Hawthorne," in MAJOR WRITERS
     OF AMERICA. Perry Miller, gen. ed. New York: Harcourt,
     Brace & World, 1962.

534 Davidson, Edward H. "The Question of History in THE SCARLET
     LETTER," in Carl F. Strauch, et al, Symposium on
     Nathaniel Hawthorne, ESQ, 25 (1961), 2-3.

535 Davidson, Edward H. "The Unfinished Romances," in
     HAWTHORNE CENTENARY ESSAYS, Roy Harvey Pearce, ed.
     Columbus: Ohio St. U. P., 1964, pp. 141-63.

536 Davidson, Frank. "Hawthorne's Hive of Honey," MLN, 61 (1946),
     14-21.

     Influences of Shakespeare and Milton.

537 Davidson, Frank. "Hawthorne's Use of Pattern from THE
     RAMBLER," MLN, 63 (1948), 545-58.

     Five sketches from the MOSSES appear to be designed
     after Nos. 82 and 105 of Johnson's RAMBLER.

538 Davidson, Frank. "Thoreau's Contribution to Hawthorne's
     MOSSES," NEQ, 20 (1947), 535-42.

539 Davidson, Frank. "Toward a Re-Evaluation of THE BLITHEDALE
     ROMANCE," NEQ, 25 (1952), 374-83.

540 Davidson, Frank. "Voltaire and Hawthorne's 'The Christmas
     Banquet,'" BPLQ, 3 (1951), 244-46.

     Hawthorne's source may have been the banquet for the
     most miserable people in Ch. XIX, Candide.

541 Davidson, Frank. "'Young Goodman Brown'--Hawthorne's Intent,"
     ESQ, 31 (1963), 68-71.

     Similarities to first two acts of "Macbeth," the
     progress of evil throught toward guilty deed.

542 Davidson, H. A. "Introductory Sketch," THE HOUSE OF THE
     SEVEN GABLES. Boston: Houghton, Mifflin & Co., 1904,
     1923, 1932, pp. v-xviii.

543 Davie, Donald. "The Legacy of Fenimore Cooper," EsCr, 9
     (1959), 222-38.

544 Davies, Horton. "Preachers and Evangelists," in A MIRROR
     OF THE MINISTRY IN MODERN NOVELS. New York: Oxford
     U. P., 1959, pp. 21-47.

     Hawthorne chose a minister for the particular role in
     THE SCARLET LETTER because the moral leader of the
     community would best show the nature of hypocrisy
     and the fatal flaw of Puritanism.

545 Davis, Joe. "The Myth of the Garden: Nathaniel Hawthorne's
     'Rappaccini's Daughter,'" SLitI, 2, i (1969), 3-12.

     Two mythic levels clarify story's ambiguity: the
     "lost Eden Paradise" and redemption of this Eden
     through selfless acts.

546 Davis, Merrell R., and William H. Gilman, eds. THE LETTERS
     OF HERMAN MELVILLE. New Haven: Yale U.P., 1960.

     Melville's letters to Hawthorne.

547 Davis, Richard Beale. "The Americanness of American
     Literature: Folk and Historical Themes and Materials
     in Formal Writing." LC, 3 (1959), 10-22.

     American writers' use of Merry Mount.

548 Davis, Richard Beale. "Hawthorne, Fanny Kemble, and 'The
     Artist of the Beautiful,'" MLN, 70 (1955), 589-92.

     A paragraph of Kemble's JOURNAL a likely source for
     Hawthorne's story.

549 Davison, Richard Allan. "Redburn, Pierre, and Robin:
     Melville's Debt to Hawthorne?" ESQ, 47 (1967), 32-34.

550 Davison, Richard Allan. "The Villagers in 'Ethan Brand,'"
     SSF, 4 (1967), 260-62.

     The stage-agent, the lawyer, and the doctor as
     failures serve as microcosmic reflectors of the
     main theme embodied in Ethan Brand. For Ethan they
     provide examples of the "inhumanity of his own
     desperate search."

551 Dawson, Edward. HAWTHORNE'S KNOWLEDGE AND USE OF NEW
     ENGLAND HISTORY: A STUDY OF SOURCES. Diss. Vanderbilt:
     1938.

552 Dawson, Wm. James. "American Novelists," /N. Hawthorne/ in
     THE MAKERS OF ENGLISH FICTION. New York: Revell, 1905,
     pp. 291-98.

553 DeBakey, Lois Elizabeth. "The Physician-Scientist as
     Character in Nineteenth-Century American Literature,"
     DA, 24 (Tulane: 1963), 3333.

554 De Casseres, Benjamin. "Hawthorne: Emperor of Shadows,"
     Critic, 45 (1904), 37-44. Also in FORTY IMMORTALS.
     New York: Lawren, 1926, pp. 303-10.

     Pictures and Portraits.

     Cf., "Hawthorne, A Century After His Birth," AmRR,
     30 (1904), 232-33.

555 Deegan, Dorothy Yost. THE STEREOTYPE OF THE SINGLE WOMAN
     IN AMERICAN NOVELS: A SOCIAL STUDY WITH IMPLICATIONS
     FOR THE EDUCATION OF WOMEN. New York: Columbia U. P.,
     1951.

     Discussion of various women characters in Hawthorne.

     Rev. by Ima Honaker, AL, 33 (1952), 521-522.

556 DeHayes, R. "Charting Hawthorne's Invisible World,"
     CEA, 27 (1965), 5-6.

557 Delaune, Henry M. "The Beautiful of 'The Artist of the
     Beautiful.'" XUS, 1 (1961), 94-99.

558 De Logu, Pietro. "Il Diario di Hawthorne," in ARTE E
     MORALE: SAGGI DI LETTERATURE AMERICANA DALL'-OTTOCENTO
     AI GIORNI NOSTRI. Genoa: Di Stefano, pp. 19-30.

559 Denny, Margaret and William H. Gilman, eds. THE AMERICAN
     WRITER AND THE EUROPEAN TRADITION. Minneapolis:
     Minn. U. P., 1950.

560 Desmond, Mary E. "Associations of Hawthorne," CathW, 74
     (1902), 455-65.

561 Dhaleine, L. N. HAWTHORNE, SA VIE ET SON OEUVRE. [Thèse pour
     le doctorat, soutenue devant le Faculté des Lettres de
     l'Université de Paris.] Paris: Hachette & Cie, 1905.

563.1 Dickson, W. "Hawthorne's 'Young Goodman Brown,'" Expl. 29
     (1971), Item 44.

562 Dicey, Edward. "Three Great Authors," excerpt from "Six
     Months in the Federal States," AMERICA THROUGH BRITISH
     EYES, Allan Nevins, ed. New York: Oxford U. P., 1948,
     pp. 285-87.

     The "worker" and the "dreamer" merge in the writer of
     romance, Nathaniel Hawthorne.

563 Dichmann, Mary E. "Hawthorne's 'Prophetic Pictures,'"
     AL, 23 (1951), 188-202.

564 Dillingham, William B. "Arthur Dimmesdale's Confession,"
     SLitI, 2, 1 (1969), 21-26.

     Dimmesdale's confession consistent with his alienated
     existence.

565 Dillingham, William B. "Structure and Theme in THE HOUSE OF THE SEVEN GABLES," NCF, 14 (1959), 59-70. Repr. in STUDIES IN THE HOUSE OF THE SEVEN GABLES. Roger Asselineau, comp. Columbus, Ohio: Charles E. Merrill Publishing Co., 1970, pp. 74-85.

565.1 Dobbs, Jeannine. "Hawthorne's Dr. Rappaccini and Father George Rapp," AL, 43 (1971), 427-30.

566 Donohue, Agnes McNeill, ed. A CASEBOOK ON THE HAWTHORNE QUESTION. New York: Thomas Y. Crowell, 1963.

567 Donohue, Agnes McNeill. "'The Endless Journey to No End': Journey and Eden Symbolism in Hawthorne and Steinbeck," in A CASEBOOK ON THE GRAPES OF WRATH. Agnes McNeill Donohue, ed. New York: Crowell, 1968, pp. 257-66.

568 Donohue, Agnes McNeill. "'From Whose Bourn No Traveller Returns': A Reading of 'Roger Malvin's Burial,'" NCF, 18 (1963), 1-19.

The story has structure of a morality play.

569 Donohue, Agnes McNeill. "'The Fruit of that Forbidden Tree': A Reading of 'The Gentle Boy,'" in A CASEBOOK ON THE HAWTHORNE QUESTION. Agnes McNeill Donohue, ed. New York: Thomas Y. Crowell, 1963, pp. 158-70.

570 Dony, Françoise. "Romantisme et Puritanisme chez Hawthorne, à propos de la 'Lettre Pourpre,'" EA, 4 (1940), 15-30.

571 Dorson, Richard M. "Five Directions in American Folklore," MF, 1 (1951), 149-65.

572 Doubleday, Neal Frank. "Classroom Consideration of Hawthorne's Tales," in Carl F. Strauch, et al., Symposium on Nathaniel Hawthorne, ESQ, 25 (1961), 4-6.

573 Doubleday, Neal Frank, ed. HAWTHORNE: TALES OF HIS NATIVE LAND. Boston: Heath, 1962.

574 Doubleday, Neal Frank. "Hawthorne and Literary Nationalism," AL, 12 (1941), 447-53.

In his literary maturity, Hawthorne did not glorify American materials in the manner of Scott, for instance.

575 Doubleday, Neal Frank. HAWTHORNE'S APPRAISAL OF NEW ENGLAND LIFE AND THOUGHT. Diss. Wis.: 1938.

576 Doubleday, Neal Frank. "Hawthorne's Criticism of New England Life," CE, 2 (1941), 639-53.

577 Doubleday, Neal Frank. "Hawthorne's Estimate of His Early Work," AL, 37 (1966), 403-09.

578 Doubleday, Neal Frank. "Hawthorne's Hester and Feminism," PMLA, 54 (1939), 825-28.

The "consecration" of Hester's love is not the theme and moral of THE SCARLET LETTER.

579 Doubleday, Neal Frank. "Hawthorne's Inferno," CE, 1 (1940), 658-70.

Hawthorne saw pride as a sin, punishment of which was solitude.

580 Doubleday, Neal Frank. "Hawthorne's Satirical Allegory," CE, 3 (1942), 325-37.

581 Doubleday, Neal Frank. "Hawthorne's Use of Three Gothic Patterns," CE, 7 (1946), 258-59.

Repr., with changes in his HAWTHORNE: TALES OF HIS NATIVE LAND. Boston: Heath, 1962, pp. 77-78.

The three patterns are: (1) Mysterious portraits; (2) witchcraft; (3) the "wandering Jew" motif; elixir of life and allied occult experiments.

582 Doubleday, Neal Frank. "The Theme of Hawthorne's 'Fancy's Show Box,'" AL, 10 (1938), 341-43.

Parallels between Hawthorne's story and Jeremy Taylor's DUCTOR DUBITANTIUM.

583 Douglas, Harold J., and Robert Daniel. "Faulkner and the Puritanism of the South," TSL, 2 (1957), 5-10.

584 Dowling, Joseph A. "Introduction," THE DEMOCRATIC IMAGINATION: A GUIDE TO AN EXHIBITION OF RARE BOOKS BY RALPH WALDO EMERSON, HENRY DAVID THOREAU, NATHANIEL HAWTHORNE, WALT WHITMAN, HERMAN MELVILLE. Bethlehem, Pa.: Rare Book Room, Lehigh Univ. Library, October 1, 1968.

585 Drake, Samuel Adams. A BOOK OF NEW ENGLAND LEGENDS AND FOLK LORE IN PROSE AND POETRY. Boston: Little Brown & Co., 1906.

The Salem legends and their part in THE HOUSE OF THE SEVEN GABLES. Also, Swampscott is scene of Hawthorne's "Village Uncle."

585 Drummond, Andrew L. THE CHURCHES IN ENGLISH FICTION.
    Leicester: Edgar Backus, 1950.

586.1 Dryden, E. A. "Hawthorne's Castle in the Air: Form and
    Theme in THE HOUSE OF THE SEVEN GABLES," ELH, 38 (1971),
    294-317.

586.2 Duerksen, Roland A. "The Double Image of Beatrice Cenci in
    THE MARBLE FAUN," MichA, 1 (1969), 47-55.

587 Duffey, Bernard I. "Hawthorne Seen in a Steeple," ChS, 38
    (1955), 134-41.

588 Duggan, Francis X. "Doctrine and the Writers of the American
    Renaissance," ESQ, 39 (1965), 45-51.

589 Duggan, Francis X. "Paul Elmer More and the New England
    Tradition," AL, 34 (1963), 542-61.

    Hawthorne "the symbolist of the religious imagination."

590 Dunlap, Leslie W. "The Letters of Willis Gaylord Clark and
    Lewis Gaylord Clark," BNYPL, 42 (1938), 455-76; 523-48;
    613-36; 753-79; 857-81.

    Letters to Hawthorne and others.

590.1 Dunne, Michael F. "Order and Excess in Hawthorne's Fiction,"
    DAI, 30 (La. State: 1970), 3003A-04A.

590.2 Durham, Frank. "Hawthorne and Goldsmith: A Note," JAmS,
    4 (1970), 103-105.

591 Durr, Robert Allen. "Feathertop's Unlikely Love Affair,"
    MLN, 72 (1957), 492-93.

592 Durr, Robert Allen. "Hawthorne's Ironic Mode," NEQ, 30
    (1957), 486-95.

593 Durston, J. H. "14 Unknown Hawthorne Works Reported Found
    by Collector," NYHTBR, 12 (1948), 15.

594 Dusenbery, Robert. "Hawthorne's Merry Company: The Anatomy
    of Laughter in the Tales and Short Stories," PMLA, 82
    (1967), 285-88.

    Mirthful laughter foreshadows disillusionment. More
    evil characters laugh fiendishly.

595   Dwight, Marianne. LETTERS FROM BROOK FARM 1844-1847. Amy L. Reed, ed. Poughkeepsie, New York: Vassar College, 1928.

595.1 Dwight, Sheila. "Hawthorne and the Unpardonable Sin," SNNTS, 2 (1970), 449-58.

596   Eagle, Nancy L. "An Unpublished Hawthorne Letter," AL, 23 (1951), 360-62.

To James T. Fields, February 22, 1851, in which Hawthorne attributes the vogue of THE SCARLET LETTER to "The Custom House" introduction.

596.1 Eakin, Paul John. "Hawthorne's Imagination and the Structure of 'The Custom House,'" AL, 43 (1971), 346-58.

597 Earnest, Ernest. "The Ambivalent Puritan: Nathaniel Hawthorne," in EXPATRIATES AND PATRIOTS: AMERICAN ARTISTS, SCHOLARS, AND WRITERS IN EUROPE. Durham, N. C.: Duke U. P., 1968, pp. 152-81.

598 Eaton, Anne Thaxter. "Foreword," THE GOLDEN TOUCH. Illustrated by Paul Galdone. New York, Toronto, London, Sydney: McGraw-Hill Book Co., 1959.

599 Eaton, Clement. "The Brighton Cattle Fair," in THE LEAVEN OF DEMOCRACY: THE GROWTH OF THE DEMOCRATIC SPIRIT IN THE TIME OF JACKSON. Clement Eaton, ed. New York: Braziller, 1963, pp. 124-26.

600 Edel, Leon. "Hawthorne's Symbolism and Psychoanalysis," in HIDDEN PATTERNS. Leonard Falk and Eleanor B. Manheim, eds. New York: Macmillan, 1966, pp. 93-111.

601 Edel, Leon. THE MODERN PSYCHOLOGICAL NOVEL. New York: Grove Press, Inc., 1955), 115.

Remarks that when Henry James was accused of making a cruel caricature of Miss Peabody, Hawthorne's sister-in-law, James replied that the character was drawn from his "moral consciousness."

602 Edel, Leon, Thomas H. Johnson, et al., eds. MASTERS OF AMERICAN LITERATURE. New York: Houghton Mifflin, 1959.

604 Edgren, C. Hobart. "Hawthorne's 'The Ambitious Guest': An Interpretation," NCF, 10 (1955), 151-56.

The family is the collective protagonist, and their fate, not the guest's, is central to Hawthorne's intention.

605 "Editing Hawthorne's Notebooks: Selections from Mrs. Hawthorne's Letters to Mr. and Mrs. Fields, 1864-1868," More Books, 20 (1945), 312.

606 Eisenstein, Samuel A. "Literature and Myth," CE, 29 (1968), 369-73.

607 Eisinger, Chester E. "Hawthorne as Champion of the Middle Way," NEQ, 27 (1954), 27-52.

608 Eisinger, Chester E. "Pearl and the Puritan Heritage," CE, 12 (1951), 323-29.

Pearl an embodiment of Puritan conception of nature and the state. Cf. Darrel Abel, "Hawthorne's Pearl," ELH, 18 (1951), 50-66.

609 Elder, Marjorie J. NATHANIEL HAWTHORNE: TRANSCENDENTAL SYMBOLIST. Athens: Ohio U. P., 1969.

Rev. by Millicent Bell, AL, 43 (1971), 287-89.

609.1 Elias, Helen L. "Alice Doane's Innocence: The Wizard Absolved," ESQ, 62 (1971), 28-32.

610 Eliot, T. S. "On Henry James: The Hawthorne Aspect," LittleR, 5 (1918), 51, 53. Also in THE QUESTION OF HENRY JAMES, A COLLECTION OF CRITICAL ESSAYS. F. W. Dupee, ed. New York: Henry Holt, 1946, pp. 112-19. Repr. in B. Bernard Cohen's THE RECOGNITION OF NATHANIEL HAWTHORNE. Ann Arbor, Michigan: Michigan U. P., 1969, pp. 157-63. Excerpted in STUDIES IN THE HOUSE OF THE SEVEN GABLES. Roger Asselineau, comp. Columbus, Ohio: Charles E. Merrill Publishing Co., 1970, pp. 113-14.

611 Ellen, Sister Francis. "Creative Work Suggested by Hawthorne's THE HOUSE OF THE SEVEN GABLES," CathSJ, 53 (1953), 220-21.

612 Elliott, Robert E. "THE BLITHEDALE ROMANCE," in HAWTHORNE CENTENARY ESSAYS. Roy Harvey Pearce, ed. Columbus: Ohio St. U. P., 1964, pp. 103-17.

613 Ellis, James. "Frost's 'Desert Places' and Hawthorne," EngRec, 15 (1965), 15-17.

614 Ellison, Ralph. "The Evil Now Stares Out of the Bright
      Sunlight," in THE IDEA OF AN AMERICAN NOVEL. Louis D.
      Rubin and John Rees Moore, eds. New York: Thomas Y.
      Crowell Co., 1961, p. 170.

      A comic aspect in the controversy over what a novel
      should be is the implicit assumption held by
      Hawthorne and others that "society was created mainly
      so that novelists could write about it."

615 Ellison, Ralph. "Society, Morality, and the Novel," in
      THE LIVING NOVEL: A SYMPOSIUM. Granville Hicks, ed.
      New York: 1957, pp. 58-91.

616 Embler, Weller. "American Literature Revisited." CE, 12
      (1951), 406-07.

      Hawthorne and Melville, insisting upon the tragic view
      of life, are closer to readers today, but Hawthorne as
      novelist of seventeenth-century Puritan New England is
      of mild historical interest only.

617 Embree, Frances B. "Nathaniel Hawthorne," NCRev, 8 (1900),
      122-28.

618 Emerson, Edward Waldo. "Address," [at Hawthorne Centenary],
      EIHC, 41 (1905), 31-38.

619 Emerson, Edward Waldo. "Nathaniel Hawthorne," in EARLY
      YEARS OF THE SATURDAY CLUB, 1855-1870. New York:
      Houghton Mifflin Co., 1918, pp. 207-16.

620 Emerson, Edward Waldo, and W. E. Forbes, eds. JOURNALS OF
      RALPH WALDO EMERSON. Boston: 1914, X, 39-41.

      Emerson's account of funeral services for Hawthorne.

621 Emerson, Everett H. "Hawthorne in General Education," CEA
      25 (1963), 6.

622 Emerson, Ralph Waldo. THE HEART OF EMERSON'S JOURNALS,
      1820-1824. Bliss Perry, ed. New York: Houghton
      Mifflin Co., 1926; republished, New York: Dover,
      1958.

623 Emerson, Ralph Waldo. THE JOURNALS AND MISCELLANEOUS
      NOTEBOOKS OF RALPH WALDO EMERSON. William H. Gilman
      and Alfred R. Ferguson, eds. Cambridge, Mass.: The
      Belknap Press of Harvard U. P., 1963.

624 Emry, Hazel Thornburg. "Two Houses of Pride: Spenser's and Hawthorne's," PQ, 33 (1954), 91-94.

Spenser's House of Pride and THE HOUSE OF THE SEVEN GABLES.

625 "English Notes about Early Settlers in New England," EIHC, 39 (1903), 365-80.

An account of the Hawthorne family.

626 Ensor, Allison. "'Whispers of the Bad Angel': A SCARLET LETTER Passage as a Commentary on Hawthorne's 'Young Goodman Brown,'" SSF, ? (1970), 467-69.

627 Erikson, Ruth L. "Studying 'The Great Stone Face,'" Instr, 54 (1947), 33, 69.

628 Erlich, Gloria C. "Deadly Innocence: Hawthorne's Dark Women," NEQ, 41 (1968), 163-79.

629 Erskine, John. "Hawthorne," in CAMBRIDGE HISTORY OF AMERICAN LITERATURE. New York, 1933. I, 26-28.

630 Erskine, John. "Nathaniel Hawthorne," in LEADING AMERICAN NOVELISTS. New York: Henry Holt, 1910, 179-273.

631 ESSAY AND GENERAL LITERATURE INDEX, 1900-1970. New York: The H. W. Wilson Company.

632 ESSEX INSTITUTE. Exercises in Commemoration of the Centennial of the Birth of Nathaniel Hawthorne by the Essex Institute, Salem, Mass., Thursday afternoon, June 23, 1904. (Salem, 1904).

632.1 Estrin, Mark W. "Dramatizations of American Fiction: Hawthorne and Melville on Stage and Screen," DAI, 30 (N. Y. U.: 1970), 3428A.

633 Evanoff, Alexander. "Some Principal Themes in THE SCARLET LETTER," Discourse, 5 (1962), 270-77.

The novel is more concerned with hypocrisy than adultery.

634 Evans, Oliver. "Allegory and Invest in 'Rappaccini's Daughter,'" NCF, Hawthorne Centenary Issue, 19 (1964), 185-95.

636 Everett, L. B. "How the Great Ones Did It: Glimpse into Methods of Plot-making from the Heart of Hawthorne's Journals," Overland, 88 (1930), 88.

637 Fadiman, Cliftonn, ed. THE AMERICAN TREASURY, 1455-1955. New York: Harper & Bros., 1955.

638 Fairbanks, Henry G. "Citizen Hawthorne and the Perennial Problems of American Society," RUO, 29 (1959), 26-38.

639 Fairbanks, Henry G. "Hawthorne Amid the Alien Corn," CE, 17 (1956), 263-68.

Hawthorne's concept and treatment of the artist in America.

640 Fairbanks, Henry G. "Hawthorne and the Atomic Age," RUO, 31 (1961), 436-51.

Hawthorne's view of science.

641 Fairbanks, Henry G. "Hawthorne and the Catholic Church," BUSE, 1 (1955), 148-65.

642 Fairbanks, Henry G. "Hawthorne and Confession," CathHR, 43 (1957), 38-45.

643 Fairbanks, Henry G. "Hawthorne and the Machine Age," AL 28 (1956), 155-63.

644 Fairbanks, Henry G. "Hawthorne and the Nature of Man: Changing Personality Concepts in the Nineteenth Century," RUO, 28 (1958), 309-22.

645 Fairbanks, Henry G. "Hawthorne and the Vanishing Venus," UTSE, 36 (1957), 52-70.

646 No entry

647 Fairbanks, Henry G. THE LASTING LONELINESS OF NATHANIEL HAWTHORNE: A STUDY OF THE SOURCES OF ALIENATION IN MODERN MAN. Albany, New York: Magi Books, 1965.

Rev. by Terence Martin, AL, 38 (1966), 250-51; and by Booklist, 62 (1965), 131.

648 Fairbanks, Henry G. "Hawthorne's 'Catholic' Critique," DA, 15 (Notre Dame: 1955), 265-66.

649 Fairbanks, Henry G. "Man's Separation from Nature: Hawthorne's Philosophy of Suffering and Death," ChS, 42 (1959), 51-63.

Hawthorne was no worshipper of "old Pan." For Hawthorne "reality was still primarily spiritual."

650 Fairbanks, Henry G. "Sin, Free Will, and 'Pessimism' in Hawthorne," PMLA, 71 (1956), 975-89.

See Joseph T. McCullen and John C. Guilds, "The Unpardonable Sin in Hawthorne: A Re-Examination," NCF, 15 (1960), 221-37; and James E. Miller, Jr., "Hawthorne and Melville: The Unpardonable Sin," PMLA, 70 (1955), 91-114.

651 Fairbanks, Henry G. "Theocracy to Transcendentalism in America," ESQ, 44 (1966), 45-59.

652 Fales, Dean A., Jr. Introduction to "Special Hawthorne Issue," EIHC, 100 (1964), 233-34.

653 Falk, Robert P. "The Literary Criticism of the Genteel Decades, 1870-1900," in THE DEVELOPMENT OF AMERICAN LITERARY CRITICISM. Floyd Stovall, ed. Chapel Hill, N. C.: North Carolina U. P., 1955, pp. 113-58.

654 Falk, Robert P. "The Rise of Realism, 1871-1891," in TRANSITIONS IN AMERICAN LITERARY CRITICISM. Harry Hayden Clark, ed. Durham, N. C.: Duke U. P., 1953.

655 Farmer, Norman, Jr. "Maule's Curse and the Rev. Nicholas Noyes: A Note on Hawthorne's Source," N&Q, 11 (1964), 224-25.

See George Monteiro for comment: "Maule's Curse and Julian Hawthorne," N&Q, 14 (1967), 62-63.

655.1 Fass, Barbara. "Rejection of Paternalism: Hawthorne's 'My Kinsman, Major Molineux' and Ellison's INVISIBLE MAN," CLAJ, 14 (1971), 313-23.

656 Faust, Bertha. HAWTHORNE'S CONTEMPORANEOUS REPUTATION: A STUDY OF LITERARY OPINION IN AMERICA AND ENGLAND, 1828-1864. Diss. Pa.: 1937. Privately printed: Philadelphia: 1939. Reprinted, New York: Octagon Books, 1968.

Contains chronological list of reviews, notices, and articles relating to Hawthorne's work, 1828-1864.

Rev. by Randall Stewart, AL, 12 (1940-41), 373-74.

657 Feidelson, Charles, Jr. "Hawthorne," SYMBOLISM AND AMERICAN LITERATURE. Chicago: Chicago U. P., 1953, pp. 6-16.

658 Feidelson, Charles, Jr. SYMBOLISM AND AMERICAN LITERATURE. Chicago: Chicago U. P., 1953, passim.

659 Feidelson, Charles, Jr. "THE SCARLET LETTER," in HAWTHORNE CENTENARY ESSAYS. Roy Harvey Pearce, ed. Columbus: Ohio State U. P., 1964, pp. 31-77.

660 Feidelson, Charles, Jr., and Paul Brodtkorb, Jr., eds. INTERPRETATIONS OF AMERICAN LITERATURE. New York: Yale U. P., 1959.

661 Fenson, Harry, and Hildreth Kritzer, eds. WRITING ABOUT SHORT STORIES. New York: Free Press, 1966, pp. 61-62.

662 Ferguson, J. D. "The Earliest Translation of Hawthorne," Nation, 100 (1915), 14-15.

Earliest recorded translations are the German versions of THE SCARLET LETTER and THE HOUSE OF SEVEN GABLES in 1851. A German version of TWICE-TOLD TALES occurs in 1852, and three Tales ("David Swan," "Rappaccini's Daughter," and "Mr. Higginbotham's Catastrophe") in French, 1853.

663 Ferguson, J. D. "Nathaniel Hawthorne," AMERICAN LITERATURE IN SPAIN. New York: Columbia U. P., 1916, pp. 87-108.

Chapter published in Nation, 100 (1915), 14-15.

664 Ferguson, J. M., Jr. "Hawthorne's 'Young Goodman Brown,'" Expl. 28 (1969), Item 32.

665 Ferrell, Margaret J. "Dissolving the Gross Actuality of Fact: Hawthorne's Attack on Matter," DA, 28 (Okla.: 1967), 1432A

666 Ficatier, Marc Etienne. "Le puritanisme américain chez Nathaniel Hawthorne," RPsyP (France), 6 (1951), 144-71.

667 Fick, Leonard J. THE LIGHT BEYOND: A STUDY OF HAWTHORNE'S THEOLOGY. Westminster, Maryland: Newman P., 1955.

Revs., CE, 19 (1957), 43-44;
Alfred S. Reid, ESQ, 6 (1957), 39-40;
Hyatt H. Waggoner, AL, 28 (1956), 384-85.

668 Fick, Leonard J. THE THEOLOGY OF NATHANIEL HAWTHORNE. Diss. Ohio State: 1951.

[669]Fiedler, Leslie A. "An American Abroad," PR, 33 (1966), 77-91.

[670] Fiedler, Leslie A. "American Literature," CONTEMPORARY LITERARY SCHOLARSHIP, Lewis Leary, ed. New York: Appleton-Century-Crofts, Inc., 1958, 157-85.

[671] Fiedler, Leslie A. "Boys Will Be Boys," NewL, 41 (1958), 23-26.

[672] Fiedler, Leslie A., ed. "The Custom House, Introductory," ART OF THE ESSAY. New York: 1958, pp. 99-122.

[673] Fiedler, Leslie A. AN END TO INNOCENCE. Boston: Beacon Press, 1955.

[674] Fiedler, Leslie A. "Le viol des /sic/ Temple: de Richardson à Faulkner," Preuves, 138 (1962), 78-81.

[675] Fiedler, Leslie A. NO! IN THUNDER: ESSAYS ON MYTH AND LITERATURE. Boston: Beacon Press, 1960.

[676] Fiedler, Leslie A. "Scarlet Letter: Woman as Faust," in LOVE AND DEATH IN THE AMERICAN NOVEL. New York: World, 1960; Revised ed. New York: Stein and Day, 1966.

Rev. by Allen Hayman, NEQ, 34 (1961), 261-63; Willard Thorp, NY Herald Trib Bk Rev. April 10, 1960, 5.

[677] Fields, Annie. NATHANIEL HAWTHORNE. Boston: Small, Maynard, 1899.

Contains bibliography, pp. 133-36.

[677.1] Fields, James T. HAWTHORNE. Boston: J. R. Osgood, 1876.

[678] Fields, James T. "Hawthorne," YESTERDAYS WITH AUTHORS. Boston: Osgood, 1872, pp. 41-124. Repr. in HAWTHORNE AMONG HIS CONTEMPORARIES. Kenneth Walter Cameron, ed. Hartford, Conn.: Transcendental Books, 1968, pp. 308-32.

[679] Finch, I. W. A STUDY OF THE RELATIONSHIP BETWEEN HAWTHORNE AND HENRY JAMES. Diss. Harvard: 1939.

[680]First Editions of Hawthorne, LitC, 8 (1904), 109-116.

681 FIRST EDITIONS OF TEN AMERICAN AUTHORS COLLECTED BY J. CHESTER
CHAMBERLAIN. New York: Anderson Auction Company,
February 16-17, 1909, Part I, 18-38. Sale catalogue.

682 FIRST EDITIONS OF THE WORKS OF NATHANIEL HAWTHORNE TOGETHER WITH
SOME MANUSCRIPTS, LETTERS, AND PORTRAITS. New York:
The Grolier Club, 1904.

683 "First Editions of the Writings of Nathaniel Hawthorne,"
KIHC, 41 (1905), 111-12.

684 Fisher, Arthur W. NATHANIEL HAWTHORNE: A STUDY. Diss.
Cornell: 1907.

685 Fisher, Marvin. "The Pattern of Conservatism in Johnson's
RASSELAS and Hawthorne's Tales," JHI, 19 (1958), 173-96.

686 Fitch, George Hamlin. "Hawthorne's Somber Puritan Romances,"
GREAT SPIRITUAL WRITERS OF AMERICA. Elder, 1916, pp.
37-47.

687 Flanagan, John T. "The Durable Hawthorne," JEGP, 49 (1950),
88-96.

688 Flanagan, John T. "Point of View in THE MARBLE FAUN,"
NS, 11 (1962), 218-23.

689 Flanagan, John T., and Arthur P. Hudson. FOLKLORE IN
AMERICAN LITERATURE. Evanston, Ill.: Row, Peterson,
1958, p. 105.

690 Fletcher, Angus. "The Cosmic Image," in ALLEGORY: THE THEORY
OF A SYMBOLIC MODE. Ithaca: Cornell U. P., 1964.

691 Flint, Allen. "Hawthorne and the Slavery Crisis," NEQ, 41
(1968), 393-408.

692 Flint, Allen. "Hawthorne's Political and Social Themes,"
DA, 27 (Minn.: 1966), 1820A.

693 Foerster, Norman. AMERICAN CRITICISM: A STUDY IN LITERARY
THEORY FROM POE TO THE PRESENT. New York: Houghton
Mifflin, 1928.

Emerson's "terrible approval" of Hawthorne is quoted:
"His reputation as a writer is a very pleasing fact,
because his writing is not good for anything, and this
is a tribute to the man."

694 Foerster, Norman. IMAGE OF AMERICA. South Bend: Notre Dame
U. P., 1962.

695 Foerster, Norman. NATURE IN AMERICAN LITERATURE: STUDIES
IN THE MODERN VIEW OF NATURE. New York: Russell &
Russell, 1923, 1950, pp. 32, 132.

696 Foerster, Norman, ed. THE REINTERPRETATION OF AMERICAN
LITERATURE. New York: Harcourt, Brace, 1928; reissued
1955, 1959.

Rev. by Henry Seidel Canby, AL, 1 (1929-30), 79-85;
SatRL, March, 1929.

697 Fogarty, Robert S. "A Utopian Literary Canon," NEQ, 38
(1965), 386-91.

Attitudes of Oneida Community towards Hawthorne
and Thoreau.

698 Fogle, Richard Harter. "Ambiguity and Clarity in Hawthorne's
'Young Goodman Brown," NEQ, 18 (1945), 448-65.

699 Fogle, Richard Harter. "An Ambiguity of Sin or Sorrow,"
NEQ, 21 (1948), 342-49.

Repr. in Fogle's HAWTHORNE'S FICTION: THE LIGHT AND
THE DARK. Norman, Okla.: Okla. U. P., 1952, pp. 33-40.

700 Fogle, Richard Harter. "Hawthorne," in AMERICAN LITERARY
SCHOLARSHIP: AN ANNUAL, 1965. James Woodress, ed.
Durham, N. C.: Duke U. P., 1967, pp. 15-27.

700.1 Fogle, Richard Harter. "Hawthorne and Coleridge on
Credibility," *Criticism*, 13 (1971), 234-41.

701 Fogle, Richard Harter. HAWTHORNE'S FICTION: THE LIGHT AND THE
DARK. Norman, Okla.: Okla. U. P., 1952.

Revs. by Walter E. Bezanson, NEQ, 26 (1953), 403-05;
C. T. Houpt, CSM (1953), 7;
J. V., SFC (1953), 11;
Hugo McPherson, QQ, 61 (1954), 280-81;
Sherman Paul, NMQ, 23 (1953), 339-42;
Randall Stewart, AL, 25 (1953), 246-27;
Warfel, Harry R, CC, 70 (1953), 19.

702 Fogle, Richard Harter. HAWTHORNE'S FICTION: THE LIGHT AND THE DARK. Norman, Okla.: Okla. U. P., 1964.

Addition of interpretations to 1952 edition, and omission of annotated bibliography.

Revs., AL, 37 (1965), 228; Choice, 2 (1965), 226; J. Merrill, FSF, 29 (1965), 73.

703 Fogle, Richard Harter. HAWTHORNE'S IMAGERY: THE 'PROPER LIGHT AND SHADOW' IN THE MAJOR ROMANCES. Norman: Okla. U. P., 1969.

Rev. by Edward H. Davidson, AL, 42 (1970), 400-01.

703.1 Fogle, Richard Harter. "Hawthorne's Pictorial Unity," ESQ, 55 (1969), 71-76.

704 Fogle, Richard Harter. "Introduction," THE HOUSE OF THE SEVEN GABLES. New York: Collier Books, 1962.

705 Fogle, Richard Harter. "Nathaniel Hawthorne," in EIGHT AMERICAN WRITERS: AN ANTHOLOGY OF AMERICAN LITERATURE. Norman Foerster and Robert P. Falk, gen. eds. New York: W. W. Norton, 1963, pp. 582-93.

706 Fogle, Richard Harter. "Nathaniel Hawthorne: THE HOUSE OF THE SEVEN GABLES," in LANDMARKS OF AMERICAN WRITING. Hennig Cohen, ed. New York and London: Basic Books, 1969, pp. 111-20.

707 Fogle, Richard Harter. "Organic Form in American Criticism: 1840-1870," in THE DEVELOPMENT OF AMERICAN LITERARY CRITICISM. Floyd Stovall, ed. Chapel Hill: North Carolina U. P., 1955, pp. 75-111.

708 Fogle, Richard Harter. "The Problem of Allegory in Hawthorne's 'Ethan Brand,'" UTQ, 17 (1948), 190-203.

709 Fogle, Richard Harter, ed. THE ROMANTIC MOVEMENT IN AMERICAN WRITING. New York: Odyssey Press, 1966.

710 Fogle, Richard Harter. "Simplicity and Complexity in THE MARBLE FAUN," TSE, 2 (1950), 103-20.

711 Fogle, Richard Harter. "Weird Mockery: An Element of Hawthorne's Style," Style, 2 (1968), 191-202.

712 Fogle, Richard Harter. "The World and the Artist: A Study of Hawthorne's 'The Artist of the Beautiful,'" TSE, 1 (1949), 31-52.

712.1 Foley, Marie L. "'The Key of Holy Sympathy': Hawthorne's
Social Ideal," DAI, 30 (Tulane: 1970), 4409A.

713 Foley, Patrick Kevin. "Bibliography of Hawthorne," in
AMERICAN AUTHORS, 1795-1895, A BIBLIOGRAPHY OF FIRST
AND NOTABLE EDITIONS CHRONOLOGICALLY ARRANGED WITH
NOTES, 1897. New York: Milford House, Inc., 1969,
pp. 117-121.

714 Folsom, James K. MAN'S ACCIDENTS AND GOD'S PURPOSES:
MULTIPLICITY IN HAWTHORNE'S FICTION. New Haven, Conn.:
College and U. P., 1963, 1966.

Revs., Richard Harter Fogle, AL, 36 (1964), 370-71;
Sidney P. Moss, ABC, 15 (1965), 6;
Roy Harvey Pearce, NCF, 19 (1964), 99-100.

715 Folsom, James K. "The Principle of Multiplicity in Hawthorne's
Fiction," DA, 20 (Princeton: 1960), 3726.

715.1 Fossum, Robert H. HAWTHORNE'S INVIOLABLE CIRCLE: THE
PROBLEM OF TIME. Deland, Florida: Everett/Edwards,
Inc., 1972.

716 Fossum, Robert H. "The Inviolable Circle: The Problem of
Time in Hawthorne's Tales and Sketches," DA, 24
(Claremont Gr. S.: 1963), 2477.

717 Fossum, Robert H. "The Shadow of the Past: Hawthorne's
Historical Tales," ClareQ, 11 (1963), 45-56.

718 Fossum, Robert H. "The Summons of the Past: Hawthorne's
'Alice Doane's Appeal,'" NCF, 23 (1968), 294-303.

719 Fossum, Robert H. "Time and the Artist in 'Legends of the
Province House,'" NCF, 21 (1967), 337-48.

The four legends of the Province House reflect
Hawthorne's views on history.

720 Foster, Charles Howell. "Hawthorne's Literary Theory,"
PMLA, 57 (1942), 241-54.

The purpose of literature is to convey spiritual truth.

721 Foster, Richard. "Introduction," SIX AMERICAN NOVELISTS OF
THE NINETEENTH CENTURY: AN INTRODUCTION. Richard
Foster, ed. Minneapolis, Minn.: Minn. U. P., 1968,
pp. 3-9.

Rev. by Richard Lehan, NCF, 23 (1968), 373-74.

722 Fraiberg, Louis. PSYCHOANALYSIS AND AMERICAN LITERATURE CRITICISM. Detroit: Wayne St. U. P., 1960, pp. 152-55, 132.

Hawthorne entangled in guilt.

722.1 Frakes, James R., and Isadore Traschen. SHORT FICTION: A CRITICAL ANTHOLOGY. Englewood Cliffs, New Jersey: 1969, pp. 232-35.

"Young Goodman Brown."

723 Frank, Frederick S. "Perverse Pilgrimage: The Role of the Gothic in the Works of Charles Brockden Brown, Edgar Allan Poe, and Nathaniel Hawthorne," DA, 29 (Rutgers: 1968), 1866A-67A.

724 Frankenstein, Alfred V. "Charles Ives: Essays Before a Sonata," in LANDMARKS OF AMERICAN WRITING. Hennig Cohen, ed. New York and London: Basic Books, Inc., 1969, pp. 270-78.

Discusses the Hawthorne movement of the Concord Sonata.

724.1 Franklin, Benjamin, V. "Hawthorne's Non-Fiction: His Attitude Toward America," DAI, 31 (Ohio: 1970), 1226A-27A.

725 Franklin, Howard Bruce. FUTURE PERFECT: AMERICAN SCIENCE FICTION OF THE NINETEENTH CENTURY. New York: Oxford U. P., 1966, pp. 3-23.

726 Franklin, Howard Bruce. "Hawthorne and Science Fiction," CentR, 10 (1966), 112-30.

Repr. in Franklin's FUTURE PERFECT: AMERICAN SCIENCE FICTION OF THE NINETEENTH CENTURY. New York: Oxford U. P., 1966), 9-16.

Hawthorne's science fiction fantastical, but based on theories of his contemporaries.

727 Franklin, Howard Bruce. "Introduction," THE SCARLET LETTER AND RELATED WRITINGS. Philadelphia: Lippincott, 1967.

728 Frederick, John T. "Hawthorne and the Workhouse Baby," ArQ, 24 (1968), 169-73.

729 Frederick, John T. "Nathaniel Hawthorne," THE DARKENED SKY: NINETEENTH-CENTURY AMERICAN NOVELISTS AND RELIGION. Notre Dame, Ind.: Notre Dame U. P., 1969, pp. 27-78.

Rev. by Robert E. Spiller, AL, 41 (1970), 618-19.

729.1 Freehafer, John. "Hawthorne Publications Since the Centenary Year," JA, Band 15 (1970), 293-98.

729.2 Freehafer, John. "THE MARBLE FAUN and the Editing of Nineteenth-Century Texts," SNNTS, 2 (1970), 487-503.

730 Freeman, Eleanor. "Motivating the Reading Lesson: A Study of Hawthorne's 'The Great Stone Face,'" GrT, 51 (1933), 50-51; 70-71; 73.

730.1 French, Allen. HAWTHORNE AT THE OLD MANSE. Concord: Privately printed, n. d.

731 French, Daniel Chester. Portrait of bust Sculptured by Daniel Chester French, CurH, 30 (1929), 422.

732 French, Joseph Lewis. "Nathaniel Hawthorne," (Poem), NEM, n.s., 34 (1906), 101.

733 Friedrich, Gerhard. IN PURSUIT OF MOBY DICK. Wallingford, Penn.: Pendle Hill P. No. 98, p. 32.

Suggests that the name "Ishmael" may have its source in Hawthorne's "The Gentle Boy."

734 Friedrich, Gerhard. "A Note on Quakerism and MOBY DICK: Hawthorne's 'The Gentle Boy' as a Possible Source," QH, 54 (1965), 94-102.

735 Friedrich, Gerhard. "A New College Course in American Literature," CE, 18 (1957), 212-14.

736 Friesen, Menno M. "The Mask in Nathaniel Hawthorne's Fiction," DA, 25 (Denver: 1965), 5276.

737 Frohock, W. M. THE NOVEL OF VIOLENCE IN AMERICA, 1920-1950. Dallas, Texas: 1950, pp. 3, 120.

Renewed interest in authors like Hawthorne and Melville can be explained in part by the fact that in our life-time something "very like a personification of evil has walked the earth."

738 Frye, Prosser Hall. "Hawthorne's Supernaturalism," LITERARY REVIEWS AND CRITICISMS. New York: G. P. Putnam's Sons, 1908, pp. 114-29.

738.1 Fuller, Frederick T. "Hawthorne and Margaret Fuller Ossoli,"
      LitW, 16 (1885), 11-15.

739 Fullerton, Bradford Morton. SELECTIVE BIBLIOGRAPHY OF
      AMERICAN LITERATURE, 1775-1900: A BRIEF ESTIMATE OF
      THE MORE IMPORTANT AMERICAN AUTHORS AND A DESCRIPTION
      OF THEIR REPRESENTATIVE WORKS. New York: William
      Tarquar Payson, 1932, pp. 131-34.

740 Fumento, Rocco. "The Atmospheric Story," in INTRODUCTION
      TO THE SHORT STORY. New York: Ronald Press, 1962,
      pp. 127-41.

741 Furst, Clyde, ed. Notes Revised by H. Y. Moffett. THE
      HOUSE OF THE SEVEN GABLES. New York: Macmillan,
      1930.

742 Fussell, Edwin. FRONTIER: AMERICAN LITERATURE AND THE
      AMERICAN WEST. Princeton: Princeton U. P., 1965,
      pp. 69-131, 350-75.

743 Fussell, Edwin. "Hawthorne, James and 'The Common Doom,'"
      AQ, 10 (1958), 438-53.

744 Fussell, Edwin. "Neutral Territory: Hawthorne and the
      Figurative Frontier," in HAWTHORNE CENTENARY ESSAYS.
      Roy Harvey Pearce, ed. Columbus, Ohio: Ohio St. U. P.,
      1964, pp. 297-314.

745 Gale, Robert L. "Evil and the American Short Story,"
      AIUO-SG, 1 (1958), 183-202.

746 Gale, Robert L. "THE MARBLE FAUN and THE SACRED FOUNT:
      A Resemblance," SA, 8 (1962), 151-99.

747 Gale, Robert L. PLOTS AND CHARACTERS IN THE FICTION AND
      SKETCHES OF NATHANIEL HAWTHORNE. Foreword Norman H.
      Pearson, Hamden, Conn.: Archon, 1968.

      Rev. by Sydney J. Krause in NEQ, 43 (1970), 152-54.

748 Gale, Robert L. "Rappaccini's Baglioni," SA, 9 (1963),
      83-87.

749 Gallagher, Edward J. "History in 'Endicott and the Red
      Cross,'" ESQ, 50 Sup. (1968), 62-65.

750 Gallagher, Edward J. "Sir Kenelm Digby in Hawthorne's 'The Man of Adamant,'" N&Q, 17 (1970), 15-16.

Richard Digby possibly derived from account by Sir Kenelm Digby (1658) of a petrified city, its inhabitants having turned to stone. Hawthorne's character similarly transformed.

751 Gallup, Donald Clifford. "On Hawthorne's Authorship of 'The Battle-Omen,'" NEQ, 9 (1936), 690-99.

A contribution to the SALEM GAZETTE, VIII, New Series, No. 88 (November 2, 1830), 1, is ascribed to Hawthorne, but is considered possibly inferior to other sketches by Hawthorne to the GAZETTE.

752 Gannon, Frederic Augustus. HAWTHORNE AND THE CUSTOM HOUSE. Boston: Salem Books Co., 1955.

753 Gannon, Frederick Augustus. HOUSES IN WHICH HAWTHORNE LIVED, THOUGHT AND WROTE. Boston: Salem Books Co., 1955.

754 Gardiner, John, and Lennis Dunlap. THE FORMS OF FICTION. New York: Random House, 1962, pp. 53-62.

755 Gargano, James W. "Hawthorne's 'The Artist of the Beautiful,'" AL, 35 (1963), 225-30.

Theme of story is growth of the artist through conflict between materialism and artistic dream. Conclusion shows artist so mature that destruction of the butterfly is unimportant.

756 Garlitz, Barbara. "Pearl: 1850-1955," PMLA, 72 (1957), 689-99.

A survey of the criticism of Pearl in THE SCARLET LETTER which shows the changes in attitude toward her.

See Anne Marie McNamara, "The Character of Flame: the Function of Pearl in THE SCARLET LETTER," AL, 27 (1956), 537-53.

757 Garlitz, Barbara. "Teaching All of Hawthorne," in Carl F. Strauch, et al., Symposium on Nathaniel Hawthorne, ESQ, 25 (1961), 6-8.

758 Gaston, Warren. "'Young Goodman Brown': A Criticism," Lit, 6 (1965), 26-30.

759 Gates, Lewis E. "Hawthorne," STUDIES AND APPRECIATIONS.
New York: Macmillan, 1900, pp. 92-109.

Hawthorne is sincere in dealing with sin, disease,
and death, the "grisliest facts of human destiny,"
but Hawthorne is also a dreamer who "dreams true,"
but who nevertheless merely dreams, whose world has
the intangibility of all dream worlds.

760 Gauss, John Dennis Hammond. HAUNTS OF HAWTHORNE IN SALEM,
MASSACHUSETTS. Priv. Pr. Salem: The Naumkeag Trust Co.,
n. d.

761 Gavigan, Walter V. "Hawthorne and Rome," CathW, 135 (1932),
555-59.

762 Geismar, Maxwell. HENRY JAMES AND THE JACOBITES. New York:
Hill and Wang, 1962, 1963.

"Miss Birdseye" of THE BOSTONIANS probably Elizabeth
Peabody, Hawthorne's sister-in-law.

763 Geismar, Maxwell. THE LAST OF THE PROVINCIALS - THE AMERICAN
NOVEL, 1915-1925. Boston: Houghton Mifflin, 1943; 1947;
1949, p. 358.

764 Geismar, Maxwell. REBELS AND ANCESTORS: THE AMERICAN
NOVEL, 1890-1915. Boston: Houghton Mifflin, 1953,
p. 406.

The opposition of the "dark" and "light" women is
a standard theme in the work of Hawthorne and Melville,
or in any literature overshadowed by Puritan ethics.

765 Geist, Stanley. "Fictitious Americans: A Preface to
'Ethan Brand,'" HudR, 5 (1952), 199-211.

766 Gerber, John C. "A Critical Exercise in the Teaching of
THE HOUSE OF THE SEVEN GABLES," in Carl F. Strauch,
et al., Symposium on Nathaniel Hawthorne, ESQ, 25
(1961), 8-11.

767 Gerber, John C. "Form and Content in THE SCARLET LETTER,"
NEQ, 17 (1944), 25-55.

See G. Thomas Tanselle, NCF, 17 (1962), 283-85.

768 Gerber, John C. "Introduction," THE SCARLET LETTER. New
York: Modern Lib., 1950, i-xxxi.

769 Gerber, John C. "Introduction," TWENTIETH-CENTURY INTERPRE-
TATIONS OF THE SCARLET LETTER: A COLLECTION OF CRITICAL
ESSAYS. John C. Gerber, ed. Englewood Cliffs, N. J.:
Prentice-Hall, Inc., 1968, pp.1-15.

770 Gerstenberger, Donna, and George Hendrick. THE AMERICAN
NOVEL 1789-1959: A CHECKLIST OF TWENTIETH-CENTURY
CRITICISM. Denver: Alan Swallow, 1961, pp. 105-118.

771 Gerould, Gordon Hall. "Interpreters: I, Hawthorne,
Melville, and the Brontes," in THE PATTERNS OF ENGLISH
AND AMERICAN FICTION, A HISTORY. Boston: Little,
Brown & Co., 1942, pp. 341-66; 440-41, passim.

772 Gerould, Katherine Fullerton. "Call It Holy Ground,"
AtlM, 163 (1939), 74-81.

773 [Getchell, E. L.] "'The Wayside,' Concord, Massachusetts,"
Educ, 52 (1931), 114.

774 Gettman, Royal, and Bruce Harkness. TEACHER'S MANUAL FOR
"A BOOK OF STORIES." New York: Rinehart, 1955.

775 "The Ghost of Doctor Harris," 19C, 47 (1900), 88-93.

        Also in Liv Age, 224 (1900), 345-49; Critic, 36 (1900),
        368-72.

776 Gibbens, Victor E. "Hawthorne's Note to 'Dr. Heidegger's
Experiment,'" MLN, 60 (1945), 408-09.

        History and refutation of the charge that Hawthorne
        borrowed from Alexander Dumas.

777 Gibson, William M. "The Art of Nathaniel Hawthorne: An
Examination of THE SCARLET LETTER," in AMERICAN
RENAISSANCE [Henrick, George, ed. THE AMERICAN
RENAISSANCE, THE HISTORY OF AN ERA: ESSAYS AND
INTERPRETATIONS (NS, Beiheft 9) Frankfurt: Diesterweg
[1961], pp. 97-106.

778 Gibson, William M. "Faulkner's THE SOUND AND THE FURY,"
Expl, 22 (1964), Item 33.

        Faulkner might have found the basic motivation of
        Quentin Compson in Dante's INFERNO or in Hawthorne's
        THE SCARLET LETTER.

779 Gibson, William M., and George Arms. "Nathaniel Hawthorne,"
TWELVE AMERICAN WRITERS. William M. Gibson and George
Arms, eds. New York: Macmillan, 1962, pp. 133-189.

780   Gleason, Arthur Huntington. "The Love Letters of Hawthorne,"
      <u>Colliers</u>, 42 (1909), 10-11.

781 Gleckner, Robert F. "James's MADAME DE MAUVES and
      Hawthorne's THE SCARLET LETTER," MLN, 73 (1958), 580-86.

782 Glicksberg, Charles I. "The Numinous in Fiction," ArQ,
      15 (1959), 305-13.

      The "existential crisis" in Hawthorne and others
      gave the nineteenth-century novel its prominence.

783 Gohdes, Clarence. AMERICAN LITERATURE IN NINETEENTH CENTURY
      ENGLAND. New York: Columbia U.P., 1944.

      Rev. by Harold Blddgett, AL, 16 (1944), 243-47;
      Henry Nash Smith, MLN, 60 (1945), 69-71.

784 Gohdes, Clarence. BIBLIOGRAPHICAL GUIDE TO THE STUDY OF
      LITERATURE OF THE UNITED STATES OF AMERICA. Durham,
      North Carolina: Duke U. P., 1959, 1963; 3rd ed., rev.
      and enlarged, 1970.

785 Gohdes, Clarence. "British Interest in American Literature
      During the Latter Part of the Nineteenth Century as
      Reflected by Mudie's Select Library," AL, 13 (1941-42),
      356-57.

      The catalogue of 1862 carried five titles of Hawthorne:
      THE BLITHEDALE ROMANCE, MOSSES FROM AN OLD MANSE,
      TWICE-TOLD TALES, TANGLEWOOD TALES, and TRANSFORMATION.

786 Gohdes, Clarence. "A Brook Farm Labor Record," AL, 1
      (1929-30), 297-303.

      P. 297, n.1: Gohdes relates that Hawthorne is supposed
      to have left the Farm in disgust but that in an obituary
      notice published at Boston in THE COMMONWEALTH, May 27,
      1864, the statement is made that Hawthorne proposed to
      one of his friends to found another /community/ on a
      smaller scale.

787 Gohdes, Clarence. "The Reception of Some Nineteenth-Century
      American Authors in Europe," THE AMERICAN WRITERS AND
      THE EUROPEAN TRADITION. Minneapolis: Minneapolis U. P.,
      pub. for Rochester U., 1950, p. 109.

      Hawthorne's popularity in England.

788 Gohlke, Elli. "Das Problem der Intersubjektivität in Leben
      und Werken Nathaniel Hawthornes," Freie Univ. (West
      Berlin).

[788.1] Goldfarb, Clare R. "THE MARBLE FAUN and Emersonian Self-Reliance," ATQ, 1 (1969), 19-23.

[789] Goldstein, J. S. "The Literary Source of Hawthorne's FANSHAWE," MLN, 60 (1945), 1-8.

Suggests Maturin's MELMOTH, THE WANDERER, as source.

[790] Collin, Rita Kaplan. "Dream and Reverie in the Writings of Nathaniel Hawthorne," DA, 22 (Minn.: 1961), 1156.

[791] Goodman, Paul. "'The Minister's Black Veil': Mystery and Sublimity," in THE STRUCTURE OF LITERATURE. Chicago: Chicago U. P., 1954, pp. 253-57.

[791.1] Goodrich, Samuel Griswold. RECOLLECTIONS OF A LIFETIME, OR MEN AND THINGS I HAVE SEEN. New York: Miller, Orton & Mulligan, 1856; repr., Detroit: Gale, 1967, 2 vols.

"Peter Parley," a "great pioneer in educational writing," tells his life story.

[792] Goodspeed, Charles Eliot. "Nathaniel Hawthorne and the Museum of the East India Marine Society," AmN, 5 (1945), 266-72.

[793] Goodspeed, Charles Eliot. NATHANIEL HAWTHORNE AND THE MUSEUM OF THE SALEM EAST INDIA MARINE SOCIETY: OR, THE GATHERING OF A VIRTUOSO'S COLLECTION. Peabody Museum, 1946.

[794] Gordan, Caroline, and Allen Tate. "Nathaniel Hawthorne: 'Young Goodman Brown'" in THE HOUSE OF FICTION: AN ANTHOLOGY OF THE SHORT STORY. With Commentary. New York: Charles Scribner's Sons, 1950, 1960, pp. 27-38.

[795] Gordan, John D. "An Anniversary Exhibition: The Henry W., and Albert A. Berg Collection, 1940-1965," BNYPL, 69 (1965), 665-77.

[796] Gordan, John D. "Nathaniel Hawthorne, The Years of Fulfillment, 1804-1853," BNYPL, 59, Part I (March, 1955), 154-65; Part II (April, 1955), 198-217; Part III (May, 1955), 259-69; Part IV (June, 1955), 316-21.

[797] Gordan, John D. NATHANIEL HAWTHORNE, THE YEARS OF FULFILLMENT, 1804-1853: AN EXHIBITION FROM THE BERG COLLECTION. FIRST EDITIONS, MANUSCRIPTS, AUTOGRAPH LETTERS. New York: New York Public Library, 1954.

798 Gordan, John D. "Novels in Manuscript: An Exhibition from the Berg Collection," BNYPL, 69 (1965), 317-29.

799 Gordon, I. "Nathaniel Hawthorne," Hobbies, 53 (1948), 133-34.

800 Gordon, Joseph T. "Nathaniel Hawthorne and Brook Farm," ESQ, 33 (1963), 51-61.

According to all the evidence THE BLITHEDALE ROMANCE cannot be regarded as an actual record. It is a fusion of fact and fiction, removed from Hawthorne's experience at West Roxbury.

801 Gorman, Herbert. HAWTHORNE: A STUDY IN SOLITUDE. New York: George H. Doran Co., 1927; Biblo and Tannen, 1966.

802 Gorman, Herbert. "Hawthorne's Notebooks are Rescued from Distortion," NYTBR, Dec. 25 1932, p. 3.

803 Gottfried, Alex, and Sue Davidson. "Utopia's Children: An Interpretation of Three Political Novels," WPQ, 15 (1962), 17-32.

Hawthorne's THE BLITHEDALE ROMANCE, M. McCarthy's THE OASIS, and Harvey Swados' FALSE COIN are dominated by a single political idea whose "characteristic components" are the same in each of the three novels.

804 Gottschalk, Jane. "The Continuity of American Letters in THE SCARLET LETTER and THE BEAST IN THE JUNGLE," WisSL, 4 (1967), 39-45.

Both works show "continuing tradition" in that both depend on non-material values, both subordinate action and dialogue to analysis of conduct, and both have universal application.

805 Grabo, Carl H. "The Omniscent Author--THE SCARLET LETTER," THE TECHNIQUE OF THE NOVEL. New York: Charles Scribner's Sons, 1928, pp. 44-53.

806 Granger, Bruce Ingham. "Arthur Dimmesdale as Tragic Hero," NCF, 19 (1964), 197-203.

807 Grant, Douglas. "Introduction," THE SCARLET LETTER: A ROMANCE. New York: Oxford U. P., 1965.

807.1 Grant, Douglas. PURPOSE AND PLACE: ESSAYS ON AMERICAN WRITERS. London: Macmillan, 1965, pp. 21-33.

808 Grant, Douglas. "Sir Walter Scott and Nathaniel Hawthorne," ULR, 8 (1962), 35-41.

809 Gray, Maxwell. "Hawthorne the Mystic," NC&A, 87 (1920), 118-25

810 "'The Great Stone Face' - Some Suggestions for Teaching It," GrT, 68 (1951), 54-77.

811 Green, Julien. UN PURITAIN HOMME DE LETTRES: NATHANIEL HAWTHORNE. Editions des cahiers libres. Toulouse: 1928.

812 Green, Martin. "The Hawthorne Myth: A Protest," E&S, 16 (1963), 16-36.

Repr. in RE-APPRAISALS: SOME COMMONSENSE READINGS IN AMERICAN LITERATURE. New York: W. W. Norton & Co., 1963, 1965, pp. 61-85.

Hawthorne's work is not "an allegorical articulation of the deepest and darkest experience of the American psyche." Hawthorne employed stock devices of Victorian fiction, displayed vulgarity of thought, and confused characters and incidents of his fables.

813 Green, Martin. "Style in American Literature," CamR, 84 (1967), 385-87.

Rev. art. of Richard Poirier, A WORLD ELSEWHERE. New York: Oxford U. P., 1966.

814 Green, Roger Lancelyn. "Postscript," in THE COMPLETE GREEK STORIES OF NATHANIEL HAWTHORNE FROM THE WONDER BOOK AND TANGLEWOOD TALES. Illustrated by Harold Jones. Foreword by Kathleen Lines. New York: Franklin Watts, Inc., 1963.

815 Greene, Maxine. "Man Without God in American Fiction," Humanist, 25 (1965), 125-28.

816 Gribble, Francis. "Hawthorne from an English Point of View," Critic, 45 (1904), 60-66.

817 Gribble, Francis. "Two Centenaries: Nathaniel Hawthorne and George Sand," FnR, 82 (1904), 260-78.

818 Griffith, Albert J. "Heart Images in Hawthorne's Names," ESQ, 43 (1966), 78-79.

819 Griffith, Ben W., Jr. "Old Books: THE HOUSE OF THE SEVEN GABLES by Nathaniel Hawthorne," GaR, 8 (1954), 235-37.

820 Griffith, Clark. "Caves and Cave Dwellers: The Study of
        a Romantic Image," JEGP, 62 (1963), 551-68.

        Hawthorne and others made extensive use of cave-
        imagery.

821 Griffith, Clark. "'Emersonianism' and 'Poeism': Some
        Versions of Romantic Sensibility," MLQ, 22 (1961),
        125-34.

822 Griffith, Clark. "Substance and Shadow: Language and
        Meaning in THE HOUSE OF THE SEVEN GABLES," MP, 51
        (.953), 187-95.

823 Griffith, Kelley, Jr. "Form in THE BLITHEDALE ROMANCE,"
        AL, 40 (1968), 15-26.

        First half objectively realistic; second half, Coverdale's
        dreams. First half anticipates the dreams of the second
        half, while second half reaches catastrophe by reference to
        a few objective occurrences. Thus Hawthorne successfully
        presents us subjective reality.

824 Griffiths, Thomas Morgan. MAINE SOURCES IN THE HOUSE OF THE
        SEVEN GABLES. Maine State Historian. Waterville,
        Maine: 1945.

        See article in NEQ, 16 (1943), 432-43, from which this
        is expanded.

        See also "Brief Mention," AL. 17 (1946), 377.

        Rev. by Milton Ellis, NEQ, 19 (1946), 281.

825 Griffiths, Thomas Morgan. "'Montpelier' and 'Seven Gables':
        Knox's Estate and Hawthorne's Novel," NEQ, 16 (1943),
        432-43.

826 Grilley, Virginia. A BRIEF HISTORY OF THE HAWTHORNE FAMILY AND
        THE ANCIENT COTTAGE AT 27 UNION STREET, WHERE THE GREAT
        ROMANCER NATHANIEL HAWTHORNE WAS BORN ON JULY 4, 1804.
        Salem: Seven Gables Book Shop, 1959.

827 Griswold, M. Jane. "American Quaker History in the Works
        of Whittier, Hawthorne, and Longfellow," Americana,
        34 (1940), 220-63.

828 Grolier Club. FIRST EDITIONS OF THE WORKS OF NATHANIEL
        HAWTHORNE, TOGETHER WITH SOME MANUSCRIPTS, LETTERS AND
        PORTRAITS EXHIBITED AT THE GROLIER CLUB FROM DECEMBER 8,
        TO DECEMBER 24, 1904. New York: The Grolier Club, 1904.

829 Gross, Robert Eugene. "Hawthorne's First Novel: The Future
        of a Style," PMLA, 78 (1963), 60-68.

830 Gross, Robert Eugene. "A Study of Hawthorne's FANSHAWE and THE MARBLE FAUN: The Texture of Significance," DA, 21 (New York: 1961), 2274.

831 Gross, Seymour L. "Four Possible Additions to Hawthorne's 'Story Teller,'" PBSA, 51 (1957), 90-95.

832 Gross, Seymour L. "Hawthorne and the Shakers," AL, 29 (1958), 457-63.

833 Gross, Seymour L. "Hawthorne Versus Melville," BuR, 14, iii (1966), 89-109.

Resemblances in the works of Hawthorne and Melville are more apparent than real.

834 Gross, Seymour L. "Hawthorne's 'Alice Doane's Appeal,'" NCF, 10 (1955), 232-36.

835 Gross, Seymour L. "Hawthorne's Income from THE TOKEN," SB, 8 (1956), 236-38.

836 Gross, Seymour L. "Hawthorne's 'Lady Eleanore's Mantle' as History," JEGP, 54 (1955), 549-54.

Repr. in STUDIES IN MEMORY OF JOHN JAY PERRY. Urbana: Illinois U. P., 1955, pp. 89-94.

837 Gross, Seymour L. "Hawthorne's Moral Realism," in Carl F. Strauch, et al., Symposium on Hawthorne, NEQ, 25 (1961), 11-13.

838 Gross, Seymour L. "Hawthorne's 'My Kinsman, Major Molineux': History as Moral Adventure," NCF, 12 (1957), 97-109.

Repr. in Agnes Donohue, ed., A CASEBOOK ON THE HAWTHORNE QUESTION. New York: Crowell, 1963, 51-63; and in Ray B. Brown and Martin Light, eds. CRITICAL APPROACHES TO AMERICAN LITERATURE, New York: Crowell, 1965, I, 212-22.

839 Gross, Seymour L. "Hawthorne's Revision of 'The Gentle Boy,'" AL, 26 (1954), 196-208.

840 Gross, Seymour L. "Hawthorne's 'Vision of the Fountain' as a Parody," AL, 27 (1955), 101-05.

The original version as it appeared in the NEW ENGLAND MAGAZINE, 9 (August, 1834), 99-100, probably shows Hawthorne's intent.

841 Gross, Seymour L. "Introduction," THE HOUSE OF THE SEVEN
GABLES. Seymour L. Gross, ed. New York: Norton, 1967,
pp. vii-x.

842 Gross, Seymour L. "Nathaniel Hawthorne: Absurdity of
Heroism," YR, 57 (1968), 182-95.

843 Gross, Seymour L. "Prologue to THE SCARLET LETTER: Hawthorne's
Fiction to 1850," in A SCARLET LETTER HANDBOOK, Seymour L.
Gross, ed. Belmont, Calif.: Wadsworth Pub. Co., 1960,
pp. 1-14.

844 Gross, Seymour L. "'Solitude, and Love, and Anguish': The
Tragic Design in THE SCARLET LETTER," CLAJ, 3 (1960),
154-65.

845 Gross, Seymour L. "The Technique of Hawthorne's Short
Stories," DA, 14 (Ill.: 1954), 1720.

846 Gross, Seymour L., and Alfred J. Levy. "Some Remarks on the
Extant Manuscripts of Hawthorne's Short Stories,"
SB, 14 (1961), 254-57.

847 Gross, Seymour L., and Randall Stewart. "The Hawthorne
Revival," in HAWTHORNE CENTENARY ESSAYS, Roy Harvey
Pearce, ed. Columbus, Ohio: Ohio St. U. P., 1964,
335-66.

847.1 Gross, Theodore L. "Nathaniel Hawthorne: The Absurdity
of Heroism," YR, 57 (1968), 182-95.

847.2 Gross, Theodore, L., and Stanley Wertheim. HAWTHORNE, MELVILLE,
AND STEPHEN CRANE: A CRITICAL BIBLIOGRAPHY. New York:
Free Press, 1971.

847.3 Grossman, J. "Vanzetti and Hawthorne," AQ, 22 (1970), 902-07.

848 Grover, P. R. "A Tanner in the Works," CamR, 89A (1968),
430-31.

A rev. art. of Henry James's HAWTHORNE, ed. by Tony
Tanner, London: 1967. Says that Tanner over-
emphasized Hawthorne's influence on James, especially
as to imagery and symbolism.

849 Guidi, Augusto. "Le Ambiguità di Hawthorne," SA, 1 (1955),
125-42.

850 Guilds, John C. "Miriam of THE MARBLE FAUN: Hawthorne's
Subtle Sinner," CaiSE (1960), 61-68.

[851] Gullace, Giovanni. "Péche et pécheurs dans LA LETTRE
ÉCARLATE et LE FAUNE DE MARBRE." EA, 15 (1962), 113-21.

[852] Gupta, R. K. "Hawthorne's Ideal Reader." IJAS, 1 (1969),
97-99.

[852.1] Gupta, R. K. "Hawthorne's Theory of Art." AL, 40 (1968),
309-24.

Technique, though important, secondary to artist's
vision.

[852.2] Gupta, R. K. "Hawthorne's Treatment of the Artist." NEQ,
45 (1972), 65-80.

[853] Guttman, Allen. THE CONSERVATIVE TRADITION IN AMERICA.
Cambridge, Mass.: Oxford U. P., 1967.

The "survival of Conservatism" in literature extends
from Hawthorne and others far into the twentieth century.

Rev. by John D. Lewis, NEQ, 41 (1968), 455-57.

[854] Guttmann, Allen. "Images of Value and the Sense of the
Past." NEQ, 35 (1962), 15.

[855] Gwynn, Frederick L. "Hawthorne's 'Rappaccini's Daughter,'"
NCF, 7 (1952), 217-19.

Giovanni, a weak male character, fails to resolve
Hawthorne's dualism of Head vs. Heart. Giovanni
and Dimmesdale have Heart, but not sufficiently to
be mature, admirable men.

[856] H., R. "Hawthorne in More Cheerful Mood." CSMM, 27 (1935), 7.

[857] Hadsell, S. R. "Introduction." THE HOUSE OF THE SEVEN GABLES.
S. R. Hadsell, ed. New York: 1932.

[857.1] Hagiwara, Tsutomu. "Symbolic and Signific Functions in
Hawthorne's Fiction - With Special reference to THE
SCARLET LETTER." SELit, 46 (1970), 129-40.

[858] Hagopian, John V. "My Kinsman, Major Molineux," in INSIGHT I:
ANALYSES OF AMERICAN LITERATURE. John V. Hagopian and
Martin Dolch, eds. Frankfurt: Hirschgraben, 1962,
pp. 69-73.

859 Hahn, Emily. ROMANTIC REBELS: AN INFORMAL HISTORY OF
BOHEMIANISM IN AMERICA. Boston: Riverside Press
Cambridge; Houghton Mifflin, 1966.

860 Hakutani, Yoshinobu. "Hawthorne and Melville's 'Benito
Cereno,'" HSELL, 10 (1963), 58-64.

861 Hale, Nancy. NEW ENGLAND DISCOVERY. A PERSONAL VIEW.
New York: Coward-McCann, Inc., 1963). 309-15; 371-741

Hawthorne's "Brook Farm," pp. 309-315.
"Lincoln in War Time," which had appeared in Atl.Mo.,
July, 1862, signed "A Peaceable Man," later published
as "Chiefly About War Matters," discussed pp. 371-374.

862 Hall, Lawrence Sargent. "Hawthorne: Critic of Society.
The Making of an American Philosophy," SatRL, 26
(1943), 28, 30, 32.

863 Hall, Lawrence Sargent. HAWTHORNE: CRITIC OF SOCIETY.
New Haven: Yale U. P., 1944.

Hawthorne as an observer of his own time.

Rev. by R. E. Spiller, "The Coming Out of a Recluse,"
SatRL, 27 (1944), 20; Reply by Lawrence Sargent Hall,
"The Author Takes Issue," SatRL, 27 (1944), 15.

Revs. by Newton Arvin, NEQ, 17 (1944), 453-55;
Manning Hawthorne, AL, 16 (1944-45), 238-40.

864 Hall, Lawrence Sargent. HAWTHORNE AS CRITIC OF NINETEENTH-
CENTURY AMERICA. Diss. Yale: 1941.

864.1 Hall, Spencer. "Beatrice Cenci: Symbol and Vision in THE
MARBLE FAUN," NCF, 25 (1970), 85-95.

865 Hall, Susan Corwin. HAWTHORNE TO HEMINGWAY: AN ANNOTATED
BIBLIOGRAPHY ABOUT NINE AMERICAN WRITERS. Robert H.
Woodward, ed. New York: Garrett Pub., 1965.

866 Halleck, Reuben Post. "Nathaniel Hawthorne," HISTORY OF
AMERICAN LITERATURE. New York: American Book Co., 1911,
pp. 204-11.

Hawthorne gave the Puritan to literature; both shared
the same concern--"the human soul in its relation to
the judgment day."

867 Halliburton, David G. "The Grotesque in American Literature:
Poe, Hawthorne and Melville," DA, 27 (Calif., Riverside:
1967), 3840A-41A.

868 Hamada, Masajiro, "Gothic Romance in THE HOUSE OF THE SEVEN GABLES," SEL, 45 (1968), 49-61.

869 Hamada, Masajiro. "THE SCARLET LETTER - A Tale of Three Prisoners," BungR, 13 (1960), 1-18.

870 Hamblen, Abigail Ann. "Protestantism in Three American Novels," ForumH, 3 (1960), V, 40-43.

871 Hammond, Lewis, Dieter Sattler, and Emil Lehnartz, eds. GEIST EINER FREIEN GESELLSCHAFT: FESTSCHRIFT ZU EHREN VON SENATOR JAMES WILLIAM FULBRIGHT AUS ANLASS DES ZEHNJAHRIGEN BESTEHENS DES DEUTSCHEN FULBRIGHT-PROGRAMMS. Heidelberg: Quelle and Meyer, 1962.

872 Haney, John Louis. THE STORY OF OUR LITERATURE. Boston: 1923.

873 Hannigan, D. F. "Hawthorne's Place in Literature," Lit, 9 (1901), 387-88; LivA, 231 (1901), 720-24; EclM, 138 (1902), 225-29.

874 Hanscom, Elizabeth Deering. "Introduction," THE SCARLET LETTER. New York: 1927.

875 Haraszti, Zoltán. "Brook Farm Letters," More Books, BBPL, 12 (1937), 62.

876 Haraszti, Zoltán. "Hawthorne Forecasts Franklin Pierce's Career," BPLQ, 3 (1951), 83-86.

877 Haraszti, Zoltán. THE IDYLL OF BROOK FARM. Boston: Public Library, 1937.

878 Harding, Walter. "American History in the Novel, 1585-1900. The Period of Expansion, 1815-1861," MwJ, 8 (1956), 393-98.

THE BLITHEDALE ROMANCE among the historical novels recommended.

879 Harding, Walter. "Another Source for Hawthorne's 'Egotism; or, the Bosom Serpent,'" AL, 40 (1969), 537-38.

An article "Snake in a Man's Stomach!" in YEOMAN'S GAZETTE, Concord, Mass., April 3, 1836, probably the source for Hawthorne's story.

880 Harding, Walter. A THOREAU HANDBOOK. New York: New York U. P., 1959.

881 Harris, Elean, and Rhoda Prosser. "The Great Stone Face,"
        SierEN, 35 (1939), 15-16.

882 Harris, Julia Collier, ed. JOEL CHANDLER HARRIS, EDITOR AND
        ESSAYIST: MISCELLANEOUS LITERARY, POLITICAL AND SOCIAL
        WRITINGS. Chapel Hill: North Carolina U. P., 1931,
        pp. 185-88, 89.

883 Hart, Francis Russell. "The Experience of Character in the
        English Gothic Novel," in EXPERIENCE IN THE NOVEL:
        SELECTED PAPERS FROM THE ENGLISH INSTITUTE. Roy
        Harvey Pearce, ed. New York: Columbia U. P., 1968,
        pp. 83-105.

        Hawthorne's characters must exist for the reader as
        mimetic characters, characters to be understood in
        terms of psychological probability.

884 Hart, James D. "Hawthorne's Italian Diary," AL, 34 (1963),
        562-67.

885 Hart, James D. THE OXFORD COMPANION TO AMERICAN LITERATURE.
        New York: Oxford U. P., 1941, 1948, 1956, pp. 312-13.

886 Hart, James D. THE POPULAR BOOK: A HISTORY OF AMERICA'S
        LITERARY TASTE. New York: Oxford U. P., 1950.

        Hawthorne deemed a failure by more usual publishing
        standards.

        Rev. by Louis Filler, NEQ, 24 (1951), 396-97.

887 Hart, John E. "THE SCARLET LETTER - One Hundred Years After,"
        NEQ, 23 (1950), 381-95.

888 Hart, Walter Morris. "Hawthorne and the Short Story,"
        UnCh, 3 (1900), 177ff.

889 Hartley, L. P. "The Novelist's Responsibility," E&S, 15
        (1962), 88-100.

        The novelist's responsibility is his acceptance of
        ethical standards. Hawthorne and others used their
        own personalities or their moral predicaments as raw
        material for their novels.

889.1 Hartley, L. P. "Nathaniel Hawthorne," THE WRITER'S
        RESPONSIBILITY. London: Hamish Hamilton, 1967, pp. 56-141.

890 Hartwick, Harry. THE FOREGROUND OF AMERICAN FICTION. New York: American Book Co., 1934, passim.

891 Harwell, Richard Barksdale. HAWTHORNE AND LONGFELLOW: A GUIDE TO AN EXHIBIT. Brunswick, Me.: Bowdoin Coll., 1966.

892 Haselmeyer, L. A. "Hawthorne and the Cenci," Neophil, 25 (1941), 59-64.

893 Haskell, Raymond I. "The Great Carbuncle," NEQ, 10 (1937), 533-35.

894 Haskell, Raymond I. "Sensings and Realizations on Reading 'The Great Stone Face,'" Educ, 43 (1923), 544-50.

895 Hassan, Ihab. RADICAL INNOCENCE: STUDIES IN THE CONTEMPORARY AMERICAN NOVEL. Princeton, N. J.: Princeton U. P., 1961.

896 Hastings, Louise. "An Origin for 'Dr. Heidegger's Experiment,'" AL, 9 (1938), 403-10.

Parallels between Hawthorne's story and "The First and Last Dinner" in Samuel P. Newman's A PRACTICAL SYSTEM OF RHETORIC (1829).

897 Hathaway, Richard D. "Hawthorne and the Paradise of Children," WHR, 15 (1961), 161-72.

898 Haugh, Robert F. "The Second Secret and THE SCARLET LETTER," CE, 17 (1956), 269-71.

Reply by Francis W. Lovett, Jr., CE, 17 (1956), 492.

899 Havens, Elmer A. "The 'Golden Branch' as Symbol in THE HOUSE OF THE SEVEN GABLES," MLN, 74 (1959), 20-22.

900 Havighurst, Walter. "Symbolism and the Student," CE, 16 (1955), 429-34, 461.

901 [Hawthorne Centenary] Brown, E. B. Harpers, 48 (1904), 986-7.

902 [Hawthorne Centenary] Gribble, F. FortRev, 82 (1904), 260-69.

903 [Hawthorne Centenary] A List of Souvenirs of Nathaniel Hawthorne Exhibited at the Essex Institute in Connection with the Hawthorne Centennial, the property of the Institute when Not Otherwise Designated. EIHC, 41 (1905), 93-98.

904 /Hawthorne Centenary7 Munger, T. T. Century, 68 (1904), 482-83.

905 /Hawthorne Centenary7 Perry, B. AtlM, 94 (1904), 195-206.

906 "The Hawthorne Centenary," Outlook, 77 (1904), 483-85.

907 "Hawthorne, a Century after His Birth," AmRR, 30 (1904), 232-33.

See DeCasseres, Benjamin, "Hawthorne: Emperor of Shadows," CRITIC, 45 (1904), 37-44.

908 Hawthorne, Hildegarde. "Hawthorne and Melville," LitR, 2 (1922), 406.

909 Hawthorne, Hildegarde. "The Most Unforgettable Character I've Met," ReadD, 56 (1950), 21-25.

About Rose Hawthorne Lathrop.

910 Hawthorne, Hildegarde. ROMANTIC REBEL: THE STORY OF NATHANIEL HAWTHORNE. New York: Appleton-Century, 1932, 1938.

911 Hawthorne, Julian. BookN, 22 (1905), 577.

912 Hawthorne, Julian. "Books of Memory," Bookman, 61 (1925), 567-69.

913 Hawthorne, Julian. "A Daughter of Hawthorne," Atl, 142 (1928), 372-77.

915 Hawthorne, Julian. "Hawthorne," in SHOCK OF RECOGNITION, Edmund Wilson, ed. Garden City, New York: Doubleday, 1947; Farrar, Straus, 1955.

914 Hawthorne, Julian. "A Group of Hawthorne Letters," Harpers, 108 (1904), 602-07.

916 Hawthorne, Julian. HAWTHORNE AND HIS CIRCLE. New York: 1903; Archon Books, 1968.

Rev. by J. W. Chadwick, Nation, 77 (1903), 410-11; W. H. Johnson, Dial, 35 (1903), 466-67; Athenaeum, (May 21, 1904), 650; W. H. Mayhew, NChR, 11 (1904), 385; Richard Lehan, NCF, 24 (1969), 123-26.

917 Hawthorne, Julian. "Hawthorne, Man of Action," SatRL, 3
(1927), 727-28.

A review-article of Lloyd Morris's THE REBELLIOUS
PURITAN. London: Constable, 1928. See also
Discussion, 3 (May 28, June, 1927), 866, 916.

918 Hawthorne, Julian. HAWTHORNE READING. Cleveland, Ohio:
The Rowfant Club, 1902.

919 Hawthorne, Julian. "Hawthorne's Last Years," Critic, 45
(1904), 67-71.

919.1 Hawthorne, Julian. "Hawthorne's Philosophy," CentM, 32
(1886), 83-93. Repr. in HAWTHORNE AMONG HIS
CONTEMPORARIES. Kenneth Walter Cameron, ed. Hartford:
Transcendental Books, 1968, pp. 289-96.

920 Hawthorne, Julian. "The Making of 'THE SCARLET LETTER,'"
Bookman, 74 (1931), 401-11.

921 Hawthorne, Julian. THE MEMOIRS OF JULIAN HAWTHORNE.
Edith Garrigues Hawthorne, ed. New York: Macmillan,
1938.

Shows the family life of Nathaniel Hawthorne and
his children.

Rev. by Randall Stewart, AL, 10 (1938-39), 380.

922 Hawthorne, Julian. NATHANIEL HAWTHORNE AND HIS WIFE: A
BIOGRAPHY. 2 vols. Cambridge, Mass.: Osgood, 1884,
1885; Boston and New York: Houghton Mifflin, 1884,
1897; Vols. 14 and 15 in THE WORKS OF NATHANIEL HAWTHORNE.
George Parsons Lathrop, ed. Boston and New York:
Houghton Mifflin, 1884; London Chatto & Windus, 1884,
1885; Grosse Pointe, Mich.: Scholarly P., 1968;
Archon Books, 1968.

Rev. by Richard Lehan, NCF, 24 (1969), 123-26.

923 Hawthorne, Julian. "Nathaniel Hawthorne's Blue Cloak: A
Son's Reminiscences," Bookman, 75 (1932), 501-06.

923.1 Hawthorne, Julian. "Nathaniel Hawthorne's 'Elixir of Life,'"
Lipp, 45 (January, February, March, April, 1890), 66-76,
224-35, 412-25, 548-61.

923.2 Hawthorne, Julian. "New Light on Hawthorne and a Salem Pepys,"
LitD-IBR, 4 (1926), 411-14.

924 Hawthorne, Julian. "A New Order of Things...," in THE IDEA OF AN AMERICAN NOVEL. L. D. Rubin, Jr., and John Rees Moore, eds. New York: 1961, pp. 66-67.

925 Hawthorne, Julian. "Problems of THE SCARLET LETTER," AtlM, 57 (1886), 471-85.

925.1 Hawthorne, Julian. "The Salem of Hawthorne," CentM, 28 (1884), 3-17. Repr. in HAWTHORNE AMONG HIS CONTEMPOR-ARIES. Kenneth Walter Cameron, ed. Hartford: Transcendental Books, 1968, pp. 245-52.

925.2 Hawthorne, Julian. "Scenes of Hawthorne's Romances," CentM, 28 (1884), 380-97. Repr. in HAWTHORNE AMONG HIS CONTEMPORARIES. Kenneth Walter Cameron, ed. Hartford: Transcendental Books, 1968, pp. 252-63.

926 Hawthorne, Julian. "Such Is Paradise, The Story of Sophia and Nathaniel Hawthorne," Century, 115 (1927), 157-69.

927 Hawthorne, Julian, and Leonard Lemmon. "Nathanial Hawthorne," in AMERICAN LITERATURE, A TEXT BOOK FOR THE USE OF SCHOOLS AND COLLEGES. Boston: D. C. Heath, 1902, pp. 155-67.

928 Hawthorne, Julian, and John Russell Young, John Porter Lamberton, Oliver H. G. Leigh, eds. "Nathaniel Hawthorne" in THE MASTERPIECES AND THE HISTORY OF LITERATURE, ANALYSIS, CRITICISM, CHARACTER AND INCIDENT. New York: E. R. Du Mont, 1903, IX, 155-71.

929 "Hawthorne, Man and Author," EdinR, 203 (1905-06), 210-35; LivA, 249 (1906), 458-76.

930 Hawthorne, Manning. "Aunt Ebe: Some Letters of Elizabeth M. Hawthorne," NEQ, 20 (1947), 209-31.

931 Hawthorne, Manning. "The Concord Writers," in AMERICAN LITERARY SCENE. Bombay: Popular Book Depot, 1962, pp. 1-13.

932 Hawthorne, Manning. "The Friendship between Hawthorne and Longfellow," EJ, 28 (1939), 221-23; ELeaf, 39 (1940), 25-30.

A review of the relationship over a period of twenty-seven years.

933 Hawthorne, Manning. "A Glimpse of Hawthorne's Boyhood," EIHC, 83 (1947), 178-84.

Repr. of article from the New York OBSERVER, August 4, 1887, by Mrs. Lucy Ann Bradley who visited the Hawthorne home between 1812 and 1820.

934 Hawthorne, Manning. "Hawthorne," in THE READER'S
ENCYCLOPEDIA OF AMERICAN LITERATURE. Max J. Herzberg,
ed. New York: Crowell, 1962, pp. 439-41.

935 Hawthorne, Manning. "Hawthorne and 'The Man of God,'"
Colophon, 2 (1937), 262-82.

Recollections of Hawthorne by Horace L. Conolly
including a new version of the story about the
source of Longfellow's Evangeline.

936 Hawthorne, Manning. "Hawthorne and Utopian Socialism:
Two Letters Written to David Mack," NEQ, 12 (1939),
726-30.

Hawthorne declined to enter an experiment in
socialized living in Northampton in 1842. His
Brook Farm experience may have been a factor in
his decision.

937 Hawthorne, Manning. "Hawthorne's Early Years," EIHC,
74 (1938), 1-21.

938 Hawthorne, Manning. "THE HOUSE OF THE SEVEN GABLES and
Hawthorne's Family History," LitHY, 7, 1 (1966), 61-66.

939 Hawthorne, Manning. "Maria Louisa Hawthorne," EIHC, 75
(1939), 103-34.

The career of Hawthorne's sister.

940 Hawthorne, Manning. "Nathaniel and Elizabeth Hawthorne,
Editors," Colophon, New Graphic Series I, 3 (1939),
35-46.

Letters written by Hawthorne to his sister Elizabeth
between January and June, 1836, when he was editor
of the AMERICAN MAGAZINE OF USEFUL AND ENTERTAINING
KNOWLEDGE.

941 Hawthorne, Manning. "Nathaniel Hawthorne at Bowdoin,"
NEQ, 13 (1940), 246-79.

Hawthorne's college years.

942 Hawthorne, Manning. "Nathaniel Hawthorne Prepares for
College; with Letters, 1819-1821," NEQ, 11 (1938),
66-88.

A continuation of "Hawthorne's Early Years," EIHC,
74 (1938), 1-21; see also, EIHC, 11 (1938), 66-68.

943   Hawthorne, Manning. "Parental and Family Influence on
Hawthorne," EIHC, 76 (1940), 1-13.

The picture of Mrs. Hawthorne as a recluse, started
by Elizabeth Peabody and "embellished" by George
Edward Woodberry, is not borne out by the view of
relatives.

944   Hawthorne, Manning. "THE SCARLET LETTER," LitHY, 2 (1966),
37-39.

Theme is sanctity of the human heart.

945   Hawthorne, Manning, and Dana, H. W. L. "Origin of
Longfellow's Evangeline," PBSA, 41 (1947), 165-203.

NATHANIEL HAWTHORNE

COMPLETE COLLECTIONS, CHRONOLOGICALLY ARRANGED

946   WORKS OF NATHANIEL HAWTHORNE. Globe Edition. Boston:
Houghton Mifflin and Company. The Riverside Press,
Cambridge: 1881. 6 Vols.

947   Hawthorne, Nathaniel. THE COMPLETE WORKS OF NATHANIEL
HAWTHORNE. Introductory Notes by George Parsons
Lathrop. Cambridge, Mass.: Houghton Mifflin, 1883,
12 vols. "Riverside Edition."

948   THE COMPLETE WRITINGS. Autograph Edition. Boston and New
York: Houghton Mifflin and Company, The Riverside
Press, Cambridge: 1900.

Signed by Rose Hawthorne Lathrop and the publishers.

TWICE-TOLD TALES, Repr. (Vols. 1 and 2)
THE SNOW IMAGE AND OTHER TWICE-TOLD TALES, Repr.
MOSSES FROM AN OLD MANSE, Vol. 1, Repr., Vol. 2, Repr.
THE SCARLET LETTER, Repr.
THE HOUSE OF THE SEVEN GABLES, Repr.
THE BLITHEDALE ROMANCE, Repr.
THE MARBLE FAUN, Vols. 1 and 2, Repr.
OUR OLD HOME, Repr.
THE WHOLE HISTORY OF GRANDFATHER'S CHAIR AND BIOGRAPHICAL
     STORIES, Repr.
A WONDER BOOK FOR GIRLS AND BOYS AND TANGLEWOOD TALES, Repr.
THE DOLLIVER ROMANCE AND KINDRED TALES, Repr.
DOCTOR GRIMSHAWE'S SECRET, Repr.

TALES AND SKETCHES, Repr.
"The Haunted Quack," prior pub., in TOKEN, 1831.

948 THE COMPLETE..., cont.

"The New England Village," pub., TOKEN, 1831
"The Bald Eagle," sometimes attributed to Hawthorne
MISCELLANIES BIOGRAPHICAL AND OTHER SKETCHES AND LETTERS,
    Repr. except for first collected appearance of Hawthorne's
    Preface to Delia Bacon's PHILOSOPHY OF THE PLAYS OF
    SHAKESPEARE UNFOLDED
An Ontario Steamboat (first book publication)
Nature of Sleep
Bells
Hints to Young Ambition
The Duston Family (this its earliest book appearance in
    America; and an earlier appearance in London: MEMOIR OF
    NATHANIEL HAWTHORNE WITH STORIES, 1872)
PASSAGES FROM THE AMERICAN NOTE-BOOKS, Repr.
NOTES OF TRAVEL. Repr., Vols. 1 and 2, 3, and 4, 1901.

949 THE COMPLETE WRITINGS OF NATHANIEL HAWTHORNE. Horace E.
    Scudder, ed. The Old Manse Edition, 22 vols. Boston:
    1900.

949.1 THE WORKS OF NATHANIEL HAWTHORNE. Julian Hawthorne, ed.
    3 vols. New York: Collier, 1900.

950 THE CENTENARY EDITION OF THE WORKS OF NATHANIEL HAWTHORNE.
    William Charvat, et al, eds. Columbus: Ohio St. U. P.,
    1962-68. (In progress.)

    Rev. by Joseph Katz, NEQ, 39 (1966), 412-13.

PARTIAL COLLECTIONS, CHRONOLOGICALLY ARRANGED:

951 "The Canterbury Pilgrims, and Other Twice-Told Tales."
    London: Knight & Son, (n. d., 1852?).

952 NATHANIEL HAWTHORNE'S TALES. In Two Volumes. London:
    Bell & Daldy, 1866.

953 NATHANIEL HAWTHORNE'S TALES; TWICE TOLD TALES, FIRST AND
    SECOND SERIES; SNOW IMAGE, AND OTHER TALES. London:
    Bell & Daldy, 1866 (ca. 1868).

    A collection made up of TWICE-TOLD TALES, first and
    second series; and THE SNOW-IMAGE, AND OTHER TALES.

954   TALES OF THE WHITE HILLS...
      Boston: James R. Osgood and Company, 1877.

955   A VIRTUOSO'S COLLECTION, AND OTHER TALES...
      Boston: James R. Osgood and Company, 1877.

956   HAWTHORNE, By James T. Fields.   TALES OF THE WHITE HILLS,
      LEGENDS OF NEW ENGLAND, by Nathaniel Hawthorne.
      Boston: Houghton Mifflin /1879/

      An omnibus volume of James T. Fields's HAWTHORNE, 1876;
      Hawthorne's TALES OF THE WHITE HILLS, 1877; and,
      LEGENDS OF NEW ENGLAND, 1877.

957   SKETCHES AND STUDIES...
      Boston: Houghton Mifflin. The Riverside Press,
      Cambridge: /1883/

958   LITTLE DAFFYDOWNDILLY AND OTHER STORIES...
      Boston: Houghton Mifflin; New York: The Riverside
      Press, Cambridge: 1887.

959   THE GRAY CHAMPION AND OTHER STORIES AND SKETCHES.
      Boston and New York: Houghton Mifflin. The Riverside
      Press, Cambridge: 1889.

960   TALES OF THE WHITE HILLS AND SKETCHES...
      Boston: Houghton Mifflin; New York: The Riverside
      Press: 1889.

961   THE OLD MANSE AND A FEW MOSSES. Boston: Houghton Mifflin;
      New York: 11 East Seventeenth Street; Chicago: The
      Riverside Press, Cambridge: /1894/

962   COLONIAL STORIES. Boston: Joseph Knight, 1897.

963   THE CUSTOM HOUSE AND MAIN STREET.   Boston: Houghton
      Mifflin; Chicago: The Riverside Press, Cambridge,
      /1899/.

964   ETHAN BRAND by Nathaniel Hawthorne; THE CHAMBERED NAUTILUS
      by Oliver Wendell Holmes.   Boston: Houghton Mifflin;
      New York: /1900/.

965   ETHAN BRAND: OR, THE UNPARDONABLE SIN...AND OTHER STORIES.
      New York: The Arundel Print. /n. d., ca. 1900/.

966   THE GENTLE BOY AND OTHER TALES.   Boston: Houghton Mifflin;
      New York: 11 East Seventeenth Street; Chicago: The
      Riverside Press, Cambridge, /1900/.

967   IN COLONIAL DAYS. Boston: L. C. Page & Co., 1906.

968   NATHANIEL HAWTHORNE: REPRESENTATIVE SELECTIONS, WITH
INTRODUCTION, BIBLIOGRAPHY, AND NOTES BY AUSTIN WARREN.
New York: American Book Co., 1934.

969   THE COMPLETE NOVELS AND SELECTED TALES OF NATHANIEL HAWTHORNE.
Introduction by Norman Holmes Pearson, ed. New York:
Modern Library, 1937.

970   HAWTHORNE AS EDITOR: SELECTIONS FROM HIS WRITINGS IN THE
AMERICAN MAGAZINE OF USEFUL AND ENTERTAINING KNOWLEDGE,
by Arlin Turner. Louisiana: Louisiana St. U.P., 1941.

971   HAWTHORNE'S SHORT STORIES. Introduction by Newton Arvin, ed.
New York: Alfred A. Knopf, 1946.

972   THE BEST OF HAWTHORNE. Introduction by Mark Van Doren, ed.
New York: Ronald Press, 1951.

973   Hawthorne, Nathaniel. NATHANIEL HAWTHORNE: SELECTED TALES
AND SKETCHES. Introduction by Hyatt H. Waggoner, ed.
New York: Rinehart, 1956.

974   Hawthorne, Nathaniel. TWICE-TOLD TALES AND OTHER SHORT
STORIES. Introduction by Quentin Anderson. New York:
Washington Sq., P., 1960.

975 HAWTHORNE IN ENGLAND. SELECTIONS FROM "OUR OLD HOME" and
"THE ENGLISH NOTE-BOOKS." Cushing Strout, ed. Ithaca:
Cornell U. P., 1965.

975.1 Hawthorne, Nathaniel THE PORTABLE HAWTHORNE. Malcolm Cowley,
ed. New York: Viking Press, 1948, 1958; rev. ed., 1969.

975.2 Hawthorne, Nathaniel. SELECTED TALES AND SKETCHES. 3rd ed.
Introduction by Hyatt Howe Waggoner. New York: Holt,
Rinehart and Winston, 1970.

976   THE HAWTHORNE DIARY OF 1859. William L. Reenan, ed.
Privately printed. Freelands, 1931.

DIARIES, LETTERS, NOTEBOOKS

977 HAWTHORNE'S FIRST DIARY: WITH AN ACCOUNT OF ITS DISCOVERY
AND LOSS. By Samuel T. Pickard. Boston and New York:
Houghton Mifflin, 1897. Authenticity unresolved.

978 TWENTY DAYS WITH JULIAN AND LITTLE BUNNY: A DIARY BY
     NATHANIEL HAWTHORNE NOW FIRST PRINTED FROM THE
     ORIGINAL MANUSCRIPT. New York: /Stephen H. Wakeman/,
     1904.

979 Hawthorne, Nathaniel. Autograph Letters and Manuscripts of
     /Nathaniel Hawthorne/, EIHC, 41 (1905), 99-110.

980 Hawthorne, Nathaniel. LETTERS OF HAWTHORNE TO WILLIAM D.
     TICKNOR, 1851-1864. Newark: The Carteret Book Club,
     1910.

981 Hawthorne, Nathaniel. Love-Letters of Hawthorne. Nation,
     85 (1907), 160.

982 Hawthorne, Nathaniel. LOVE LETTERS OF NATHANIEL HAWTHORNE.
     Chicago: Society of the Dofobs, 1907.

983 Hawthorne, Nathaniel. LOVE LETTERS OF NATHANIEL HAWTHORNE.
     Cleveland: Bell & Howell, 1907.

984 PASSAGES FROM THE AMERICAN NOTE-BOOKS OF NATHANIEL HAWTHORNE.
     Sophia Hawthorne, ed. Boston: Ticknor and Fields, 1868.

985 PASSAGES FROM THE /AMERICAN/ NOTE-BOOKS OF THE LATE NATHANIEL
     HAWTHORNE. With an Introduction by Moncure D. Conway.
     London: John Camden Hotten, 1869.

986 PASSAGES FROM THE AMERICAN NOTE-BOOKS. Boston: James R.
     Osgood and Company, 1876.

     LITTLE CLASSIC EDITION.

987 Hawthorne, Nathaniel. THE AMERICAN NOTEBOOKS BY NATHANIEL
     HAWTHORNE. BASED UPON THE ORIGINAL MANUSCRIPTS IN THE
     PIERPOINT MORGAN LIBRARY. Randall Stewart, ed. New
     Haven: Yale U. P., 1932.

987.1 THE AMERICAN NOTEBOOKS. Claude M. Simpson, ed. THE CENTENARY
     EDITION OF THE WORKS OF NATHANIEL HAWTHORNE. Vol. 8.
     Columbus, Ohio: Ohio St. U. P., 1971.

988 PASSAGES FROM THE ENGLISH NOTE-BOOKS OF NATHANIEL HAWTHORNE.
     Sophia Hawthorne, ed. Boston: Fields, Osgood & Co.,
     1870; London: Strahan, 1870.

989   PASSAGES FROM THE ENGLISH NOTE-BOOKS. Boston: James R.
      Osgood and Company, 1876.

      LITTLE CLASSIC EDITION.

990

    Hawthorne, Nathaniel. THE ENGLISH NOTEBOOKS BY NATHANIEL
    HAWTHORNE. BASED UPON THE ORIGINAL MANUSCRIPTS IN THE
    PIERPONT MORGAN LIBRARY. Randall Stewart, ed. New
    York: Modern Language Association of America, 1941.
    Reprinted, New York: Russell & Russell, 1962.

      Rev. by Manning Hawthorne, AL, 14 (1942-43), 84-87;
      V. S. Pritchett, NS&N, 24 (1942), 275- Townsend
      Scudder, NEQ, 15 (1942), 166-67; Arlin Turner, SR,
      50 (1942), 275-77.

991   PASSAGES FROM THE FRENCH AND ITALIAN NOTE-BOOKS OF NATHANIEL
      HAWTHORNE. Una Hawthorne, ed. London: Strahan & Co.,
      1871; Boston: James R. Osgood & Co., Late Ticknor &
      Fields, Osgood & Co., 1872.

992 PASSAGES FROM THE FRENCH AND ITALIAN NOTE-BOOKS. Boston:
      James R. Osgood and Company, 1876.

      LITTLE CLASSIC EDITION.

        WORKS: ROMANCES, COLLECTED STORIES, BIOGRAPHY

993 BIOGRAPHICAL STORIES FOR CHILDREN.

      Boston: Tappan and Dennet, 1842.
      Reissued, 1842, as HISTORICAL TALES FOR YOUTH.
      Reissued, 1851, as TRUE STORIES FROM HISTORY AND
        BIOGRAPHY.

    Grandfather's Chair: A History for Youth. Boston: E. P.
      Peabody, 1841.
    Famous Old People: Being the Second Epoch of Grandfather's
      Chair. Boston: E. P. Peabody, 1841.
    The Liberty Tree: With the Last Words of Grandfather's
      Chair. Boston: E. P. Peabody, 1841. Second edition,
      Boston: Tappan and Dennet, 1842.

994 ...BIOGRAPHICAL STORIES...
      Boston: Houghton Mifflin; New York: The Riverside
      Press, Cambridge: 1883.

994.1
    TRUE STORIES FROM HISTORY AND BIOGRAPHY. Introduction by
    Roy Harvey Pearce; Fredson Bowers, textual editor.
    THE CENTENARY EDITION OF THE WORKS OF NATHANIEL
    HAWTHORNE. Vol. 6. Columbus, Ohio: Ohio St. U. P.,
    1971.

995
    THE BLITHEDALE ROMANCE.
      Boston: Ticknor, Reed, and Fields, 1852;
      London: Chapman and Hall, 1852.

996
THE BLITHEDALE ROMANCE. Boston: James R. Osgood and
Company, Late Ticknor & Fields, and Fields, Osgood, &
Co., 1876.

LITTLE CLASSIC EDITION.

997
Hawthorne, Nathaniel. THE BLITHEDALE ROMANCE. Introduction
by Ernest Rhys, ed. New York: Dutton, 1912.

998
Hawthorne, Nathaniel. THE BLITHEDALE ROMANCE. Introduction
by Arlin Turner, ed. New York: Norton, 1958.

999
Hawthorne, Nathaniel. THE BLITHEDALE ROMANCE. Introduction
by David Levin, ed. New York: Dell Pub. Co., 1962.

1000
Hawthorne, Nathaniel. THE BLITHEDALE ROMANCE and FANSHAWE.
William Charvat, Roy Harvey Pearce, Claude M. Simpson,
gen eds.; Fredson Bowers, Matthew J. Bruccoli, L. Neal
Smith, textual eds. THE CENTENARY EDITION OF THE WORKS
OF NATHANIEL HAWTHORNE. III. Columbus: Ohio St. U. P.,
1964.

1001
DOCTOR GRIMSHAWE'S SECRET: A ROMANCE. Edited with Preface and
Notes by Julian Hawthorne. Boston and New York: Houghton
Mifflin, 1882; Boston: Osgood, 1883; London: Longmans,
Green, 1883.

1002
Hawthorne, Nathaniel. DR. GRIMSHAWE'S SECRET. With
Introduction and Notes by Edward H. Davidson, ed.
Cambridge, Mass.: Harvard U. P., 1954; New York:
1955.

1003
THE DOLLIVER ROMANCE AND OTHER PIECES. Sophia Hawthorne, ed.
Boston: James R. Osgood and Company, 1876.

An Old Woman's Tale, SG, December 21, 1830, 1-2.
Doctor Bullivant, SG, January, 1831.
My Visit to Niagara, NEM, 1835.
Graves and Goblins, NEM, June, 1835.
Fragments From the Journal of a Solitary Man, AmMMag,
     July, 1837.
The Antique Ring, SarNMM, February, 1843.
A Book of Autographs, DemR, November, 1844.

1004
THE DOLLIVER ROMANCE, FANSHAWE, AND SEPTIMIUS FELTON.
London: Kegan Paul, 1883.

1005
Hawthorne, Nathaniel. THE DOLLIVER ROMANCE; FANSHAWE; AND
SEPTIMIUS FELTON With an Appendix Containing THE
ANCESTRAL FOOTSTEP BY NATHANIEL HAWTHORNE. (First
published 1883), repr., Freeport, New York: Books
for Libraries Press, 1970.

1006
FANSHAWE, A TALE. Boston: Marsh & Capen, 1828.

1007
FANSHAWE AND OTHER PIECES. Boston: James R. Osgood, 1876.

Pieces added:
Sir William Phips, SG (November 23, 1830), 1-2.
Mrs. Hutchinson, SG (December 7, 1830), 4.
Jonathan Cilly, DemR (1838).
Thomas Green Fessenden, AmMMag. 5 (1838), 30-41.

1008
THE HOUSE OF THE SEVEN GABLES.
. Boston: Ticknor, Reed, and Fields, 1851.
London: Bohn, 1851.

Four publications, 1851-1852: Two in April, 1851;
May, 1851; and September, 1852.

1009
THE HOUSE OF THE SEVEN GABLES. Boston: James R. Osgood and
Company, 1876.

1010
Hawthorne, Nathaniel. THE HOUSE OF THE SEVEN GABLES.
Introductory Sketch by H. A. Davidson. Boston:
Houghton Mifflin, 1904, 1923, 1932.

1011
Hawthorne, Nathaniel. THE HOUSE OF THE SEVEN GABLES.
Introduction by J. R. Castleman. New York: Charles
E. Merrill, 1907.

1012
Hawthorne, Nathaniel. THE HOUSE OF THE SEVEN GABLES.
Introduction by A. Marion Merrill. Boston: 1923.

1013
Hawthorne, Nathaniel. THE HOUSE OF THE SEVEN GABLES.
Clyde Furst, ed. Notes Revised by H. Y. Moffett.
New York: Macmillan, 1930.

1014
Hawthorne, Nathaniel. THE HOUSE OF THE SEVEN GABLES.
S. R. Hadsell, ed. New York: 1932.

1015
Hawthorne, Nathaniel. THE HOUSE OF THE SEVEN GABLES.
Introduction by Roy Harvey Pearce. New York: Dent, 1954.

1016
Hawthorne, Nathaniel. THE HOUSE OF THE SEVEN GABLES.
Introduction by Charles Angoff, ed. Fine Editions
Club, 1956.

1017
Hawthorne, Nathaniel. THE HOUSE OF THE SEVEN GABLES.
Introduction by Philip Young. New York: Holt,
Rinehart and Winston, 1957; Repr. with new Introduction
and Note by Philip Young, Holt, Rinehart and Winston,
1970.

1018 Hawthorne, Nathaniel. THE HOUSE OF THE SEVEN GABLES.
      Afterward by Edward C. Sampson. New York: New
      American Lib., 1961.

1019 Hawthorne, Nathaniel. THE HOUSE OF THE SEVEN GABLES.
      Introduction by Richard Harter Fogle. New York:
      Collier Books, 1962.

1020 Hawthorne, Nathaniel. THE HOUSE OF THE SEVEN GABLES.
      Introduction by David Levin, ed. New York: Dell
      Pub. Co., 1962.

1021 Hawthorne, Nathaniel. THE HOUSE OF THE SEVEN GABLES. With
      a Life of Hawthorne, Notes and Other Aids to Study by
      A. Marion Merrill, ed. Boston: Allyn, 1964.

1022 Hawthorne, Nathaniel. THE HOUSE OF THE SEVEN GABLES.
      Introduction by Hyatt H. Waggoner, ed. Boston: Houghton
      Mifflin Co., 1964.

1023 Hawthorne, Nathaniel. THE HOUSE OF THE SEVEN GABLES.
      William Charvat, Roy Harvey Pearce, Claude M. Simpson,
      gen. eds.; Fredson Bowers, Matthew J. Bruccoli,
      L. Neal Smith, textual eds. THE CENTENARY EDITION OF
      THE WORKS OF NATHANIEL HAWTHORNE, II. Columbus: Ohio
      St. U. P., 1965.

1024 Hawthorne, Nathaniel. THE HOUSE OF THE SEVEN GABLES.
      Introduction by Seymour L. Gross, ed. New York:
      Norton, 1967.

1025 Hawthorne, Nathaniel. THE HOUSE OF THE SEVEN GABLES.
      Introduction by Harry Levin. Columbus, Ohio: Charles
      E. Merrill, 1969.

1025.1 Hawthorne, Nathaniel. THE HOUSE OF THE SEVEN GABLES.
        Introduction by James Franklin Beard. Barre, Mass.:
        Imprint Society, 1970.

1026 LIFE OF FRANKLIN PIERCE. Boston: Ticknor, Reed, and Fields,
      1852.

1027 LIFE OF FRANKLIN PIERCE. New York: Garrett Press, Inc.,
      1969.

1027.1 Hawthorne, Nathaniel. THE LIFE OF FRANKLIN PIERCE. Foreword
        by Richard C. Robey. New York: Garrett, 1970.

1028

THE MARBLE FAUN: OR, THE ROMANCE OF MONTE BENI...IN TWO VOLUMES. Boston: Ticknor and Fields, 1860.

Reissued with added "Conclusion," 1860.

1029

THE MARBLE FAUN. Boston: James R. Osgood and Company, 1876.

LITTLE CLASSIC EDITION.

1030

Hawthorne, Nathaniel. THE MARBLE FAUN. Introduction by Annie Russell. Boston: 1901, 1925.

1031

Hawthorne, Nathaniel. THE MARBLE FAUN. Introduction by Leslie Stephens. Ernest Rhys, ed. New York: Everyman's Lib., 1910.

1032

Hawthorne, Nathaniel. THE MARBLE FAUN. Introduction by David Levin. New York: Dell, 1960.

1033

Hawthorne, Nathaniel. THE MARBLE FAUN: OR, THE ROMANCE OF MONTE BENI. Afterword by Murray Krieger. New York: New American Library, 1961.

1034

Hawthorne, Nathaniel. THE MARBLE FAUN. Introduction by David Levin. New York: Dell Pub. Co., 1962.

1035

Hawthorne, Nathaniel. THE MARBLE FAUN: OR, THE ROMANCE OF MONTE BENI. William Charvat, Roy H. Pearce, Claude M. Simpson, Matthew J. Bruccoli, Fredson Bowers, and L. Neal Smith, eds. THE CENTENARY EDITIONS OF THE WORKS OF NATHANIEL HAWTHORNE. Vol. 4. Columbus: Ohio St. U. P., 1968.

1035.1

Hawthorne, Nathaniel. THE MARBLE FAUN. Richard H. Rupp, ed. Indianapolis, Ind.: Bobbs-Merrill, 1971.

1036

MOSSES FROM AN OLD MANSE. New York and London: Wiley and Putnam, 1846, 2 vols.

1036 MOSSES FROM..., cont.

P's Correspondence, DemR, 16 (April, 1845), 337–45;
Rappaccini's Daughter, DemR, (December, 1844), as "Writings of
 Aubepine";
Roger Malvin's Burial, Token (1832), 161-88;
A Select Party, DemR, 15 (July, 1844), 33-40;
Sketches from Memory. By a Pedestrian. No. I. The Notch. Our
 Evening Party Among The Mountains, NEM, 9 (November), 1835;
 321-26;
Sketches from Memory. By a Pedestrian, No. II. The Canal-Boat.
 The Inland Port. Rochester. An Afternoon Scene. A Night
 Scene, NEM, 9 (December, 1835), 398-409;
The Story Teller. No. I. At Home. A Flight In the Fog. A
 Fellow-Traveler, NEM, 7 (November, 1834), 352-58;
The Story Teller, No. II. The Village Theatre. Mr. Higginbotham's
 Catastrophe, NEM, 7 (December, 1834), 449-59;
A Virtuoso's Collection, BM, 1 (May, 1842), 193-200;
Writings of Aubepine (See "Rappaccini's Daughter"), DemR, 15
 (December, 1844), 545-60;
Young Goodman Brown, NEM, 8 (April, 1835), 249-60.

The Artist of the Beautiful, DemR, 14 (June, 1844), 605-17;
The Birthmark, Pioneer, 1 (March, 1843), 113-19;
Buds and Bird-Voices, DemR, 12 (June, 1843), 640-08;
The Canal Boat, NEM (December, 1835);
The Celestial Railroad, DemR, 12 (May, 1843), 515-23;
The Christmas Banquet, DemR, 14 (January, 1844), 78-87;
Drowne's Wooden Image, GMLB, 29 (July, 1844), 13-17;
Earth's Holocaust, GM, 25 (May, 1844), 193-200;
Egotism; or The Bosom Serpent, DemR, 12 (March, 1843), 255-61;
Feathertop, IMM, 5 (February, March, 1852), 182-86; 333-37;
Fire-Worship, DemR, 13 (December, 1843), 627-30;
The Hall of Fantasy, Pioneer, 1 (February, 1843), 49-55;
The Intelligence Office, DemR, 14 (March, 1844), 269-75;
Monsieur du Miroir, Token (1837), 49-64;
Mrs. Bullfrog, Token (1837), 66-75;
The New Adam and Eve, DemR, 12 (February, 1843), 146-55;
The Notch of the White Mountains, NEM, (November, 1835);
The Old Apple Dealer, SarNMM, 1 (January, 1843), 21-24;
The Old Manse, MOM, 1846;
Our Evening Party in the White Mountains, NEM (1835);
The Procession of Life, DemR, 12 (April, 1843), 360-66;

1037 MOSSES FROM AN OLD MANSE.
 New York: George P. Putnam, 1850.

1038 MOSSES FROM AN OLD MANSE. Boston: Ticknor and Fields, 1854.
 2 Vols. Repr., Books for Libraries, ISBN, 1970.

1039 MOSSES FROM AN OLD MANSE. Boston: James R. Osgood and
 Company, 1876.

1040 MOSSES FROM AN OLD MANSE. Freeport, New York: Books for
 Libraries, 1970.

1041 THE SCARLET LETTER, A ROMANCE.
      Boston: Ticknor, Reed, and Fields, 1850; second
         edition with added "Preface," 1850.
      London: Walker /pirated/, 1851.

1042 THE SCARLET LETTER. Boston: James R. Osgood and Company,
      Late Ticknor & Fields, and Fields, Osgood, & Co., 1875.

      LITTLE CLASSIC EDITION.

1043 THE SCARLET LETTER, A ROMANCE. Edinburgh: William
      Paterson, /n. d., 1883/.

1044 Hawthorne, Nathaniel. THE SCARLET LETTER. Introduction by
      Claire Soule Seay. New York: 1920.

1045 Hawthorne, Nathaniel. THE SCARLET LETTER. Introduction by
      Elizabeth Deering Hanscom. New York: 1927.

1046 Hawthorne, Nathaniel. THE SCARLET LETTER. Introduction by
      William Lyon Phelps. New York: Mod. Lib., 1927.

1047 Hawthorne, Nathaniel. THE SCARLET LETTER. Ernest E. Leisy,
      ed. New York: 1929.

1048 Hawthorne, Nathaniel. THE SCARLET LETTER. Introduction by
      Austin Warren. New York: Holt, Rinehart and Winston,
      1947, 1963.

1049 Hawthorne, Nathaniel. THE SCARLET LETTER. Foreword and
      Descriptive Captions by Basil Davenport. New York:
      Dodd, Mead, 1948.

1050 Hawthorne, Nathaniel. THE SCARLET LETTER. Introduction by
      Newton Arvin. Harper's Modern Classics, 1950.

1051 Hawthorne, Nathaniel. THE SCARLET LETTER. Introduction by
      John C. Gerber. New York: Modern Lib., 1950.

1052 Hawthorne, Nathaniel. THE SCARLET LETTER. Introduction by
      Roy Harvey Pearce. New York: J. M. Dent & Sons,
      Everyman's Lib., 1957.

1053 Hawthorne, Nathaniel. THE SCARLET LETTER. Introduction by
      Leo Marx, ed. New York: New American Lib. (Signet),
      1959.

1054   Hawthorne, Nathaniel. THE SCARLET LETTER. Foreword by
      Louise Bogan. New York: Barnes & Noble, 1960.

1055   Hawthorne, Nathaniel. THE SCARLET LETTER. Introduction by
      David Levin. New York: Dell Pub. Co., 1960.

1056   Hawthorne, Nathaniel. THE SCARLET LETTER. Introduction by
      Harry Levin, ed. Boston: Houghton Mifflin Co., 1960.

1057   Hawthorne, Nathaniel. THE SCARLET LETTER AND OTHER TALES
      OF THE PURITANS. General Introduction by Harry Levin, ed.
      Boston: Houghton Mifflin, 1961.

1058   Hawthorne, Nathaniel. THE SCARLET LETTER. An Annotated
      Text, Backgrounds and Sources, Essays in Criticism,
      Sculley Bradley, R. C. Beatty, E. H. Long, Compilers.
      New York: Norton, 1962.

1059   Hawthorne, Nathaniel. THE SCARLET LETTER. William Charvat,
      Roy Harvey Pearce, Claude M. Simpson, gen. eds.;
      Fredson Bowers, Matthew J. Bruccoli, textual eds.
      Columbus: Ohio St. U. P., 1962.

1060   Hawthorne, Nathaniel. THE SCARLET LETTER. Introduction by
      Willard Thorp. New York: Collier Books, 1962.

1061   Hawthorne, Nathaniel. THE SCARLET LETTER. Introduction by
      William Charvat. Boston: Houghton Mifflin, 1963.

1062   Hawthorne, Nathaniel. THE SCARLET LETTER. Introduction by
      Larzer Ziff, ed. Indianapolis: Robbs-Merrill, 1963.

1063   Hawthorne, Nathaniel. THE SCARLET LETTER: A ROMANCE.
      Introduction by Douglas Grant. New York: Oxford
      U.P., 1965.

1064   Hawthorne, Nathaniel. THE SCARLET LETTER. Introduction by
      Hyatt H. Waggoner and George Monteiro. San Francisco:
      Chandler, 1968.

1065   Hawthorne, Nathaniel. THE SCARLET LETTER. Introduction by
      Edwin Harrison Cady. Columbus, Ohio: Merrill, 1969.

1065.1   Hawthorne, Nathaniel. THE SCARLET LETTER and YOUNG GOODMAN
      BROWN. Introduction by Alfred Kazin. New York:
      Anchor Books, 1970.

1065.2

Hawthorne, Nathaniel. THE SCARLET LETTER. With Reader's Guide by Solomon Schlakman. Amsco School Publications, 1970.

1065.3

Hawthorne, Nathaniel. THE SCARLET LETTER. Compiled by Arlin Turner. Charles E. Merrill Studies. Columbus, Ohio: Charles E. Merrill, 1970.

1066

SEPTIMIUS: A ROMANCE. Una Hawthorne and Robert Browning, eds. London: Henry S. King & Co., 1872.

1067

SEPTIMIUS FELTON; OR THE ELIXIR OF LIFE. Una Hawthorne and Robert Browning, eds., Boston: James R. Osgood & Co., 1872.

1068

SEPTIMIUS FELTON. Boston: James R. Osgood and Company, 1876.

LITTLE CLASSIC EDITION.

1069

THE SNOW-IMAGE, AND OTHER TALES. London: Henry G. Bohn, 1851.

The title story first appeared in a "Memorial" for Mrs. Osgood. New York: 1851. Also, printed separately.

1069 THE SNOW-IMAGE..., cont.

My Kinsman, Major Molineux, Token (1832), 89-116.
Wives of the Dead/The Two Widows/. Token (1832), 74-82.
The Canterbury Pilgrims, Token (1833), 153-66.
The Colonial Newspaper, NEM (February, 1835).(Old News, No. I)
The Old French War, NEM, 8 (March, 1835) (Old News, No. II)
The Old Tory, NEM, 8 (May, 1835), (Old News, No. III)
The Devil in Manuscript, NEM, 9 (November, 1835), 340-45.
Old Ticonderoga, AmMMag, 1 (February, 1836), 138-42.
The Man of Adamant, an Apologue, Token (1837), 119-28.
A Bell's Biography, KbM, 9 (March, 1837), 219-23.
Sylph Etherege, TokenAS (1838), 22-32.
John Inglefield's Thanksgiving, DemR, 7 (March, 1840), 209-12.
Little Daffydowndilly, BGM, 2 (August, 1843), 120-25.
Main Street, AEsthetic Papers, 1849.
The Great Stone Face, NE, 4 (January 24, 1840), 16.
The Snow Image, IMM (October, 1850.("The Snow-Image. A
   Childish Miracle" in THE MEMORIAL. New York: Putnam, 1851.
Ethan Brand, IM (May, 1851; first appeared in THE BOSTON
   MUSEUM (January 5, 1850) as "The Unpardonable Sin."

1070

THE SNOW-IMAGE, AND OTHER TWICE-TOLD TALES. Boston: Ticknor, Reed, and Fields, 1852.

1071

"The Snow-Image: A Childish Miracle." New York: James G. Gregory, 1864.

1072 THE SNOW-IMAGE....
      Boston: James R. Osgood and Company, 1876.

      LITTLE CLASSIC EDITION.

1073 Hawthorne, Nathaniel. THE SNOW IMAGE AND OTHER TWICE-TOLD
      TALES. Introduction by Richard Burton. 1899.
      Reprint, Freeport, New York: Books for Libraries,
      1970.

1074 TANGLEWOOD TALES, FOR GIRLS AND BOYS: BEING A SECOND WONDER-
      BOOK. Boston: Ticknor, Reed, and Fields, 1853;
      London: Chapman and Hall, 1853.
      New York: repr., except for "The Wayside," in COMPLETE
      GREEK STORIES OF NATHANIEL HAWTHORNE FROM THE WONDER
      BOOK AND TANGLEWOOD TALES. Franklin Watts, Inc., 1963.

        The Wayside
        The Minotaur
        The Pygmies
        The Dragon's Teeth
        Circe's Palace
        The Pomegranate Seeds
        The Golden Fleece

1074.1 [TANGLEWOOD TALES] A WONDER BOOK and TANGLEWOOD TALES.
      Introduction by Roy Harvey Pearce. THE CENTENARY EDITION
      OF THE WORKS OF NATHANIEL HAWTHORNE. Vol. 7. Columbus,
      Ohio: Ohio St. U. P., 1971.

1075 TRANSFORMATION: OR, THE ROMANCE OF MONTE BENI - IN THREE
      VOLUMES. London: Smith, Elder, 1859; 2nd edition,
      London: Smith, Elder, 2 vols., 1860.

1076 TWICE-TOLD TALES. Boston: American Stationers Co.,
      John B. Russell, 1837.

      Publication dates of individual stories of TWICE-TOLD
      TALES of 1837 and 1842 editions follow:

      The Ambitious Guest, NEM, 8 (June, 1835), 424-31.
      Chippings With A Chisel, DemR, 3 (September, 1838), 18-26.
      David Swan, A Fantasy, Token (1837), 147-55.
      Dr. Heidegger's Experiment, KbM, 9 (January, 1837), as
        "The Fountain of Youth," and SG (March, 1837).
      Edward Fane's Rosebud, KbM, 10 (September, 1837), 195-99.
      Edward Randolph's Portrait, DemR (July, 1838).
      Endicott and the Red Cross, Token (1838), 69-78; SG
        (November, 1837).
      Fancy's Show Box, Token (1837), 177-84.

1076 TWICE-TOLD..., cont.

Foot-Prints On The Sea-Shore, DemR, 1 (January, 1838),
190-97.
The Fountain of Youth: see Dr. Heidegger's Experiment.
The Gentle Boy, Token (1832), 193-240.
The Gray Champion, NEM, 8 (January, 1835), 20-26.
The Great Carbuncle, Token (1837), 156-75.
The Haunted Mind, Token (1835), 76-82.
The Hollow of the Three Hills, SG (November 12, 1830), 1.
Howe's Masquerade, DemR (May, 1838).
Lady Eleanore's Mantle, DemR (December, 1838).
The Lily's Quest, SoRose (January 19, 1839), 161-64.
Little Annie's Ramble, YK (1835).
The May-Pole of Merry Mount, Token (1836), 283-97.
The Minister's Black Veil, Token (1836), 302-20.
Mr. Higginbotham's Catastrophe, NEM, 7 (December, 1834),
450-59, one of a group designated "The Story-Teller."
Night Sketches, Beneath an Umbrella, TokenAS (1838), 81-89.
Old Esther Dudley, DemR (January, 1839).

The Old Maid in the Winding-Sheet, NEM, 9 (July, 1835),
8-16; in TTT (1842), as "The White Old Maid."
Peter Goldthwait's Treasure, TokenAS (1838), 37-65.
The Prophetic Pictures, Token (1837), 289-307.
A Rill from The Town-Pump, NEM, 8 (June, 1835), 473-78.
The Seven Vagabonds, Token (1833), 49-77.
The Shaker Bridal, TokenAS (1838), 117-25.
Sights from a Steeple, Token (1831), 41-51.
The Sister Years, SG (January, 1839).
Snow-Flakes, DemR, 1 (February, 1838), 355-59.
Sunday at Home, Token (1837), 88-96.
Legends of the Province-House, No. II. Edward Randolph's
Portrait, DemR, 2 (July, 1838), 360-69.
Legends of the Province-House, No. I. Howe's Masquerade,
DemR, 2 (May, 1838), 129-40.
Legends of the Province-House, No. III. Lady Eleanore's
Mantle, DemR, 3 (December, 1838), 321-32.
Legends of the Province-House, No. IV. Old Esther Dudley,
DemR, 5 (January, 1839), 51-59.

The Three-Fold Destiny, AmMMag, 5 (March, 1838), 228-35.
The Toll-Gatherer's Day, DemR, 1 (October, 1837), 31-35.
The Village Uncle: An Imaginary Retrospect. Published
anonymously with title The Mermaid: A Reverie,
Token (1835).
The Vision of the Fountain, NEM, 9 (August, 1835), 99-104.
Wakefield, NEM, 8 (May, 1835), 341-47.
The Wedding Knell, Token (1836), 113-24.
The White Old Maid (see The Old Maid in the Winding-Sheet).

1077 TWICE-TOLD TALES. Boston: Munroe, 1842, reissued with
added material.

1078 TWICE-TOLD TALES.
London: William Tegg and Co., Cheapside; 1850.

1079   TWICE-TOLD TALES. Boston: Ticknor, Reed, and Fields, 1851,
       repr. with added "Preface."
       London: Bohn, 1851.

1080   TWICE-TOLD TALES. Boston: Ticknor and Fields, 1865.

       A repr., except for a note in Vol. 1 in which
       Hawthorne refutes the suggestion that he had
       based his "Dr. Heidegger's Experiment" on a story
       by Alexandre Dumas.

1081   TWICE-TOLD TALES...
       Boston: James R. Osgood and Company, 1876.

       LITTLE CLASSIC EDITION.

1082   Hawthorne, Nathaniel. THE TWICE-TOLD TALES BY NATHANIEL
       HAWTHORNE. With Introductory Note by George Parsons
       Lathrop. J. Hubert Scott, ed. New York: Houghton
       Mifflin Co., 1882, 1907.

1083   Hawthorne, Nathaniel. TWICE-TOLD TALES. Introduction by
       Roy Harvey Pearce. London: Dent & Co., Everyman's
       Lib., 1955.

       INDIVIDUAL SHORT WORKS AND BRIEF COLLECTIONS

1084   "Alice Doane's Appeal," Token (1835), 84-101.

1085   THE AMERICAN MAGAZINE OF USEFUL AND ENTERTAINING KNOWLEDGE.
       Boston: Boston Bewick Co., 1836. Vol. II. Nos. 7-12,
       March to August, were edited and virtually written by
       Hawthorne and his sister.

1086   "The Ancestral Footstep," AtlM, 50-51 (December, 1882;
       February, 1883), 823-39; 47-63, 180-95.

1087   "The Battle Omen," SG, 8, New Series, No. 88 (November 2,
       1830), 1.

       See Donald Clifford Gallup, "On Hawthorne's Authorship
       of 'The Battle-Omen,'" NEQ, 9 (1936), 690-99.

1088   "Biographical Sketch of Jonathan Cilley," DemR, 3 (September,
       1838), 69-76.

1089   "Browne's Folly," THE DOLLIVER ROMANCE AND OTHER PIECES.
       Boston: Osgood, 1876, pp. 209-13. First appeared
       in THE WEAL-REAF, 1860, as "Letter From Hawthorne."

1090   "The Celestial Railroad."

      DemR, 12 (May, 1843), 515-23.
      Boston: Wilder and Co., 1843; also Boston: James F.
         Fish, 1843. (The Wilder imprint possibly earlier.)
      Also, Lowell, 1843.
      As "A Visit to the Celestial City," Philadelphia:
         /1844/, a reprint with one anecdote deleted.
      London: Houston and Stoneman, 1846.
      MOM, 1846.

1091   "The Celestial Railroad...with Additions and Alternations."
      Boston: J. V. Himes, 1860.

      The "alternations" possibly are not by Hawthorne.

1092   "Celestial Railroad; or, Modern Pilgrim's Progress. After
      the Manner of Bunyan...with Additions and alterations.
      Buchanan, Michigan: Published by the W. A. C. P. Assn.,
      1867.

1093   "Chiefly About War-Matters," AtlM, 10 (July, 1862), 43-61.

1094   "Eastern Lands," THE ESSEX BANNER AND HAVERHILL ADVERTISER
      (November 17, 1838), p. 1. Attributed.

1095   FAMOUS OLD PEOPLE: BEING THE SECOND EPOCH OF GRANDFATHER'S
      CHAIR. Boston: E. P. Peabody, 1841.

1096   FAMOUS OLD PEOPLE: BEING THE SECOND EPOCH OF GRANDFATHER'S
      CHAIR. Boston: Tappan & Dennet, 1842.

1097   "The Fated Family," THE TOKEN. Boston: Gray and Bowen, 1831,
      pp. 57-82. Attributed.

1098   "The First and Last Dinner," A PRACTICAL SYSTEM OF RHETORIC,
      by Samuel P. Newman. Portland: Shirley & Hyde;
      Andover: Newman, 1829, pp. 218-21. Attributed.

1099   "Footprints on the Seashore." Boston: Samuel E. Cassino,
      1892.

1100   "Fragments From The Journal Of A Solitary Man. My Return
      Home," AmMMag, 4 (July, 1837), 45-56.

1101   THE GENTLE BOY: A THRICE TOLD TALE. Boston: Jordan & Co.,
      New York and London: Wiley & Putnam, 1839.

      Prior publication in The Token, 1832, and TWICE-TOLD
      TALES, 1837.

1102 THE GHOST OF DOCTOR HARRIS. New York: The Tucker Publishing Co., 1900.

Issued as THE BALZAC LIBRARY, No. 1, February 19, 1900.

1103 THE GHOST OF DOCTOR HARRIS. New York: Printed for Gratuitous Distribution by the Goerck Art Press, Lewis W. Goerck, Prop., /n. d., 1910/.

1104 THE GOLDEN TOUCH. Boston and New York: Houghton, Mifflin Co., /n. d., 1912?/.

1105 THE GOLDEN TOUCH. Dansville, New York: F. A. Owen Publishing Co., 1915.

1106 THE GOLDEN TOUCH. San Francisco: The Grabhorn Press, 1927.

1107 Hawthorne, Nathaniel. THE GOLDEN TOUCH. Illustrated by Paul Galdone. Foreword by Anne Thaxter Eaton. New York, Toronto, London, Sydney: McGraw-Hill Book Co., 1959.

1108 "A Good Man's Miracle," CF, 1 (February, 1844), 151-56.

1109 GRANDFATHER'S CHAIR: A HISTORY FOR YOUTH. Boston: E. P. Peabody. New York: Wiley & Putnam, 1841.

1110 GRANDFATHER'S CHAIR: A HISTORY FOR YOUTH. 2nd Edition. Revised and Englarged. Boston: Tappan and Dennet, 1842.

1111 "The Haunted Quack. A Tale of a Canal Boat," THE TOKEN. Boston: Gray and Bowen, 1831, pp. 117-37. Attributed.

1112 HAWTHORNE'S HISTORICAL TALES FOR YOUTH. Boston: Tappan & Dennet, 1842(?).

A two-volume set including "Grandfather's Chair," 1842; "Famous Old People," 1842; "Liberty Tree," 1842; and "Biographical Stories," 1842.

1113 "Hints to Young Ambition," NEM, 2 (1832), 513-14. Attributed.

1114 "Howe's Masquerade," in THE BOSTON BOOK. BEING SPECIMENS OF METROPOLITAN LITERATURE. Boston: George W. Light, 1841.

Collected in TWICE-TOLD TALES, 1842.

1115 "The Interrupted Nuptials," SG, (October 12, 1827), p. 1.
Attributed.

1116 JOURNAL OF AN AFRICAN CRUISER by Horatio Bridge, edited by
Nathaniel Hawthorne. New York and London: Wiley and
Putnam, 1845.

1117 LEGENDS OF NEW ENGLAND...
Boston: James R. Osgood and Company, 1877.

1118 LEGENDS OF THE PROVINCE HOUSE...
Boston: James R. Osgood and Company, 1877.

1119 LIBERTY TREE: WITH THE LAST WORDS OF GRANDFATHER'S CHAIR
Boston: E. P. Peabody, 1841.

1120 "The Lily's Quest," in THE PICTURESQUE POCKET COMPANION, AND
VISITOR'S GUIDE, THROUGH MOUNT AUBURN. Boston:
Otis, Broaders and Company, 1839.

Collected in TWICE-TOLD TALES, 1842.

1121 "Little Annie's Ramble," YOUTH'S KEEPSAKE. Boston:
Broaders, 1835, pp. 147-59.

1122 "Little Annie's Ramble, and Other Tales."
Halifax: Milner and Sowerby, 1853.

1123 "Little Annie's Ramble." Cedar Rapids, Iowa: Privately
Printed for Jean and Josephine Fisher and Their
Friends, 1913.

1124 "Little Pansie," in GOOD COMPANY FOR EVERY DAY IN THE YEAR.
Boston: Ticknor and Fields, 1866, pp. 288-304.

1125 "Main-Street," AESTHETIC PAPERS. E. P. Peabody, ed. Boston:
The Editor, 1849, pp. 145-74.

1126 Reissued, Preface by Julian Hawthorne, Canton, Pa.: Kirgate
Press, 1901.

See SNOW-IMAGE.

1127 MAIN STREET. Preface by Julian Hawthorne. Canton,
Pennsylvania: Kirgate Press, 1901.

1128 "The Maypole of Merrymount," [Boston:] With Greetings for
the Year 1947 to the Friends of the Merrymount Press.

1129 MR. HIGGINBOTHAM'S CATASTROPHE...
Boston: The Berkeley Printers, /1931/.

1130 THE NEW ADAM AND EVE...BEING SECOND SERIES OF MOSSES FROM AN
OLD MANSE. Edinburgh: William Paterson, 1883.

1131 THE NEW ADAM AND EVE. London: F. Tennyson Neely, Publisher;
New York: /1899?/

1132 "The New England Village," THE TOKEN. Boston: Gray and
Bowen, 1831, pp. 155-76. Attributed.

1133 THE OLD MANSE. /Cambridge, Mass./. The Riverside Press, 1904.

1134 "An Old Woman's Tale," SG (December 21, 1830), pp. 1-2.

1135 OUR OLD HOME: A SERIES OF ENGLISH SKETCHES. Boston: Ticknor
and Fields, 1863. London: Smith, Elder, 1863, 2 Vols.

1136 OUR OLD HOME. Boston: James R. Osgood and Company, 1876.

LITTLE CLASSIC EDITION.

1136.1
OUR OLD HOME: A SERIES OF ENGLISH SKETCHES. With L. Neal
Smith, associate textual editor. Introduction by Claude
M. Simpson. Textual Introduction by Fredson Bowers.
THE CENTENARY EDITION OF THE WORKS OF NATHANIEL HAWTHORNE.
Vol. 5. Columbus, Ohio: Ohio St. U. P., 1970.

1137 PANDORA'S BOX; THE PARADISE OF CHILDREN. New York: McGraw,
1967.

1138 PANSIE: A FRAGMENT. THE LAST LITERARY EFFORT OF NATHANIEL
HAWTHORNE. London: John Camden Hotten, /1864/.

First published in AtlM, July, 1864. First American
publication, Good Company, 1866. Collected in
DOLLIVER ROMANCE, 1876, under title, "A Scene from
the Dolliver Romance," Boston: Osgood.

1139 PETER PARLEY'S UNIVERSAL HISTORY, ON THE BASIS OF GEOGRAPHY.
Boston: American Stationers' Company. John B. Russell,
1837. 2 Vols.

1140 PETER PARLEY'S COMMON SCHOOL HISTORY. Boston: American
Stationers' Company. J. B. Russell, 1838; London: Parker,
1837. 1 Vol. ed., slightly revised.

1141 "Preface," THE PHILOSOPHY OF THE PLAYS OF SHAKSPERE UNFOLDEN, by Delia Bacon. London: Groombridge, 1857, pp. vii-xv. Boston: Ticknor and Fields, 1857, pp. vii-xv.

1142 "Recollections of a Gifted Woman," AtlM, 11 (January, 1863), 43-58.

1143 "The Rill from the Town Pump."

In Arc, May, 1841: "The Rill from the Town Pump, the best known of Hawthorne's sketches, was stolen by a cunning London bookseller, the author's name omitted, and circulated as a temperance tract."

The sketch was first collected in TWICE-TOLD TALES, 1837; issued as a separate in 1857.

1144 "A Rill from the Town Pump" with Remarks by Telba.

Published for the Albion Society, by W. and F. G. Cash, Bishopsgate Without. 1857.

1145 THE SEVEN VAGABONDS. Boston and New York: Houghton Mifflin, The Riverside Press, 1916.

1146 "Sir William Pepperell," THE TOKEN. Boston: Gray and Bowen, 1833, pp. 124-34.

1147 "Sir William Phips," SG (November 23, 1830), pp. 1-2.

1148 THE SISTER YEARS; BEING THE CARRIER'S ADDRESS, TO THE PATRONS OF THE SALEM GAZETTE, FOR THE FIRST OF JANUARY, 1839. Salem, Massachusetts: SALEM GAZETTE, 1839. Pamphlet.
Collected in TWICE-TOLD TALES, 1842.

1149 "Thomas Green Fessenden," AmMMag, 5 (January, 1838), 30-41.

1150 TIME'S PORTRAITURE, BEING THE CARRIER'S ADDRESS TO THE PATRONS OF THE SALEM GAZETTE FOR THE FIRST OF JANUARY, 1838. Salem, Massachusetts, January 1, 1838.

Reissued, 1853, as 8-page pamphlet. Collected in THE DOLLIVER ROMANCE, 1876.

1151 TRUE STORIES FROM HISTORY AND BIOGRAPHY. Boston: Ticknor, Reed, and Fields, 1851.

1152 TRUE STORIES FROM HISTORY AND BIOGRAPHY... Boston: James R. Osgood and Company, 1876.

LITTLE CLASSIC EDITION.

1153 TRUE STORIES FROM NEW ENGLAND HISTORY, 1620-1692...GRAND-
FATHER'S CHAIR, Part I. Boston: Houghton Mifflin,
New York: The Riverside Press, Cambridge; 1883.

1154 TRUE STORIES FROM NEW ENGLAND HISTORY, 1692-1763...GRAND-
FATHER'S CHAIR, PART II. Boston: Houghton, Mifflin;
New York: The Riverside Press, Cambridge: 1883.

1155 TRUE STORIES FROM NEW ENGLAND HISTORY, 1763-1803...GRAND-
FATHER'S CHAIR, PART III. Boston: Houghton Mifflin;
New York: The Riverside Press, Cambridge: 1883.

1156 "A Visit to the Celestial City."
Revised by the Committee of Publication of the
American Sunday-School Union. Philadelphia: American
Sunday-School Union, No. 146 Chestnut Street. 1852.

Anonymous. A revised reprint (by the Committee of
Publication of the American Sunday-School Union) of
Hawthorne's "The Celestial Rail-Road," 1843.

1157 "A Visit to the Clerk of the Weather," AmMMag, 1 (May, 1836),
483-87. Attributed.

1158 "Visit to an Old English Abbey," in THE ATLANTIC ALMANAC 1868.
Oliver Wendell Holmes and Donald G. Mitchell, eds.
Boston: Ticknor and Fields, Office of the ATLANTIC
MONTHLY, 1867, pp. 44-45.

Collected in PASSAGES FROM THE ENGLISH NOTE-BOOKS,
1870, Vol. 1, pp. 186-191, as "Furness Abbey."

1159 THE WEAL-REAF. A RECORD OF THE ESSEX INSTITUTE FAIR, HELD
AT SALEM, September 4, 5, 6, 7, 8, with Two Supplementary
Numbers, September 10, 11, 1860.

Contains letter from Hawthorne, August 28, 1860, in
No. 2, p. 14; No. 3, p. 24. Collected in THE
DOLLIVER ROMANCE, 1876, as "Browne's Folly."

1160 THE WHOLE HISTORY OF GRANDFATHER'S CHAIR OR TRUE STORIES
FROM NEW ENGLAND HISTORY, 1620-1803.
Boston: Houghton Mifflin; New York: 11 East Seventeenth
Street; Chicago: The Riverside Press, [1896].

1161 A WONDER BOOK FOR GIRLS AND BOYS. Boston: Ticknor, Reed,
and Fields, 1852; London: Bohn, 1852.

Repr., THE COMPLETE GREEK STORIES OF NATHANIEL HAWTHORNE
FROM THE WONDER BOOK AND TANGLEWOOD TALES. New York:
Franklin Watts, Inc., 1963.

The Gorgon's Head
The Golden Touch
The Paradise of Children
The Three Golden Apples
The Miraculous Pitcher
The Chimaera

1162
A WONDER-BOOK....
Boston: James R. Osgood and Company, 1876.

LITTLE CLASSIC EDITION.

1162.1
A WONDER BOOK AND TANGLEWOOD TALES. Introduction by Roy
Harvey Pearce. THE CENTENARY EDITION OF THE WORKS OF
NATHANIEL HAWTHORNE. Vol. 7. Columbus, Ohio: Ohio
St. U. P., 1971.

1163 "The Young Provincial," THE TOKEN. Boston: Carter and
Hendee, 1830, pp. 127-45. Attributed.

1164
THE YARN OF A YANKEE PRIVATEER. Nathaniel Hawthorne, ed.
Introduction by Clifford Smyth. New York and London:
Funk & Wagnalls Company, 1926.
Repr., from DemR (Jan-Sept., 1846).

Benjamin Frederick Brown, the presumed author.
See EIHC, 13, Part II (April, 1875), as to authorship,
and Hawthorne's part in the publication.

1165 YOUTH'S KEEPSAKE. A CHRISTMAS AND NEW YEAR'S GIFT FOR YOUNG
PEOPLE. Boston: E. R. Broaders, 1835.

Little Annie's Ramble (Collected in TWICE-TOLD TALES,
1837).

1166 "Hawthorne Relics," EIHC, 41 (1905), 113-16.

1167 "Hawthorne Resurrected," Newsweek, 32 (1948), 100, 102.

1168 "Hawthorne's Bowdoin College Bills," EIHC, 76 (1940), 13.

1169 Hawthorne, Sophia. Letter, YR, n. s. 23 (1933), 214-15.

1170 Hawthorne, Sophia. "Mrs. Hawthorne to Mrs. Fields,"
BPLQ, 9 (1957), 143-54.

1170.1 Hawthorne, Sophia. NOTES IN ENGLAND AND ITALY. New York:
G. P. Putnam, 1869. Repr. by Houghton Mifflin, 1891.

1171
"Hawthorne's Opinions," Bookman, 38 (1913), 217-18.

1172 "Hawthorne's Place in Literature," LivA, 231 (1901), 720.

1173 "The Hawthorne Statue," Atl, 94 (1904), 140-41.

1174 Hayford, Harrison. HAWTHORNE AND MELVILLE: A BIOGRAPHICAL
AND CRITICAL STUDY. Diss. Yale: 1945.

1175 Hayford, Harrison. "Hawthorne, Melville, and the Sea,"
NEQ, 19 (1946), 435-52.

Hawthorne's interest in the sea may have attracted
him to Melville.

1176 Hayford, Harrison. "Nathaniel Hawthorne," CLASSIC AMERICAN
WRITERS. Harrison Hayford, ed. Boston: Little Brown
& Co., 1962, pp. 109-58.

1177 Hayford, Harrison. "The Significance of Melville's 'Agatha'
Letter," ELH, 13 (1946), 299-310.

1178 Hazard, Lucy Lockwood. "Hawthorne: The Reluctant Puritan:
The Timid Pioneer," THE FRONTIER IN AMERICAN LITERATURE.
New York: Frederick Ungar, 1927, 1961, pp. 27-40, passim.

Deals with reformers, bluestockings, transcendentalism,
and Puritanism. Hawthorne was at once "a product of
his ancestry and a living protest against it."

1179 Hedges, Elaine. "Howells on a Hawthornesque Theme," TSLL,
3 (1961), 129-43.

1180 Hedges, William L. "Hawthorne's BLITHEDALE: The Function
of the Narrator," NCF, 14 (1960), 303-16.

1181 Heeney, Sister St. Agnes, S. S. J. "The Cathedral in Four
Major New England Authors: A Study in Symbolical
Inspiration," DA, 17 (Penn.: 1957), 1083-84.

1182 Heilman, Robert B. "Hawthorne's 'The Birthmark': Science
as Religion," SAQ, 48 (1949), 575-83.

1183 Heimert, Alan. "Moby-Dick and American Political Symbolism,"
AQ, 15 (1963), 498-534.

1184 Heinitz, Kenneth L. HAWTHORNE'S THEORY OF ART. Diss.
Loyola U. (Chicago: 1963).

1185 Heiser, M. F. "The Decline of Neoclassicism, 1801-1848," in
TRANSITIONS IN AMERICAN LITERARY CRITICISM. Harry
Hayden Clark, ed. Durham, N. C.: Duke U. P., 1953.

Our attention is focused on Hester, Hepzibah, Miriam,
and Zenobia.

1186 Helmstadter, Frances, comp. "Nathaniel Hawthorne," PICTURE BOOK OF AMERICAN AUTHORS. New York: Sterling Pub. Co., 1962.

1187 Hendrick, George. "William Sloane Kennedy Looks to Emerson and Thoreau," ESQ, 26 (1962), 28-31.

Kennedy's diary reveals that he visited the Old Manse and Hawthorne's grave during the 1878-1879 pilgrimages to Concord.

1188 "Henpecked Immortals," Nation, 135 (1932), 604.

1189 Henry, George H. "The Idea of Coverage in the Teaching of Literature," EJ, 54 (1965), 480.

1190 "Herbert Read on Hawthorne," N&Q 184 (1943), 211-12.

1191 Hergenhan, L. T. "The Strange World of Sir William Heans (and the Mystery of William Hay)," Southerly, 27 (1967), 118-37.

Hay's reading of Hawthorne and others reveals his interest in character regeneration.

1192 Herndon, Jerry A., and Sidney P. Moss. "The Identity and Significance of the German Jewish Showman in Hawthorne's 'Ethan Brand,'" CE, 23 (1962), 362-63.

1193 Herring, Thelma. "The Escape of Sir William Heans: Hay's Debt to Hawthorne and Melville," Southerly, 26 (1966), 75-92.

1194 Herzberg, Max J., and the Staff of the Thomas Y. Crowell Company. "Nathaniel Hawthorne," THE READERS ENCYCLOPEDIA OF AMERICAN LITERATURE. New York: Thomas Y. Crowell Co., 1962, 439-41.

1195 Hetherington, Hugh W. MELVILLE'S REVIEWERS: BRITISH AND AMERICAN, 1846-1891. Chapel Hill, N. C.: North Carolina, U. P., 1961.

Hawthorne on Melville's works.

1196 Hewett-Thayer, Harvey S. AMERICAN LITERATURE AS VIEWED IN GERMANY, 1818-1861. STUDIES IN COMPARATIVE LITERATURE, 22. Chapel Hill: North Carolina U. P., 1958.

1197Hewitt, Augustine F. "Hawthorne's Attitude Toward Catholicism,"
CathW, 42 (1885), 21-34. Repr. in HAWTHORNE AMONG HIS
CONTEMPORARIES.. Kenneth Walter Cameron, ed. Hartford:
Transcendental Books, 1968, pp. 269-74.

1198 Hiatt, David. "Hawthorne and the Romantic Tradition,"
WisSL, 1 (1964), 77-84.

Hawthorne's closeness to romanticism indicated in
THE SCARLET LETTER by view taken of nature and its
relation to man.

1199 Hibbard, Addison, ed. WRITERS OF THE WESTERN WORLD. Boston
and New York: Houghton Mifflin Co., 1942, pp. 764-78.

1200 Hicks, Granville. "Afterword: The Enemies of the Novel,"
in THE LIVING NOVEL. Granville Hicks, ed. New York:
Macmillan, 1957, pp. 212-24.

1201 Hicks, Granville. "A Conversation in Boston," SR, 39
(1931), 129-42.

1202 Hicks, Granville. THE GREAT TRADITION: AN INTERPRETATION
OF AMERICAN LITERATURE SINCE THE CIVIL WAR. New York:
Macmillan, 1935.

Hawthorne, more than other men of his day, kept
himself most remote from his own period.

1203Higginson, Thomas Wentworth, ed. THE HAWTHORNE CENTENARY
CELEBRATION AT THE WAYSIDE, CONCORD, MASSACHUSETTS,
July 4-7, 1904. Boston: 1905.

1203.1 Higginson, Thomas Wentworth. "A Precursor of Hawthorne,"
Indep, 40 (1888), 385-86.

1204 Higginson, Thomas Wentworth, and Henry Walcott Boynton.
A READER'S HISTORY OF AMERICAN LITERATURE. Boston:
Houghton, Mifflin & Co., 1903.

1205 Hilda, Sister M., I. H. M. "John Erskine's 'Hester of Troy,'"
PMASAL, 48 (1963), 665-74.

1206Hillman, Mary V. "Hawthorne and Transcendentalism," CathW,
93 (1911), 199-212. Repr. in HAWTHORNE AMONG HIS
CONTEMPORARIES. Kenneth Walter Cameron, ed. Hartford:
Transcendental Books, 1968, pp. 538-42.

Hawthorne undoubtedly skeptical as to transcendentalism.

1207 Hillway, Tyrus. HERMAN MELVILLE. New Haven, Con.: College and
Univ. P., Twayne U. S. Authors Series, 1963).

1208   Hillway, Tyrus. INTRODUCTION TO RESEARCH, 2nd ed. Boston: Houghton Mifflin & Co., 1956, 1964, 123-24; 152.

1209   Hillway, Tyrus. "Pierre, the Fool of Virtue," AL, 21 (1949), 200-11.

1210   Hilton, Earl. "The Body in Hawthorne's Fountain," PMASAL, 52 (1967), 383-89.

1210.1   Hilton, Earl. "Hawthorne, the Hippie, and the Square," SNNTS, 2 (1970), 425-39.

1211   Hoagland, Clayton. "The Diary of Thoreau's 'Gentle Boy,'" NEQ, 28 (1955), 473-89.

     Account of excursions of Thoreau and his friends in a boat which Thoreau used, the "Musketaquid," which Hawthorne later purchased and renamed.

1212   Hodgkins, Louise Manning. "Guide to the Study of Nathaniel Hawthorne," in GUIDE TO THE STUDY OF NINETEENTH CENTURY AUTHORS, 1890, Part 2, pp. 15-20.

1213   Hoeltje, Hubert H. "Captain Nathaniel Hawthorne: Father of the Famous Salem Novelist," EIHC, 89 (1953), 329-56.

     The novelist's father was an indirect influence on the reflective nature of the writer.

1214   Hoeltje, Hubert H. "Emerson, Citizen of Concord," AL, 11 (1940), 367-78.

1215   Hoeltje, Hubert H. "A Forgotten Hawthorne Silhouette," AL, 28 (1957), 510-11.

1216   Hoeltje, Hubert H. "Hawthorne as Senior at Bowdoin," EIHC, 94 (1958), 205-28.

1217   Hoeltje, Hubert H. "Hawthorne, Melville, and 'Blackness,'" AL, 37 (1965), 41-51. Repr. in THE RECOGNITION OF NATHANIEL HAWTHORNE. B. Bernard Cohen, ed. Ann Arbor, Michigan: Michigan U. P., 1969, pp. 257-67.

1218   Hoeltje, Hubert H. "Hawthorne's Review of Evangeline," NEQ, 23 (1950), 232-35.

     Hawthorne's skill in writing expository prose.

1219 Hoeltje, Hubert H. INWARD SKY: THE HEART AND MIND OF
NATHANIEL HAWTHORNE. Durham, N. C.: Duke U. P., 1962.

Revs. by Booklist, 59 (1962), 27;
Richard Harter Fogle, NCF, 18 (1963), 94-95;
Granville Hicks, SatR, 45 (1962), 26;
Edward M. Holmes, NEQ, 36 (1963), 115-17;
LaVern Kohl, LJ, 87 (1962), 1126;
Harro H. Kühnelt, Erasmus, 16 (1964), 277-79;
Michael Millgate, MLR, 58 (1963), 251-52;
S. P. M., ABC, 13 (1962), 3;
Robert Shulman, MLQ, 24 (1963), 413-14;
Randall Stewart, AL, 34 (1963), 577-78;
TLS (August, 1962), 642;
Edward Wagenknecht, CST (June, 1962), 5;
YR, 52 (1962), xviii, xx.

1220 Hoeltje, Hubert H. "The Writing of THE SCARLET LETTER,"
NEQ, 27 (1954), 326-46.

1221
Hoffman, Daniel G. FORM AND FABLE IN AMERICAN FICTION.
New York: Oxford U. P., 1961.

Rev. by Wallace W. Douglas, CE, 23 (1961), 239;
by Allen Guttman in NEQ, 35 (1962), 115-17, who
says Hoffman's analyses of Hawthorne's stories are
the best he has ever read.

1222 Hoffman, Daniel G. "Myth, Romance, and the Childhood of
Man," in HAWTHORNE CENTENARY ESSAYS. Roy Harvey
Pearce, ed. Columbus, Ohio: Ohio St. U. P., 1964,
pp. 197-219.

1223 Hoffman, Daniel G. "William Faulkner: 'The Bear,'" in
LANDMARKS OF AMERICAN WRITING. Hennig Cohen, ed.
New York and London: Basic Books, Inc., 1969,
pp. 341-52.

1224 Hoffman, Daniel G. "Yankee Bumpkin and Scapegoat King,"
SR, 69 (1961), 48-60.

Repr. in A CASEBOOK ON THE HAWTHORNE QUESTION, Agnes
Donohue, ed. New York: Crowell, 1963, 62-71.
Three levels in "My Kinsman": psychological--Robin
(the Great American Boob) witnesses destruction of
the father image; political--Robin is the American
child breaking with paternal authority; cultural--
significance of story lies in Scapegoat King ritual.

1225 Hoffmann, Charles G. THE DEVELOPMENT TOWARD THE SHORT
NOVEL FORM IN AMERICAN LITERATURE WITH SPECIAL
REFERENCE TO HAWTHORNE, MELVILLE, AND JAMES. Diss.
Wis.: 1952.

1226 Holaday, Clayton A. "Re-examination of 'Feathertop' and RLR," NEQ, 27 (1954), 103-105.

Significance of "RLR" in Hawthorne's notebooks in regard to ideas for a story corresponding to "Feathertop."

See A. A. Kern, "Hawthorne's Feathertop and RLR," PMLA, 52 (1937), 503-11; and Randall Stewart, THE AMERICAN NOTEBOOKS, p. 304, n. 268.

1227 Hollenbeck, Mary Opal. "'The Great Stone Face': Another Study of a Required Reading," GrT, 62 (1944), 64, 66, 94.

1228 Hollister, Michael A. "Gloom to Glory: Hawthorne's Mythology," DA, 28 (Stanford: 1968), 4632A.

1229 Holman, C. Hugh. "'Cheap Books' and the Public Interest: Paperbound Book Publishing in Two Centuries," in FRONTIERS OF AMERICAN CULTURE. Ray B. Browne, et al., eds. Lafayette, Ind.: Purdue Univ. Studies, 1968, pp. 25-37.

1230 Holman, C. Hugh. "The Defense of Art: Criticism Since 1930," in THE DEVELOPMENT OF AMERICAN LITERARY CRITICISM, Floyd Stovall, ed. Chapel Hill: North Carolina U. P., 1955, pp. 242, 245.

In modern criticism, place of transcendentalists gives way to Hawthorne and Melville.

1231 Holman, C. Hugh. "Nathaniel Hawthorne," in THE AMERICAN NOVEL THROUGH HENRY JAMES. C. Hugh Holman, Compiler. New York: Appleton-Century-Crofts, 1966, pp. 33-39.

1232 Holmes, Edward M. "Hawthorne and Romanticism," NEQ, 33 (1960), 476-88.

The framework of Hawthorne's stories is almost always orthodox in the Christian sense.

1233 Homan, John, Jr. "Hawthorne's 'The Wedding Knell' and Cotton Mather," ESQ, 43 (1966), 66-67. __

1234 Honig, Edwin. DARK CONCEIT: THE MAKING OF ALLEGORY. Evanston, Ill.: Northwestern U. P., 1959.

The use of allegory by Romantic and contemporary writers, especially Hawthorne, Melville, and Kafka.

1235 Honig, Edwin. "In Defense of Allegory," KR, 20 (1958), 1-19.

1236 Hopkins, Vivian Constance. PRODIGAL PURITAN: A LIFE OF
      DELIA BACON. Cambridge, Mass.: Belknap Press of
      Harvard U. P., 1959.

      Rev. by Elizabeth Bancroft Schlesinger, NEQ, 33
      (1960), 278-80.

1237 Horne, Lewis B. "The Growth of Awareness in the Novels of
      Hawthorne and Hardy," DA, 27 (Mich.: 1967), 2153A-54A.

1238 Horne, Lewis B. "The Heart, the Hand, and 'The Birthmark,'"
      ATQ, 1 (1969), 38-41.

1238.1 Horne, Lewis B. "Of Place and Time: A Note on THE HOUSE OF
      THE SEVEN GABLES," SNNTS, 2 (1970), 459-67.

1239 Horton, Rod W., and Herbert W. Edwards. BACKGROUNDS OF
      AMERICAN LITERARY THOUGHT. New York: 1952.

      Elementary historical treatments of Puritanism, the
      Enlightenment, Transcendentalism, Evolution and
      Pragmatism, Gentility and Revolt, Imperialism,
      Naturalism, and Freudianism.

1240 Horwill, Herbert W. "Hawthorne's America Fifty Years After,"
      Critic, 45 (1904), 71-73.

1241 Hosmer, Elizabeth. HAWTHORNE'S INTEREST IN SCIENCE AND
      PSEUDO-SCIENCE. Diss. Ill.: 1948.

1242 Houston, Neal B. "Hester Prynne as Eternal Feminine,"
      Discourse, 9 (1966), 230-44.

1243 Houston, Neal B. "Nathaniel Hawthorne and the Eternal
      Feminine," DA, 26 (Tex. Tech. Col.: 1966), 4659-60.

1243.1 Houston, Neal B., and Roy E. Cain. "Holgrave: Hawthorne's
      Antithesis to Carlyle's Teufelsdrockh," RS, 38 (1970),
      36-45.

1244 Hovey, Richard B. "Love and Hate in 'Rappaccini's Daughter,'"
      UKCR, 29 (1962), 137-45.

      When the fears of the immature, Puritanical Giovanni
      are heightened to hatred, he kills Beatrice by a
      rejection of her love.

1245 Howard, Anne B. "Hawthorne's Magnetic Chain: The Achievement
      of Humanity," DA, 27 (N. M.: 1966), 1823A.

1246 Howard, David. "THE BLITHEDALE ROMANCE and a Sense of Revolution," in TRADITION AND TOLERANCE IN NINETEENTH-CENTURY FICTION: CRITICAL ESSAYS ON SOME ENGLISH AND AMERICAN NOVELS. David Howard, John Lucas, and John Goode, eds. London: Routledge and Kegan Paul, 1966; New York: Barnes and Noble, 1967, pp. 55-97.

1247 Howard, David. "The Fortunate Fall and Hawthorne's THE MARBLE FAUN," in ROMANTIC MYTHOLOGIES, Ian Fletcher, ed. London: Routledge and K. Paul, 1967; New York: Barnes and Noble, 97-136.

1248 Howard, Leon. "Americanization of the European Heritage," THE AMERICAN WRITER AND THE EUROPEAN TRADITION. A Series of Essays by Louis B. Wright, Theodore Hornberger, Robert E. Spiller, Stanley T. Williams, and others. Minneapolis: Minn. U. P., pub. for Rochester U., 1950, pp. 78-89.

1249 Howard, Leon. "The Centenary Edition of Hawthorne," NCF, 22 (1967), 191-95.

1250 Howard, Leon. "Hawthorne's Fiction," NCF, 7 (1953), 237-50.

1251 Howard, Leon. HERMAN MELVILLE: A BIOGRAPHY. Berkeley and Los Angeles: Calif. U. P., 1951, passim.

1252 Howard, Leon. "The Late Eighteenth Century: An Age of Contradictions," in TRANSITIONS IN AMERICAN LITERARY CRITICISM. Harry Hayden Clark, ed. Durham, N. C.: 1953.

1253 Howard, Leon. LITERATURE AND THE AMERICAN TRADITION. Garden City, New York: Doubleday, 1960, 1963, pp. 114-28.

A short comprehensive history, attempts to seek out "those attitudes of mind which controlled the creative imagination and helped shape country's literature toward a recognizable national character."

1254 Howard, Leon, L. B. Wright, and C. Bode. AMERICAN HERITAGE - BOOK OF GREAT HISTORIC PLACES. New York: American Heritage Pub. Co., Inc., in cooperation with Simon and Schuster, Inc., 1957, pp. 560-68.

1255 Howe, Irving. "Anarchy and Authority in American Literature," DenQ, 2 (1967), 5-30.

Hawthorne and others depict the conflict between authority as embodied in the FEDERALIST PAPERS and a "vision of human community" beyond necessity for government and law.

1256 Howe, Irving. "Hawthorne and American Fiction," AmM, 68 (1949), 367-74.

Hawthorne's finest work a blending of "allegory and surface realism" which was subordinated to his "moral realism."

1257 Howe, Irving. "Hawthorne: Pastoral and Politics," NR, 133 (1955), 17-20.

THE BLITHEDALE ROMANCE as a political novel.

1258 Howe, Irving. "Nathaniel Hawthorne (1804-1864)," in THE LITERATURE OF AMERICA: NINETEENTH CENTURY. Irving Howe, ed. New York: McGraw-Hill, 1970, pp. 398-401.

Hawthorne's moral sense largely detached from the traditional context of Puritan orthodoxy.

1259 Howe, Irving. "Some American Novelists: The Politics of Isolation," POLITICS AND THE NOVEL. New York: Horizon Press, 1957, pp. 163-175.

What might have tempted Hawthorne in Brook Farm was the reformers' idealism and faith in possibility of human communication.

1260 Howe, M. A. DeWolfe. "Hawthorne, Emerson and the Old Manse," in WHO LIVED HERE? Boston: Little, Brown & Co., 1952, pp. 76-87.

1261 Howe, M. A. DeWolfe, ed. LATER YEARS OF THE SATURDAY CLUB. Boston and New York: Houghton, Mifflin Co., 1927.

1262 Howe, M. A. DeWolfe. MEMORIES OF A HOSTESS: A CHRONICLE OF EMINENT FRIENDSHIPS DRAWN CHIEFLY FROM THE DIARIES OF MRS. JAMES T. FIELDS. Boston: Atlantic Monthly P., 1922.

1263 Howe, M. A. DeWolfe. "The Tale of Tanglewood," YR, n. s., 32 (1942), 323-36.

1264 Howe, M. A. DeWolfe. "With Hawthorne at Tanglewood," CSMM, 38 (1946), 6.

1265 Howells, William Dean. "A Conjecture of Intensive Fiction," NAR, 204 (1916), 869-81.

Howells preferred "intensive" fiction which portrayed one character in dramatic encounter with a few other persons.

1266 Howells, William Dean. "Editor's Easy Chair." <u>Harpers</u>, 139 (1919), 605-08.

"We question if such a very great artist as Hawthorne will be torturing the consciences of the twenty-first century and subduing them to the spell which THE SCARLET LETTER laid upon those of the nineteenth;...."

1267 Howells, William Dean. "Hawthorne's Heroines." HarpB, 33 (October 20, 1900), 1543-48; (November 3, 1900), 1671-77.

1268 Howells, William Dean. HEROINES OF FICTION. New York and London: Harper & Row, 1901, I, 161-89. Partly repr. in THE RECOGNITION OF NATHANIEL HAWTHORNE. B. Bernard Cohen, ed. Ann Arbor, Michigan: Michigan U. P., 1969, 134-37.

1269 Howells, William Dean. IMAGINARY INTERVIEWS. New York, 1910.

1270 Howells, William Dean. "My First Visit to New England," in LITERARY FRIENDS AND ACQUAINTACES: A PERSONAL RETROSPECT OF AMERICAN AUTHORSHIP. New York: Harper, 1900; David F. Hiatt and Edwin H. Cady, eds. Indiana U. P., 1968. (A selected edition.)

1271 Howells, William Dean. MY LITERARY PASSIONS AND CRITICISM AND FICTION. New York and London: Library Edition, Harper & Bros., 1891, 1895, 1910, p. 139.

1272 Howells, William Dean. "The Personality of Hawthorne." NAR, 177 (1903), 880-82.

1273 Hull, Raymona E. "Hawthorne's Efforts to Help Thoreau." ESQ, 33 (1963), 24-28.

Old and new evidence indicate Hawthorne's respect for Thoreau.

1274 Hungerford, Edward B. "Hawthorne Gossips about Salem." NEQ, 6 (1933), 445-69.

Three new letters by Hawthorne, written in 1830-31 about Salem, his family, and himself.

1275 Hurley, Paul J. "Young Goodman Brown's 'Heart of Darkness.'" AL, 37 (1966), 410-19.

1276 Hutton, Richard Holt. "Nathaniel Hawthorne." LITERARY ESSAYS. London: Macmillan, 1871, 1908, pp. 437-90.

1277 Hutton, Richard Holt. ESSAYS IN LITERARY CRITICISM. Philadelphia, Pa.: J. H. Coates & Co., [1876], 98-155.

1278
Huzzard, John A. "Hawthorne's THE MARBLE FAUN," *Italica*,
35 (1958), 119-24.

1279
Hyman, Lawrence W. "Moral Values and the Literary Experience."
JAAC, 24 (1966), 538-47.

1280
Ibershoff, C. H. "Hawthorne's Philosophy of Life,"
Outlook, 126 (1920), 124.

1281
Inman, H. Portrait by. InternS, 75 (1922), 469.

1282
Irwin, W. R. "The Survival of Pan," PMLA, 76 (1961), 159-67.

1283
Isaacs, Neil B., and Louis H. Leiter. APPROACHES TO THE
SHORT STORY. San Francisco: Chandler, 1963, pp.
115-42.

Comparison of "Ethan Brand" with modern short stories.

1284
Iseri, Tatsunari. "'Pearl' and Pearl," in MAEKAWA SHUNICHI
KYOJU KANREKI KINEN-RONBUNSHU /Essays and Studies in
Commemoration of Professor Shunichi Maekawa's Sixty-
First Birthday/ 1. Tokyo: Eihosha, 1968.

1285
Ito, Kiyoshi. "Similarity of Wordings in Hawthorne's Two
Works," in STUDIES IN ENGLISH GRAMMAR AND LINGUISTICS:
A MISCELLANY IN HONOUR OF TAKANOBU OTSUKA. Kazuo
Araki, et al., eds. Tokyo: Kenkyusha, 1958, pp.
275-88.

1286
Ives, Charles. "Hawthorne," in ESSAYS BEFORE A SONATA AND
OTHER WRITINGS. Howard Boatwright, ed. New York:
Knickerbocker Press, 1920, pp. 46-50; W. W. Norton &
Co., 1961, 1962, pp. 39-42.

1287
Izzo, Carlo. CIVILTÀ AMERICANA: Vol. I - Saggi; Vol. II -
Impressioni e Note. Rome: Edizioni di Storia e
Letteratura, 1967.

Influence of Italian literature on American writers.

Rev. by James Woodress, AL, 41 (1969), 136-37.

1288
Izzo, Carlo. "Un Metafisico della narrazione: Nathaniel
Hawthorne," SA, 1 (1955), 97-124.

1289
Jackson, Holbrook. DREAMERS OF DREAMS: THE RISE AND FALL
OF 19th CENTURY IDEALISM. London: Faber and Faber,
1948.

1290 Jacobs, Leland B. "Feathertop: A Detailed Study of a
      Required Reading," GrT, 56 (1939), 44, 72-73.

1291 Jacobs, Leland B. "Literature Studies: Test on 'The Pine
      Tree Shillings,'" GrT, 56 (1938), 58-59.

1292 Jacobson, Richard J. HAWTHORNE'S CONCEPTION OF THE CREATIVE
      PROCESS. Cambridge, Mass.: Harvard U. P., 1965.

1292.1 Jaffe, Adrian H., and Virgil Scott. Instructor's Manual to
        Accompany STUDIES IN THE SHORT STORY. New York: Holt,
        Rinehart and Winston, 1968, pp. 62-65.

        "My Kinsman, Major Molineux."

1293 Jaffé, David. "The Miniature that Inspired Clifford
      Pyncheon's Portrait," EIHC, 98 (1962), 278-82.

1293.1 James, Henry. THE AMERICAN ESSAYS OF HENRY JAMES. Leon
        Edel, ed. New York: Vintage Books, 1956, pp. 3-31.

1294 James, Henry. THE AMERICAN NOVELS AND STORIES OF HENRY JAMES.
      Ed. and with Introduction by F. O. Matthiessen. New York:
      Alfred A. Knopf, 1956.

1295 James, Henry. THE AMERICAN SCENE. New York: Harper & Bros.,
      1907.

      Describes places associated with Hawthorne and his
      novels.

1296 James, Henry. HAWTHORNE. John Morley, ed. ENGLISH MEN
      OF LETTERS SERIES. New York: Harper, 1879, 1887, 1907.

1297 James, Henry. HAWTHORNE. Tanner, Tony, ed. London:
      1967.

      See rev. art. by P. R. Grover, CamR, 89A (1968),
      430-31.

1298 James, Henry. "Hawthorne: Early Manhood," LITERATURE IN
      AMERICA. Philip Rahv, ed. New York: World Pub. Co.,
      1957, 1967, pp. 84-100.

1299 James, Henry. "Hawthorne: THE SCARLET LETTER," in PORTABLE
      HENRY JAMES. Edited with Introduction by Morton Zabel.
      New York: Viking Press, 1921, pp. 440-53.

1300 James, Henry. "Hawthorne," in SHOCK OF RECOGNITION. Edmund
Wilson, ed. Garden City, New York: Doubleday & Co.,
1947.

Hawthorne's early years, pp. 427-45; early manhood,
445-66; Brook Farm and Concord, 484-506; early writing,
466-84.

1301 James, Henry. Letter from, on June 10, 1904, on occasion
of Hawthorne Centennial, EIHC, 41 (1905), 55-62.

1302 James, Henry. THE LETTERS OF HENRY JAMES. Percy Lubbock, ed.
New York: 1920, I, 72.

1303 James, Henry. NOTES OF A SON AND BROTHER. New York:
Charles Scribner's Sons, 1914.

1304 James, Stuart B. "The Politics of Personal Salvation: The
American Literary Record," DenQ, 4 (1969), 19-45.

Hawthorne's Hester Prynne a literary figure, not merely
historical. American literature does not provide "heroes
who think as well as feel."

1304.1 Janssen, James G. "Dimmesdale's 'Lurid Playfulness,'"
ATQ, 1 (1969), 30-34.

1304.2 Janssen, James G. "Hawthorne's Seventh Vagabond: 'The
Outsetting Bard,'" ESQ, 62 (1971), 22-28.

1305 Janssen, James G. "Hawthorne's Treatment of the Theme of
Pride in His Major Short Stories and Novels," DA, 28
(Wis.: 1967), 678A-79A.

1306 Jepson, George Edwin. "Hawthorne in the Boston Custom House,
Some Lately Discovered Facts Which Are at Variance with
the Hitherto Accepted Data of His Biographers," Bookman,
19 (1904), 573-80. Repr. in HAWTHORNE AMONG HIS
CONTEMPORARIES. Kenneth Walter Cameron, ed. Hartford:
Transcendental Books, 1968, pp. 514-18.

1307 Jessup, Alexander, and Henry Seidel Canby, eds. THE BOOK
OF THE SHORT STORY. New York and London: D. Appleton,
1903, 1918.

Suggests Hawthorne's debt to Hoffman, E. T. A.,
"Weird Tales."

1308 Johnson, Evelyn Cleone. HAWTHORNE AND THE SUPERNATURAL.
Diss. Stanford, 1938.

1309 Johnson, George W. "Frank Norris and Romance," AL, 33
(1961), 52-63.

1310 Johnson, Lionel. "Hawthorne," (Poem). LivA, 242 (1904), 64.

1311 Johnson, Merle. MERLE JOHNSON'S AMERICAN FIRST EDITIONS.
      BIBLIOGRAPHIC CHECK LISTS OF THE WORKS OF 199 AMERICAN
      AUTHORS. Rev. by Jacob Blanck. New York: R. R. Bowker,
      1936, pp. 208-212.

1312 Johnson, Thomas H., ed. LITERARY HISTORY OF THE UNITED STATES.
      New York: Macmillan, 1948, 1953, 1963, III, 544-53.

      Bibliography

1313 Johnson, W. H. "A New Book About Hawthorne," Dial, 35
      (1903), 466-67.

      Rev. art. of Julian Hawthorne's HAWTHORNE AND HIS
      CIRCLE.

1314 Johnson, W. Stacy. "Hawthorne and THE PILGRIM'S PROGRESS,"
      JEGP, 50 (1951), 156-66.

      Hawthorne's "echoes of Bunyan are striking."

1315 Johnson, W. Stacey. "Sin and Salvation in Hawthorne,"
      HJ, 50 (1951), 39-47.

1316 Johnston, Helen. "American Boy and Nathaniel Hawthorne--Now,"
      EducR, 54 (1917), 413-14.

1317 Joline, Adrian Hoffman. MEDITATIONS OF AN AUTOGRAPH
      COLLECTOR. New York and London: 1902, pp. 39-41, 158.

      Contains two letters.

1318 Jones, Bartlett C. "The Ambiguity of Shrewdness in 'My
      Kinsman, Major Molineux,'" MASJ, 3 (1962), 42-47.

1319 Jones, Buford. A CHECKLIST OF HAWTHORNE CRITICISM, 1951-1966.
      Hartford, Conn.: Transcendental Books, 1967.

1320 Jones, Buford. "A Checklist of Hawthorne Criticism, 1951-
      1966," ESQ, 52 Sup. (1968), 1-90.

1321 Jones, Buford. "The FAERY LAND of Hawthorne's Romances,"
      ESQ, 48 (1967), 106-24.

1322 Jones, Buford. "'The Hall of Fantasy' and the Early Hawthorne-
      Thoreau Relationship," PMLA, 83 (1968), 1429-38.

      Two versions of "The Hall of Fantasy" indicate intellectual
      exchange between Hawthorne and Thoreau more extensive and
      formative than hitherto supposed.

1322.1 Jones, Buford. "Hawthorne Studies: The Seventies," SNNTS, 2 (1970), 504-18.

1323 Jones, Buford. "Hawthorne's Coverdale and Spenser's Allegory of Mutability," AL, 39 (1967), 215-19.

Hawthorne used contest between goddesses Nature and Mutability from Spenser's FAERIE QUEENE as an "ironic background" for criticizing the dream of Utopia in THE BLITHEDALE ROMANCE.

1324 Jones, Buford. "Melville's Buccaneers and Crébillon's Sofa," ELN, 2 (1964), 122-26.

1325 Jones, Buford. NATHANIEL HAWTHORNE AND ENGLISH RENAISSANCE ALLEGORY. Diss. Harvard: 1962.

1326 Jones, Dennis M. "From Moralist to Psychologist to Maker of Myth: A Study of Hawthorne's Use of Regional History," DA, 27 (Iowa: 1967), 3011A-12A.

1327 Jones, Gardner Maynard. NATHANIEL HAWTHORNE: A COMPLETE LIST OF HAWTHORNE'S WRITINGS, WITH FULL CONTENTS, AND OF BOOKS AND MAGAZINE ARTICLES ABOUT HAWTHORNE. In Salem Public Library. Bulletin, October, 1891, Vol. 1, pp. 46-48.

1328 Jones, Howard Mumford. BELIEF AND DISBELIEF IN AMERICAN LITERATURE. Chicago: Chicago U. P., 1967.

Rev. by Arnold Smithline in CE, 29 (1968), 581-83.

1329 Jones, Howard Mumford. IDEAS IN AMERICA. Cambridge, Mass.: Harvard U. P., 1945.

1330 Jones, Howard Mumford. THE THEORY OF AMERICAN LITERATURE. Ithaca, New York: Cornell U. P., 1948.

Rev. by James D. Hart, AL, 21 (1949-50), 364-65.

1331 Jones, Howard Mumford, et al., eds. MAJOR AMERICAN WRITERS. New York: Harcourt, Brace & Co., 1935, 1952, pp. 485-576.

1332 Jones, Joseph. "Introduction," to AESTHETIC PAPERS, (1849). Elizabeth P. Peabody, ed. Gainesville: Scholars' Facsimiles and Reprints, 1957.

The Elizabeth Peabody circle and the composition of "Main Street."

1333 Jones, Joseph, et al. AMERICAN LITERARY MANUSCRIPTS: A CHECKLIST OF HOLDINGS IN ACADEMIC, HISTORICAL AND PUBLIC LIBRARIES IN THE UNITED STATES. Austin: Texas U. P., 1960, pp. 163-64.

1334 Jones, Llewellyn. "Mr. Hawthorne's SCARLET LETTER," Bookman, 58 (1924), 622-25.

1335 Jordan, Alice Mabel. "Dawn of Imagination in American Books for Children" in FROM ROLLO TO TOM SAWYER; AND OTHER PAPERS. Boston: Horn Books, 1948), 92-101.

1336 Jordan, Gretchen G. "Hawthorne's 'Bell': Historical Evolution through Symbol," NCF, Hawthorne Centenary Issue, 19 (1964), 123-39.

1337 Joseph, Brother. "Art and Event in 'Ethan Brand,'" NCF, 15 (1960), 249-57.

"Ethan Brand" the story of a dying generation and a living one.

1338 Joseph, Sister M. Evelyn, I. H. M. "Substance as Suggestion: Ambiguity in Hawthorne," Ren, 17 (1965), 216-20.

1339 Josephs, Lois. "One Approach to the Puritans," EJ, 50 (1961), 183-87.

1340 Josipovici, G. D. "Hawthorne's Modernity," CritQ, 8 (1966), 351-66.

A rev. art., of A. N. Kaul, ed., HAWTHORNE: A COLLECTION OF CRITICAL ESSAYS, and Frederick C. Crews, THE SINS OF THE FATHERS: HAWTHORNE'S PSYCHOLOGICAL THEMES.

1341 Junkins, Donald. "Hawthorne's HOUSE OF SEVEN GABLES: A Prototype of the Human Mind," L&P, 17 (1967), 193-210.

The house is a symbol of the human mind, the four inhabitants are symbols of four basic psychological functions of the mind, and emergence of these characters at conclusion is symbolic of "individuation as it occurs in the regenerative human psyche."

1342 Just, Walter. DIE ROMANTISCHE BEWEGUNG IN DER AMERIKANISCHEN LITERATUR: BROWN, C. B., POE, HAWTHORNE: EIN BEITRAG ZUR GESCHICHTE DER ROMANTIK. Diss. Munster: 1910.

1343 Justus, James. "Beyond Gothicism: WUTHERING HEIGHTS and an American Tradition," TSL, 5 (1960), 25-33.

The tradition includes Hawthorne, Melville, and Faulkner.

1344 Kaftan, Robert A. "A Study of the Gothic Techniques in the Novels of Nathaniel Hawthorne," DA, 29 (Mich. State: 1968), 1899A.

1344.1 Kamogawa, Takahiro. "On the Family Name 'Pyncheon' in THE HOUSE OF THE SEVEN GABLES," HSELL, 16 (1969), 41-47.

1345 Kamogawa, Takahiro. "Rome in THE MARBLE FAUN," KAL 11 (1968), 32-43.

1346 Kane, Robert J. "Hawthorne's 'The Prophetic Pictures' and James's 'The Liar,'" MLN, 65 (1950), 257-58.

Similarity of theme.

1347 Kariel, Henry S. "Man Limited: Nathaniel Hawthorne's Classicism," SAQ, 52 (1953), 528-42.

Hawthorne worked with the drama of man torn between "his vision of evil and his knowledge of perfection."

1347.1 Karita, Motoshi. "Shosetsu to Denki no Shudai-sentaku to Imi," SophiaT, 17 (1968), 29-45.

Matter and meaning in fiction and biography in Hawthorne and Henry James.

1348 Karrfalt, David H. "Anima in Hawthorne and Haggard," AN&Q, 2 (1964), 152-53.

Jungian elements in "Rappaccini's Daughter" and SHE.

1349 Kasegawa, Koh. "Emerson, Thoreau, Melville," AJGE, 5 (1964), 15-24.

Also includes Hawthorne.

1350 Katz, Seymour. "'Character,' 'Nature,' and 'Allegory,' in THE SCARLET LETTER," NCF, 23 (1968), 3-17.

1351 Kaufman, Paul. "Defining Romanticism: A Survey and a Program," MLN, 40 (1925).

1352 Kaul, A. N. "Character and Motive in THE SCARLET LETTER," CritQ, 10 (1968), 373-84.

Hester's inner conflict, not the organic world of Puritans, but non-organic human society of loneliness, despair and dislocated relationships.

1353 Kaul, A. N. "Introduction," HAWTHORNE: A COLLECTION OF CRITICAL ESSAYS. A. N. Kaul, ed. Englewood Cliffs, N. J.: Prentice-Hall, 1966, pp. 1-10.

Rev. by G. D. Josipovici, CritQ, 8 (1966), 351-60; Philip Rahv, NYRB, 7 (1966), 21-23.

1354 Kaul, A. N. "Nathaniel Hawthorne: Heir and Critic of the Puritan Tradition," THE AMERICAN VISION: ACTUAL AND IDEAL SOCIETY IN NINETEENTH-CENTURY FICTION. New Haven: Yale U. P., 1963, pp. 139-213. ..

Rev. by Richard Coander, NCF, 18 (1963), 300-02.

1354.1 Kay, Donald. "Hawthorne's Use of Laughter in Selected Short Stories," XUS, 10 (1971), 27-32.

1355 Kazin, Alfred. "Hawthorne: The Artist of New England," AtlM, 218 (1966), 109-113. Repr. as "Introduction" to SELECTED SHORT STORIES OF NATHANIEL HAWTHORNE. Greenwich, Conn.: Fawcett, 1966.

Hawthorne has almost no influence on today's writers. His importance for our time and modern literature remains to be established.

1356 Kazin, Alfred. "Introduction," SELECTED SHORT STORIES OF NATHANIEL HAWTHORNE. Greenwich, Conn.: Fawcett, 1966, pp. 7-19.

1357 Kazin, Alfred. "On Hawthorne," NYR, 11 (1968), 26-28.

1358 Kazin, Alfred. ON NATIVE GROUNDS: AN INTERPRETATION OF MODERN AMERICAN PROSE LITERATURE. New York: Raynal & Hitchcock, 1942).

1359 Kearns, Francis E. "Margaret Fuller as a Model for Hester Prynne," JA, 10 (1965), 191-97.

1360 Keating, L. Clark. "Julien Green and Nathaniel Hawthorne," FR, 28 (1955), 485-92.

Parallels in works of both authors between FANSHAWE and Green's LE VOYAGEUR SUR LA TERRE. Green's gloomy mansion resembles THE HOUSE OF THE SEVEN GABLES.

1361 Kehl, D. G. "Hawthorne's 'Vicious' Circles: The Sphere-Circle Imagery in the Four Major Novels," BRMMLA, 23 (1969), 9-20.

1362 Kehler, Harold F. "The Making of the Scarlet A: A Study of Hawthorne's Technique of the Central Symbol," DA, 29 (Ohio U.: 1969), 314A-44A.

1363 Keller, I. C. "Hawthorne and the Puritan Soul," in LITERATURE AND RELIGION. Rindge, New Hampshire: Richard R. Smith, 1956, pp. 48-50.

1364 Kelly, George. "Poe's Theory of Unity," PQ, 37 (1958), 34-44.

1365 Kelly, Richard. "Hawthorne's 'Ethan Brand,'" Expl. 28
        (1970), Item 47.

1366 Kempton, Kenneth. THE SHORT STORY. Cambridge: Harvard U. P.,
        1947.

1367 Kenton, Edna. "Henry James in the World," THE QUESTION OF
        HENRY JAMES: A COLLECTION OF CRITICAL ESSAYS. F. W.
        Dupee, ed. New York: Henry Holt, 1945, pp. 133-34.

        James diagnosed the American artist who stayed home,
        even when he went abroad.

1368 Kern, Alfred A. "Hawthorne's Feathertop and 'R. L. R,'"
        PMLA, 52 (1937), 503-11.

        R. L. R., in an outline of "Feathertop" in the
        AMERICAN NOTEBOOKS, probably a satirical reference
        to Richard S. Rogers.

        See Clayton A. Holaday, "Re-examination of 'Feathertop'
        and RLR," NEQ, 27 (1954), 103-05; and Randall Stewart,
        AMERICAN NOTEBOOKS, p. 304, n. 268.

1369 Kern, Alfred A. "The Sources of Hawthorne's 'Feathertop,'"
        PMLA, 46 (1931), 1253-59.

1370
      Kern, Alexander C. "A Note on Hawthorne's Juveniles."
        PQ, 39 (1960), 242-46.

        Letter of Mary Peabody to Horace Mann, March 3, 1838,
        shows pecuniary problems of a major American author and
        the "romantic sensibility" of the second quarter of the
        19th century.

1371 Kern, Alexander C. "The Rise of Transcendentalism, 1815-1860,"
        in TRANSITIONS IN AMERICAN LITERARY CRITICISM. Harry
        Hayden Clark, ed. Durham, N. C.: Duke U. P., 1953.

        Hawthorne and Melville were affected by Transcendentalism,
        "if negatively."

1372
      Kerr, J. "Nathaniel Hawthorne: A Notable Son of New
        England," NatlR, 131 (1948), 367-70.

1373 Kesselring, Marion L. "Hawthorne's Reading, 1828-1850,"
        BNYPL, 53 (February, 1949), 55-71; (March, 1959), 121-38;
        (April, 1959), 173-94.

1374 Kesselring, Marion L. HAWTHORNE'S READING, 1828-1850, A
        TRANSCRIPTION AND IDENTIFICATION OF TITLES RECORDED IN
        THE CHARGE-BOOKS OF THE SALEM ATHENAEUM. New York:
        The New York Public Library, 1949.

1375 Kesterson, David B. "Hawthorne and Nature: Thoreauvian Influence?" ELN, 4 (1967), 200-06.

Questions Thoreau's influence on Hawthorne.

1375.1 Kesterson, David B. "Nature and Theme in 'Young Goodman Brown.'" DickR, 2 (1970), 42-46.

1376 Kesterson, David B. "Nature in the Life and Works of Nathaniel Hawthorne," DA, 26 (Ark.: 1965), 1023.

1376.1 Kesterson, David B. STUDIES IN THE NOVEL. Columbus: Charles E. Merrill Publishing Co., 1971.

1377 Killinger, John. "The Death of God in American Literature," SHR, 2 (1968), 149-72.

American roots include the 17th century quarrel between Calvinistic theocrats and atheists, 18th century Deism, 19th century Unitarianism, and the vision of evil associated with Puritan godliness in Hawthorne and Melville.

1378 Kim, Yong-Chol. "A Note on Hawthorne's 'My Kinsman, Major Molineux,'" ELL, 19 (1966), 85-88.

1379 Kimball, LeRoy Elwood. "Miss [Delia] Bacon Advances Learning," Colophon. n. s., 2 (1937), 338-54.

Three letters to Charles Butler (1802-1897), her financial backer, which contain references to Emerson and Hawthorne and their interest in her theory.

1380 Kimbrough, Robert. "The Actual and the Imaginary: Hawthorne's Concept of Art in Theory and Practice," TWA, 50 (1961), 277-93.

1381 Kimmey, John L. "PIERRE and Robin: Melville's Debt to Hawthorne," ESQ, 38 (1965), 90-92.

1382 Kingery, R. E. "Disastrous Friendship: Pierce and Hawthorne," Hobbies, 45 (1941), 98.

1383 Kingsley, Mary E. "Outline Study of Twice-Told Tales," Educ, 41 (1921), 398-410.

1384 Kingsley, Mary E. "Examination Questions for THE HOUSE OF THE SEVEN GABLES," Educ, 33 (1913), 382-83.

1385 Kirk, Russell. "The Moral Conservatism of Hawthorne,"
     ContempR, 182 (1952), 361-66.

     Analysis of Hawthorne's political conservatism and
     preoccupation with sin.

1386 Kirk, Russell. "Transitional Conservatism: New England
     Sketches," in THE CONSERVATIVE MIND FROM BURKE TO
     SANTAYANA. Chicago: H. Regnery Co., 1953. pp. 218-26.

1387 Kjørven, Johannes. "Hawthorne and the Significance of History,"
     in AMERICANA NOVEGICA: NORWEGIAN CONTRIBUTIONS TO
     AMERICAN STUDIES. Sigmund Skard and Henry H. Wasser, eds.
     Philadelphia: Pennsylvania U. P., 1966, I, 110-60.

1388 Kling, Carlos. "Hawthorne's View of Sin," Person. 13 (1932),
     119-30.

     Hawthorne's view of sin more aesthetic than Puritan.

1388.1 Klinkowitz, Jerome F. "In Defense of Holgrave," ESQ, 62
     (1971), 4-8.

1388.2 Klinkowitz, Jerome F. "The Significance of the Ending to
     THE HOUSE OF THE SEVEN GABLES. DAI, 31 (Wis.: 1970),
     392A.

1389 Kloeckner, A. J. "The Flower and the Fountain: Hawthorne's
     Chief Symbols in 'Rappaccini's Daughter,'" AL, 38
     (1966), 323-36.

     Description of love scenes in MARBLE FAUN, THE HOUSE
     OF THE SEVEN GABLES, and "Rappaccini's Daughter" have
     common traits. Likely source is PARADISE LOST, III,
     351-64. Giovanni's flaw is his inability to cope with
     a mixed world.

1390 Knight, Grant C. AMERICAN LITERATURE AND CULTURE. New
     York: Ray Lacy and Richard R. Smith, Inc., 1932,
     pp. 203-14.

1391 Knight, Grant C. THE CRITICAL PERIOD IN AMERICAN LITERATURE.
     Chapel Hill: North Carolina U. P., 1951.

1392 Knight, Grant C. THE STRENUOUS AGE IN AMERICAN LITERATURE.
     Chapel Hill: North Carolina U. P., 1954.

1393 Knoll, Robert E. INSTRUCTOR'S MANUAL FOR "CONTRASTS." 2nd ed.
     New York: Harcourt, Brace, 1959, pp. 69-70.

1394 Knox, George. "Dissonance Abroad: Julian Hawthorne's Saxon Studies," EIHC, 96 (1960), 131-139.

Footnote 8, reference to ENGLISH NOTEBOOKS.

1395 Knox, George. "The Hawthorne-Lowell Affair," NEQ, 29 (1956), 493-502.

Julian Hawthorne's Memoirs omits a misunderstanding with Lowell.

See Carl J. Weber, "Lowell's 'Dead Rat in the Wall,'" NEQ, 9 (1936), 686-88; and Evan Charteris, THE LIFE AND LETTERS OF SIR EDMUND GOSS. New York; 1931, p. 200.

1396 Koizumi, Ichiro. "The 'Artist' in Hawthorne," SELit, 40 (1964), 35-53.

1397 Koskenlinna, Hazel M. "Sir Walter Scott and Nathaniel Hawthorne: Parallels and Divergencies," DA, 28 (Wis.: 1968), 5059A.

1398 Kotker, Norman. "The Literary Road to Rome," Horizon, 9 (1967), 18-30.
Rome inspired Hawthorne to write THE MARBLE FAUN.

1399 Kouwenhoven, John A. "Hawthorne's Notebooks and DOCTOR GRIMSHAWE'S SECRET," AL, 5 (1934), 349-58.

Hawthorne made use of notebook jottings.

1400 Kraft, Quentin G. "The Central Problem of James's Fictional Thought: From THE SCARLET LETTER to RODERICK HUDSON," ELH, 36 (1969), 416-39.

1401 Kreuter, Kent Kirby. "The Literary Response to Science, Technology and Industrialism: Studies in the Thought of Hawthorne, Melville, Whitman and Twain," DA, 24 (Wis.: 1963), 2446.

1402 Krieger, Murray. "Afterword," THE MARBLE FAUN: OR, THE ROMANCE OF MONTE BENI. New York: New American Library, 1961, pp. 335-46.

Repr. as "THE MARBLE FAUN and the International Theme," in THE PLAY AND PLACE OF CRITICISM. Baltimore: The Johns Hopkins P., 1967, pp. 79-90.

1403 Krumpelmann, John T. "Hawthorne's 'Young Goodman Brown' and Goethe's 'Faust,'" NS, 5, Heft 11 (1956), 516-21.

1404 Krusell, Cynthia, Chairman, Marshfield Historical Commission, Marshfield, Mass. "Making the Natives Restless." Letter to the Editor. *Time*, 96 (1970), 4.

See Melvin Maddocks. "Rituals--The Revolt against the Fixed Smile," *Time*, 96 (1970), 42-43.

1405 Krutch, Joseph Wood. "Is Our Common Man Too Common?" THE SATURDAY REVIEW TREASURY. Selected from files by John Haverstick and editors of THE SATURDAY REVIEW. New York: Simon & Schuster, 1957, p. 48.

The year that Hawthorne earned $144.09 in royalty was the year his publisher paid Susan Warner $4,500, and another publisher sold 70,000 copies of a work of Fanny Fern.

1406 Kuhlmann, Susan. "The Window of Fiction," CEA, 30 (1967), 15-16.

1407 Kuhn, Anna. WATCHING AT MY GATES. Bruce Publishing Co., 1948, pp. 11-50.

Rose (Hawthorne) Lathrop, Mother Mary Alphonsa.

1407.1 Kummings, Donald D. "Hawthorne's 'The Custom House' and the Conditions of Fiction in America," CEA, 33 (1971), 15-18.

1408 L. S. L. "Hawthorne's Diary for 1859," *Nation*, 94 (1912), 434-35.

1409 Labaree, Benjamin W., and B. Bernard Cohen. "Hawthorne at the Essex Institute," EIHC, 94 (1958), 297-308.

List of Hawthorne letters at the Essex Institute, with a catalog of ten books once in Hawthorne's possession.

1410 Lagemann, John K. "Husband to the Month of May," CSMM, 38 (1946), 4-5. Also in *ReadD*, 49 (1946), 122-26.

The love story of Hawthorne and Sophia Peabody.

1411 Lamont, John H. "Hawthorne's Unfinished Works," HMAB, 36 (1962), 13-20.

Psychoanalysis of the uncompleted romances in terms of Oedipal themes of parricide and incest.

1412 Lane, Lauriat, Jr. "Allegory and Character and THE SCARLET LETTER," in Carl F. Strauch, et al. Symposium on Nathaniel Hawthorne. ESQ, 25 (1961), 13-16.

1413 Lang, Andrew. "An Appreciation of Hawthorne," EIHC, 41
(1905), 63-65.

1414 Lang, Andrew. "Hawthorne's Tales of Old Greece,"
Indep, 62 (1904), 792-94.

1415 Lang, Andrew. "Nathaniel Hawthorne," ADVENTURES AMONG
BOOKS. Longmans, 1905, pp. 211-223.

1416 Lang, Hans-Joachim. "THE BLITHEDALE ROMANCE: A HISTORY OF
IDEAS APPROACH," in LITERATUR UND SPRACHE DER VEREINIGTEN
STAATEN: AUFSÄTZE ZU EHREN VON HANS GALINSKY. Hans
Helmcke, Klaus Lubbers, and Renate Schmidt-von
Bardeleben, eds, Heidelberg: Winter, 1969, 88-106.

1417 Lang, Hans-Joachim. "Ein Ärgerteufel bei Hawthorne und
Melville: Quellenuntersuchung zu THE CONFIDENCE MAN,"
JA, 12 (1967), 246-51.

Hawthorne's "Seven Vagabonds" a source for Melville's
THE CONFIDENCE MAN.

1418 Lang, Hans-Joachim. "How Ambiguous is Hawthorne?" FreieG,
(1962), 195-220.

Also in HAWTHORNE: A COLLECTION OF CRITICAL ESSAYS,
A. N. Kaul, ed. Englewood Cliffs: Prentice-Hall,
1966, 93-95.

1419 Lang, Hans-Joachim. "The Authorship of 'David Whicher,'"
JA, 7 (1962), 293-96.

See Irving T. Richards, "A Note on the Authorship
of 'David Whicher,'" JA, 7 (1962), 293-96.

1420 Lang, Hans-Joachim. "The Turns in THE TURN OF THE SCREW,"
JA, 9 (1963), 111-28.

Study of the Gothic novel provides insight into
technique from Poe and Hawthorne to James.

1421 Lansdale, Nelson. "Literary Landmarks, U. S. A.," SatR
41 (1958), 28.

Description of the Hawthorne home "Tanglewood," near
Lennox, Massachusetts.

1422 Laser, Marvin. HAWTHORNE AND THE CRAFT OF FICTION: A STUDY
IN ARTISTIC DEVELOPMENT. Diss. Northwestern: 1948.

1423 Laser, Marvin. "'Head,' 'Heart,' and 'Will' in Hawthorne's Psychology," NCF, 10 (1955), 130-40.

Characterizations in Hawthorne may have been influenced by Thomas C. Upham.

1424 Lasser, Michael L. "Mirror Imagery in THE SCARLET LETTER," EJ, 56 (1967), 274-77.

Mirrors reveal obscured reality and enable characters to look into themselves and others.

1424.1 Lathrop, George Parsons. "The Hawthorne Manuscripts," AtlM, 51 (1883), 363-75. Repr. in HAWTHORNE AMONG HIS CONTEMPORARIES. Kenneth Walter Cameron, ed. Hartford: Transcendental Books, 1968, pp. 232-39.

1425 Lathrop, George Parsons. Introductory Notes by. THE COMPLETE WORKS OF NATHANIEL HAWTHORNE. Cambridge, Mass.: Houghton Mifflin, 1883, 12 vols. "Riverside Edition."

1426 Lathrop, George Parsons. "Nathaniel Hawthorne's College Days," YouthC, (1954), 624-31.

1426.1 Lathrop, George Parsons. "Poe, Irving, Hawthorne," ScbM, 11 (1876), 799-808.

1427 Lathrop, George Parsons. A STUDY OF HAWTHORNE. Boston: James R. Osgood & Co. Late Ticknor & Fields, 1876; Republished, St. Clair Shores, Mich.: Scholarly P., 1970.

1427.1 Lathrop, Rose Hawthorne. "My Father's Literary Methods," LadHJ, 11 (1894), 1-2. Repr. in HAWTHORNE AMONG HIS CONTEMPORARIES. Kenneth Walter Cameron, ed. Hartford: Transcendental Books, 1968, pp. 371-74.

1427.2 Lathrop, Rose Hawthorne. MEMORIES OF HAWTHORNE. Boston: Houghton, Mifflin, 1897. Repr. New York: AMS Press, 1969.

1428 Latimer, George D. "The Tales of Poe and Hawthorne," NEM, 30 (1904), 692-703.

1429 Lauber, John. "Hawthorne's Shaker Tales," NCF, 18 (1963), 82-86.

1429.1 Laverty, Carroll D. "Some Touchstones of Hawthorne's Style," ESQ, 60 (1970), 30-36.

1430 [Law, Frederick Houk] "Eight Great Short Stories from American Literature, with Introductions by Frederick Houk Law." - "The Ambitious Guest" by Nathaniel Hawthorne, <u>Indep.</u> 89 (1917), 454-56.

1431 Lawrence, David Herbert. "Studies in Classic American Literature - Nathaniel Hawthorne," <u>EngR</u>, 28 (1919), 404-17.

1432 Lawrence, David Herbert. STUDIES IN CLASSICAL AMERICAN LITERATURE. New York: Thomas Seltzer, Inc., 1923, pp. 121-162; Garden City, New York: Doubleday, 1951, pp. 92-120.

Chapters 7 and 8 ("Nathaniel Hawthorne and THE SCARLET LETTER" and "Hawthorne's BLITHEDALE ROMANCE,") deal directly with Hawthorne. Other comments are made throughout. Excerpts and reprints are included in THE SYMBOLIC MEANING: THE UNCOLLECTED VERSIONS OF STUDIES IN CLASSIC AMERICAN LITERATURE. Armin Arnold, ed. Viking, 1962, 1964; SELECTED LITERARY CRITICISM, Anthony Beal, ed. New York: Viking, 1956; SHOCK OF RECOGNITION, Edmund Wilson, ed. Garden City, New York: Doubleday, 1947.

1433 Lawson, Alvin H. "Hawthorne and the Limits of Intellect," DA, 27 (Stanford: 1967), 4257A.

1434 Lawton, William C. "Hawthorne," THE NEW ENGLAND POETS. New York: 1898, pp. 48-104.

1435 Lawton, William C. "Nathaniel Hawthorne," A STUDY OF AMERICAN LITERATURE. New York: Globe Sch. Bks., 1907, 151-72.

1436 Le, Van-Diem. "Puritan Idealism and the Transcendental Movement," DA, 21 (Minn.: 1961), 1929.

1437 Leaf, Munro. "THE HOUSE OF THE SEVEN GABLES, By Nathaniel Hawthorne, Who Had Ghosts in His Own Garrett," AmMag, 131 (1941), 62.

A humorous "take off" of the story: "Never sign a two-year lease until you are sure about the ghosts and the plumbing."

1438 Leary, Lewis, ed. CONTEMPORARY LITERARY SCHOLARSHIP: A CRITICAL REVIEW. New York: Appleton-Century-Crofts, 1958.

1439 Leary, Lewis. "Nathaniel Hawthorne," ARTICLES ON AMERICAN LITERATURE, 1900-1950. Durham, N. C.: Duke U. P., 1954, pp. 128-34.

In the half century of entries, those on Hawthorne increased from 120 to 260.

Rev. by Nelson F. Adkins, AL, 27 (1955), 449-50.

1440   Lease, Benjamin. "Hawthorne and BLACKWOOD'S in 1849: Two
Unpublished Letters," JA, 14 (1969), 152-54.

Letters by Horatio Bridge and John Jay.

1440.1
Lease, Benjamin. "Hawthorne and 'A Certain Venerable
Personage': New Light on 'The Custom-House,'"
JA, 15 (1970), 201-07.

1441 Lease, Benjamin. "The Chemistry of Genius: Herman Melville
and Anton Bruckner," Person, 48 (1967), 224-41.

Both Melville and Bruckner inspired by Nathaniel
Hawthorne and Richard Wagner, respectively.

1441.1
Lease, Benjamin. "Salem vs. Hawthorne: An Early Review of
THE SCARLET LETTER," NEQ, 44 (1971), 110-17.

1441.2
Lease, Benjamin. "'The Whole Is a Prose Poem': An Early
Review of THE SCARLET LETTER," AL, 44 (1972), 128-30.

1442 Leavis, Q. D. "Hawthorne as Poet," SR, 59 (Spring, 1951),
180-205; 59 (Summer, 1951), 426-58.

Hawthorne classed with George Eliot, Tolstoi, and
Conrad.

Repr. in Charles Feidelson and Paul Brodtkorb, eds.
INTERPRETATIONS OF AMERICAN LITERATURE. New York:
Oxford U. P., 1959, 44-49; Agnes Donohue, ed. A
CASEBOOK ON THE HAWTHORNE QUESTION. New York: Crowell,
1963, 313-318; A. N. Kaul, ed. HAWTHORNE: A COLLECTION
OF CRITICAL ESSAYS. Englewood Cliffs: Prentice-Hall,
1966, 25-63.

1443   Leavitt, Charles Loyal. "Hawthorne's Use of Pageantry,"
DA, 22 (Wis.: 1961), 871-72.

1444 Leavitt, Charles Loyal. Review Notes and Study Guide to
Hawthorne's THE SCARLET LETTER. New York: Monarch
Press, 1966.

1445
Ledger, Marshall A. "George Eliot and Nathaniel Hawthorne,"
N&Q, 11 (1964), 225-26.

A comparison between Eliot and Hawthorne earlier than
any previously noted--in Edinburgh Review, July 1859--
in an anonymous review of Adam Bede.

1446
Lefcowitz, Allan, and Barbara Lefcowitz. "Some Rents in the
Veil: New Light on Priscilla and Zenobia in THE
BLITHEDALE ROMANCE," NCF, 21 (1966), 263-75.

The ambiguity with which Hawthorne presents fair
Priscilla and dark Zenobia is not sustained when the
story is reduced to moral allegory; the two are
turned into abstract counterparts.

1447 Le Gallienne, Richard. "Imperishable Fiction," VANISHING
ROADS AND OTHER ESSAYS. New York: G. P. Putnam's
Sons; Knickerbocker P., 1915, pp. 333-34.

1448 Le Gallienne, Richard. "Re-Reading Hawthorne," in
ATTITUDES AND AVOWALS WITH SOME RETROSPECTIVE REVIEWS.
Lane, 1910, 267-84.

1449 Leib, Amos Patten. "Hawthorne as Scenic Artist," DA, 24
(Tulane: 1964), 3338-39.

1450 Leibowitz, Herbert A. "Hawthorne and Spenser: Two Sources."
AL, 30 (1959), 459-66.

1451 Leisy, Ernest E. THE AMERICAN HISTORICAL NOVEL. Norman,
Okla.: Okla. U. P., 1950.

  Rev. by Kenneth B. Murdock, AL, 22 (1950), 527-28;
  and Sterling Lanier, NEQ, 23 (1950), 418-19.

1452 Leisy, Ernest E. AMERICAN LITERATURE: AN INTERPRETATIVE
SURVEY. New York: Thomas Y. Crowell, 1929.

  Hawthorne, a "reflective Puritan," reinspired by
  Transcendentalism.

  Rev. by Gregory Paine, AL, 1 (1929-30), 327-30.

1453 Leisy, Ernest E. "Folklore in American Literature,"
CE, 8 (1946), 122-29.

1454 Leisy, Ernest E., ed. THE SCARLET LETTER. New York: 1929.

1455 Lemon, Lee T. APPROACHES TO LITERATURE. New York: Oxford
U. P., 1969.

1456 Lesser, Simon O. "The Attitude of Fiction," MFS, 2
(1956), 47-55.

1457 Lesser, Simon O. FICTION AND THE UNCONSCIOUS. Boston:
Beacon Press, 1957.

  Excerpt, "Hawthorne and Anderson: Conscious and
  Unconscious Perception," in PSYCHOANALYSIS AND
  AMERICAN FICTION, Irving Malin, ed., New York:
  Dutton, 1965, pp. 87-110.

1458 Lesser, Simon O. "The Image of the Father: A Reading of
'My Kinsman, Major Molineux' and 'I Want to Know Why,'"
PR, 22 (1955), 372-90.

  Psychoanalytic interpretations of stories by
  Hawthorne and Anderson.

  Essay also in FIVE APPROACHES OF LITERARY CRITICISM.
  Wilbur Stewart Scott, ed. New York: Macmillan, 1962;
  and in ART AND PSYCHOANALYSIS. Williams Phillips, ed.
  Criterion Books, 1957.

1459 Levi, Joseph. "Hawthorne's THE SCARLET LETTER: A Psychoanalytic Interpretation," AI, 10 (1953), 291-306.

1460 Levin, David. "Introduction," THE BLITHEDALE ROMANCE.
David Levin, ed. New York: Dell Pub. Co., 1962,
pp. 7-19.

1461 Levin, David. "Introduction," THE HOUSE OF THE SEVEN GABLES.
David Levin, ed. New York: Dell Pub. Co., 1962, pp.
7-20. .

1462 Levin, David. "Introduction," THE MARBLE FAUN. New York:
Dell Pub. Co., 1962, pp. 7-19.

1463 Levin, David. "Introduction," THE SCARLET LETTER. New
York: Dell, 1960, pp. 7-20.

1464 Levin, David. "Introduction," WHAT HAPPENED IN SALEM?
David Levin, ed. New York: Harcourt, Brace & World,
Inc., 1960.

1465 Levin, David. "Nathaniel Hawthorne, THE SCARLET LETTER," in
THE AMERICAN NOVEL FROM JAMES FENIMORE COOPER TO
WILLIAM FAULKNER. Wallace Stegner, ed. New York:
Basic Books, 1965.

1466 Levin, David. "Shadows of Doubt: Specter Evidence in
Hawthorne's 'Young Goodman Brown,'" AL, 34 (1962),
344-52.

1466.1 Levin, Gerald. THE SHORT STORY: AN INDUCTIVE APPROACH.
New York: Harcourt, Brace & World, 1967.

"The Celestial Railroad," pp. 260-62;
"Roger Malvin's Burial," pp. 82-83.

1467 Levin, Harry. "Introduction," THE HOUSE OF THE SEVEN GABLES.
Columbus, Ohio: Charles E. Merrill, 1969, pp. v-xv.

1468 Levin, Harry. "Introduction," THE SCARLET LETTER. Harry
Levin, ed. Boston: Houghton Mifflin Co., 1960.

1469 Levin, Harry. "Introduction," THE SCARLET LETTER AND OTHER
TALES OF THE PURITANS. Harry Levin, ed. Boston:
Houghton Mifflin Co., 1961, pp. vii-xxi.

1470 Levin, Harry. THE POWER OF BLACKNESS: HAWTHORNE, POE AND
MELVILLE. New York: Alfred A. Knopf, 1958.

Rev. by Newton Arvin, AL, 30 (1958), 380-81;
Richard H. Fogle, NCF, 13 (1958), 167-70.

1471   Levin, Harry. "The Quintessence of Hawthorne," NYTBR,
       June 16, 1946.

1472   Levin, Harry. "Statues from Italy: THE MARBLE FAUN," in
       HAWTHORNE CENTENARY ESSAYS. Columbus: Ohio St. U. P.,
       1964, pp. 119-140.

       Repr., in REFRACTIONS: ESSAYS IN COMPARATIVE LITERATURE.
       Fairlawn, New Jersey: Oxford U. P., 1966, pp. 192-211.

1473   Levy, Alfred J. "'Ethan Brand' and the Unpardonable Sin,"
       BUSE, 5 (1961), 185-90.

1474   Levy, Alfred J. "THE HOUSE OF THE SEVEN GABLES: The
       Religion of Love," NCF, 16 (1961), 189-203.

1475   Levy, Alfred J. "Nathaniel Hawthorne's Attitude Toward Total
       Depravity and Evil," DA, 17 (Wis.: 1957), 1751.

       Hawthorne neither a believer in total depravity nor
       a transcendentalist. He was a "Christian dualist"
       who believed man was made of "marble and mud."

1476   Levy, Leo B. "THE BLITHEDALE ROMANCE: Hawthorne's 'Voyage
       Through Chaos,'" SIR, 8 (1968), 1-15.

       THE BLITHEDALE ROMANCE a sociological novel whose
       characters and themes portray society in the process
       of changing from agrarian to urban order.

1477   Levy, Leo B. "Criticism Chronicle: Hawthorne, Melville,
       and James," SoR, 2, n. s. (1966), 427-42.

1477.1 Levy, Leo B. "FANSHAWE: Hawthorne's World of Images,"
       SNNTS, 2 (1970), 440-48.

1478   Levy, Leo B. "Hawthorne and the Idea of 'Bartleby,'"
       ESQ, 47 (1967), 66-69.

1479   Levy, Leo B. "Hawthorne and the Sublime," AL, 37 (1966),
       391-402.

1480   Levy, Leo B. "Hawthorne, Melville, and the MONITOR,"
       AL, 37 (1965), 33-40.

1481   Levy, Leo B. "Hawthorne's 'The Canal Boat': An Experiment in
       Landscape," AQ, 16 (1964), 211-15.

1432   Levy, Leo B. "Hawthorne's 'Middle Ground,'" SSF, 2 (1964),
       56-60.

1483   Levy, Leo B. "The Landscape Modes of THE SCARLET LETTER,"
       NCF, 23 (1969), 377-92.

1484 Levy, Leo B. "THE MARBLE FAUN: Hawthorne's Landscape of the
        Fall," AL, 42 (1970), 139-56.

1485 Levy, Leo B. "The Mermaid and the Mirror: Hawthorne's 'The
        Village Uncle,'" NCF, Hawthorne Centenary Issue, 19,
        (1964), 205-11.

1486 Levy, Leo B. "Picturesque Style in THE HOUSE OF THE SEVEN
        GABLES," NEQ, 39 (1966), 147-60.

1487 Levy, Leo B. "The Temple and the Tomb: Hawthorne's 'The
        Lily's Quest,'" SSF, 3 (1966), 334-42.

1488 Lewin, Walter. "Nathaniel Hawthorne," Bookman (London), 26
        (1904), 121-28.

1489 Lewis, R. W. B. "Introduction," HERMAN MELVILLE. R. W. B.
        Lewis, ed. New York: Dell, 1962, pp. 7-35.

      Part One - Melville and Hawthorne," pp. 37-81.

1490 Lewis, R. W. B. "The Return into Time: Hawthorne," THE
        AMERICAN ADAM: INNOCENCE, TRAGEDY, AND TRADITION IN
        THE NINETEENTH CENTURY. Chicago: Chicago U. P.,
        1955. pp. 110-26.

      Hawthorne more than his contemporaries saw in
      American experience the recreation of the story of
      Adam.
      Rev. by Sherman Paul, NEQ, 29 (1956), 254-58.

1491 Lewis, R. W. B. "The Tactics of Sanctity: Hawthorne and
        James," HAWTHORNE CENTENARY ESSAYS, Roy Harvey Pearce, ed.
        Columbus, Ohio: Ohio St. U. P., 1964), 271-95.

1492 Lewisohn, Ludwig. EXPRESSION IN AMERICA. New York: Harper &
        Brothers, 1932, pp. 168-86.

      A psychoanalytical interpretation.

      Rev. by Ernest E. Leisy, AL, 5 (1933-34), 285-286,
      who says an appropriate title for the book would be
      REPRESSION IN AMERICA.

1493 Lewisohn, Ludwig. "The Troubled Romancers," in CREATIVE
        AMERICA: AN ANTHOLOGY. Ludwig Lewisohn, ed. New York:
        Harper, 1933, 218ff.

1494 Leyda, Jay. THE MELVILLE LOG: A DOCUMENTARY LIFE OF HERMAN
        MELVILLE, 1819-1891. 2 Vols. New York: Harcourt, Brace
        & Co., 1951.

1494.1 Lid, R. W., ed. Instructor's Manual for THE SHORT STORY:
CLASSIC AND CONTEMPORARY. New York: J. B. Lippincott,
1967.

"Young Goodman Brown," pp. 30-32.

1494.2 Liebman, Sheldon W. "Ambiguity in 'Lady Eleanore's Mantle,'"
ESQ, 58 (1970), 97-101.

1495 Liebman, Sheldon W. "The Design of THE MARBLE FAUN,"
NEQ, 40 (1967), 61-78.

Central metaphor in THE MARBLE FAUN is the sarcophagus.
Like Rome, it contains the dead; around it carved
figures dance, displaying innocence and experience.

1496 Liebman, Sheldon W. "Hawthorne and Milton: The Second Fall
in 'Rappaccini's Daughter,'" NEQ, 41 (1968), 521-35.

1497 Lind, Sidney E. "Emily Dickinson's 'Further in Summer than
the Birds' and Nathaniel Hawthorne's THE OLD MANSE,"
AL, 39 (1967), 163-69.

We can assume that the poet read Hawthorne's essay.
Best commentary on the poem is Hawthorne's mystical
description of fusion of beauty and coming decay in
THE OLD MANSE.

1498 Lines, Kathleen. "Foreword," THE COMPLETE GREEK STORIES OF
NATHANIEL HAWTHORNE FROM THE WONDER BOOK AND TANGLEWOOD
TALES. Illustrated by Harold Jones, with postscript by
Roger Lancelyn Green. New York: Franklin Watts, Inc.,
1963.

1499 Link, Franz H. Die Erzahlkunst Nathaniel Hawthornes: Eine
Interpretation seiner Skizzen, Erzahlungen und Romance.
FAGAAS, 7, Heidelberg: Carl Winter.

Rev. by Wilfred Edener, NS, 12 (1963), 383-84.

1500 Link, Franz H. "Hawthorne's Skizzen," NS, 8, Heft 12
(1959), 537-46.

1501 Little, George T. "Bowdoin and Her Sons," MunM, 28
(1903), 576-85.

1502 Little, George T. "Hawthorne's FANSHAWE and Bowdoin's Past,"
BowQ (1904).

1503 Litzinger, Boyd. "Mythmaking in America: 'The Great Stone
Face' and RAINTREE COUNTY," TSL, 8 (1963), 81-84.

1504
Lloyd Michael. "Hawthorne, Ruskin, and the Hostile Tradition,"
EM, 6 (1955), 109-33.

1505
Lockwood, F. C. "Hawthorne as a Literary Artist," MethR, 64
(1904), 738.

1506
Loggins, Vernon. THE HAWTHORNES: THE STORY OF SEVEN
GENERATIONS OF AN AMERICAN FAMILY. New York:
Columbia U. P., 1951.

Revs. by A. L. Bader, CST (1952), 12;
Alice M. Baldwin, SAQ, 53 (1954), 585-87;
Bookmark, 11 (1952), 131;
Katherine Burton, Cw, 54 (1951), 628-29;
W. E. G., CC, 68 (1951), 1078;
B. R. McElderry, Person, 34 (1953), 208;
NY, 27 (1951), 167;
Stewart Mitchell, AHR, 57 (1952), 765-66;
Winnifred King Rugg, NEQ, 25 (1952), 106-07;
K. Stewart, MLN, 67 (1952), 287-88;
Louise Hall Tharp, NYTBR (1951), 28;
USQBR, 7 (1951), 340;
George F. Whicher, NYHTBR (1951), 7;
Stanley T. Williams, AL, 24 (1952), 243-44;
TLS (February, 1952), 110.

1507
Lohmann, Christoph. "The Burden of the Past in Hawthorne's
American Romances," SAQ, 66 (1967), 92-104.

Conflict between past and present a major theme in
Hawthorne's fiction. Man cannot avoid past's burden
of sin and guilt.

1507.1
Lohmann, Christoph. "Nathaniel Hawthorne: The American
Janus," DAI, 30 (Pa.: 1969), 1172A.

1508
Lombardo, Agostino. "Il primo romanzo di Hawthorne," SA, 1
(1955), 73-95. Repr. in La ricerca del vero: saggi
sulla tradizione letteraria americana. Rome: Edizioni
di Storia e Letteratura, 1961, pp. 145-70.

FANSHAWE contains the "leitmotifs" of all Hawthorne's
novels.

1509
Lombardo, Agostino. "I racconti di Hawthorne." IL SIMBOLISMO
NELLA LETTERATURA NORD-AMERICANA: ATTI DEL SYMPOSIUM
TENUTO A FIRENZE 27-29 novembre 1964. Praz, Mario, et al.
(Pubblicazioni dell'Ist. di Studi Americani, U. degli
Studi di Firenze, 1.) Firenze: La Nuova Italia, 1965,
pp. 69-160.

1510
Lombardo, Agostino. LA RICERCA DEL VERO: SAGGI SULLA
TRADIZIONE LETTERARIA AMERICANA. Roma: Ed di storia
e letteratura, 1961.

Rev. by J. Chesley Mathews, AL, 34 (1963), 592-93.

1511 Long, Orie William. LITERARY PIONEERS: EARLY AMERICAN
EXPLORERS OF EUROPEAN CULTURE. Cambridge, Mass.:
Harvard U. P., 1935, p. 62.

Quotes Hawthorne's description of George Ticknor in 1850.

1512 Long, Robert Emmet. "'THE AMBASSADORS' and The Genteel
Tradition: James's Correction of Hawthorne and
Howells." NEQ, 42 (1969), 44-64.

1513 Long, Robert Emmet. "The Society and the Maska: THE
BLITHEDALE ROMANCE and THE BOSTONIANS," NCF,
Hawthorne Centenary Issue, 19 (1964), 105-22.

1514 Long, William J. "Nathaniel Hawthorne," OUTLINES OF
ENGLISH AND AMERICAN LITERATURE. New York: Ginn & Co.,
1917, 487-98.

Hawthorne is a man who never laughs and seldom smiles
in his work; he passes over a hundred normal, cheerful
homes to pitch upon some gloomy habitation.

1515 Longfellow, Henry Wadsworth. "Hawthorne," in THE GROWTH OF
AMERICAN LITERATURE. Edwin Harrison Cady, et al, eds.
New York: American Book Co., 1956, pp. 532-33.

The poem "Hawthorne" is included. The editors remark
that Longfellow interprets Hawthorne as a "lonely,
wondrous, romantically distant writer." They suggest
we compare this "portrait" with the one modern
biographers give us.

1515.1 Longfellow, Henry Wadsworth. "Hawthorne's TWICE-TOLD TALES"
/1837/ in his PROSE WORKS. Boston: Houghton Mifflin,
1886, V, 360-67. Repr. in THE RECOGNITION OF
NATHANIEL HAWTHORNE. B. Bernard Cohen, ed. Ann
Arbor: 1969, pp. 9-12.

1516 Loring, G. B. "Hawthorne's SCARLET LETTER," in THE TRANS-
CENDENTALISTS: AN ANTHOLOGY. Perry Miller, ed.
(Partially analyzed) Cambridge, Mass.: Harvard U. P.,
1950, 475-82.

1516.1 Loring, G. B. "Hawthorne," in PAPYRUS LEAVES. William F.
Gill, ed. New York: R. Worthington, 1880, pp. 249-68.
Repr. in HAWTHORNE AMONG HIS CONTEMPORARIES. Kenneth
Walter Cameron, ed. Hartford: Transcendental Books,
1968, pp. 213-18.

1517 Lothrop, Margaret Mulford. "Under Hawthorne's Many Roofs,"
THE WAYSIDE: HOME OF AUTHORS. New York: American
Bk. Co., 1940, 79-149.

1518 Lothrop, Margaret Mulford. "The Wayside, Home of Three
Authors," ElER, 10 (1933), 98-100, 111.

1519   Lovecraft, Howard Phillips. SUPERNATURAL HORROR IN
         LITERATURE. With Introduction by August Derleth.
         New York: Ben Abramson, Pub., 1945, pp. 61-66, 100.

         Rev. by Fred Lewis Pattee, AL, 18 (1946), 175-77.

1520   Lovejoy, David S. "Lovewell's Fight and Hawthorne's 'Roger
         Malvin's Burial,'" NEQ, 27 (1954), 527-31.

         Hawthorne not only relied upon Symmes' memoir and a
         popular ballad but also upon "Indian Troubles at
         Dunstable" (1823) by "J. B. H."
         See Gail H. Bickford, "Lovewell's Fight, 1725-1958,"
         AQ, 10 (1958), 358-66.

1521   Lowell, James Russell. "Fable for Critics," in LOWELL
         ESSAYS, POEMS AND LETTERS. Selected and edited by
         William Smith Clark, II. New York: Odyssey P., 1948,
         pp. 212-13.

         Passage on Hawthorne in "Fable for Critics," ll.780ff.

1522   Lowell, James Russell. JAMES RUSSELL LOWELL: REPRESENTATIVE
         SELECTIONS. With Introduction, Bibliography and Notes
         by Harry Hayden Clark and Norman Foerster. New York:
         American Book Co., 1947, p. 477.

1523   Lowell, Robert. "Hawthorne," /poem/ in HAWTHORNE CENTENARY
         ESSAYS, Roy Harvey Pearce, ed. Columbus, Ohio: Ohio
         U. P., 1964, pp. 3-4.

1524   Lowell, Robert. "'My Kinsman, Major Molineux,'" PR, 31
         (1964), 495-514; 566-83.

         Drama based on the story.

1525   Lowell, Robert. THE OLD GLORY. New York: Farrar, Straus &
         Giroux, 1968. /Rev. ed. Theater trilogy based on two
         stories by Hawthorne and a novella by Melville./

1526   Lubbers, Klaus. "Metaphorical Patterns in Hawthorne's THE
         HOUSE OF THE SEVEN GABLES," in LITERATUR AND SPRACHE DER
         VEREINIGTEN STAATEN: AUFSATZE ZU EHREN VON HANS GALINSKY.
         Hans Helmcke, Klaus Lubbers, and Renate Schmidt-von
         Bardeleben, eds. Heidelberg: Carl Winter--Universitätsver-
         lag, 1969, pp. 107-16. Repr. in STUDIES IN THE HOUSE OF THE
         SEVEN GABLES, Roger Asselineau, comp. Columbus, Ohio:
         Charles E. Merrill Studies, 1970, pp. 60-73.

1527   Lucke, Jessie Ryon. "Hawthorne's Madonna Image in THE
         SCARLET LETTER," NEQ, 38 (1965), 391-92.

1528   Lucke, Jessie Ryon. "The Inception of 'The Beast in the
         Jungle,'" NEQ, 26 (1953), 529-32.

         Suggests a passage in THE BLITHEDALE ROMANCE.

1529 Ludwig, Richard M., ed. LITERARY HISTORY OF THE UNITED
STATES: BIBLIOGRAPHY SUPPLEMENT. New York:
1959, 1963. Selective bibliography covering the
period 1948-58, pp. 133-36.

1530 Luecke, Sister Jane Marie. "Villains and Non-Villains in
Hawthorne's Fiction," PMLA, 78 (1963), 551-558.

1531 Lueders, Edward G. "The Melville-Hawthorne Relationship in
PIERRE and THE BLITHEDALE ROMANCE," WHR, 4 (1950),
323-34.

1532 Lundblad, Jane, ed. ÅTERBERÄTTADE HISTORIER FRAN AMERIKA
OCH DAGBOKSBLAD FRAN EUROPA. Stockholm: Tiden.

1533 Lundblad, Jane. NATHANIEL HAWTHORNE AND THE EUROPEAN LITERARY
TRADITION, ESSAYS AND STUDIES ON AMERICAN LANGUAGE AND
LITERATURE, No. VI, Diss. Upsala, 1947.

Rev. by F. C. Marston, Jr., AL, 21 (1949), 248-50.

Repr. NATHANIEL HAWTHORNE AND EUROPEAN LITERARY
TRADITION. New York: Russell and Russell, 1965.

1534 Lundblad, Jane. "Nathaniel Hawthorne and the Tradition of
Gothic Romance," ESSAYS AND STUDIES ON AMERICAN
LANGUAGE AND LITERATURE, 4, American Institute University,
Upsala, 1946; SN, 19 (1946), 1-92; Cambridge, Mass.:
Harvard U. P., 1947.

Gothic romance formed an important substratum of
Hawthorne's work, ever present and often employed
for definite artistic purposes.

1534.1 Lycette, Ronald L. "Diminishing Circumferences: Feminine
Responses in Fiction to New England Decline," DAI, 31
(Purdue: 1970), 1764A.

1535 Lynch, James J. "The Devil in the Writings of Irving,
Hawthorne, and Poe," NYFQ, 8 (1952), 111-31.

Because of his interest in the workings of the human
mind and spirit, Hawthorne usually treats his devil
psychologically.

1536 Lynch, James J. "Structure and Allegory in 'The Great Stone
Face,'" NCF, 15 (1960), 137-46.

1537 Lynd, Robert. "Hawthorne," in BOOKS AND AUTHORS. London:
1922; Travellers' Library, 1929, pp. 117-24.

1538 Lynd, Robert. "Hawthorne," NStm, 19 (1922), 68-70.

1539 Lynn, Kenneth S. "Nathaniel Hawthorne," THE COMIC TRADITION IN AMERICA. Foreword and Notes by Kenneth S. Lynn, ed. New York: Doubleday, 1958, pp. 235-57.

1540 Lynn, Kenneth S. THE SCARLET LETTER, TEXT, SOURCES, CRITICISM. New York: Harcourt, Brace & World, Inc., 1961.

1541 Mabie, Hamilton Wright. "Hawthorne in the New World," BACKGROUNDS OF LITERATURE. New York: Macmillan, 1904, pp. 305-28.

Hawthorne, the "most perfect artist in our literature-- all things considered."

1542 Mabie, Hamilton Wright. "Nathaniel Hawthorne," NAR, 179 (1904), 13-23.

1543 MacCarthy, Desmond. "Nathaniel Hawthorne, (1931)," HUMANITIES. Preface by Lord David Cecil. New York: Oxford U. P., 1954, pp. 167-71.

1544 MacLean, Hugh N. "Hawthorne's SCARLET LETTER: 'The Dark Problem of This Life,'" AL, 27 (1955), 12-24.

1545 Macomber, H. E. STORY OF HAWTHORNE. Boston and New York: Educational Pub. Co., 1912.

1546 MacShane, Frank. "The House of the Dead: Hawthorne's Custom House and THE SCARLET LETTER," NEQ, 35 (1962), 93-101.

1547 Macy, John. THE SPIRIT OF AMERICAN LITERATURE. New York: Boni & Liveright, Inc., 1911; Garden City: Doubleday, Page & Co., 1913.

1548 Madden, Edward H. CIVIL DISOBEDIENCE AND MORAL LAW IN NINETEENTH-CENTURY AMERICAN PHILOSOPHY. Seattle: Washington U. P., 1968.

Challenges Randall Stewart on Hawthorne.

Rev. by Richard P. Haynis, AL, 40 (1969), 585-86.

1549 Madden, Edward H. "G. W. Curtis: Practical Transcendentalist," Person, 40 (1959), 369-79.

Curtis' dissatisfaction with Hawthorne's views on the Civil War.

1550 Maddocks, Melvin. "Rituals--The Revolt against the Fixed Smile," *Time*, 96 (1970), 42-43.

Provides survey of Maypole festivity and recalls that in Hawthorne's story the "peal of psalm from Plymouth" would occasionally collide with the "chorus of a jolly catch" from Merry Mount. Raises the question as to whether a "little band of displaced Americans had lived exactly in the middle of culture and counterculture."

1551 Maes-Jelinek, Hena. "Roger Chillingworth: An Example of the Creative Process in THE SCARLET LETTER," ES, 49 (1968), 341-48.

Takes issue with A. S. Reid's statement (THE YELLOW RUFF AND THE SCARLET LETTER: A SOURCE OF HAWTHORNE'S NOVEL, Gainesville, Fla.: 1955) that Roger Chillingworth has much in common with William Chillingworth, the author of THE RELIGION OF PROTESTANTS: A SAFE WAY TO SALVATION (1637). More likely Roger's character was suggested by the Puritan Francis Cheynell who attempted to force William Chillingworth to confess his errors on his death bed. Also, William Prynne may have suggested Hester's surname but not her character.

1552 Magalaner, Marvin, and Edmond L. Volpe, eds. TEACHER'S MANUAL TO ACCOMPANY "TWELVE SHORT STORIES." New York: Macmillan, 1961. pp. 1-2.

A teaching aid for "Young Goodman Brown."

1553 Magginis, Mary A. HAWTHORNE'S COMMENTS ON THE ARTS AS EVIDENCE OF AN AESTHETIC THEORY. Diss. North Carolina: 1948.

1554 Magginis, Mary Amelia. "Hawthorne on Church Architecture," FSUS, 2 (1953), 54-74.

1555 Mahan, Helen Rose Selkis. "Hawthorne's THE MARBLE FAUN: A Critical Introduction and Annotations," DA, 27 (Rochester: 1966), 1341A.

1556 "Main Street," GoldB, 13 (1931), 33-39.

Hawthorne the first to see the developing small town as symbolic of something peculiarly and exclusively American.

1557 Male, Roy R. "Criticism of Bell's 'Hawthorne's "Fire-Worship": Interpretation and Source,'" AL, 25 (1953), 85-87.

See M. Bell's "Hawthorne's 'Fire-Worship': Interpretation and Source," AL, 24 (1952), 31-39.

1558 Male, Roy R. "The Dual Aspects of Evil in 'Rappaccini's Daughter,'" PMLA, 69 (1954), 99-109.

1559 Male, Roy R. "'From the Innermost Germ,' the Organic
Principle in Hawthorne's Fiction," ELH, 20 (1953),
218-36.

The organic principle is an essential aspect of
Hawthorne's fiction and complements his tragic sense.

1560 Male, Roy R. "Hawthorne," in AMERICAN LITERARY SCHOLARSHIP:
AN ANNUAL, 1968. J. Albert Robbins, ed. Durham, N. C.:
Duke U. P., 1970, pp. 19-29.

1561 Male, Roy R. "Hawthorne and the Concept of Sympathy,"
PMLA, 68 (1953), 138-49.

Puts Hawthorne in the context of romanticism by
showing what sympathy meant for him.

See Carl F. Strauch, "Emerson and the Doctrine of
Sympathy," SIR, 6 (1967), 153, n. 1.

1562 Male, Roy R. "Hawthorne's Allegory of Guilt and Redemption,"
in Carl F. Strauch, et al., Symposium on Nathaniel
Hawthorne, ESQ, 25 (1961), 16-18.

1563 Male, Roy R. "Hawthorne's THE BLITHEDALE ROMANCE," Expl,
28 (1970), Item 56.

1564 Male, Roy R. HAWTHORNE'S TRAGIC VISION. Austin, Texas:
1957.

Revs., CE, 21 (1960), 504;
Richard Harter Fogle, NCF, 12 (1957), 251;
W. Gordon Milne, BA, 32 (1958), 82;
Lewis Leary, SatR (1957), 31;
Ernest E. Leisy, SWR, 42 (1957), 356;
Harry Levin, AL, 29 (1958), 491-92;
Alfred S. Reid, ESQ, 12 (1958), 52;
Hyatt H. Waggoner, MLN, 73 (1958), 369-71;
D. S. R. Welland, MLR, 53 (1958), 571-72.

1565 Male, Roy R. "The Sins of the Fathers: An Exchange,"
NCF, 22 (1967), 106-10.

1566 Male, Roy R. "The Story of the Mysterious Stranger in
American Fiction," Criticism, 3 (1961), 281-94.

1567 Male, Roy R. "Toward 'The Wasteland': The Theme of THE
BLITHEDALE ROMANCE," CE, 16 (1955), 277-83.

The real subject of the romance is social and psychological disintegration. Most of the characters are "hollow
men."

1568 Malin, Irving. NEW AMERICAN GOTHIC. Carbondale: So. Ill.
U. P., 1962, pp. 6-7, 79.

1569 Malone, Ted. (Pseud., Frank Alden Russell)
"Nathaniel Hawthorne," SHOULD OLD ACQUAINTANCE.
Haddonfield, New Jersey: Bookmark P., 1942, 1943,
pp. 51-64.

Formerly, "Nathaniel Hawthorne," AMERICAN PILGRIMAGE.
New York: Dodd, Mead & Co., 1942, pp. 51-64.

1570 "Man and Author," EdinbR, 203 (1905-06), 210-235.

Also in LivA, 249 (1906), 458-76.

1570.1 Manierre, William R. "Some Apparent Confusions in THE
SCARLET LETTER," CEA, 33 (1971), 9-13.

1570.2 Manley, Seon. NATHANIEL HAWTHORNE: CAPTAIN OF THE IMAGINATION.
New York: Vanguard, 1967.

1571 Mann, Robert W. "Afterthoughts on Opera and THE SCARLET
LETTER," SA, 5 (1959), 339-350.

1572 Mann, Robert W. "THE SCARLET LETTER: Libretto in Four
Acts and Nine Scenes," SA, 5 (1959), 351-381.

1573 Manning, Clarence Augustus. "Hawthorne and Dostoyevsky,"
SlavonR, 14 (1936), 417-24.

The two writers are different superficially, but both
grasped a central truth, that man must be judged by
his motives rather than by his actions.

1574 Manning, Clarence Augustus. "New England in Lesya Ukrainka's
IN THE WILDERNESS," CL, 8 (1956), 136-41.

Influence of Hawthorne.

1575 Mansfield, Luther S. "The Emersonian Idiom and the Romantic
Period in American Literature," ESQ, 35 (1964), 23-28.

1576 Marble, Annie Russell. "Gloom and Cheer in Hawthorne,"
Critic, 45 (1904), 28-34.

1577 Marble, Annie Russell. "Introduction," THE MARBLE FAUN.
Boston: 1901, 1925.

1578 Marcus, Fred H. "THE SCARLET LETTER: The Power of Ambiguity,"
EJ, 51 (1962), 449-58.

1579 Marenco, Franco. "Nathaniel Hawthorne e il BLITHEDALE
ROMANCE," SA, 6 (1960), 135-82.

1580 Mariani, Giuseppe, ed. LA LETTERA SCARLATTA. With Introd.
Modena: Edizioni Paoline.

1581 Marks, Alfred H. "German Romantic Irony in Hawthorne's
Tales," Symposium, 7 (1953), 274-305.

Hawthorne's debt to Schlegel, Tieck, et al.

1582 Marks, Alfred H. HAWTHORNE AND ROMANTIC IRONY. Diss.
Syracuse: 1953.

1583 Marks, Alfred H. "Hawthorne's Daguerreotypist: Scientist,
Artist, Reformer," BSTCF, 3 (1962), 61-74.

1583.1 Marks, Alfred H. "Ironic Inversion in THE BLITHEDALE
ROMANCE," ESQ, 55 (1969), 95-102.

1584 Marks, Alfred H. "Two Rodericks and Two Worms: 'Egotism; or,
The Bosom Serpent' as Personal Satire," PMLA, 74 (1959),
607-12.

Roderick Ellison was intended to suggest Poe.

1585 Marks, Alfred H. "Who Killed Judge Pyncheon? The Role of the
Imagination in THE HOUSE OF THE SEVEN GABLES," PMLA,
71 (1956), 355-69.

1586 Marks, Barry A. "The Origin of Original Sin in Hawthorne's
Fiction," NCF, 14 (1960), 359-62.

Hawthorne's work raised and refused to answer the
question of "ultimate guilt for specific actions."

1587 Marks, William S., III. "The Psychology of the Uncanny in
Lawrence's 'The Rocking-Horse Winner," MFS, 11 (1965),
381-92.

Comparison: Pearl and Hester - Hester and Paul.

1587.1 Marovitz, Sanford E. "RODERICK HUDSON: James's MARBLE
FAUN," TSLL, 11 (1970), 1427-43.

1588 Marsh, Philip. "Hawthorne and Griswold," MLN, 63 (1948),
132-33.

Postscript to letter from Hawthorne to James T. Fields,
August 20, 1850, completes record of Hawthorne's con-
tribution to memorial volume for Mrs. Fanny Osgood which
Griswold was editing.

1589 Marshall, Thomas F. AN ANALYTICAL INDEX TO AMERICAN
LITERATURE. Vols. I-XX (March 1929-January 1949).
Durham, North Carolina: Duke U. P., 1954, pp. 30-31.

1590 Martin, Harold C. "The Development of Style in Nineteenth-
Century American Fiction," EIE, (1958), 114-41.

Comparison of style in "Rappaccini's Daughter"
with that of Irving's BRACEBRIDGE HALL.

1591 Martin, Robert K. "Hawthorne's THE BLITHEDALE ROMANCE," Expl, 28 (1969), Item 11.

1592 Martin, Terence. "Adam Blair and Arthur Dimmesdale: A Lesson from the Master," AL, 34 (1962), 274-79.

On James's comparison of THE SCARLET LETTER to John Gibson Lockhart's ADAM BLAIR.

1593 Martin, Terence. "The Emergence of the Novel in America," DA, 20 (Okla St.: 1954).

1594 Martin, Terence. "The Haunted Mind," THE INSTRUCTED VISION - SCOTTISH COMMON SENSE PHILOSOPHY AND THE ORIGINS OF AMERICAN FICTION. Bloomington: Indiana U. P., 1961.

1595 Martin, Terence. "The Imagination at Play: Edgar Allan Poe," KR, 28 (1966), 194-209.

1596 Martin, Terence. "The Method of Hawthorne's Tales," in HAWTHORNE CENTENARY ESSAYS, Roy Harvey Pearce, ed. Columbus, Ohio: Ohio St. U. P., 1964, pp. 7-30.

1597 Martin, Terence. NATHANIEL HAWTHORNE. New York: Twayne Publishers and New Haven: College and U. P., 1965.

Rev., Booklist, 61 (1965), 779; Choice, 2 (1965), 227-28; Sidney P. Moss, ABC, 16 (1965), 4; Richard Harter Fogle, AL, 37 (1965), 355.

1598 Martineau, Stephen F. "Opposition and Balance: A Characteristic of Structure in Hawthorne, Melville, and James," DA, 28 (Columbia: 1967), 1441A.

1599 Marx, Leo. HAWTHORNE AND EMERSON: STUDIES IN THE IMPACT OF THE MACHINE TECHNOLOGY UPON THE AMERICAN WRITERS. Diss. Harvard: 1950.

1600 Marx, Leo. "Introduction," THE SCARLET LETTER. Leo Marx, ed. New York: New American Lib. (Signet), 1959.

1601 Marx, Leo. "The Machine in the Garden," NEQ, 29 (1956), 27-42.

The response of American writers before 1880 to the Industrial Revolution, with attention to Hawthorne's "Ethan Brand."

1602 Marx, Leo. THE MACHINE IN THE GARDEN: TECHNOLOGY AND THE PASTORAL IDEAL IN AMERICA. New York: Oxford U. P., 1964, pp. 265-77, passim.

1603 Masback, Frederic Joseph. "The Child Characters in Hawthorne
and James," DA, 21 (Syracuse: 1960), 338.

1604 Matenko, Percy. "Ludwig Tieck and America," UNCSGLL, 12
(1954).

Does not give explicit answer as to Tieck's
influence on Hawthorne.

Rev. by Henry A. Pochmann, AL, 27 (1955), 444-45.

1604.1 Matenko, Percy. "Tieck, Poe, and Hawthorne," in his
LUDWIG TIECK AND AMERICA. Chapel Hill: North
Carolina U. P., 1954, pp. 71-88.

1605 Mather, Edward A. NATHANIEL HAWTHORNE: A MODEST MAN.
New York: Thomas Y. Crowell Co., 1940; repr. Westport,
Conn.: Greenwood Press, 1970.

Rev. by Randall Stewart, AL, 13 (1941-42), 73-74.

Contains bibliography together with a list of first
editions of Hawthorne's works.

1606 Matherly, E. P. "Poe and Hawthorne as Writers of the Short
Story," Educ, 40 (1920), 294-306.

1606.1 Mathews, J. Chesley. "Hawthorne," in BIBLIOGRAPHICAL
SUPPLEMENT: A SELECTIVE CHECK LIST, 1955-1962. EIGHT
AMERICAN AUTHORS: A REVIEW OF RESEARCH AND CRITICISM.
Jay B. Hubbell, et al, eds. New York: W. W. Norton &
Company, 1956, 1963, pp. 428-34.

1607 Mathews, J. Chesley. "Hawthorne's Knowledge of Dante,"
UTSE, #20, No. 4026 (1940), 157-65.

Hawthorne probably read the Inferno as well as the
Purgatorio and Paradiso.

1608 Mathews, J. Chesley. "The Interest in Dante Shown by
Nineteenth-Century Men of Letters," SA, 11 (1965),
77-104.

1609 Mathews, James W. "Antinomianism in 'Young Goodman Brown,'"
SSF, 3 (1965), 73-75.

1610 Mathews, James W. "Hawthorne and the Chain of Being,"
MLQ, 18 (1957), 282-94.

1611 Mathews, James W. "Hawthorne and Howells: The Middle Way
in American Fiction," DA, 21 (Tenn.: 1961), 1941-42.

1612 Mathews, James W. "The Heroines of Hawthorne and Howells,"
TSL, 7 (1962), 37-46.

1613 Matsuyama, Nobunao. "Hawthorne's THE HOUSE OF THE SEVEN GABLES and Nature--An Interpretation," SH, 75 (1964), 58-90.

1614 Matsuyama, Nobunao. "Nature in Hawthorne's Major Novels," Jimb, 43 (1967), 41-69.

1615 Matsuyama, Nobunao. "Solitude in Hawthorne: A Comment on Isolation," SELit, 42 (1966), 171-92.

1616 Mattfield, Mary S. "Hawthorne's Juvenile Classics," Discourse, 12 (1969), 346-64.

1617 Matthews, Brander. AN INTRODUCTION TO THE STUDY OF AMERICAN LITERATURE. New York: American Book Co., 1896.

1618 Matthiessen, Francis O. AMERICAN RENAISSANCE: ART AND EXPRESSION IN THE AGE OF EMERSON AND WHITMAN. New York: Oxford U. P., 1941.

1619 Matthiessen, Francis O. HENRY JAMES: THE MAJOR PHASE. New York: Oxford U. P., 1944.

1620 Matthiessen, Francis O. "The Isolation of Hawthorne," NR, 61 (1930), 281-282.

1620.1 Matthiessen, Francis O. "Nathaniel Hawthorne," in his THE RESPONSIBILITIES OF THE CRITIC. New York: Oxford U. P., 1952, pp. 209-11.

1621 Matthiessen, Francis O. SARAH ORNE JEWETT. Boston and New York: Houghton Mifflin Co., Riverside Press, Cambridge, 1929.

Sarah Orne Jewett is the "daughter" of Hawthorne's style.

Rev. by Fred Lewis Pattee, AL, 1 (1929-30), 335-36.

1622 Matthiessen, Francis O. "Tradition and the Individual Talent," AMERICAN CRITICAL ESSAYS: TWENTIETH CENTURY. Harold Beaver, ed. London: 1959.

1623 Maurois, André. "Un Puritan," NL, No. 1311 (1952), 1, 5.

1624 Maxwell, Desmond Ernest Stewart. "The Tragic Phase: Melville and Hawthorne." AMERICAN FICTION: THE INTELLECTUAL BACKGROUND. New York: Columbia U. P., 1963, 141-91.

1625 Maynard, Theodore. A FIRE WAS LIGHTED. New York: Bruce Pub. Co., 1948.

Rev. by John B. Harcourt, NEQ, 22 (1949), 119-21.

1626 Maynard, Theodore. GREAT CATHOLICS IN AMERICAN HISTORY. Hanover House, 1957, pp. 223-33.

Nathaniel Hawthorne's daughter, Rose Hawthorne Lathrop - Mother Mary Alphonsa.

1627 Maynard, Theodore. "The Hawthorne Year," CathW, 168 (1949), 283-86.

1628 McAleer, John J. "Biblical Symbols in American Literature: A Utilitarian Design," ES, 46 (1965), 310-22.

1629 McAleer, John J. "Hester Prynne's Grave," Descant, 5 (1961), 29-33.

In the center of King's Chapel burial ground where it is thought the grave of Isaac Johnson was located, is a grave of Hannah Dinsdale, wife of Adam Dinsdale.

1630 McAleer, John J. "Transcendentalism and the Improper Bostonian," ESQ, 39 (1965), 73-81.

Suggests themes of incest.

1631 McCabe, Bernard. "Narrative Technique in 'Rappaccini's Daughter,'" MLN, 74 (1959), 213-17.

1632 McCall, Dan E. "Citizen of Somewhere Else: The Achievement of THE SCARLET LETTER," DA, 28 (Columbia: 1967), 1790A.

1633 McCall, Dan E. "The Design of Hawthorne's 'Custom-House,'" NCF, 21 (1967), 349-558.

Organic connection between the "Custom-House" and THE SCARLET LETTER lies in conflicting artistic and social responsibilities. Movement from social concerns to imagination and romance parallels Hawthorne's increasing commitment to writing in face of troubled relations with Salem and his job.

1634 McCall, Dan E. "Hawthorne's 'Familiar Kind of Preface,'" ELH, 35 (1968), 422-39.

1635 McCall, Dan E. "'I Felt a Funeral in My Brain' and 'The Hollow of the Three Hills,'" NEQ, 42 (1969), 432-35.

1636 McCall, Dan E. "Robert Lowell's 'Hawthorne,'" NEQ, 39 (1966), 237-39.

1636.1 McCarthy, Harold T. "Hawthorne's Dialogue with Rome: THE MARBLE FAUN," SA, 14 (1968), 97-112.

1637 McCarthy, Paul. "The Extraordinary Man as Idealist in Novels by Hawthorne and Melville," ESQ, 54 (1969), 43-51.

1638 McCorquodale, Marjorie Kimball. "Melville's Pierre as Hawthorne," UTSE, 33 (1954), 97-102.

1639 McCullen, J. T., Jr. "Ancient Rites for the Dead and Hawthorne's 'Roger Malvin's Burial,'" SFQ, 30 (1966), 313-22.

1640 McCullen, J. T., Jr. "Influences on Hawthorne's 'The Artist of the Beautiful,'" ESQ, 50 (1968), 43-46.

1641 McCullen, J. T. "Young Goodman Brown: Presumption and Despair," Discourse, 2 (1959), 145-57.

1642 McCullen, J. T. "Zenobia: Hawthorne's Scornful Sceptic," Discourse, 4 (1961), 72-80.

1643 McCullen, J. T., and John C. Guilds. "The Unpardonable Sin in Hawthorne: A Re-Examination," NCF, 15 (1960), 211-37.

Unpardonable sinners are Digby, Chillingworth, and Ethan Brand.

See Henry G. Fairbanks, "Sin, Free Will, and 'Pessimism' in Hawthorne," PMLA, 71 (1956), 975-89; and James E. Miller, Jr., "Hawthorne and Melville: The Unpardonable Sin," PMLA, 70 (1955), 91-114.

1643.1 McDonald, John J. HAWTHORNE AT THE OLD MANSE. Diss. (Princeton: 1972).

1644 McDonald, Walter R. "Coincidence in the Novel: A Necessary Technique," CE, 29 (1968), 373-88.

1645 McDowell, Tremaine, ed. "Nathaniel Hawthorne," in THE ROMANTIC TRIUMPH; AMERICAN LITERATURE FROM 1830-to 1860. New York: Macmillan, 1933, 1949, II, 294-376.

1646 McDowell, Tremaine. "Nathaniel Hawthorne and the Witches of Colonial Salem," N&Q, 166 (1934), 152.

1647 McElderry, B. R., Jr. "The Transcendental Hawthorne," MQ, 2 (1961), 307-23.

As with the Transcendentalists, an important part of Hawthorne's power comes from "a deep awareness of original virtue."

1647.1 McElroy, John. "The Brand Metaphor in 'Ethan Brand,'" AL, 43 (1972), 633-37.

1648 McElroy, John. IMAGES OF THE SEVENTEENTH-CENTURY PURITAN
IN AMERICAN NOVELS, 1823-1860. Diss. Duke: 1966.

1649 McHaney, Thomas L. "The Textual Editions of Hawthorne and
Melville," SLitI, 2 (1969), 27-41.

The two new textual editions of Hawthorne and Melville
are "monuments of hard work and solid scholarship....
In spite of their detractors, notably Edmund Wilson,
these texts are enormously useful and should be used."

1650 McInerney, Thomas Joseph. "Nathaniel Hawthorne, 1825-1850:
Literary Apprentice, Magazinist, and Experimental
Craftsman," DA, 20 (Wash.: 1959), 3019.

1651 McKiernan, John Thomas. "The Psychology of Nathaniel
Hawthorne," DA, 17 (Penn. St.: 1957), 3019.

1652 McKeithan, D. M. "Hawthorne's 'Young Goodman Brown': An
Interpretation," MLN, 67 (1952), 93-96.

1653 McMurray, William. "Point of View in Howells's THE LANDLORD
AT LION'S HEAD," AL, 34 (1962), 207-14.

The Lion's Head is an allusion to Hawthorne's "The
Great Stone Face."

1654 McNamara, Anne Marie. "The Character of Flame: The
Function of Pearl in THE SCARLET LETTER," AL, 27 (1956),
537-53.

See Sampson, Edward C. "Motivation in THE SCARLET
LETTER," AL, 28 (1957), 511-13, for discussion of
above article.

See also Barbara Garlitz, "Pearl: 1850-1955," PMLA,
72 (1957), 689-99.

1655 McPherson, Hugo A. HAWTHORNE AND THE GREEK MYTHS: A STUDY IN
IMAGINATION. Diss. Toronto: 1956.

1656 McPherson, Hugo A. HAWTHORNE AS MYTH-MAKER: A STUDY IN
IMAGINATION. (U. of Toronto Dept. of Eng. Studies and
Texts 16.) Toronto: U. of Toronto P., 1969.

1657 McPherson, Hugo A. "Hawthorne's Major Source for His
Mythological Tales," AL, 30 (1958), 364-65.

1658 McPherson, Hugo A. "Hawthorne's Mythology: A Mirror for
Puritans," UTQ, 28 (1959), 267-78.

1659 Mehta, R. N. "' Mr. Higginbotham's Catastrophe': An Unusual Hawthorne Story." INDIAN ESSAYS IN AMERICAN LITERATURE: PAPERS IN HONOUR OF ROBERT E. SPILLER. Sujit Mukherjee, and D. V. K. Raghavacharyulu, eds. /William Mulder, "Foreword," iii-viii; Sujit Mukherjee and D. V. K. Raghavacharyulu, "Robert E. Spiller: A Personal Note," ix-xii; "Spiller: 70 /incl. "Select List of Dr. Spiller's Writings in Chronological Order'/" xiii-xvi./ 1969, 113-19.

1660 Meigs, Cornelia, and Anne Eaton, Elizabeth Nesbitt, and Ruth Hill Viguers. A CRITICAL HISTORY OF CHILDREN'S LITERATURE. New York: The Macmillan Co., 1953.

1660.1 Meixsell, Anne B. "Symbolism in THE MARBLE FAUN," DAI, 30 (Penn State: 1969), 1174A.

1661 Melchiori, Barbara. "Scenografie di Hawthorne e il dilemma dell' artista," SA, No. 2 (1956), 67-81.

1662 Melchiori, Giorgio. "The English Novelist and the American Tradition (1955)," Tr. B. M. Arnett, SR, 68 (1960), 502-15. Repr. from SA, No. 1 (1955),

Influence of Hawthorne and James on L. P. Hartley's view of sin.

1663 Melchiori, Giorgio. "Locksley Hall Revisited: Tennyson and Henry James," REL, 6 (1965), 9-25.

1664 Melchiori, Giorgio. "Tradizione americana e romanzo inglese," SA, 1 (1955), 55-71.

1665 /Melville, Herman/ "Hawthorne and His Mosses," LITERARY WORLD, 1850. Variously reprinted: THE PORTABLE MELVILLE. Jay Leyda, ed. New York: Viking Press, 1952, 1967.

1666 Mencken, H. L. "The American Novel," LITERARY OPINION IN AMERICA. Morton Dauwen Zabel, ed. New York: Harper, 1937, 1951. Repr. from PREJUDICES; Fourth Series. Alfred A. Knopf, 1924, p. 158.

Hawthorne and Cooper, though occupied with American themes, showed "no evidence of an American point of view."

1667 Mencken, H. L. PREJUDICES: SECOND SERIES. New York: Alfred A. Knopf, 1920.

Plays down importance of Hawthorne.

1668 Mengeling, Marvin E. "Moby-Dick: The Fundamental Principles," ESQ, 38 (1965), Part 2, 74-87.

1669 Merideth, Robert. "The Critic, the Editor, and the Organization Scholar," MRR, 1 (1964-65), 74-77.

1670 Merrill, A. Marion, ed. THE HOUSE OF THE SEVEN GABLES WITH
A LIFE OF HAWTHORNE, NOTES AND OTHER AIDS TO STUDY.
Boston: Allyn, 1964.

1671 Merrill, A. Marion. "Introduction," THE HOUSE OF THE SEVEN
GABLES. Boston: 1923, p. xix.

1672 Merrill, Louis Taylor. "The Puritan Policeman," ASocR, 10
(1945), 766-76.

1673 Merrill, Walter M. "Introduction," Special Hawthorne
Issue, EIHC, 94 (1958), 169.

1674 Metcalf, Eleanor Melville. HERMAN MELVILLE, CYCLE AND
EPICYCLE. Cambridge: Harvard U. P., 1953.

1675 Metzger, Charles R. "*Effictio* and *Notatio*: Hawthorne's
Technique of Characterization," WHR, 14 (1960), 224-26.

Hawthorne never abandoned these two devices.

1676 Metzdorf, Robert F. "Hawthorne's Suit Against Ripley and
Dana," AL, 12 (1940), 235-41

Shows Hawthorne business-like in collecting money
due him.

1677 Michaud, Régis. "How Hawthorne Exorcised Hester Prynne,"
THE AMERICAN NOVEL TODAY. Boston: Little Brown & Co.,
1928, p. 32.

Hawthorne is Freudian in many respects but mostly in
THE SCARLET LETTER.

1678 Michel, Pierre. "Hawthorne Rehabilitated," ES, 45 (1964), 44-48.

1679 Miller, Harold P. HAWTHORNE AS A SATIRIST. Diss. Yale:
1936.

1680 Miller, Harold P. "Hawthorne Surveys His Contemporaries,"
AL, 12 (1940), 228-35.

1681 Miller, James E., Jr. "Hawthorne and Melville: No! in Thunder,"
QUESTS SURD AND ABSURD: ESSAYS IN AMERICAN LITERATURE.
Chicago: Chicago U. P., 1967, pp. 186-208.

Rev. by Richard P. Adams, AL, 40 (1969), 581-82.

1682   Miller, James E., Jr. "Hawthorne and Melville: The
Unpardonable Sin," PMLA, 70 (1955), 91-114.
Repr. in QUESTS SURD AND ABSURD: ESSAYS IN AMERICAN
LITERATURE. Chicago: Chicago U. P., 1967, pp. 209-38.

Sees a pattern in treatment of the unpardonable sin
which has significance not only for study of Hawthorne's
fiction, but for study of writers influenced by
Hawthorne. The theme of isolation, important in
fiction of a later day, may be illuminated by a study
of Hawthorne's pattern.

See Henry G. Fairbanks, "Sin, Free Will, and 'Pessimism'
in Hawthorne," PMLA, 71 (1956), 975-89; and Joseph T.
McCullen and John C. Guilds, "The Unpardonable Sin in
Hawthorne: A Re-Examination," NCF, 15 (1960), 221-37.

1683 Miller, James E., Jr. "Uncharted Interiors: The American
Romantics Revisited," ESQ, 35 (1964), 34-39.
Repr. in QUESTS SURD AND ABSURD: ESSAYS IN AMERICAN
LITERATURE. Chicago: Chicago U. P., 1967, pp. 249-59.

The meeting ground of Emerson, Thoreau, and Whitman
is in their transcendental mysticism--spirit; the
meeting ground of Poe, Hawthorne, and Melville in
their psychological drama--mind.

1684   Miller, Louise. "THE HOUSE OF THE SEVEN GABLES as Literature
for Secondary Schools," SchRv, 17 (1909), 495-97.

1685   Miller, Paul W. "Hawthorne's 'Young Goodman Brown':
Cynicism or Meliorism?" NCF, 14 (1959), 255-64.

Hawthorne urges that Puritan rigorism in society be
sloughed off and replaced by a striving for virtue
starting from confession of common human weakness.

1686   Miller, Perry. "Introduction," in THE GOLDEN AGE OF AMERICAN
LITERATURE. An Anthology selected and with notes by
Perry Miller, ed. New York: George Braziller, Inc.,
1959, pp. 1-28.

The "compulsive theme" throughout Hawthorne's writing
is human isolation. His work pervaded by this agony
of alienation from common nature.

1687   Miller, Perry. THE NEW ENGLAND MIND FROM COLONY TO PROVINCE.
Cambridge, Mass.: Harvard U. P., 1953, p. 404.

The Puritan mind was given to Bunyanesque allegory,
as Hawthorne demonstrates.

1688   Miller, Perry. THE RAVEN AND THE WHALE: THE WAR OF WORDS AND
WITS IN THE ERA OF POE AND MELVILLE. New York: Harcourt,
Brace, 1956, passim.

1689 Miller, Perry, ed. THE TRANSCENDENTALISTS: AN ANTHOLOGY.
Cambridge, Mass.: Harvard U.P., 1950, pp. 475-82.

See as to Hawthorne and transcendentalism.

1690 Miller, Raymond A., Jr. "Representative Tragic Heroines in
the work of Brown, Hawthorne, Howells, James and Dreiser,"
DA, 17 (Wis.: 1957), 2612-13.

1691 Miller, William B. "A New Review of the Career of Paul
Akers, 1825-1861," ColLQ, 7 (1966), 227-56.

Deals with sculptures in THE MARBLE FAUN.

1692 Mills, Barriss. "Hawthorne and Puritanism," NEQ, 21 (1948),
78-102.

Hawthorne discarded the whole Puritan exegesis as too
coldly intellectual, but he was not a sceptic nor a
transcendentalist. Even his belief in universal
depravity was colored by an un-Puritan sympathy for
the sinner.

1693 Milne, Gordon. GEORGE WILLIAM CURTIS AND THE GENTEEL
TRADITION. Bloomington: Indiana U. P., 1956.

Friendship and correspondence between two Brook
farmers and Concord citizens.

1694 Milton, John R. "The American Novel: The Search for Home,
Tradition, and Identity," WHR, 16 (1962), 169-80.

The house in America is a temporary status symbol,
characterizing the spiritual quest of the American
for a new home. A parallel theme concerns the loss or
destruction of innocence.

1695 Minter, David L. THE INTERPRETED DESIGN AS STRUCTURAL
PRINCIPLE IN AMERICAN PROSE. London and New Haven:
Yale U. P., 1969, pp. 137-60.

Rev. by Nina Baym, JEGP, 69 (1970), 323-25.

1696 Mitchell, Donald Grant. Letter from - on occasion of
Hawthorne centenary. EIHC, 41 (1905), 70.

1697 Mitchener, Hope. "'The Great Stone Face': A Study of
Hawthorne's Most Famous Tale," GrT, 55 (1937), 78, 90.

1698 Mizener, Arthur. "Nathaniel Hawthorne: THE SCARLET LETTER,"
in TWELVE GREAT AMERICAN NOVELS. New York: New American
Library, 1967, pp. 9-18.

Rev. by William Braswell, AL, 40 (1968), 423-24.

1699 Möhle, Günter. DAS EUROPABILD MARK TWAIN'S: GRUNDLAGEN UND
BILDUNGSELEMENTE: IRVING, HAWTHORNE, MARK TWAIN. Diss.
Bonn: 1940.

1699.1 Montégut, Emile. "Un Roman Socialiste en Amerique,"
RDM, 16 (December 1, 1852), 809-41.

THE BLITHEDALE ROMANCE

1699.2 Montégut, Emile. "Un Romancier Pessimiste en Amerique.
Nathaniel Hawthorne," RDM, 28 (August 1, 1860),
668-703.

See Reino Virtanen. "Emile Montégut as a Critic of
American Literature," PMLA, 63 (1948), 1265-75.

1700 Monteiro, George. "Additions to the Bibliography of Julian
Hawthorne," BB, 25 (1967), 64.

1701 Monteiro, George. "First Printing for a Hawthorne Letter,"
AL, 36 (1964), 346.

1702 Monteiro, George. "Hawthorne, James, and the Destructive Self,"
TSLL, 4 (1962), 58-71.

Antecedent in THE BLITHEDALE ROMANCE of the hero in
"The Beast of the Jungle."

1702.1 Monteiro, George. "Hawthorne's Letters in Old Catalogues,"
ATQ, 1 (1969), 122.

1703 Monteiro, George. "Hawthorne's 'The Minister's Black Veil,'"
Expl, 22 (1963), Item 9.

1704 Monteiro, George. "Maule's Curse and Julian Hawthorne,"
N&Q, 14 (1967), 62-63.

Curse reflected in THE HOUSE OF THE SEVEN GABLES
has its source in an episode involving Rev. Nicholas
Noyes and Sarah Good.

1705 Monteiro, George. "A Non Literary Source for Hawthorne's
'Egotism; or the Bosom Serpent,'" AL, 41 (1970), 575-77.

1706 Montgomery, Elizabeth Rider. STORY BEHIND GREAT BOOKS.
McBride, 1947, pp. 41-44; 163-68.

1707 Moore, Helen-Jean. THE AMERICAN CRITICISM OF HAWTHORNE,
1938-1948. Diss. Pittsburgh: 1952.

1708 Moore, Jack B. "The First Narrative of the Unpardonable Sin," Discourse, 10 (1967), 274-83; 310-11.

Refers to a short story in THEOLOGICAL MAGAZINE, II (Sept.-Oct., 1796), 17-20, which explores the consequences of the same transgressions committed by Ethan Brand.

1709 Moore, John Brooks, ed. "Nathaniel Hawthorne," SELECTIONS FROM POE'S LITERARY CRITICISM. New York: F. S. Crofts & Co., 1926, 111-25.

1710 Moore, L. Hugh, Jr. "Hawthorne's Ideal Artist as Presumptuous Intellectual," SSF, 2 (1965), 278-83.

1711 Moorman, Charles. "Melville's PIERRE and the Fortunate Fall," AL, 25 (1953), 13-30.

1712 Mor, Antonio. "I Taccuini Di Hawthorne," NA (Roma), 1551 (1951), 304-10.

1713 Mordell, Albert, ed. NOTORIOUS LITERARY ATTACKS. Ed with Introd. by Albert Mordell. New York: Boni & Liveright, 1926, 122-37.

1714 More, Paul Elmer. "Hawthorne: Looking Before and After," Indep, 56 (1904), 1489-94.

Reprinted and excerpted in: SHELBURNE ESSAYS. Vol. II Boston: Houghton Mifflin Co., 1905; SHELBURNE ESSAYS, Second Series. New York: G. P. Putnam's Sons, The Knickerbocker P., 1905; LITERATURE IN AMERICA. Philip Rahv, ed. New York: Meridian, 1957; SHELBURNE ESSAYS ON AMERICAN LITERATURE. Daniel Aaron, ed. New York: Harcourt, 1963.

1715 More, Paul Elmer. "The Origins of Hawthorne and Poe," Indep, 54 (1902), 2453-60.

Reprinted and excerpted in: SHELBURNE ESSAYS, First Series. New York: G. P. Putnam's Sons, 1904, 1906; SHELBURNE ESSAYS ON AMERICAN LITERATURE. Daniel Aaron, ed. New York: Harcourt, 1963.

1716 More, Paul Elmer. "The Solitude of Nathaniel Hawthorne," AtlM, 88 (1901), 588-599.
Reprinted in SHELBURNE ESSAYS, First Series. New York: G. P. Putnam's Sons, 1904.

1717 Morison, Samuel E., ed. "Melville's 'Agatha' Letter to Hawthorne," NEQ, 2 (1929), 296-307.

1718 Morley, George. "Hawthorne's Warwickshire Haunts," LivA, 225 (1900), 379-83.

Also in CentM, n. s., 65 (1900), 408-13; and EclM, 135 (1900), 28.

1719 Morooka, Aiko. "A Man of Solitude: Nathaniel Hawthorne," Kam, 5 (1962), 17-25.

1720 Morris, Lloyd. THE REBELLIOUS PURITAN: PORTRAIT OF MR. HAWTHORNE. London: Constable, Ltd., 1928; New York: 1927.

See Augustine Birrell, "Nathaniel Hawthorne," ET CETERA. London: 1930, pp. 199-222; and Julian Hawthorne, "Hawthorne, Man of Action, SRL, 3 (1927), 727-28.

1721 Morris, Wright. THE TERRITORY AHEAD. New York: Harcourt, Brace & Co., 1958; Atheneum, paperback, 1963.

Introductory and concluding chapters first appeared as a single essay in THE LIVING NOVEL: A SYMPOSIUM, ed. by Granville Hicks, 1957.

Wright Morris discusses our literature in relation to the myth of a "state of Nature." This idealized "Nature," he considers the typical American myth, which "from Hawthorne to Faulkner" has generated what is memorable in our literature.

Rev. by Frederick I. Carpenter, AL, 31 (1959-60), 364-65.

1722 Morrow, Patrick. "A Writer's Workshop: Hawthorne's 'The Great Carbuncle,'" SSF, 6 (1969), 157-64.

1723 Morsberger, Robert E. "'I Prefer Not to': Melville and the Theme of Withdrawal," UCQ, 10 (1965), 24-29.

1724 Morton, Paul. Toronto, Canada, "The Other Mortons," Letter to the Editor, Time, 96 (1970), 4.

See Melvin Maddocks. "Rituals--The Revolt against the Fixed Smile," Time, 96 (1970), 42-43.

1725 Moses, W. R. "A Further Note on 'The Custom House,'" CE, 23 (1962), 396.

Cf., Sam S. Baskett, CE, 22 (1961), 231-28; CE, 23 (1961), 62; and Allen Austin, CE, 23 (1961), 61.

1726 Moss, Sidney P. "'Cock-A-Doodle-Doo!' and Some Legends in Melville Scholarship," AL, 40 (1968), 192-210.

Melville less akin to ultimate defeatism of Hawthorne than to the self-reliance of the Transcendentalists.

1727 Moss, Sidney P. "The Mountain God of Hawthorne's 'The Ambitious Guest,'" ESQ, 47 (1967), 74-75.

1728 Moss, Sidney P. POE'S LITERARY BATTLES: THE CRITIC IN THE CONTEXT OF HIS LITERARY MILIEU. Durham, N. C.: Duke U. P., 1963.

1729 Moss, Sidney P. "The Problem of Theme in THE MARBLE FAUN," NCF, 18 (1964), 393-99.

1730 Moss, Sidney P. "A Reading of 'Rappaccini's Daughter,'" SSF, 2 (1965), 145-56.

1731 Moss, Sidney P. "The Symbolism of the Italian Background in THE MARBLE FAUN." NCF, 23 (1968), 332-36.

1732 Motoda, Shuichi. "The Witches' Sabbath in 'Young Goodman Brown,'" SELL, 42 (1966), 73-86.

1733 Mott, Frank Luther. A HISTORY OF AMERICAN MAGAZINES, 1865-1885. Cambridge, Mass.: Belknap P. of Harvard U. P., 1957, pp. 224, 225.

1734 Mowat, Robert B. "Americans and English in the Eighteen-Fifties," AMERICANS IN ENGLAND. New York: Houghton, Riverside P., 1935, pp. 155-85.

1735 Moyer, Patricia. "Time and the Artist in Kafka and Hawthorne," MFS, 4 (1958-59), 295-306.

1736 Mugridge, Donald H., and Blanche P. McCrum. A GUIDE TO THE STUDY OF THE UNITED STATES OF AMERICA: REPRESENTATIVE BOOKS REFLECTING THE DEVELOPMENT OF AMERICAN LIFE AND THOUGHT. Washington: Library of Congress, 1960, pp. 37-29.

1737 Mulder, Arnold. "An Immoral Moral," Freeman, 5 (1922), 517-18.

1737.1 Mulqueen, James E. "Conservatism and Criticism: The Literary Standards of the American Whigs, 1845-1852," AL, 41 (1969), 355-72.

Study of relationship between political and literary principles of American Whigs. Among others, discusses Whig reaction to novels of Hawthorne.

1738 Mumford, Lewis. THE GOLDEN DAY: A STUDY IN AMERICAN EXPERIENCE AND CULTURE. New York: Boni & Liveright, 1926, passim.

Hawthorne, an afterglow of the Seventeenth Century. With him came the twilight of Puritanism as a spiritual force.

1739 Mumford, Lewis. HERMAN MELVILLE. New York: Literary Guild of America, 1929, pp. 145-147.

Repeats legend that in Ethan Brand Hawthorne drew a portrait of Herman Melville.

In this connection, see E. K. Brown, "Hawthorne, Melville, and 'Ethan Brand,'" AL, 3 (1932-33), 72-75.

1740 Mumford, Lewis. "The Writing of Moby-Dick: Hawthorne's Influence on Herman Melville," AmM, 15 (1928), 482-90.

1741 Munger, Theodore T. "The Centenary of Hawthorne," Century, 68 (1904), 482-83.

1742 Munger, Theodore T. "Notes on THE SCARLET LETTER," AtlM, 93 (1904), 521-35.
Repr. in ESSAYS FOR THE DAY. New York: Houghton Mifflin, 1904, pp. 104-53.

1743 Murakami, Fujio. "Hawthorne and Transcendentalism," StH, 13 (1962), 105-25.

1744 Murphy, John J. "The Function of Sin in Hawthorne's Novels," ESQ, 50 (1968), 65-71.

1745 Murphy, Morris. "Wordsworthian Concepts in 'The Great Stone Face,'" CE, 23 (1962), 364-65.

1746 Murray, Peter B. "Myth in THE BLITHEDALE ROMANCE," in MYTH AND LITERATURE: CONTEMPORARY THEORY AND PRACTICE. John B. Vickery, ed. Lincoln: Nebr. U.P., 1966, pp. 213-20.

1747 Murray, Peter B. "Mythopoesis in THE BLITHEDALE ROMANCE," PMLA, 75 (1960), 591-96.

1748 Musser, Paul H. JAMES NELSON BARKER, 1784-1858. With a Reprint of His Comedy, TEARS AND SMILES. Philadelphia: 1929, p. 95.

See G. Harrison Orians, "The Angel of Hadley in Fiction: A Study of the Sources of Hawthorne's 'The Gray Champion'," AL, 4 (1932), 257-69. Says Musser thought Barker's SUPERSTITION was source of the tale, but notes that Hawthorne used the regicide story in 1833 as subject of "The Gray Champion."

1749 Myers, Gustavus. "Hawthorne and the Myths about Puritans," AmSp, 2 (1934), 1.

1750 Nakata, Yuji. "THE HOUSE OF THE SEVEN GABLES: A Study in
Isolation with an Emphasis on Name Symbolism,"
KAL, 11 (1968), 11-31.

1751 Natale, Eleonora Taglioni. "Solitudine di Hawthorne,"
NA, 491 (1964), 373-85.

1752 "Nathaniel Hawthorne," PICTURE BOOK OF AMERICAN AUTHORS.
Visual History Series. New York: Sterling Pub. Co., Inc.,
1962, pp. 23-25.

1753 "Nathaniel Hawthorne (1804-1864)," THE DEMOCRATIC IMAGINATION:
A GUIDE TO AN EXHIBITION OF RARE BOOKS BY RALPH WALDO
EMERSON, HENRY DAVID THOREAU, NATHANIEL HAWTHORNE, WALT
WHITMAN, HERMAN MELVILLE. Bethlehem, Pa.: Rare Book
Room, Lehigh Univ. Library, October 1, 1968.

1754 Nayyar, Sewak. "Sin and Redemption in THE SCARLET LETTER,"
VARIATIONS ON AMERICAN LITERATURE. Darshan Singh
Maini, ed. New Delhi: U. S. Educ. Foundation in
India, 1968, pp. 53-57.

1755 Neff, Merlin L. SYMBOLISM AND ALLEGORY IN THE WRITING OF
NATHANIEL HAWTHORNE. Diss. Washington (Seattle:
1939).

1756 Nelson, Truman. "The Matrix of Place," EIHC, 95 (1959),
176-85.

Hawthorne's alienation from Salem.

1757 Nevins, Winfield S. "Nathaniel Hawthorne's Removal from
the Salem Custom House," EIHC, 53 (1917), 97-132.

1758 Nevius, Blake R. "The Hawthorne Centenary," NCF, Hawthorne
Centenary Issue, 19 (1964), 103-04.

1759 Newcomer, Alphonso G. "Nathaniel Hawthorne," AMERICAN
LITERATURE. Chicago: Scott, Foresman & Co., 1904,
129-46.

1760 Newlin, Paul A. "The Uncanny in the Supernatural Short
Fiction of Poe, Hawthorne and James," DA (U. C. L. A.:
1968), 5064A-65A.

1761 Newman, Franklin B. "'My Kinsman, Major Molineux': An
Interpretation," UKCR, 21 (1955), 203-12.

Emphasis on Hawthorne's "hypnagogic" technique which
seems to agree with Freud's views of dream formulation.

1762 Nichols, Lewis. "Hawthorne," NYTBR (April 30, 1961), p. 8.

1763 Nichols, Roy Franklin. FRANKLIN PIERCE: YOUNG HICKORY OF THE GRANITE HILLS. Philadelphia: Pa. U. P., 1931.

Biographical references to Hawthorne.

1764 Niess, Robert J. "Hawthorne and Zola—An Influence?" RLC, 27 (1953), 446-52.

Influence of THE SCARLET LETTER on THÉRÈSE RAQUIN.

1765 Niikura, Ryuichi. "On THE MARBLE FAUN," EiK, 13 (1963), 91-103.

1765.1 Nilon, Charles H. "Nathaniel Hawthorne," BIBLIOGRAPHY OF BIBLIOGRAPHIES OF AMERICAN LITERATURE. New York and London: R. R. Bowker Company, 1970, pp. 92-95.

1765.2 Nirenberg, Morton. "Hawthorne's Reception in Germany," JA, 15 (1970), 141-61.

1766 Noble, David W. "Jeremiahs: James Fenimore Cooper, Nathaniel Hawthorne, Herman Melville," in THE ETERNAL ADAM AND THE NEW WORLD GARDEN: THE CENTRAL MYTH IN THE AMERICAN NOVEL SINCE 1830. New York: Braziller, 1968.

Hawthorne asked his readers to discover that they were accommodating their lives to a transcendent script written by European theoreticians who hated the historical experience of mankind.

Rev. by Walter E. Bezanson, AL, 41 (1969), 120-21.

1767 Nolte, William H. "Hawthorne's Dimmesdale: A Small Man Gone Wrong," NEQ, 38 (1965), 168-86.

1768 Norlin, George. THE QUEST OF AMERICAN LIFE: THE UNIVERSITY OF COLORADO STUDIES, Series B, Vol. 2, No. 3. Boulder, Colorado: 1945.

Refers to the intellectual awakening in the East that produced Emerson, Hawthorne, and others.

Rev. by Floyd Stovall, AL, 17 (1946), 52-53.

1769 Normand, Jean. "L'univers interdit de Nathaniel Hawthorne," InfD, 204 (1964), 38-45.

1770 Normand, Jean. NATHANIEL HAWTHORNE: ESQUISSE D'UNE ANALYSE
DE LA CREATION ARTISTIQUE. Paris: Presses Universi-
taires de France, 1964. Repr., NATHANIEL HAWTHORNE:
AN APPROACH TO AN ANALYSIS OF ARTISTIC CREATION. Trans.
by Derek Coltman. Foreword by Henri Peyre. Cleveland,
Ohio: Case Western U. P., 1969.

Rev. by Henri Peyre, Criticism, 8 (1966), 203-08.

1771 Normand, Jean. "Thoreau et Hawthorne à Concord: Les
Ironies de la Solitude," Europe, 45 (1967), 162-69.

1772 Oberndorff, C. P. "The Psychoanalytic Insight of Nathaniel
Hawthorne," PsyR, 29 (1942), 373-85.

1773 O'Brien, Edward J. "Hawthorne and Melville," THE ADVANCE
OF THE AMERICAN SHORT STORY. New York: Dodd, Mead &
Co., 1923, pp. 42-65.

1774 O'Brien, Edward. SHORT STORY CASE BOOK. New York: Farrar,
Rinehart, 1935.

1775 O'Connor, E. M. J. AN ANALYTICAL INDEX TO THE WORKS OF NATHANIEL
HAWTHORNE WITH A SKETCH OF HIS LIFE. Boston: Houghton,
Mifflin, 1882. Reprinted with Introduction by C. E. Frazer
Clark, Jr. Detroit: Gale, 1967.

1776 O'Connor, Flannery. "Mary Ann, The Story of a Little Girl,"
Jubilee, 9 (1961), 28-35.

1777 O'Connor, William Van. "Conscious Naivete in THE BLITHEDALE
ROMANCE," RLV, 20 (1954), 37-45.

1778 O'Connor, William Van. THE GROTESQUE: AN AMERICAN GENRE, AND
OTHER ESSAYS. Preface by Harry T. Moore. Carbondale:
So. Ill. U. P., 1916, 1956, 1962.

Includes three chapters: "Hawthorne and Faulkner:
Some Common Ground," pp. 59-77, repr. in VQR, 33 (1957),
105-23; "The Hawthorne Museum: Dialogue," pp. 193-231;
"The Narrator as Distorting Mirror," pp. 78-91.

1779 O'Dea, Richard J. "THE FATHERS, A Revaluation," TCL, 12
(1966), 87-95.

Like Hawthorne, Tate's novel depicts man as good but
not wholly good; he seeks some protection against evil,
but is never completely successful.

1780 O'Donnell, Charles R. "Hawthorne and Dimmesdale: The Search for the Realm of Quiet," NCF, 14 (1960), 317-332.

"Civilization-wilderness dichotomy" represents pull of opposite areas of experience on the fictional artist. THE SCARLET LETTER makes a clear distinction between the market place and the forest.

1781 O'Donnell, Charles R. "The Mind of the Artist: Cooper, Thoreau, Hawthorne, Melville," DA, 17 (1957), 1752.

1782 Ogden, Merlene Ann. "Nathaniel Hawthorne and John Bunyan," DA, 25 (Neb.: 1964), 2964-65.

1782.1 Okamoto, Katsumi. "Hawthorne--Hatashi naki Kikyu," EigoS, 114 (1968), 801-02.

1783 Okamoto, Katsumi. "THE SCARLET LETTER: Struggle Toward Integrity," SELit, 46 (1969), 45-61.

1784 Oldham, Ellen M, ed. "Mrs. Hawthorne to Mrs. Fields," BPLQ, 9 (1957), 143-54.

Letters.

1785 Olenjeva, B. "Amerikans' ka novela epoxy romantyzmu," RLs, 11 (1967), 45-55.

American short story during the Romantic period.

1786 Olfson, Lewy. "THE HOUSE OF THE SEVEN GABLES BY NATHANIEL HAWTHORNE Adapted for Radio," Plays, 14 (1955), 87-96.

1787 Olsen, Frederick Bruce. "Hawthorne's Integration of Methods and Materials," DA, 21 (Ind.: 1961), 3458.

1788 O'Neill, Edward H. BIOGRAPHY BY AMERICANS, 1658-1936. Philadelphia: Pa. U. P., 1939.

A list of biographies written by Americans up to 1936. It may be noted that there were sixteen biographies of Hawthorne.

1789 Oomoto, Goshi. "Solitude and Society in Hawthorne's Twice-Told Tales," RikR, 22 (1961), 37-54.

1790 Orel, Harold. "The Double Symbol," AL, 23 (1951), 1-6.

Hawthorne's fascination with the framework of a crime story matures into THE MARBLE FAUN.

1791   Orians, G. Harrison. "The Angel of Hadley in Fiction: A
        Study of the Sources of Hawthorne's 'The Gray Champion,'"
        AL, 4 (1932), 257-69.

        Cf., Paul H. Musser. JAMES NELSON BARKER, 1784-1858.
        With Reprint of His Comedy, TEARS AND SMILES. Philadelphia:
        1929.

1792   Orians, G. Harrison. "Hawthorne and 'The Maypole of Merry
        Mount,'" MLN, 53 (1938), 159-67.

        Sources of the story with reference to Hawthorne's
        feeling for history.

1793   Orians, G. Harrison. "Hawthorne and Puritan Punishments,"
        CE, 13 (1952), 424-32.

        Historical data on punishments used by Hawthorne in
        his fiction.

1794   Orians, G. Harrison. "New England Witchcraft in Fiction,"
        AL, 2 (1930), 54-71.

        On sources for "Young Goodman Brown."

1795   Orians, G. Harrison. "The Rise of Romanticism, 1805-1855,"
        in TRANSITIONS IN AMERICAN LITERARY CRITICISM. Harry
        Hayden Clark, ed. Durham, N. C.: Duke U. P., 1953,
        pp. 207-08.

1796   Orians, G. Harrison. "Scott and Hawthorne's FANSHAWE,"
        NEQ, 11 (1938), 388-95.

        See Fred Lewis Pattee, "Nathaniel Hawthorne," THE
        DEVELOPMENT OF THE AMERICAN SHORT STORY. New York:
        Harper, 1923, pp. 91-115.

1797   Orians, G. Harrison. "The Source of Hawthorne's 'Roger
        Malvin's Burial,'" AL, 10 (1938), 313-18.

1798   Orians, G. Harrison. "The Sources and Themes of Hawthorne's
        'The Gentle Boy,'" NEQ, 14 (1941), 664-78.

1799   Osborne, John Ball. "Nathaniel Hawthorne as American Consul,"
        Bookman, 16 (1903), 461-64.

        Two volumes of Hawthorne's official correspondence in
        the State Department show Hawthorne to have been a
        conscientious and efficient consul.

1800   Ota, Saburo. "Hawthorne's Conception of Literature,"
        Gak, 275 (1962), 57-64.

1801 Oursler, Fulton. WHY I KNOW THERE IS A GOD. New York: Doubleday, 1950, pp. 85-99.

Concerning Rose Lathrop, daughter of Nathaniel Hawthorne, (Mother Mary Alphonsa).

1802 Overton, Grant. "Hawthorne; Melville," AN HOUR OF THE AMERICAN NOVEL. Philadelphia: 1929.

1803 Page, H. A. [Alexander Hay Japp] MEMOIR OF NATHANIEL HAWTHORNE WITH STORIES NOW FIRST PUBLISHED IN THIS COUNTRY. London: Henry S. King & Co., 1872.

The Duston Family (Collected in COMPLETE WRITINGS, Vol. 17);
April Fools (Uncollected);
A Prize from the Sea (a version of The Sunken Treasure);
Grandfather's Chair, 1841, in THIRTEEN AUTHOR COLLECTIONS OF THE NINETEENTH CENTURY, Vol. 1, Wilson. (Error in identifying "A Prize from the Sea" with "Sir William Phips.")

1804 Paltsits, Victor Hugo. LIST OF BOOKS, ETC., BY AND RELATING TO NATHANIEL HAWTHORNE PREPARED AS AN EXHIBITION [at the Lennox Library, New York, July-August, 1904] to Commemorate the Centenary of His Birth. BNYPL, 8 (1904), 312-22.

1805 Pancoast, Henry S. "Nathaniel Hawthorne (1804-1864)," AN INTRODUCTION TO AMERICAN LITERATURE. New York: Henry Holt & Co., 1898, 1900, 190-99.

1806 Pannwitt, Barbara, ed. THE ART OF SHORT FICTION. Boston: Ginn, 1964.

1807 Parcher, Adrian. "Hawthorne's THE SCARLET LETTER," Expl, 21 (1963), Item 48.

Since the bewitched Pearl is humanized only after Dimmesdale's confession, the evil genius which has possessed her must be regarded as the minister's secret guilt rather than simply the sin of adultery.

1808 Paris, Bernard J. "Optimism and Pessimism in THE MARBLE FAUN," BUSE, 2 (1956), 95-112.

1809 Parkes, Henry Bamford. THE AMERICAN EXPERIENCE, AN INTERPRETATION OF THE HISTORY AND CIVILIZATION OF THE AMERICAN PEOPLE. New York: Alfred A. Knopf, 1947, 1949, pp. 198-200, passim.

The image of the judge condemning the witch appears explicitly or by implication in each Hawthorne novel, each a different rendering of the same central theme. Because of the symbolic meaning of this theme, the novels are a significant commentary on American character in its Puritan manifestations.

1810 Parkes, Henry Bamford. "Freedom and Order in Western
         Literature," DenQ, 4 (1969), 1-18.

1811 Parkes, Henry Bamford. "Poe, Hawthorne, Melville: An
         Essay in Sociological Criticism," PR, 16 (1949), 157-65.

         These authors commonly dealt with characters who
         show isolation and sexual immaturity.

1812 Parks, Edd W. ANTE-BELLUM SOUTHERN CRITICS. Athens, G.:
         Ga. U. P., 1962.

1813 Parks, Edd W., et al. "Problems of the Complete or Collected
         Edition," MissQ, 15 (1962), 95-125.

1814 Parrington, Vernon L. "Foufouville, Excelsior and Blithedale,"
         AMERICAN DREAMS: A STUDY OF AMERICAN UTOPIAS. Providence,
         Rhode Island: Brown University Studies, American Series,
         1947, pp. 35-42. 2nd ed. enlarged with a Postscript.
         New York: Russell & Russell, Inc., 1964, pp. 37-40.

1815 Parrington, Vernon L. MAIN CURRENTS IN AMERICAN THOUGHT,
         3 Vols. New York: 1927-30; 1954; Vol. 3, only, 1963.

         Survey of political and social philosophy of American
         authors from colonial times to about 1880. Last
         volume unfinished. (This work often mistaken for
         a history of American literature.)

1816 Parrington, Vernon L. "Nathaniel Hawthorne, Skeptic,"
         ROMANTIC REVOLUTION IN AMERICA, 1800-1860: MAIN
         CURRENTS IN AMERICAN THOUGHT. New York: Harcourt,
         Brace & Co., 1927, 1954, II, 434-42.

         There was much of the skeptic in Hawthorne although
         he retained much of the "older Calvinist view of
         life and human destiny."

1817 Passerini, Edward M. "Hawthornesque Dickens," DiS, 2 (1966),
         18-25.

1818 Pattee, Fred Lewis. "A Call for a Literary Historian," in
         THE REINTERPRETATION OF AMERICAN LITERATURE. Norman
         Foerster, ed. New York: Harcourt, Brace & Co., 1928;
         reissued, 1955, 1959.

         Repr. from AmM, June, 1924.

1819 Pattee, Fred Lewis. "Hawthorne," in THE FIRST CENTURY OF
         AMERICAN LITERATURE, 1770-1870. New York: D. Appleton-
         Century, 1935, pp. 537-51.

         Rev. by Ernest E. Leisy, AL, 7 (1935-56), 481-83.

1820 Pattee, Fred Lewis. A HISTORY OF AMERICAN LITERATURE SINCE 1870. New York: The Century Co., 1915.

1821 Pattee, Fred Lewis. "Nathaniel Hawthorne," THE DEVELOPMENT OF THE AMERICAN SHORT STORY. New York: Harper & Bros., 1923, pp. 91-115.

Asserts that the NATIONAL REVIEW of 1861 was the first to note that all of Hawthorne's tales "embody single ideal situations." If true, then Hawthorne, rather than Poe, stands as father of the short story.

See G. Harrison Orians, "Scott and Hawthorne's FANSHAWE," NEQ, 11 (1938), 388-94, for discussion of above reference.

1822 Pattison, Joseph C. "'The Celestial Railroad' as Dream-Tale," AQ, 20 (1968), 224-36.

1823 Pattison, Joseph C. "The Guilt of the Innocent Donatello," ESQ, 31 (1963), 66-68.

Because Donatello is half-animal, half-human, many consider him innocent of pushing Brother Antonio off the Tarpeian Rock. A close reading indicates he is a responsible being, capable of hating with intelligence.

1824 Pattison, Joseph C. "Point of View in Hawthorne," PMLA, 82 (1967), 363-69.

Only the logic of the dream can explain certain happenings in the stories.

1825 Paul, Louis. "A Psychoanalytic Reading of Hawthorne's 'Major Molineux': The Father Manqué and the Protégé Manqué," AI, 18 (1961), 279-88.

1826 Paul, Sherman. "Hawthorne's Debt to Ahab," N&Q, 196 (1951), 255-57.

Ethan Brand and Ahab.

1827 Paulits, Walter J. "Ambivalence in 'Young Goodman Brown,'" AL, 41 (1970), 577-84.

Ambivalence, not ambiguity, key to interpretation.

1828 Pavese, Cesare. LA LETTERATURA AMERICANA E ALTRI SAGGI. Turin: Einaudi, 1962.

1828.1 [Peabody, Elizabeth P.] "The Genius of Hawthorne," AtlM, 22 (1868), 359-74. Repr. in HAWTHORNE AMONG HIS CONTEMPORARIES. Kenneth Walter Cameron, ed. Hartford: Transcendental Books, 1968, 99-108.

1828.2 Peabody, Elizabeth P.   "The Two Hawthornes," Western, n. s.,
        1 (1875), 352-59.

1829 Pearce, Roy Harvey.   "Hawthorne and the Sense of the Past,
        or the Immortality of Major Molineux," ELH, 21 (1954),
        327-49. Repr. in Roy Harvey Pearce's HISTORICISM ONCE
        MORE. Princeton, N. J.: 1969, pp. 137-74.

1830 Pearce, Roy Harvey.   "Hawthorne and the Twilight of Romance,"
        YR, n. s., 37 (1948), 487-506.
        Repr. in HISTORICISM ONCE MORE: PROBLEMS AND OCCASIONS
        FOR THE AMERICAN SCHOLAR. Princeton U. P., 1969,
        pp. 175-99.

1831 Pearce, Roy Harvey, ed. HAWTHORNE CENTENARY ESSAYS.
        Columbus: Ohio St. U. P., 1964.

        Revs. by Richard P. Adams, JEGP, 64 (1965), 600-02;
        Maurice Charney, NEQ, 38 (1965), 106-08;
        James M. Cox, AL, 37 (1965), 80-82;
        Irving Howe, AL, 37 (1965), 80-81;
        Henry Pochmann, SAQ, 64 (1965), 419-20;
        TLS, November 19, 1964, 1041;
        Arlin Turner, SoR, 1 (1965), 961-67;
        Philip Young, "Hawthorne and 100 Years," KR, 27 (1965),
            215-32.

1832 Pearce, Roy Harvey. "Historicism Once More," KR, (1958),
        554-91.

        Repr. in Roy Harvey Pearce's HISTORICISM ONCE MORE:
        PROBLEMS AND OCCASIONS FOR THE AMERICAN SCHOLAR.
        Princeton, N. J.: Princeton U. P., 1969, pp. 3-45.

1833 Pearce, Roy Harvey. "Introduction," THE HOUSE OF THE
        SEVEN GABLES. New York: Dent, 1954.

1834 Pearce, Roy Harvey. "Introduction," THE SCARLET LETTER.
        New York: J. M. Dent & Sons, Everyman's Lib., 1957.

1835 Pearce, Roy Harvey. "Introduction to THE BLITHEDALE ROMANCE,"
        in THE CENTENARY EDITION OF THE WORKS OF NATHANIEL
        HAWTHORNE. VOL. III. THE BLITHEDALE ROMANCE AND FANSHAWE.
        William Charvat, et al, eds. Columbus: Ohio St. U. P.,
        1964, pp. xvii-xvi.

1836 Pearce, Roy Harvey. "Introduction to FANSHAWE," in THE
        CENTENARY WORKS OF NATHANIEL HAWTHORNE. VOL. III. THE
        BLITHEDALE ROMANCE AND FANSHAWE. William Charvat, et
        al, eds. Columbus: Ohio St. U. P., 1964, pp. 301-16.

1836.1
Pearce, Roy Harvey. "Introduction," TRUE STORIES FROM HISTORY AND BIOGRAPHY. Vol. VI. CENTENARY EDITION OF THE WORKS OF NATHANIEL HAWTHORNE. Columbus, Ohio: Ohio St. U. P., 1971.

1837
Pearce, Roy Harvey. "Introduction," TWICE TOLD TALES. London: Dent & Co., (Everyman's Lib.) (Reissue), 1955.

1838
Pearce, Roy Harvey. "Robin Molineux on the Analyst's Couch: A Note on the Limits of Psychoanalytic Criticism," Criticism, 1 (1959), 83-90.

Repr. in Roy Harvey Pearce's HISTORICISM ONCE MORE. Princeton, N. J.: 1969, pp. 96-106.

1839
Pearce, Roy Harvey. "Romance and the Study of History," in HAWTHORNE CENTENARY ESSAYS. Roy Harvey Pearce, ed. Columbus, Ohio: Ohio St. U. P., 1964, pp. 221-44. Repr. in Roy Harvey Pearce's HISTORICISM ONCE MORE. Princeton, N. J.: 1969, pp. 137-74.

1839.1
Pearce, Roy Harvey, and B. Bernard Cohen. HAWTHORNE'S LIBRARY. (In process)

1840
Pearson, Norman Holmes. "The American Writer and the Feeling of Community," ES, 43 (1962), 403-12.

Hawthorne and Faulkner. The common symbol of The Mansion is an affront to society just as the absence of democratic grace is typical. Pride is commonly seen to violate the ideal of brotherhood.

1841
Pearson, Norman Holmes. "Anonymous Editor," SatRL, 24 (1941), 18.

A review-article of Arlin Turner's HAWTHORNE AS EDITOR. Baton Rouge: La. State U. P., 1941.

1842
Pearson, Norman Holmes. "The College Years of Nathaniel Hawthorne," an unpublished monograph which won the Henry H. Strong Prize in American Literature at Yale University in 1932.

1843
Pearson, Norman Holmes. "Elizabeth Peabody on Hawthorne," EIHC, 94 (1958), 256-76.

1844
Pearson, Norman Holmes. "A 'Good Thing' for Hawthorne," EIHC, C, Special Hawthorne Issue (1964), 300-05.

1845
Pearson, Norman Holmes. "Hawthorne and the Mannings," EIHC, 94 (1958), 170-90.

1846 Pearson, Norman Holmes. "Hawthorne's Duel," EIHC, 94 (1958),
          229-42.

1847 Pearson, Norman Holmes. HAWTHORNE'S FRENCH AND ITALIAN
          NOTEBOOKS. Diss. Yale: 1941.

1848 Pearson, Norman Holmes. HAWTHORNE'S TWO ENGAGEMENTS.
          Northampton, Mass.: 1963.

          Sarah Freeman Clark's letter to Ednah Cheney, January 22,
          1894, evidence that Hawthorne was never engaged to
          Elizabeth Peabody.

1849 Pearson, Norman Holmes. Hawthorne's Usable Truth... and
          Other Papers Presented at the Fiftieth Anniversary of
          New York Lambda Chapter, Phi Beta Kappa. Canton,
          New York: 1950.

1850 Pearson, Norman Holmes. "Introduction," THE COMPLETE NOVELS
          AND SELECTED TALES OF NATHANIEL HAWTHORNE. Norman Holmes
          Pearson, ed. New York: Modern Library, 1937.

1851 Pearson, Norman Holmes. "The Pynchons and Judge Pyncheon,"
          EIHC, 100 (1964), 235-55.

1852 Pearson, Norman Holmes. "A Sketch by Hawthorne," NEQ, 6
          (1933), 136-44.

          "A Good man's Miracle," published in THE CHILD'S FRIEND
          (1844), is reprinted with comments.

1853 Pebworth, Ted-Larry. "The Soul's Instinctive Perception:
          Dream, Actuality, and Reality in Four Tales from
          Hawthorne's MOSSES FROM AN OLD MANSE," SCB, 23 (1963),
          18-23.

1854 Peck, Harry Thurston. "Hawthorne and THE SCARLET LETTER,"
          in STUDIES IN SEVERAL LITERATURES. Dodd, 1909, pp. 117-30.

1855 Peck, Richard, ed. NATHANIEL HAWTHORNE: POEMS. Charlottesville,
          Va.: The Bibliographical Society of the University of
          Virginia, 1967.

1856 Peckham, Morse. "Hawthorne and Melville as European Authors,"
          in MELVILLE AND HAWTHORNE IN THE BERKSHIRES: A SYMPOSIUM.
          Howard P. Vincent, ed. Kent, Ohio: Kent St. U. P., 1968,
          pp. 42-62.

1856.1 Peckham, Morse. THE TRIUMPH OF ROMANTICISM. Columbia:
          South Carolina U. P., 1970.

1857 Peckham, Morse. "Toward a Theory of Romanticism," PMLA, 66 (1951), 5-23.

Does not discuss Hawthorne per se, but offers a theory of Romanticism that many critics apply, such as Millicent Bell, Richard Jacobson, and Arthur Schwartz.
Cf., Arthur Schwartz. "The American Romantics: An Analysis," ESQ, 35 (1964), 39-44.

1858 Peden, William. THE AMERICAN SHORT STORY. FRONT LINE IN THE NATIONAL DEFENSE OF LITERATURE. Boston: Houghton Mifflin Co., Cambridge: Riverside P., 1964.

1859 Pederson, Glenn. "Blake's Urizen as Hawthorne's Ethan Brand," NCF, 12 (1958), 304-14.

1860 Pelham, Edgar. "Nathaniel Hawthorne and THE SCARLET LETTER," THE ART OF THE NOVEL FROM 1700 TO THE PRESENT TIME. New York, 1933.

1861 Pérez Gallego, Cándido. "Los prólogos de Nathaniel Hawthorne a sus novelas," RL, 29 (1966), 111-19.

1862 Perkins, George. "Howells and Hawthorne," NCF, 15 (1960), 259-62.

Howells' admiration of THE BLITHEDALE ROMANCE reflects his awareness that the aims of his own realism-theory and Hawthorne's romance-theory were not as disparate as one might think.

1863 Perry, Bliss. THE AMERICAN MIND AND AMERICAN IDEALISM. Introduction by Ada L. F. Snell. Boston: Houghton, Mifflin Co., 1913.

Hawthorne and others, "sound antiquarians," though not in sympathy with Puritan theology, have described the barrenness of the New England meeting house.

1864 Perry, Bliss. THE AMERICAN SPIRIT IN LITERATURE: A CHRONICLE OF GREAT INTERPRETERS. New Haven: Yale U. P., 1918.

Hawthorne, "typically American."

1865 Perry, Bliss. "The Centenary of Hawthorne," Atl, 94 (1904), 195-206.

Later reprinted in PARK STREET PAPERS. Boston: Houghton, Mifflin Co., 1908, pp.63-103.

1866 Perry, Bliss. "Hawthorne at North Adams," [Atl., 1893] in his
THE AMATEUR SPIRIT. Boston and New York: Houghton,
Mifflin Co., 1904, pp. 119-39. Repr. in CONTEMPORARY
ESSAYS. William Thomson Hastings, ed. New York:
Houghton, Mifflin Co., 1928, pp. 287-300.

Background for "Ethan Brand."

1867 Peterich, Werner. "Hawthorne and the GESTA ROMANORUM: The
Genesis of 'Rappaccini's Daughter' and 'Ethan Brand,'"
Galinsky, Hans, and Hans-Joachim Lang, eds. KLEINE
BEITRÄGE ZUR AMERIKANISCHEN LITERATURGESCHITE:
Arbeitsproben aus deutschen Seminaren und Instituten
Heidelberg: Carl Winter, 1961, pp. 11-18.

1868 Peters, Leonard J. HAWTHORNE AND THE FALL OF MAN. Diss.
Tulane: 1953.

1869 Peterson, Annamarie Willenbrock. "Hawthorne's Double Focus
and Its Use in THE BLITHEDALE ROMANCE," DA, 26
(UCLA: 1966), 4637.

1870 Peterson, Joseph N. (Mayor of Salem) "Introductory
Address," (Hawthorne Centenary), EIHC, 41 (1905), 7-8.

1871 Pfeiffer, Karl G. "The Prototype of the Poet in 'The
Great Stone Face,'" RS, 9 (1941), 100-08.

1872 Pfenning, Hazel T. PERIODICAL LITERARY CRITICISM, 1800-1865:
A STUDY OF THE BOOK REVIEWS FROM 1800 TO THE CLOSE OF
THE CIVIL WAR, DEALING WITH THE SUCCESSIVE WORKS OF
IRVING, COOPER, BRYANT, POE, HAWTHORNE, AND THOREAU,
WHICH APPEARED IN AMERICAN PUBLICATIONS WITHIN THE
LIFETIME OF THE INDIVIDUAL AUTHORS. Diss. New York:
1932.

1873 Phelps, William Lyon. AS I LIKE IT, Second Series. New York:
Scribner's Sons, 1924, pp. 16, 58.

1874 Phelps, William Lyon. "Introduction," THE SCARLET LETTER.
New York: Mod. Lib., 1927.

1875 Phelps, William Lyon. "Nathaniel Hawthorne and Puritanism,"
SOME MAKERS OF AMERICAN LITERATURE. Boston: Marshall
Jones, 1923, pp. 97-128.

Also: "Nathaniel Hawthorne and Puritanism,"
LaHJ, 40 (1923), 15. Contains picture "The Scarlet
Letter" painted for the Journal by W. L. Taylor.

1876 Phillips, Robert. "THE SCARLET LETTER: A Selected Checklist
of Criticism (1850-1962)," BB, 23 (1962), 213-16.

1877 Phillips, Robert, Jack Kligerman, Robert E. Long, and
Robert Hastings. "Nathaniel Hawthorne: Criticism of
the Four Major Romances, A Selected Bibliography,"
Thoth, 3 (1962), 39-50.

1878 Phillips, Williams. "Introduction," ART AND PSYCHOANALYSIS.
William Phillips, ed. New York: Criterion Books, 157.

1879 Pickard, Samuel T. HAWTHORNE'S FIRST DIARY. Boston:
1897.

An account of the Diary's discovery and loss.

1880 Pickard, Samuel T. "Is 'Hawthorne's First Diary' a
Forgery?" Dial, 32 (1902), 155.

Mr. Pickard admits he is puzzled and has lost hope
of "ever solving the mystery."

1880.1 Pikuleff, Michael J. "The Role of Community in the Major
Writings of Nathaniel Hawthorne," DAI, 31 (Wis.:
1970), 1809A-10A.

1880.2 Plank, Robert. "Heart Transplant Fiction," HSL, 2 (1970),
102-12.

Focuses on Hauff's DAS KALTE HERZ and Hawthorne's
"Ethan Brand."

1881 Plumstead, A. W. "Puritanism and Nineteenth Century
American Literature," QQ, 70 (1963), 209-22.

A thorough knowledge of the writings of New England
Puritan writers is indispensable to understanding of
American literature. They inaugurated the "American
Dream," prophesied its destruction, and produced the
rich symbolism of the American Renaissance..

1882 Pochmann, Henry A. "Hawthorne at Wisconsin," in Carl F.
Strauch, et al. Symposium on Nathaniel Hawthorne.
ESQ, 25 (1961), 18-20.

1883 Pochmann, Henry A. THE INFLUENCE OF THE GERMAN TALE ON THE
SHORT STORIES OF IRVING, HAWTHORNE, AND POE. Diss.
North Carolina: 1928.

1884 Pochmann, Henry A. "Nathaniel Hawthorne," in "German
Materials and Motifs in the Short Story," GERMAN
CULTURE IN AMERICA: PHILOSOPHICAL AND LITERARY
INFLUENCES, 1600-1900. With the assistance of Arthur
R. Schultz and others. Madison: Wisconsin U. P.,
1957, pp. 381-88.

1885 Poe, Edgar Allan. "Nathaniel Hawthorne," THE WORKS OF EDGAR ALLAN POE. New York: Redfield, 1858, III, 188-202.

1886 Poe, Edgar Allan. "Review of Hawthorne," in THE GOLDEN AGE OF AMERICAN LITERATURE. Perry Miller, ed. New York: Geo. Braziller, Inc., 1959, pp. 75-81.

1886.1 Poe, Edgar Allan. Reviews of TWICE-TOLD TALES /1842/ and "Tale Writing - Nathaniel Hawthorne," in THE RECOGNITION OF NATHANIEL HAWTHORNE. B. Bernard Cohen, ed. Ann Arbor: 1969, pp. 12-18, 21-27.

1887 Poe, Edgar Allan. "Two Reviews of 'Twice-Told Tales'," THE COMPLETE WORKS OF EDGAR ALLAN POE. James A. Harrison, ed. New York: 1902, XI, 75-81.

1888 Poirier, Richard. THE COMIC SENSE OF HENRY JAMES: A STUDY OF THE EARLY NOVELS. New York: Oxford U. P., 1960.

1889 Poirier, Richard. "Visionary to Voyeur: Hawthorne and James," A WORLD ELSEWHERE: THE PLACE OF STYLE IN AMERICAN LITERATURE. New York: Oxford U. P., 1966, pp. 93-143.

Rev. by Richard Bridgman, NCF, 22 (1967), 97-100.

1890 Policardi, Silvio. BREVE STORIA DELLA LETTERATURA AMERICANA. Milan and Varese: Instituto Editoriale Cisalpino, 1951, pp. 107-14.

1891 Pollin, Burton R. "'Rappaccini's Daughter'--Sources and Names," Names, 14 (1966), 30-35.

1892 Polt, John H. R. "Algunos símbolos de Eduardo Mallea: Mallea y Hawthorne," RHM, 26 (1960), 96-101.

1893 Porte, Joel. "Hawthorne," in THE ROMANCE IN AMERICA: STUDIES IN COOPER, POE, HAWTHORNE, MELVILLE, AND JAMES. Middletown, Conn.: Wesleyan U. P., 1969, pp. 95-151, passim.

Rev. by Nina Baym, JEGP, 68 (1969), 723-27;
Lawrence Buell, NEQ, 43 (1970), 331-33;
Harry Hayden Clark, AL, 43 (1971), 310-11.

1894 Portrait. CathW, 73 (1901), 20.

1895 Portrait. Colliers, 136 (1955), 71.

1896 Portrait. Critic, 45 (1900-04), 2.

1897 Portrait. Educ, 23 (1903), 408.

1898 Portrait. InternS, 75 (1922), 469.

1899   Portrait. LitD, 89 (1926), 34.

1900   Portrait. Mentor, 16 (1929), 28.

1901   Portrait, NEM, n. s. 31 (1904), 415.

1902   Portrait of Nathaniel Hawthorne. Arena, 32 (1904), 160.

1903   Portrait of Sophia A. Peabody - Mrs. Nathaniel Hawthorne.
       Colliers, 42 (1909), 11.

1904   Portrait. Outlook, 69 (1902), 408.

1905   Portrait. RevR, 22 (1900), 569.

1906   Portrait. SatRL, 16 (1937), 3.

1907   [Portraits] The Proceedings in Commemoration of the One-
       Hundredth Anniversary of the Birth of Nathaniel Hawthorne
       Held at Salem, Mass., June 23, 1904; Salem: 1904.
       (Contains twenty-two portraits of Hawthorne.)

1908   Portrait. Time, 28 (1936), 61.

1908.1 Poulet, Georges. STUDIES IN HUMAN TIME. Trans. by
       Elliott Coleman. Baltimore: Johns Hopkins U. P.,
       1956, pp. 326-29.

1909   Powers, Lyall H. "Hawthorne and Faulkner and the Pearl
       of Great Price," PMASAL, 52 (1967), 391-401.

1909.1 Prater, William G. "Nathaniel Hawthorne: A Self-
       Characterization in the Novels," DAI, 30 (Ohio:
       1969), 2494A-95A.

1910   Pratt, Bela L. "First Worthy Memorial of Nathaniel Hawthorne,
       Statue," CurOp, 61 (1916), 48.

       Sketch given of the statue of Hawthorne by Bela L.
       Pratt which Salem proposed to erect.

1911   Pratt, Bela L. Statue by. InternS, 59 (1916).

       The statue of Hawthorne by Bela L. Pratt which Salem
       proposed to erect.

1912 Praz, Mario. THE ROMANTIC AGONY. Angus Davidson, tr. Cleveland and New York: World Pub. Co., 1933, 1951, 1956, 1968.

Theme of persecuted woman throughout the 19th century.

1913 Praz, Mario. "Shelley, Lamartine, Hawthorne, Dostoevski a Firenze," RLMC, 8 (1955), 5-20.

1914 Prezzolini, Giuseppe. "Gli Hawthorne a Roma," NA, 85 (1950), 69-78.

1915 Price, Sherwood R. "The Heart, the Head, and 'Rappaccini's Daughter,'" NEQ, 27 (1954), 399-403.

Major conflict is not between Baglioni and Rappaccini but between Rappaccini and Giovanni, Beatrice's lover.

1916 Priestley, John Boynton. "The Novelists," LITERATURE AND WESTERN MAN. New York: Harper & Bros., 1960, pp. 222-73.

1917 "Prints of American Authors," ESQ, 28 (1962).

No. 2 is a picture of Hawthorne from the oil painting by Charles Osgood in the Essex Institute Collection.

1918 Pritchard, Francis Henry, ed. FROM CONFUCIUS TO MENCKEN: THE TREND OF THE WORLD'S BEST THOUGHT AS EXPRESSED BY FAMOUS WRITERS OF ALL TIME. New York: Harper, 1929; Albert and Charles Boni, 1936.

1919 Pritchard, John Paul. CRITICISM IN AMERICA: AN ACCOUNT OF THE DEVELOPMENT OF CRITICAL TECHNIQUES FROM THE EARLY PERIOD OF THE REPUBLIC TO THE MIDDLE YEARS OF THE TWENTIETH CENTURY. Norman, Okla.: Okla. U. P., 1956.

1920 Pritchard, John Paul. "Hawthorne's Debt to Classical Literary Criticism," ClW, 29 (1935), 41-45.

1921 Pritchard, John Paul. "Nathaniel Hawthorne," RETURN TO THE FOUNTAINS: SOME CLASSICAL SOURCES OF AMERICAN CRITICISM. Durham, N. C.: 1942, pp. 68-78, passim.

1922 Pritchett, V. S. "Books in General," NS&N, 24 (1942), 275.

1923 Pritchett, V. S. "Hawthorne at Brook Farm," NS&N, 28 (1944), 323.

1924 THE PROCEEDINGS IN COMMEMORATION OF THE ONE HUNDREDTH ANNIVERSARY OF THE BIRTH OF NATHANIEL HAWTHORNE. Salem, Mass.: 1904.

1925 "The Proceedings: On the One-Hundredth Anniversary of the Birth of Nathaniel Hawthorne," EIHC, 41 (1905), 1-2.

1926 Prochnow, Herbert V. "Housekeeper to Genius," Coronet, 27 (1949), 39.

Sophia's household savings enabled Hawthorne to write THE SCARLET LETTER.

1927 "The Property of Miss Rebecca B. Manning," AMERICAN ART ASSOCIATION ANDERSON GALLERIES SALE NUMBER 3927, (November 19-20, 1931), pp. 61-76.

1928 Prosser, Michael H. "A Rhetoric of Alienation as Reflected in the Works of Nathaniel Hawthorne," QJS, 54 (1968), 22-28.

The alienated in Hawthorne's works are guilty of too much intellect or pride, particularly the artists and scientists.

1929 Pryce-Jones, Alan. "Hawthorne in England," Lif&L, 50 (1946), 71-80.

1930 Pulos, Christos E. "Nathaniel Hawthorne and John Bunyan," DA, 25 (Nebr.: 1964), 5.

1931 "Puritan Romancer," TLS, No. 2495, 770 (1949).

1932 Putzel, Max. "The Way Out of the Minister's Maze: Some Hints for Teachers of THE SCARLET LETTER," NS, 9 (1960), 127-31.

1933 Quen, Jacques M. "Frederick C. Crew's THE SINS OF THE FATHERS: AN EXCHANGE," NCF, 22 (1967), 101-02.

Replies: Frederick C. Crews, NCF, 22 (1967), 102-05; Roy R. Male, NCF, 22 (1967), 106-10.

1934 Quinn, Arthur Hobson. A HISTORY OF THE AMERICAN DRAMA FROM THE CIVIL WAR TO THE PRESENT DAY. New York: F. S. Crofts & Co., 1937, II, passim.

Hawthorne's use of the regicide theme.

Also in REPRESENTATIVE AMERICAN PLAYS. New York: 1917, p. 111.

1935 Quinn, Arthur Hobson. "Literature, Politics, and Slavery," THE LITERATURE OF THE AMERICAN PEOPLE: AN HISTORICAL AND CRITICAL SURVEY. New York: Appleton, 1951, pp. 433-34.

1936 Quinn, Arthur Hobson. "Nathaniel Hawthorne, The Romance of the Moral Life," AMERICAN FICTION, AN HISTORICAL AND CRITICAL SURVEY. New York and London: Appleton-Century, 1936, 1964, pp. 132-48, passim.

Futility of human judgment, illumination of heredity, maturing influence of remorse, and the Puritan conscience.

Repr. in LITERATURE OF THE AMERICAN PEOPLE: AN HISTORICAL AND CRITICAL SURVEY. New York: Appleton, 1951.

1937 Quinn, Arthur Hobson. REPRESENTATIVE AMERICAN PLAYS. New York: 1917, p. 111.

One of the earliest plays based upon colonial history, SUPERSTITION, in which the theme of the regicide occurs, was written eleven years before Hawthorne published "The Gray Champion."

1938 Quinn, Arthur Hobson. "Some Phases of the Supernatural in American Literature," PMLA, 25 (1910), 114-34.

1939 Quinn, Arthur Hobson. THE SOUL OF AMERICA, YESTERDAY AND TODAY. Philadelphia: Pennsylvania U. P., 1932.

The lessons of THE SCARLET LETTER are the stronger for not being uttered. The countless editions that have come from the press since 1850 can surely not have failed to make their "impress upon the American soul."

1940 Ragan, James F. "Hawthorne's Bulky Puritans," PMLA, 75 (1960), 420-23.

No one has pointed out how Hawthorne demonstrates the progress of American society by "emblematizing the human body in his fiction."

1941 Ragan, James F. "The Irony in Hawthorne's BLITHEDALE," NEQ, 35 (1962), 239-46.

1942 Ragan, James F. "Nature in Hawthorne's Novels," DA, 15 (Notre Dame: 1955), 2214.

1943 Ragan, James F. "Social Criticism in THE HOUSE OF THE SEVEN GABLES," in LITERATURE AND SOCIETY: NINETEEN ESSAYS BY GERMAINE BRÉE AND OTHERS. Bernice Slote, ed. Lincoln: Nebr.: 1964, pp. 112-20.

1944 Rahv, Philip. "The Cult of Experience in American Writing," PR, 7 (1940), 412-24.

Reprinted in LITERARY OPINION IN AMERICA. Morton D. Zabel, ed. New York: Harper, 1951, pp. 550-60; IMAGE AND IDEA. Norfolk: New Directions, 1949.

The dilemma that confronted the early writers manifested itself in their frequent failure to integrate their inner and outer worlds.

1945 Rahv, Philip. "The Dark Lady of Salem," PR, 8 (1941), 362-81. Repr. in IMAGE AND IDEA. Norfolk: A New Directions Book, 1949, pp. 22-41.

Hawthorne's blonds are the "sexually anesthetic females to whom he officially paid homage" and his dark women a "dream-image of sexual bliss."

Rev. by Henry Nash Smith, AL, 22 (1950), 219-21.

1946 Rahv, Philip. "Introduction," DISCOVERY OF EUROPE: THE STORY OF AMERICAN EXPERIENCE IN THE OLD WORLD. Philip Rahv, ed. Boston: Houghton Mifflin Co., 1947.

Hawthorne in Rome; consular experiences; emptiness of picture-galleries; Leamington Spa.

1947 Rahv, Philip. "Introduction: The Native Bias," in LITERATURE IN AMERICA. Philip Rahv, ed. Cleveland and New York: World Publishing Co., 1957, 1967, pp. 11-22.

The real issue with Emerson and Whitman was not love of America nor disdain of it. Neither Cooper nor Hawthorne disdained it. The real issue was "availability at home of creatively usable materials."

1947.1 Rahv, Philip. LITERATURE AND THE SIXTH SENSE. Boston: Houghton, Mifflin Co., 1969, pp. 55-75, 422-29.

1948 Raleigh, John H. "Eugene O'Neill," Ramparts, 2 (1964), 72-87.

Allegory, ambiguity and other qualities place O'Neill in the "great dark tradition" of Poe, Melville and Hawthorne.

1949 Raleigh, John H. "Revolt and Revaluation in Criticism, 1900-1930," in THE DEVELOPMENT OF AMERICAN LITERARY CRITICISM, Floyd Stovall, ed. Chapel Hill: North Carolina U. P., 1955, pp. 242-45.

The transcendentalists of New England have given place before an intensive interest in Herman Melville and Nathaniel Hawthorne.

1950 Randel, William Peirce. "Hawthorne, Channing, and Margaret Fuller," AL, 10 (1939), 472-76.

Refutes theory that Hawthorne attacked Channing by slandering Margaret Fuller in THE BLITHEDALE ROMANCE.

See also: Oscar Cargill, "Nemesis and Nathaniel Hawthorne," PMLA, 52 (1937), 848-62; Austin Warren, "Hawthorne, Margaret Fuller, and 'Nemesis,'" PMLA, 54 (1939), 615-18.

1951 Rantoul, Robert S. "Opening Remarks," /Hawthorne Centenary7 EIHC, 41 (1905), 3-6.

1952 "Rappaccini's Daughter," GoldB, 19 (1934), 365-84.

Called "a curious blend of science and fantasy."

1953 Rawls, Walton. "Hawthorne's 'Rappaccini's Daughter,'" Expl. 15 (1957), Item 47.

1954 Read, Herbert. "Hawthorne," in COLLECTED ESSAYS IN LITERARY CRITICISM. London: Faber, 1938, pp. 265-79. Repr. in THE NATURE OF LITERATURE. New York: Horizon P., 1956, pp. 265-79.

1955 Read, Herbert. "Hawthorne," H&H, 3 (1930), 213-29. Also in his THE NATURE OF LITERATURE. New York: Horizon Press, 1956, 265-79.

1956 "Herbert Read on Hawthorne," N&Q, 184 (1943), 211-12.

1957 Read, Herbert. "The Puritan as an Artist," List. 29 (1943).

Also: N&Q, 184 (1943), 211-12.

1958 "Real Man's Life," Time, 52 (1948), 104-08.

An article-review of Robert Cantwell's NATHANIEL HAWTHORNE: THE AMERICAN YEARS. New York: Rinehart, 1948.

1959 Reed, Amy Louise. "Self-Portraiture in the Works of Nathaniel Hawthorne," SP, 23 (1926), 40-54.

Sources for "The Prophetic Pictures."

1960 Reenan, William L. ed. THE HAWTHORNE DIARY of 1859. Privately printed. Freelands, 1931.

1961 Rees, John O. "Elizabeth Peabody and 'The Very A B C':
A Note on THE HOUSE OF THE SEVEN GABLES." AL, 38
(1967), 537-40.

Hawthorne's statement "in our day, the very A B C
has become a science greatly too abstruse to be
any longer taught by pointing a pin from letter to
letter," is probably an ironic reference to the
linguistic theories of Elizabeth Peabody which she
gained from Charles Kraitser.

1962 Rees, John O. "Hawthorne and the Emblem," DA, 26 (Iowa: 1965),
357.

1963 Reeves, George, Jr. "Hawthorne's 'Ethan Brand,'" Expl, 14
(1956), Item 56.

1963.1 Regan, Robert. "Hawthorne's 'Plagiary': Poe's Duplicity,"
NCF, 25 (1970), 281-98.

1964 Reid, Alfred S. "Hawthorne's Ghost-Soul and the Harmonized
Life," FurmS, 12 (1964), 1-10.

Hawthorne's ghosts reflect his view of man as composed
of body and soul.

1965 Reid, Alfred S. "Hawthorne's Humanism: 'The Birthmark' and
Sir Kenelm Digby," AL, 38 (1966), 337-51.

1966 Reid, Alfred S. "A Note on the Date of THE SCARLET LETTER,"
FUB, n. s., 4 (1957), 30-39.

1967 Reid, Alfred S. "The Role of Transformation in Hawthorne's
Tragic Vision," FurmS, 6 (1958), 9-20.

Hawthorne's mature stage asserts that sin really is
man's happiness, for it is the transforming and
humanizing agent in man's life.

1968 Reid, Alfred S., ed. "SIR THOMAS OVERBURY'S VISION" (1616)
BY RICHARD NICOLLS AND OTHER ENGLISH SOURCES OF
NATHANIEL HAWTHORNE'S "THE SCARLET LETTER."
Gainesville, Fla.: Scholars' Facsimiles Repr., 1957.

Facsimiles with an Introd. [The Loseley Manuscript;
Fulke Greville's THE FIVE YEARS OF KING JAMES (1643);
State Trials.]

1969 Reid, Alfred S. THE SOURCES OF "THE SCARLET LETTER."
Diss. Florida: 1952.

1970   Reid, Alfred S.   THE YELLOW RUFF AND THE SCARLET LETTER:
A SOURCE OF HAWTHORNE'S NOVEL.   Gainesville, Fla.:
Florida U. P., 1955.

      Revs., Louis J. Budd, SAQ, 55 (1956), 389-91;
Ernest E. Leisy, AL, 28 (1956), 238-39;
John Lydenberg, NEQ, 28 (1955), 558-60;
SCN, 13 (1955), 30;
TLS (1955), 508.

      See Hena Maes-Jelinek, "Roger Chillingworth: An
Example of the Creative Process in THE SCARLET
LETTER," ES, 49 (1968), 341-48.

1971   Reid, William.   A HISTORY OF HAWTHORNE CRITICISM, 1879-1932.
MA Thesis. Colorado: 1932.

1972   Reilly, Cyril A.   "On the Dog's Chasing His Own Tail in
'Ethan Brand,'" PMLA, 68 (1953), 975-81.

1972.1   Reiss, John P., Jr.   "Problems of the Family Novel: Cooper,
Hawthorne, and Melville," DAI, 30 (Wis.: 1969),
1178A-79A.

1973   Report of the Committee on Trends in Research in American
Literature, 1940-1951, published by American Literature
Group of the Modern Language Association, Baton Route:
La. St. U., 1951.

      Rev. by Jay B. Hubbell, AL, 23 (1951-52), 390-91.

1974   Réti, Elizabeth.   HAWTHORNES VERHALTNIS ZUR NEUENGLANDTRADITION.
Diss. Gottingen, 1935.

1975   Rhys, Ernest. "Introduction," THE BLITHEDALE ROMANCE.
Ernest Rhys, ed. New York: E. P. Dutton & Co., 1912.

1976   Rhys, Ernest, ed.   THE MARBLE FAUN. New York: Everyman's
Lib., 1910.

1976.1   Ribbens, Dennis N.   "The Reading Interests of Thoreau,
Hawthorne, and Lanier," DAI, 31 (Wis.: 1970), 777A.

1976.2   Richard, Claude.   "Poe et Hawthorne," EA, 22 (1970), 351-61.

1977   Richards, Irving T.   "A Note on the Authorship of 'David
Whicher,'" JA, 7 (1962), 293-96.

      Suggests Hawthorne as possible author.

      See Hans-Joachim Lang, "The Authorship of 'David
Whicher,'" JA, 7 (1962), 293-96.

1978   Rideout, Walter B. INSTRUCTOR'S MANUAL FOR "THE EXPERIENCE OF
        PROSE." New York: Crowell, 1960.

1979   Ridout, Albert K. "THE SCARLET LETTER and Student Verse,"
        EJ, 55 (1966), 885-86.

1980   Ringe, Donald A. "Hawthorne's Psychology of the Head and
        the Heart," PMLA, 65 (1950), 120-32.

        Central theme in Hawthorne's fiction is the "problem
        of life in an evil world."

1981   Ringe, Donald A. "Teaching Hawthorne to Engineering Students,"
        in Carl F. Strauch, et al., Symposium on Nathaniel
        Hawthorne, ESQ, 25 (1961), 24-26.

1982   Ringler, Ellin J. "The Problem of Evil: A Correlative Study
        in the Novels of Nathaniel Hawthorne and George Eliot,"
        DA, 28 (Ill.: 1968), 5068A.

1982.1   Robbins, J. Albert, ed. AMERICAN LITERARY SCHOLARSHIP:
            AN ANNUAL, 1969. Durham, N. C.: Duke U. P., 1971.

1983   Roberto, Eugène. "LE LIVRE DES MERVEILLES de Nathaniel
        Hawthorne, et Paul Claudel," RUO, 37 (1967), 139-45.

        Repr. in CCC, 5 (1967), 99-108.

1984   Roberts, H. D. "Literature Appreciation Tests: THE HOUSE OF
        THE SEVEN GABLES." Atlanta, Ga.: Turner E. Smith & Co.,
        1936.

1985   Roberts, Josephine E. "Elizabeth Peabody and the Temple
        School," NEQ, 15 (1942), 497-508.

1986   Roberts, Josephine E. A NEW ENGLAND FAMILY: ELIZABETH
        PEABODY, 1809-1871, MARY T. PEABODY, 1806-1887. Diss.
        Western Reserve: 1937.

1987   Roberts, Josephine E. "Sophia Hawthorne, Editor," in
        "Letters to the Editor," SatRL, 21 (1939), 9.

1988   Robey, Richard C. "The Enchanted Ground: An Approach to the
        Tales and Sketches of Nathaniel Hawthorne," DA, 29
        (Columbia: 1969), 4467A-68A.

1988.1   Robey, Richard C. "Foreword," NATHANIEL HAWTHORNE: THE
            LIFE OF FRANKLIN PIERCE. New York: Garrett, 1970.

1989   Robillard, Douglas. "Hawthorne's 'Roger Malvin's Burial,'" Expl. 26 (1968), Item 56.

Emphasis should be on the "burial," a symbolic one.

1990   Robinson, E. Arthur. "Thoreau's Buried Short Story," SSF, 1 (1963), 16-20.

"Baker Farm" in WALDEN resembles the early sketches of Hawthorne.

1991   Robinson, E. Arthur. "The Vision of Goodman Brown: A Source and Interpretation." AL, 35 (1963), 218-25.

A possible secondary source of Hawthorne's story is Cotton Mather's MAGNALIA CHRISTI AMERICANA.

1992 Robinson, H. A. "Nathaniel Hawthorne in Wirral," ChesL, 19 (1953), 43.

Hawthorne liked the Wirral landscape.

1993   Robinson, H. M. "Materials of Romance," Cw, 10 (1929), 622-23.

1994   Robotti, Frances Diane. CHRONICLES OF OLD SALEM, A HISTORY IN MINIATURE. Foreword by Russell Leigh Jackson. New York: Bonanza Books, 1948.

Historical chronicle of Salem. Many references to Hawthorne and his family, plus background of characters and situations.

1995   Roch, John Henry. "The American Short Story, 1865-1885," DA, 19 (Columbia: 1958), 2340.

1996   Rochner, J. "Life in a Picture Gallery: Things in THE PORTRAIT OF A LADY and THE MARBLE FAUN," TSLL, 11 1969), 761-77.

1997   Rocks, James E. "Hawthorne and France: In Search of American Literary Nationalism," TSE, 17 (1969), 145-57.

1998   Rodabaugh, Delmer J. HAWTHORNE'S USE OF THE ENGLISH AND THE ITALIAN PAST. Diss. Minnesota: 1952.

1998.1   Rodnon, Stewart. "THE HOUSE OF THE SEVEN GABLES and ABSALOM, ABSALOM! Time, Tradition, and Guilt," in STUDIES IN THE HUMANITIES. William F. Grayburn, ed. 1, ii. Indiana: Indiana U. of Pa., 1970.

1999 Roe, Frederick William, and George Roy Elliott, eds.
ENGLISH PROSE: A SERIES OF RELATED ESSAYS FOR THE
DISCUSSION AND PRACTICE OF THE ART OF WRITING.
New York: Longmans, 1913, pp. 450-61.

"Dr. Heidegger's Experiment."

1999.1 Rogers, Robert. A PSYCHOANALYTIC STUDY OF THE DOUBLE IN
LITERATURE. Detroit, Mich.: Wayne State U. P., 1970.

2000 Rohrberger, Mary. "Hawthorne and the Modern Literary Short
Story: A Study in Genre," DA, 22 (Tulane: 1962), 3206-07.

2001 Rohrberger, Mary. HAWTHORNE AND THE MODERN SHORT STORY: A
STUDY IN GENRE. The Hague: Mouton, 1966.

Rev. by James W. Gargano, SSF, 6 (1969), 354-55.

2002 Rohrberger, Mary. "Hawthorne's Literary Theory and the Nature
of His Short Stories," SSF, 3 (1965), 23-30.

2003 Roper, Gordon. "Introduction," THE SCARLET LETTER AND
SELECTED PROSE WORKS. Gordon Roper, ed. New York:
Hendricks House, 1949; 1960.

2004 Roper, Gordon. "The Originality of Hawthorne's THE SCARLET
LETTER," DR, 29 (1950), 62-79.

2004.1 Rosa, Alfred F. A STUDY OF TRANSCENDENTALISM IN SALEM WITH
SPECIAL REFERENCE TO NATHANIEL HAWTHORNE. Diss.
(Mass.: 1971).

2005 Rosati, Salvatore. L'OMBRA DEI PADRI: STUDI SULLA
LETTERATURA AMERICANA. Rome: Edizioni di Storia e
Letteratura, 1958.

2005.1 Rose, Marilyn G. "Miles Coverdale as Hawthorne's Persona,"
ATQ, 1 (1969), 90-91.

2006 Rose, Marilyn G. "Theseus Motif in 'My Kinsman, Major
Molineux,'" ESQ, 47 (1967), 21-23.

2006.1 Roselle, Daniel. SAMUEL GRISWOLD GOODRICH, CREATOR OF PETER
PARLEY: A STUDY OF HIS LIFE AND WORK. Albany: New York
State U. P., 1968.

Contains chapter on Goodrich and Hawthorne.

Rev. by Neal Frank Doubleday, AL, 41 (1969), 433-34.

2007 Rosenberry, Edward H. "Hawthorne's Allegory of Science:
'Rappaccini's Daughter,'" AL, 32 (1960), 39-46.

The story ranks high among Hawthorne's tales of the
scientist as an "ethical being" and of the "ambiguous
warfare" of guilt and innocence in the human soul.

2008 Rosenberry, Edward H. "James's Use of Hawthorne in 'The
Liar,'" MLN, 76 (1961), 234-38.

2009 Rosenfeld, William. "The Divided Burden: Common Elements
in the Search for a Religious Synthesis in the Works
of Theodore Parker, Horace Bushnell, Nathaniel
Hawthorne, and Herman Melville," DA, 22 (Minnesota:
1962), 4019.

2010 Rosenthal, Melvyn. "The American Writer and His Society: The
Response to Estrangement in the Works of Nathaniel
Hawthorne, Randolph Bourne, Edmund Wilson, Norman Mailer,
Saul Bellow," DA, 29 (Conn.: 1969), 3108A.

2011 Ross, Danforth. THE AMERICAN SHORT STORY. Minneapolis:
Minn. U. P., 1961.

2011.1 Ross, Donald. "Dreams and Sexual Repression in THE
BLITHEDALE ROMANCE," PMLA, 86 (1971), 1014

2011.2 Ross, Donald. "Hawthorne and Thoreau on 'Cottage
Architecture,'" ATQ, 1 (1969), 100-01.

2012 Ross, E. C. "A Note on THE SCARLET LETTER," MLN, 37 (1922),
58-59.

2013 Ross, Maude Cardwell. "Moral Values of the American Woman
as Presented in Three Major American Authors," DA, 25
(Tex.: 1965), 5262-63. [Hawthorne, James, Faulkner.]

2014 Ross, Morton L. "Hawthorne's Bosom Serpent and Mather's
MAGNALIA," ESQ, 47 (1967), 13.

2014.1 Ross, Morton L. "What Happens in 'Rappaccini's Daughter,'"
AL, 43 (1971), 336-45.

2015 Rossky, William. "Rappaccini's Garden: Or the Murder of
Innocence," ESQ, 19 (1960), 98-100.

2016 Rourke, Constance. AMERICAN HUMOR: A STUDY OF THE NATIONAL
CHARACTER. Garden City, New York: Doubleday, 1931,
pp. 150-54, passim.

2017 Rovit, Earl. "Ambiguity in Hawthorne's SCARLET LETTER," Archiv, 198 (1961), 76-88.

2018 Rovit, Earl. "American Literature and 'The American Experience,'" AQ, 13 (1961), 115-25.

2019 Rovit, Earl. "Fathers and Sons in American Fiction," YR, 53 (1963), 248-57.

The father or father figure in literature either omitted or degraded as in Arthur Dimmesdale.

2020 Rovit, Earl. "James and Emerson: The Lesson of the Master," ASch, 33 (1964), 434-40.

Because James's feelings of insecurity prevented him from acknowledging that America could produce art, James in the 1870's and 80's praised Hawthorne and Emerson as men but disparaged their art on narrowly formalistic grounds.

2021 Rowse, Alfred Leslie. "Three Americans on England," in THE ENGLISH SPIRIT: ESSAYS IN HISTORY AND LITERATURE. New York: Macmillan, 1945, pp. 266-72; Rev. ed. Funk & Wagnalls, 1967, pp. 246-69.

Hawthorne was torn between resentment toward England, and "deep yearning of the blood for that from which it had been estranged."

2022 Royalty, Paul. "Why Read Great Books?" BSTCF, 1 (1960-61), 37-43.

2023 Rubin, Joseph Jay. "Hawthorne's Theology: The Wide Plank," ESQ, 25 (1961), 20-24.

2024 Rubin, Louis D., Jr., and John Rees Moore, eds. THE IDEA OF AN AMERICAN NOVEL. New York: Thos. Y. Crowell Co., 1961.

2025 Ruland, Richard. THE REDISCOVERY OF AMERICAN LITERATURE: PREMISES OF CRITICAL TASTE, 1900-1940. Cambridge, Mass.: Harvard U. P., 1967, passim.

Rev. by Benjamin T. Spencer, AL, 40 (1968), 235-36.

2026 Rusk, Ralph L. "Emerson in Salem, 1849," EIHC, 94 (1958), 194-95.

Emerson as a guest of Hawthorne, January 17, 1849.

2027 Russell, Jason Almus. "Hawthorne and the Romantic Indian," Educ, 48 (1928), 381-86.

2028 Russell, John. "Allegory and 'My Kinsman, Major Molineux,'" NEQ, 40 (1967), 432-40.

2029 Rust, James D. "George Eliot on THE BLITHEDALE ROMANCE," BPLQ, 7 (1955), 207-15.

2030 Rust, Richard D. "Character Change and Development in the Major Novels of Nathaniel Hawthorne," DA, 28 (Wis.: 1967), 641A-42A.

2031 Rutledge, Lyman V. THE ISLE OF SHOALS IN LORE AND LEGEND. Barre, Mass.: Barre Publishers, 1965.

  Hawthorne's notebook comments as history of the island, and remarks as to his friendship with Celia and Levi Thaxter.

2032 Ryan, Pat M., Jr. "Young Hawthorne at the Salem Theatre," EIHC, 94 (1958), 243-55.

2033 Ryskamp, Charles. "The New England Sources of THE SCARLET LETTER," AL, 31 (1959), 257-72.

2034 Sachs, Viola. "The Myth of America in Hawthorne's HOUSE OF THE SEVEN GABLES and BLITHEDALE ROMANCE," KN, 15 (1968), 267-83.

2035 Sachs, Viola. "The Myth of America in Hawthorne's THE SCARLET LETTER," KN, 14 (1967), 245-67.

2036 Safranek, William Paul. "Hawthorne's Use of Setting in His Short Stories," DA, 21 (Wis.: 1961), 3462.

2037 Sakamoto, Shigetake. "A Study of THE SCARLET LETTER," StELLit, 3 (1963), 1-18.

2038 Saito, Tadatoshi. "Notes on Romances--The Study of Nathaniel Hawthorne," JSKK, 4 (1962), 111-33.

2039 Salomon, Louis B. "Hawthorne and His Father: A Conjecture," L&P, 13 (1963), 12-17.

2040 Salomon, Louis B. "Realism as Disinheritance: Twain, Howells, and James," AQ, 16 (1964), 531-44.

2041 Sampson, Edward C. "Afterword," THE HOUSE OF THE SEVEN GABLES. New York: New Amer. Lib., 1961, pp. 279-86.

2042 Sampson, Edward C. "Motivation in THE SCARLET LETTER," AL, 28 (1957), 511-13.

Discusses article of Anne Marie McNamara, "The Character of Flame: The Function of Pearl in THE SCARLET LETTER," AL, 27 (1956), 537-53.

2043 Sampson, Edward C. "A Note on William B. Stein's HAWTHORNE'S FAUST," N&Q, 200, n. s. II (1955), 137-38.

2044 Sampson, Edward C. "The Structure of THE SCARLET LETTER and THE HOUSE OF THE SEVEN GABLES," DA, 17(Cornell: 1957), 2015.

2045 Sampson, Edward C. "Three Unpublished Letters of Hawthorne to Epes Sargent," AL, 34 (1962), 102-05.

2046 Sampson, Edward C. "The 'W' in Hawthorne's Name," EIHC, Special Hawthorne Issue, C, iv (1964), 297-99.

2047 Sampson, M. W. "Nathaniel Hawthorne." Reader, 5 (1905), 775-78.

2048 Sams, Henry W., ed. AUTOBIOGRAPHY OF BROOK FARM. Englewood Cliffs, New Jersey: Prentice-Hall, Inc., 1958.

Letters and excerpts.

2049 Samuels, C. T. "Giovanni and the Governess," AS, 37 (1968), 655-78.

2050 Sanborn, Frank B. HAWTHORNE AND HIS FRIENDS: REMINISCENCE AND TRIBUTE. Cedar Rapids, Iowa: The Torch P., 1908.

Reminiscences. Sanborn was a Transcendental School-master of Concord.

2050.1 Sanborn, Frank B. MEMORABILIA OF HAWTHORNE, ALCOTT AND CONCORD. Kenneth Walter Cameron, ed. Hartford: Transcendental Books, 1970.

2051 Sanborn, Frank B. RECOLLECTIONS OF SEVENTY YEARS. Badger: 1912.

2052 Sandeen, Ernest. "THE SCARLET LETTER as a Love Story," PMLA, 77 (1962), 425-35.

2053 Sanders, Charles. "A Note on Metamorphosis in Hawthorne's 'The Artist of the Beautiful,'" SSF, 4 (1966), 82-83.

Warland's encounter with four other characters corresponds to the stages of a butterfly.

2054 Sanford, Charles L. "Classics of American Reform Literature," AQ, 10 (1958), 295-311.

2055 Sanford, Charles L. THE QUEST FOR PARADISE. Urbana: Illinois U. P., 1961, pp. 184-85.

Hawthorne was "wistful" about failure of Brook Farm, thinking it might have succeeded if it had remained faithful to its higher spirit and not lapsed into Fourierism.

2055.1 Santangelo, G. A. "The Absurdity of 'The Minister's Black Veil,'" PCP, 5 (1970), 61-66.

2056 Santayana, George. "The Genteel Tradition in American Philosophy," WINDS OF DOCTRINE. New York: 1912.

See Carpenter, F. I. "The Genteel Tradition...." NEQ, 15 (1942), 427-33.

2057 Sato, Takami. "The Revival of TWICE-TOLD TALES--Hawthorne's Historical Tales," Sylvan, 7 (1962), 58-67.

2058 Savelli, Giovanni. "Nataniele Hawthorne e gli svolgimenti dello spirito nordamericano," LetM, 5 (1954), 306-13.

2059 Scanlon, Lawrence E. "The Heart of THE SCARLET LETTER," TSLL, 4 (1962), 198-13.

Novel structured through heart imagery and centrality of the scaffold. Secrecy and sympathy, the two major meanings of "heart."

2060 Scanlon, Lawrence E. "That Very Singular Man, Dr. Heidegger," NCF, 17 (1962), 253-63.

2061 Scherman, David Edward, and Rosemarie Redlich. AMERICA: THE LAND AND ITS WRITERS. New York: Dodd, 1956, pp. 36-38.

2062 Scherman, David Edward, and Rosemarie Redlich. LITERARY AMERICA: A CHRONICLE OF AMERICAN WRITERS FROM 1607-1952 with 173 PHOTOGRAPHS OF THE AMERICAN SCENE THAT INSPIRED THEM. New York: Dodd, Mead & Co., 1952, pp. 48-49.

2063 Schiller, Andrew. "The Moment and the Endless Voyage: A Study of Hawthorne's 'Wakefield,'" Diameter, 1 (1951), 7-12.

2064 Schlaback, Anne V. A CRITICAL STUDY OF SOME PROBLEMS DERIVED FROM HAWTHORNE'S NOVELS AND EMERSON'S REPRESENTATIVE MEN. Diss. Wis.: 1947.

2065 Schlesinger, Arthur M. THE AGE OF JACKSON. Boston, Toronto: Little, Brown & Co., 1945.

Hawthorne and others regarded themselves primarily as guardians of the "sacred flame, cherishing the purest essence of the Jeffersonian past."

2066 Schlesinger, Arthur M. "American History and American Literary History," in THE REINTERPRETATION OF AMERICAN LITERATURE, Norman Foerster, ed. New York: Harcourt, Brace & Co., 1928, 1955, 1959.

The pattern of moral conduct to which Hawthorne adhered was that of the writers in the "parlor magazines." He was preoccupied with the suffering and remorse which tormented those who rebelled against the accepted code.

2067 Schneider, Daniel J. "The Allegory and Symbolism of Hawthorne's THE MARBLE FAUN," SNNTS, 1 (1969), 38-50.

Five opposing clusters of images reinforce theme of man between two opposing worlds, the ideal and the primitive.

2068 Schneider, Herbert W. "The Democracy of Hawthorne," EUQ, 22 (1966), 123-32.

2069 Schneider, Herbert W. THE PURITAN MIND. New York: Henry Holt & Co., 1930, pp. 256-64.

Hawthorne used the theological terminology of the Puritans only metaphorically. He saw the empirical truth behind the Calvinist symbols.

2070 Schneider, Herbert W. "Young America," A HISTORY OF AMERICAN PHILOSOPHY. Columbia Studies in American Culture, No. 18. Columbia U. P., 1946, pp. 133-44.

Hawthorne's democracy was neither political nor economic, but social. He had a love of social equality and a preference for a classless society.

2070.1 Schneiderman, Leo. "Hawthorne and the Refuge of the Heart," ConnR, 3 (1970), 83-101.

2071 Schnittkind, Henry T. (Henry Thomas, pseud.) "Nathaniel Hawthorne, the Conscience of America," STORY OF THE UNITED STATES: A BIOGRAPHICAL HISTORY OF AMERICA. New York: Doubleday, Doran, 1938, pp. 119-28.

2072 Schnittkind, Henry T., and Dana A. Schnittkind /pseuds,7. "Nathaniel Hawthorne," LIVING BIOGRAPHIES OF FAMOUS NOVELISTS. Garden City, New York: Garden City Pub. Co., 1943, pp. 165-77.

2073 Schoen, Carol B. "The Pattern of Meaning: Theme and Structure in the Fiction of Nathaniel Hawthorne," DA, 29 (Columbia: 1968), 1879A.

2074 Scholes, James B. NATHANIEL HAWTHORNE'S "THE SCARLET LETTER": A STUDY GUIDE. Bound Brook, N. J.: Shelley, 1962.

2075 Schönback, Anton E. "An Estimate of Hawthorne," EIHC, 41 (1905), 66-67.

2076 Schorer, Calvin E. "Hamlin Garland's First Published Story," AL, 25 (1953), 89-92.

Notes Hawthorne's influence.

2077 Schorer, Calvin E. THE JUVENILE LITERATURE OF NATHANIEL HAWTHORNE. Diss. Chicago: 1949.

2077.1 Schorer, Mark. GALAXY: LITERARY MODES AND GENRES. New York: Harcourt, 1967.

2078 Schroeter, James. "Redburn and the Failure of Mythic Criticism," AL, 39 (1967), 279-97.

2079 Schubert, Leland. "A Boy's Journal of a Trip into New England in 1838," EIHC, 86 (1950), 97-105.

George Duyckinck and his brother are shown through Salem by Hawthorne.

2080 Schubert, Leland. HAWTHORNE, THE ARTIST: FINE-ART DEVICES IN FICTION. Chapel Hill: North Carolina U. P., 1944.

Analysis of Hawthorne's work as expression of his understanding of the technique of art.

Rev. by Walter Blair, MP (1944;
Stanley Williams, MLN, 60 (1945), 71-72;
F. O. Matthiessen, NEQ, 18 (1945), 265-68.

2081 Schubert, Leland. "Hawthorne and George W. Childs and the Death of W. D. Ticknor," EIHC, 84 (1948), 164-68.

2082 Schubert, Leland. "Hawthorne Used the Melodic Rhythm of Repetition," CSMM, 37 (1945), 6.

2083 Schueller, Herbert M. "An American in Rome: The Experiments of W. W. Story," in FRONTIERS OF AMERICAN CULTURE. Ray B. Browne, et al., eds. Lafayette, Ind.: Purdue Univ. Studies, 1968, pp. 41-68.

It is the Cleopatra of William Wetmore Story which Hawthorne describes in THE MARBLE FAUN.

2084 Schwartz, Arthur M. "The American Romantics: An Analysis," ESQ, 35 (1964), 39-44.

Hawthorne, Poe, and Melville should be considered negative Romantics, according to the Morse Peckham definition.

2085 Schwartz, Arthur M. "The Heart in Hawthorne's Moral Vision," DA, 22 (Wis.: 1961), 2006.

2086 Schwartz, Joseph. "'Ethan Brand' and the Natural Goodness of Man: A Phenomenological Inquiry," ESQ, 39 (1965), 78-81.

2087 Schwartz, Joseph. "Myth and Ritual in THE MARBLE FAUN," ESQ, 25 (1961), 26-29.

2088 Schwartz, Joseph. NATHANIEL HAWTHORNE AND FREEDOM OF THE WILL. Diss. Wis.: 1952.

2089 Schwartz, Joseph. "Nathaniel Hawthorne, 1804-1864 - God and Man in New England," in AMERICAN CLASSICS RECONSIDERED: A CHRISTIAN APPRAISAL. Harold Charles Gardiner, ed. New York: Scribners, 1958, pp. 121-45.

2090 Schwartz, Joseph. "A Note on Hawthorne's Fatalism," MLN, 70 (1955), 33-36.

Hawthorne's ambiguity on Calvinistic fatalism is a literary device, not a revelation of personal philosophy.

2091 Schwartz, Joseph. "Three Aspects of Hawthorne's Puritanism," NEQ, 36 (1963), 192-208.

The three aspects are: (1) Puritanism as a theology of predestination and universal depravity; (2) Puritanism as a way of life; (3) Puritanism as it was involved in the early struggle for political liberty in America.

2092 Schwarz, Peter. "Zwei mögliche 'Faust'--Quellen für Hawthornes Roman THE SCARLET LETTER," JA, 10 (1965), 198-205.

2093 Scott, Arthur L. "The Case of the Fatal Antidote," ArQ, 11 (1955), 38-43.

2094 Smith, J. Hubert, ed. THE TWICE-TOLD TALES BY NATHANIEL HAWTHORNE. With Introductory Note by George Parsons Lathrop. New York: Houghton Mifflin Co., 1882, 1907.

2095 Scott, Nathan A., Jr. "Judgment Marked by a Cellar: The American Negro Writer and the Dialectic of Despair," DenQ, 2 (1967), 5-35.

The cultural basis of Negro literature is not found in the African jungle but, as with Hawthorne, in the myth, secularized Calvinist pattern of the "wounded Adam."

2096 Scott, Wilbur Stewart, ed. FIVE APPROACHES OF LITERARY CRITICISM: AN ARRANGEMENT OF CONTEMPORARY CRITICAL ESSAYS. New York: Macmillan, 1962.

2097 Scoville, Samuel. "To Conceive of the Devil: Hawthorne's 'Young Goodman Brown' and Levin's 'Rosemary's Baby,'" EJ, 58 (1969), 673-75.

2098 Scrimgeour, Gary J. "THE MARBLE FAUN: Hawthorne's Faery Land," AL, 36 (1964), 271-87.

2099 Scudder, Horace E., ed. THE COMPLETE WRITINGS OF NATHANIEL HAWTHORNE, The Old Manse Edition, 22 vols. Boston: 1900.

2100 Scudder, Harold H. "Hawthorne's Use of TYPEE," N&Q, 187 (1944), 184-86.

Parallels in "The Paradise of Children" (A WONDER BOOK) with pictures in TYPEE.

2101 Sealts, Merton M., Jr. "Approaching Melville Through 'Hawthorne and His Mosses,'" in Melville Supplement, ESQ, 28 (1962), 12-15.

2102 Sealts, Merton M., Jr. "Did Melville Write 'October Mountain'?" AL, 22 (1950), 178-82.

History of the error that Melville reviewed THE SCARLET LETTER.

2103 Seay, Claire Soulé. "Introduction," THE SCARLET LETTER. New York: 1920.

2104 Secor, Robert. "Conrad's American Sharers," Conrad, 1 (1968), 59-67.

Similarities between VICTORY and THE BLITHEDALE ROMANCE, based on Conrad's affinity to what Richard Chase defines as the American consciousness.

2105 Secor, Robert. "Hawthorne, Conrad, and the Descent into Darkness," MRR, 2 (1967), 41-55.

Hawthorne's mythic journey into the heart of darkness lends itself to an analysis of the psychological nature of man better than the Adamic myth.

2106 Secor, Robert. "Hawthorne's 'The Canterbury Pilgrims,'" Expl, 22 (1963), Item 8.

2107 Seelye, John F. "The Structure of Encounter: Melville's Review of Hawthorne's MOSSES," in MELVILLE AND HAWTHORNE IN THE BERKSHIRES: A SYMPOSIUM. Howard P. Vincent, ed. Kent, Ohio: Kent State U. P., 1968, pp. 63-69.

2108 Seib, Kenneth. "A Note on Hawthorne's Pearl," ESQ, 39 (1965), 20-21.

2109 Seitz, Don C. "'FANSHAWE' at the American Top," PubW, 119 (1931), 2441.

2110 Sewall, Richard Benson. "The Scarlet Letter," in THE VISION OF TRAGEDY. New Haven: Yale U. P., 1962, pp. 86-91.

2111 Sewell, W. Stuart, ed. BRIEF BIOGRAPHIES OF FAMOUS MEN AND WOMEN. Permabooks, 1949, pp. 132-33.

2112 Shafer, Robert E. "Teaching Sequences in Hawthorne and Melville," in THE TEACHER AND AMERICAN LITERATURE: PAPERS PRESENTED AT THE 1964 CONVENTION OF THE NATIONAL COUNCIL OF TEACHERS OF ENGLISH. Lewis Leary, ed. Champaign: NCTE, 1965, pp. 110-14.

2113 Shapiro, Charles, ed. TWELVE ORIGINAL ESSAYS ON GREAT AMERICAN
       NOVELS. Wayne St. U. P., 1958.

2114 Sharf, Frederic A. "Charles Osgood: The Life and Times of
       a Salem Portrait Painter," EIHC, 102 (1966), 203-12.

       The Hawthorne portrait (1840) represents the culmination
       of Osgood's mature style.

2115 Sharf, Frederic A. "'A More Bracing Morning Atmosphere':
       Artistic Life in Salem, 1850-1859," EIHC, 95 (1959),
       149-64.

2115.1 Sharma, T. R. A. "Diabolic World and Naive Hero in 'My
       Kinsman, Major Molineux,'" IJAS, 1, i (1969), 35-43.

2116 Shea, Daniel B., Jr. SPIRITUAL AUTOBIOGRAPHY IN EARLY
       AMERICA. Princeton U. P., 1968.

       Rev. by Thomas E. Johnston, Jr., NEQ, 42 (1969), 461-63.

2116.1 Shear, W. "Characterization in THE SCARLET LETTER,"
       MQ, 12 (1971), 437-54.

2117 Sheehan, Arthur T., and Elizabeth Sheehan. ROSE HAWTHORNE:
       THE PILGRIMAGE OF NATHANIEL'S DAUGHTER. Farrar, Straus,
       1959, p. 190.

2118 Shelton, Austin J. "Transfer of Socio-Historical Symbols
       in the Interpretation of American Literature by West
       Africans," Phylon, 26 (1965), 372-79.

2119 Shepard, Odell, ed. THE JOURNALS OF BRONSON ALCOTT. Boston:
       Little, Brown & Co., 1938.

2120 Sherbo, Arthur L. "Albert Brisbane and Hawthorne's
       Holgrave and Hollingsworth," NEQ, 27 (1954), 531-34.

2121 Sherman, Stuart P. "Hawthorne: A Puritan Critic of
       Puritanism," AMERICANS. New York: Charles Scribner's
       Sons, 1923, 122-52.

       Hawthorne, a satirist of Puritanism.

2122 Shigehisa, Tokutaro. "Appendix to the Bibliography of
       Japanese Interpretations of THE SCARLET LETTER,"
       Shur, 24 (1962), 68.

2123 Shipman, Carolyn. "Illustrated Editions of THE SCARLET LETTER," Critic, 45 (1902), 49-51.

2124 Short, Raymond W. "Introduction," FOUR GREAT AMERICAN NOVELS. Raymond W. Short, ed. New York: Holt, Rinehart & Winston, 1946, 1960.

2125 Short, Raymond W., and Richard B. Sewall. A MANUAL OF SUGGESTIONS FOR TEACHERS USING "SHORT STORIES FOR STUDY." 3rd ed. New York: Holt, 1956, pp. 11-12.

2126 Shroeder, John W. "Hawthorne's 'Egotism; or, The Bosom Serpent' and Its Source," AL, 31 (1959), 150-62.

Spenser's First Book of THE FAIRIE QUEENE, "Legende of the Knight of the Red Crosse," as source.

2127 Shroeder, John W. "Hawthorne's 'The Man of Adamant': A Spenserian Source-Study," PQ, 41 (1962), 744-56.

2128 Shroeder, John W. "Miles Coverdale as Actaeon, as Faunus, and as October: With Some Consequences," PLL, 2 (1966), 126-39.

2129 Shroeder, John W. "Miles Coverdale's Calendar: or, A Major Literary Source for THE BLITHEDALE ROMANCE," EIHC, 103 (1967), 353-64.

2130 Shroeder, John W. "Sources and Symbols for Melville's Confidence-Man," PMLA, 66 (1951), 363-68.

Comparison of devices in Hawthorne's stories, particularly "The Celestial Railroad."

2131 Shroeder, John W. "'That Inward Sphere': Notes on Hawthorne's Heart Imagery and Symbolism," PMLA, 65 (1950), 106-119.

2132 Shulman, Robert. "Hawthorne's Quiet Conflict," PQ, 47 (1968), 216-36.

2133 Shuman, Edwin L. "Benjamin Frederick Brown Was Hawthorne's Yankee Privateer," NYTBR, March 20, 1927.

2134 Shuster, George N. "Wider Horizons," IIENB, 24 (1949), 3.

2135 Silver, Rollo G. "THE SCARLET LETTER by Nathaniel Hawthorne,"
      AL, 35 (1964), 538-39.

      Rev. art. of Centenary Edition, William Charvat, et al, eds.

2135.1 Simonson, Harold P. THE CLOSED FRONTIER: STUDIES IN
        AMERICAN LITERARY TRAGEDY. New York: Holt, Rinehart
        and Winston, 1970, passim.

2136 Simonson, Harold P. INSTRUCTOR'S MANUAL TO ACCOMPANY "TRIO:
      A BOOK OF STORIES, PLAYS, AND POEMS." New York:
      Harper & Row, 1965.

2137 Simpson, Claude M. "Introduction," THE MARBLE FAUN: OR THE
      ROMANCE OF MONTE BENI. in THE CENTENARY EDITION OF THE
      WORKS OF NATHANIEL HAWTHORNE. William Charvat, et al.,
      eds. Columbus: Ohio St. U. P., 1968.

2138 Simpson, Claude M. "The Practice of Textual Criticism," in
      THE TASK OF AN EDITOR: PAPERS READ AT A CLARK LIBRARY
      SEMINAR, February 8, 1969. Foreword, Vinton A.
      Dearing. Los Angeles: Wm. Andrews Clark Mem. Lib.,
      U. C. L. A., pp. 35-52.

2138.1 Simpson, Claude M. "Introduction," OUR OLD HOME: A SERIES
        OF ENGLISH SKETCHES in THE CENTENARY WORKS OF NATHANIEL
        HAWTHORNE. Vol. V. William Charvat, et al, eds.
        Columbus, Ohio: Ohio St. U. P., 1970, pp. xiii-xli.

2139 Simpson, Claude M., and Allan Nevins, eds. THE AMERICAN
      READER. Boston: Heath, 1941.

2140 Singer, David. "Hawthorne and the 'Wild Irish': A Note,"
      NEQ, 42 (1969), 425-32.

2141 Sits, Herbert A. "'The Great Stone Face': Test Questions
      for Review in the Reading Class," GrT, 53 (1936).
      42, 68.

2142 Sjöström, Victor. [A Swedish Director who in 1926 made a
      film of THE SCARLET LETTER. Lillian Gish played Hester.]

2142.1 Skaggs, Calvin, and Merrill Maguire Skaggs. Instructor's
        Manual for Mark Schorer's GALAXY: LITERARY MODES AND
        GENRES. New York: Harcourt, 1967.

        "My Kinsman, Major Molineux," pp. 1-4.

2143 Skey, Miriam. "The Letter 'A.'" KAL, 11 (1968), 1-10.

2143.1 Skinner, J. W. "Some Aspects of Emile Montégut," RLC, 3 (1923), 283-88.

2144 Smith, Charles R., Jr. "The Structural Principle of THE MARBLE FAUN," Thoth, 3 (1962), 32-38.

2145 Smith, David E. "Bunyan and Hawthorne," in JOHN BUNYAN IN AMERICA. Bloomington: Indiana U. P., 1966, pp. 45-89.

2146 Smith, David E. "John Bunyan in America: A Critical Inquiry," DA, 23 (Minn.: 1963), 4690-91.

2147 Smith, David Rodman. "Origins of the International Novel: Studies in Transatlantic Fiction, 1812 to 1865," DA, 21 (Claremont: 1960), 3101.

2148 Smith, George B. POETS AND NOVELISTS. London: 1955, p. 196.

2149 Smith, Harrison. "Hawthorne: The Somber Strain," SatRL, 33 (1950), 18, 55.

2150 Smith, Henry Nash. "The Morals of Power: Business Enterprise as a Theme in Mid-Nineteenth Century American Fiction," in ESSAYS ON AMERICAN LITERATURE IN HONOR OF JAY B. HUBBELL. Clarence Gohdes, ed. Durham, N. C.: Duke U. P., 1967, pp. 90-107.

Hawthorne emphasizes lust for wealth as a force of evil.

2151 Smith, Henry Nash. "Origins of a Native American Literary Tradition," THE AMERICAN WRITER AND THE EUROPEAN TRADITION. Minneapolis: Minnesota U. P., 1950, pp. 65-66.

Hawthorne and the artist.

2152 Smith, Julian. "THE BLITHEDALE ROMANCE -Hawthorne's New Testament of Failure," Person, 49 (1968), 540-48.

A religious allegory, a "Paradise Un-regained," in which Coverdale fails to commit himself to action beneficial to others and to himself.

2153 Smith, Julian. "Coming of Age in America: Young Ben Franklin and Robin Molineux," AQ, 17 (1965), 550-58.

2154 Smith, Julian. "Hawthorne and a Salem Enemy," EIHC, 102 (1966), 299-302.

2154.1 Smith, Julian. "A Hawthorne Source for THE HOUSE OF THE SEVEN GABLES," ATQ, 1 (1969), 18-19.

2155 Smith, Julian. "Hawthorne's LEGENDS OF THE PROVINCE HOUSE," NCF, 24 (1969), 31-44.

2156 Smith, Julian. "Keats and Hawthorne: A Romantic Bloom in Rappaccini's Garden," ESQ, 42 (1966), 8-12.

2157 Smith, Julian. "Why Does Zenobia Kill Herself?" ELN, 6 (1968), 37-39.

2158 Smith, L. N. "Manuscript of OUR OLD HOME," CEAAN (1968), 1-2.

2159 Smyth, Albert H. "Hawthorne's 'Great Stone Face,'" Chautauquan, 31 (1900), 75-79.

2160 Smyth, Albert H. "Hawthorne's MARBLE FAUN," Chautauquan, 30 (1900), 522-26.

2161 Smyth, Clifford. "Introduction," THE YARN OF A YANKEE PRIVATEER. Nathaniel Hawthorne, ed. New York and London: Funk & Wagnalls Company, 1926. Repr. from DemR. (Jan.-Sept., 1846.

Benjamin Frederick Browne, presumed author.
See EIHC, 13, Part II (April, 1875), as to authorship, and Hawthorne's part in the publication.

2162 Snell, George. "Nathaniel Hawthorne: Bystander," in his THE SHAPERS OF AMERICAN FICTION, 1798-1947. New York: E. P. Dutton & Co., 1947, pp. 117-29.

Rev. by Kenneth B. Murdock, AL, 20 (1948-49), 461-65.

2163 Snyder, Cecil K., Jr. "Mandala: A Proposed Schema for Literary Criticism," DA, 29 (Penn. State: 1969), 3588A.

2164 Sojka, Raoul. UNTERSUCHUNGEN ÜBER DAS VORHANDENSEIN GRANDLE-GENDER IDEEN ES IN AMERIKANISCHEN ROMANEN VON NATHANIEL HAWTHORNE. Diss. Vienna: 1948.

2165 Sokoloff, B. A. "Ethan Brand's Twin," MLN, 73 (1958), 413-14.

2166 Sommavilla, Guido. "Nathaniel Hawthorne: Manzoni americano," Letture, 15 (1960), 403-16.

2167 Souers, Philip Webster, et al, eds. WRITER'S READER: MODELS AND MATERIALS FOR THE ESSAY. New York: Harcourt, 1950, pp. 9-12.

2168 Speare, Morris Edmond. THE POLITICAL NOVEL: ITS DEVELOPMENT IN ENGLAND AND AMERICA. New York: Oxford U. P., 1924, pp. 196-97.

2169 Spector, Robert Donald, ed. THE SCARLET LETTER: SPECIAL AIDS. New York: Bantam, 1965.

2170 Spencer, Benjamin T. "Criticism: Centrifugal and Centripetal," Criticism, 8 (1966), 139-54.

2171 Spencer, Benjamin T. "The New Realism and a National Literature." PMLA, 56 (1941), 1116-1133.

2172 Spencer, Benjamin T. THE QUEST FOR NATIONALITY: AN AMERICAN LITERATURE CAMPAIGN. Syracuse: Syracuse U. P., 1957.

History of the nationalistic element in American literature from colonial times to 1892 with emphasis on 1830-60.

2172.1 Spigel, Helen T. "The Sacred Image and the New Truth: A Study in Hawthorne's Women," DAI, 30 (Wash.U.: 1970), 2981A.

2173 Spiller, Robert E. "The Artist in America: Poe, Hawthorne," THE CYCLE OF AMERICAN LITERATURE: AN ESSAY IN HISTORICAL CRITICISM. New York: Macmillan Company, 1957, pp. 69-75.

2174 Spiller, Robert E. "Closed Room and Haunted Chamber," SatRL, 31 (1948), 14-15.

2175 Spiller, Robert E. "The Coming Out of a Recluse," SatRL, 27 (July 8, 1944), 20.

An essay-review of L. S. Hall's HAWTHORNE: CRITIC OF SOCIETY. New Haven: Yale U. P., 1944.

See Hall's reply: "The Author Takes Issue," SatRL, 27 (1944), 15.

2176 Spiller, Robert E. "Critical Revaluations," SatRL, 10 (1934), 406.

2177 Spiller, Robert E. "The Mind and Art of Hawthorne," Outlook, 149 (1928), 650-52, 676, 678.

2178 Spiller, Robert E. THE OBLIQUE LIGHT: STUDIES IN AMERICAN LITERARY HISTORY AND BIOGRAPHY. New York: Macmillan, 1968.

Rev. by Oscar Cargill, AL, 41 (1969), 315-17.

2179 Spiller, Robert E., et al. "Bibliographical Supplement," LITERARY HISTORY OF THE UNITED STATES. New York: Macmillan, 1948.

2180 Spiller, Robert E., Willard Thorp, Thomas H. Johnson, et al, eds. LITERARY HISTORY OF THE UNITED STATES. 3 Vols. New York: 1948.

Usually referred to as LHUS. Fifty-five authors contributed one or more chapters. Third volume is devoted exclusively to bibliography.

2181 Spiller, Robert E., et al, eds. LITERARY HISTORY OF THE UNITED STATES. Rev. edition in one volume. New York: 1953.

Includes a new chapter, "Postscript at Mid-Century" and a twenty-three page BIBLIOGRAPHY. Vol. 3 of 1948 edition is not included.

2182 Spiller, Robert, Willard Thorp, Thomas H. Johnson, Henry Seidel Canby, Richard M. Ludwig, eds. LITERARY HISTORY OF THE UNITED STATES: BIBLIOGRAPHY. London and New York: Macmillan, 1946, 1963.

2183 Spiller, Robert, Willard Thorp, Thomas H. Johnson, Henry Seidel Canby, Richard M. Ludwig, eds. LITERARY HISTORY OF THE UNITED STATES: HISTORY. London: Macmillan Co., 1946, 1963.

Hawthorne references passim. Chapter 27, pp. 416-40 on Nathaniel Hawthorne.

2184 Spingarn, Lawrence P. "The Yankee in Early American Fiction," NEQ, 31 (1958), 484-95.

2184.1 Spinucci, Pietro. "Hawthorne tra presente e passato: OUR OLD HOME," SA, 14 (1968), 113-63.

2185 Spofford, Harriet. Letter from - on occasion of Hawthorne
Centenary, EIHC, 41 (1905), 68-69.

2186 Sprague, Claire. "Dream and Disguise in THE BLITHEDALE
ROMANCE," PMLA, 84 (1969), 596-97.

Dream, itself a disguise, paradoxically becomes
pertinent comment on the many disguises of the novel.
Functioning as revelation and wish-fulfillment,
Coverdale's central dream tells reader what he already
knows.

2186.1 St. Armand, Barton Levi. "Hawthorne's 'Haunted Mind,'"
Criticism, 13 (1971), 1-25.

2187 St. John-Stevas, Norman. "The Author's Struggles with the
Law," CathW, 194 (1962), 345-50.

2188 Stafford, Arnold John. "Hawthorne and Society." KAL, 6
(1963), 3-7.

2189 Stafford, John. "Henry Norman Hudson and the Whig Use of
Shakespeare," PMLA, 66 (1951), 649-61.

Background for Melville's use of Shakespeare in his essay
on Hawthorne and in MOBY DICK.

2190 Stafford, John. THE LITERARY CRITICISM OF 'YOUNG AMERICA':
A STORY IN THE RELATIONSHIP OF POLITICS AND LITERATURE
1837-1850. Berkeley and Los Angeles: California U. P.,
English Studies No. 3, 1952.

American literary nationalism of Melville's essay on
Hawthorne.

Rev. by Richard E. Amacher, NEQ, 25 (1952), 409-10.

2191 Stallman, Robert W., and Arthur Waldhorn. "Nathaniel
Hawthorne," AMERICAN LITERATURE: READINGS AND CRITIQUES.
New York: G. P. Putnam's Sons, 1961, pp. 274-333.

2192 Stallman, Robert W., and Reginald Eyre Watters, eds.
CREATIVE READER: AN ANTHOLOGY OF FICTION, DRAMA, AND
POETRY. New York: Ronald, 1954, pp. 197-206; 207-12.

Source material for "Ethan Brand."

2193 Stanton, Robert. "Dramatic Irony in Hawthorne's Romances,"
MLN, 71 (1956), 420-26.

2194   Stanton, Robert.   "Hawthorne, Bunyan, and the American
         Romances," PMLA, 71 (1956), 155-65.

2194.1 Stanton, Robert.   "THE SCARLET LETTER as Dialectic of
         Temperament and Idea," SNNTS, 2 (1970), 474-86.

2195   Stanton, Robert. THE SIGNIFICANCE OF WOMEN IN HAWTHORNE'S
         ROMANCES. Diss. Ind.: 1953.

2196   Stanton, Robert.   "The Trial of Nature: An Analysis of THE
         BLITHEDALE ROMANCE," PMLA, 76 (1961), 528-38.

2197   Stanton, Theodore, ed.   A MANUAL OF AMERICAN LITERATURE.
         New York: G. P. Putnam's Sons, 1909.

2198   Starkey, Marion L. THE DEVIL IN MASSACHUSETTS. New York:
         Alfred A. Knopf, 1949, p. 268.

2199   Stavrou, C. N.   "Hawthorne on Don Juan," GaR, 16 (1962),
         210-21.
         Hawthorne, like D. H. Lawrence and William Blake,
         believed man's greatest fulfillment was through woman,
         but one of his favorite themes in his novels was the
         man who failed woman.

2200   Stavrou, C. N.   "Hawthorne's Quarrel with Man," Person, 42
         (1961), 352-60.

2201   Stearns, Frank P.   "Hawthorne as Art Critic," CAMBRIDGE
         SKETCHES. Philadelphia: Lippincott, 1905, pp. 365-74.

2202   Stearns, Frank P.   THE LIFE AND GENIUS OF NATHANIEL HAWTHORNE.
         Philadelphia: Lippincott, 1906, 1912.

2203   Stedman, Edmund C. Letter from - on occasion of Hawthorne
         Centenary, EIHC, 41 (1905), 71-73.

2204   Steele, Oliver L.   "On the Imposition of the First Edition
         of Hawthorne's THE SCARLET LETTER," Lib, 17 (1962), 250-55.

2205   Stegner, Wallace, ed.   THE AMERICAN NOVEL FROM JAMES FENIMORE
         COOPER TO WILLIAM FAULKNER. New York: Basic Books, 1965.

2206 Stegner, Wallace, and Mary Stegner, eds. GREAT AMERICAN SHORT STORIES. New York: 1957.

2207 Stein, Roger B. JOHN RUSKIN AND AESTHETIC THOUGHT IN AMERICA, 1800-1900. Cambridge, Mass.: Harvard U. P., 1967.

Rev. by David H. Dichason, AL, 40 (1968), 241-43.

2208 Stein, William Bysshe. "'The Artist of the Beautiful': Narcissus and the Thimble," AI, 18 (1961), 35-44.

A clinical explanation of the paranoiac symptoms which characterize an individual's struggle to sublimate homosexual predispositions.

2209 Stein, William Bysshe. THE FAUST MYTH AND HAWTHORNE. Diss. Florida: 1951.

2210 Stein, William Bysshe. HAWTHORNE'S FAUST: A STUDY OF THE DEVIL ARCHETYPE. Gainesville, Florida: Florida U. P., 1953, pp. 104-22.

Rev. by Louis J. Budd, SAQ, 53 (1954), 150-52; Leon Howard, NCF, 8 (1954), 318-21; Roy Harvey Pearce, MLN, 71 (1956), 61-63; Edward C. Sampson, "A Note on William B. Stein's HAWTHORNE'S FAUST," N&Q, 2 (1955), 137-38; Randall Stewart, AL, 25 (1954), 150-52; Gordon W. Thayer, JAF, 68 (1955), 95-97; Stanley T. Williams, BA, 28 (1954), 352.

2211 Stein, William Bysshe. "The Parable of the AntiChrist in 'The Minister's Black Veil,'" AL, 27 (1955), 386-92.

2212 Stein, William Bysshe. "A Possible Source of Hawthorne's 'English Romance,'" MLN, 67 (1952), 52-55.

2213 Stein, William Bysshe. "Teaching Hawthorne's 'My Kinsman, Major Molineux,'" CE, 20 (1958), 83-86.

2214 Steinke, Russell. "The Scarlet Letters of Puritanism," UR, 31 (1965), 289-91.

2215 Steinmann, Martin, and Gerald Willen, eds. LITERATURE FOR WRITING. Belmont, Calif.: Wadsworth, 1962.

2216 Stephens, Leslie. "Introduction," THE MARBLE FAUN. Ernest Rhys, ed. New York: Everyman's Lib., 1910.

2216.1 Stephens, Rosemary. "'A' Is for 'Art' in THE SCARLET LETTER." ATQ, 1 (1969), 23-27.

2217 Stephenson, Edward R. "Hawthorne's 'The Wives of the Dead.'" Expl, 25 (1967), Item 63.

2218 Stern, Madeleine B. "Three Lives in a New England Tapestry." SatRL, 33 (1950), 8-9.

Rev. art. of Louise Hall Tharp's THE PEABODY SISTERS OF SALEM. Boston: Little, Brown & Co., 1950.

2219 Stern, Milton R., and Seymour L. Gross. AMERICAN LITERATURE SURVEY: THE AMERICAN ROMANTICS, 1800-1860. With a Prefatory Essay by Van Wyck Brooks. New York: Viking P., 1962, pp. 373-75.

2220 Stevenson, Lionel. THE ENGLISH NOVEL: A PANORAMA. Boston: Houghton Mifflin Co., 1960, pp. 339-40.

Central situation of ADAM BEDE has some resemblance to that of THE SCARLET LETTER.

2221 Stevenson, Lionel. "The Hawthorne and Browning Acquaintance: An Addendum." VN, 21 (1962), 16.

James C. Austin, "The Hawthorne and Browning Acquaintance," VN, 20 (1961), 13-18, suggests that Browning's "mesmerism" was probably inspired by a tale of Matthew Maule and Alice Pyncheon. However, Lionel Stevenson notes that a similar situation is developed in Browning's "Porphyria's Lover" (1834), in BELLS AND POMEGRANATES which Hawthorne read in 1850.

2222 Stewart, Randall. AMERICAN LITERATURE AND CHRISTIAN DOCTRINE. Baton Rouge, La. State U. P., 1958.

Rev. by Harold A. Larrabee, NEQ, 32 (1959), 258-60.

2223 Stewart, Randall, ed. THE AMERICAN NOTEBOOKS BY NATHANIEL HAWTHORNE. BASED UPON THE ORIGINAL MANUSCRIPTS IN THE PIERPONT MORGAN LIBRARY. New Haven: Yale University Press, 1932.

2224 Stewart, Randall. "The Concord Group: A Study of Relationships." SR, 44 (1936), 434-46.

2225 Stewart, Randall. A CRITICAL EDITION OF HAWTHORNE'S AMERICAN NOTEBOOKS. Diss. Yale: 1930. Yale U. P., 1932.

2226
Stewart, Randall. "Editing THE AMERICAN NOTEBOOKS,"
EIHC, 94 (1958), 277-81.

2227
Stewart, Randall. "Editing Hawthorne," in Edd W. Parks,
et al., eds., "Problems of the Complete or Collected
Edition," MissQ, 15 (1962), 97-99.

Establishing the Hawthorne canon is the first major
difficulty in editing his works.since the early
Hawthorne wrote under a variety of pen names and
in various periodicals.

2228
Stewart, Randall. "Editing Hawthorne's Notebooks: Selections
from Mrs. Hawthorne's Letters to Mr. and Mrs. Fields,
1864-1868," More Books, 20 (1945), 299-315.

2229
Stewart, Randall, ed. THE ENGLISH NOTEBOOKS BY NATHANIEL
HAWTHORNE. BASED UPON THE ORIGINAL MANUSCRIPTS IN THE
PIERPONT MORGAN LIBRARY. New York: Modern Language
Association of American, 1941. Reprinted, New York:
Russell & Russell, 1962.

Rev. by Manning Hawthorne, AL, 14 (1942-43), 84-87;
V. S. Pritchett, NS&N, 24 (1942), 275; Arlin Turner,
SR, 50 (1942), 275-77; Townsend Scudder, NEQ, 15 (1942),
166-67.

2230
Stewart, Randall. "Ethan Brand," SatRL, 5 (1929), 967.

2231
Stewart, Randall. "The Golden Age of Hawthorne Criticism,"
UKCR, 22 (1955), 44-46.

A marked interest in Hawthorne is one of the more
striking phenomena of our time.

2232
Stewart, Randall. "Hawthorne and the Civil War," SP, 34
(1937), 91-106.

Hawthorne's views of the war and certain environmental
conditions brought about by the war.

2233
Stewart, Randall. "Hawthorne and THE FAERIE QUEENE,"
PQ, 12 (1933), 196-206.

Similarities in characterization and situation between
Hawthorne and Spenser.

2234
Stewart, Randall. "Hawthorne and Faulkner," CE, 17 (1956),
258-62. Repr. in CE, 22 (1960), 128-32.

Although there are differences, man's struggle toward
redemption is the grand subject of both Hawthorne and
Faulkner, and both work in the orthodox Christian
tradition.

2235   Stewart, Randall. "Hawthorne and Politics, Unpublished
       Letters to William B. Pike, Edited by Randall Stewart,"
       NEQ, 5 (1932), 237-63.

       The letters fall in the years 1840-1857.

2236   Stewart, Randall. "Hawthorne in England: The Patriotic
       Motive in the Note-Books," NEQ, 8 (1935), 3-13.

       Hawthorne's judgment of England and the English
       often biased because of Hawthorne's Americanism.

2237   Stewart, Randall. "The Hawthornes at the Wayside, 1860-1864,"
       More Books, 19 (1944), 263-79.

       Selections from Mrs. Hawthorne's letters to
       Mr. and Mrs. James T. Fields.

       Above article continued in "Hawthorne's Last Illness
       and Death," More Books, 19 (1944), 303-13.

2238   Stewart, Randall, ed. "Hawthorne's Contributions to THE
       SALEM ADVERTISER," AL, 5 (1934), 327-41.

       The contributions, reprinted for the first time,
       include reviews of works by Calvert, Longfellow,
       Melville, and Simms, plus two comments on local
       theatrical productions.

2239   Stewart, Randall. "Hawthorne's Last Illness and Death,"
       More Books, 19 (1944), 303-13.

       This is a continuation of the article "The Hawthornes
       at the Wayside, 1860-1864," More Books, 19 (1944),
       263-79.

2240   Stewart, Randall. "Hawthorne's Speeches at Civic Banquets,"
       AL, 7 (1936), 415-23.

       Accounts in newspapers of speeches which Hawthorne
       delivered while in England.

2241   Stewart, Randall. "Introductory Essay," HAWTHORNE: THE
       AMERICAN NOTEBOOKS. New Haven: Yale U. P., 1932.

2242   Stewart, Randall. "Letters to Sophia," HLQ, 7 (1944), 387-95.

2243   Stewart, Randall. "Melville and Hawthorne," SAQ, 51 (1952),
       436-46; repr. in MOBY DICK CENTENNIAL ESSAYS. Tyrus
       Hillway and Luther S. Mansfield, eds. Dallas: Southern
       Methodist U. P., 1953, pp. 153-64.

       Declares that Melville is not portrayed in "Ethan
       Brand" nor is Hawthorne the villain of MOBY DICK.

2244 Stewart, Randall. "Moral Crisis as Structural Principle in Fiction: A Few American Examples," CS, 42 (1959), 284-89.

2245 Stewart, Randall. "Mrs. Hawthorne's Financial Difficulties: Selections from Her Letters to James T. Fields, 1865-1868," More Books, 21 (1946), 43-53.

2246 Stewart, Randall. "Mrs. Hawthorne's Quarrel with James T. Fields," More Books, 21 (1946), 254-63.

Further letters.

2247 Stewart, Randall. "Nathaniel Hawthorne," in MASTERPLOTS: CYCLOPEDIA OF WORLD AUTHORS. Frank Northen Magill, ed. Harper, 1958, I, 487-89.

2248 Stewart, Randall. NATHANIEL HAWTHORNE: A BIOGRAPHY. New Haven: Yale U. P., 1948; repr., Hamden, Conn.: Archon Books, 1970.

Rev. by Stephen E. Whicher, AL, 21 (1949-50), 354-57; Manning Hawthorne, NEQ, 22 (1949), 105-08.

2249 Stewart, Randall. "The Outlook for Southern Writing: Diagnosis and Prognosis," VQR, 31 (1955), 252-63.

Comparisons of the flowering of Hawthorne's New England and the Southern Renascence.

2250 Stewart, Randall. "'Pestiferous Gail Hamilton,' James T. Fields, and the Hawthornes," NEQ, 17 (1944), 418-23.

2251 Stewart, Randall. "Present Trends in the Study and Teaching of American Literature," CE, 18 (1957), 207-11.

2252 Stewart, Randall. "Recollections of Hawthorne by His Sister Elizabeth," AL, 16 (1945), 316-31.

Her letters to James T. Fields.

2253 Stewart, Randall. REGIONALISM AND BEYOND. ESSAYS OF RANDALL STEWART. George Core, ed. Foreword by Norman Holmes Pearson. Nashville: Vanderbilt U. P., 1968.

2254 Stewart, Randall. "Selections from Mrs. Hawthorne's Letters to Mr. and Mrs. Fields," More Books, 19 (1944), 263-79; 303-13.

2255 Stewart, Randall, ed. "Two Uncollected Reviews by Hawthorne,"
NEQ, 9 (1936), 504-09.

The reviews are of J. G. Whittier's THE SUPERNATURALISM
OF NEW ENGLAND (1847), and Charles Wilkins Webber's
THE HUNTER-NATURALIST (1851).

2256 Stewart, Randall. "The Vision of Evil in Hawthorne and Melville,"
in THE TRAGIC VISION AND THE CHRISTIAN FAITH, Nathan A.
Scott, Jr., ed. New York: Association Press, 1957, pp.
238-63; reprinted, substantially, in his AMERICAN LITERATURE
AND CHRISTIAN DOCTRINE. Baton Rouge: Louisiana State
U. P., 1958, pp. 73-102.

2257 Stewart, Randall and Dorothy Bethurum, eds. "Nathaniel
Hawthorne," in LIVING MASTERPIECES OF AMERICAN LITERATURE.
Chicago: Scott, Foresman & Co., 1963, pp. 55-175.

2258 Stewart, Randall, with Seymour L. Gross. "The Hawthorne
Revival," in HAWTHORNE CENTENARY ESSAYS. Roy Harvey
Pearce, ed. Columbus: Ohio St. U. P., 1964, pp.
335-66.

2259 Stibitz, E. Earle. "Ironic Unity in Hawthorne's 'The
Minister's Black Veil,'" AL, 34 (1962), 182-90.

2260 Stock, Ely. "The Biblical Context of 'Ethan Brand,'"
AL, 37 (1965), 115-34.

2261 Stock, Ely. "History and the Bible in Hawthorne's 'Roger
Malvin's Burial,'" EIHC, Special Hawthorne Issue, 100
(1964), 279-96.

2262 Stock, Ely. "Studies in Hawthorne's Use of the Bible,"
DA, 28 (Brown: 1967), 645A-46A.

2263 Stocking, David M. "An Embroidery on Dimmesdale's Scarlet
Letter," CE, 13 (1952), 336-37.

2264 Stoddard, Richard Henry. "My Acquaintance with Hawthorne,"
RECOLLECTIONS, PERSONAL AND LITERARY. New York:
A. S. Barnes & Co., 1903, pp. 116-33.

Contains letter to Stoddard showing Hawthorne's
cynicism concerning political appointments.

2265 Stoddard, Richard Henry. NATHANIEL HAWTHORNE. New York:
Scribners, 1879.

2266 Stoddard, Richard Henry. "Reminiscences of Hawthorne and Poe," Indep. 54 (1902), 2756-58.

2267 Stoehr, Taylor. "Hawthorne and Mesmerism," HLQ, 33 (1969), 33-60.

2268 Stoehr, Taylor. "'Young Goodman Brown' and Hawthorne's Theory of Mimesis," NCF, 23 (1969), 393-412.

2268.1 Stokes, E. "BLEAK HOUSE and THE SCARLET LETTER," AUMLA, 32 (1969), 177-89.

2269 Stone, Edward. "The Antique Gentility of Hester Prynne," PQ, 36 (1957), 90-96.

2269.1 Stone, Edward. "The Devil Is White," in ESSAYS ON DETERMINISM IN AMERICAN LITERATURE. Sydney J. Krause, ed. Kent State U. P., 1964, pp. 55-66.

2270 Stone, Edward. "On Last Teaching Hawthorne," CE, 19 (1958), 257. (A poem.)

2271 Stone, Edward. "Two More Glimpses of Hawthorne," ELN, 3 (1965), 52-55.

2272 Stone, Geoffrey. MELVILLE. New York: Sheed and Ward, 1949.

2273 Stone, Herbert Stuart. /First Editions of Nathaniel Hawthorne7 in FIRST EDITIONS OF AMERICAN AUTHORS, 1893, pp. 91-94.

2273.1 Stouck, David. "The Surveyor of the Custom-House: A Narrator for THE SCARLET LETTER," CentR, 15 (1971), 309-29.

2274 Stovall, Floyd. "Contemporaries of Emerson," AMERICAN IDEALISM. Norman, Okla.: Okla. U. P., 1943, pp. 55-78, passim.

2275 Stovall, Floyd. "The Decline of Romantic Idealism, 1855-1871," TRANSITIONS IN AMERICAN LITERARY CRITICISM. Harry Hayden Clark, ed., Durham, N. C.: Duke U. P., 1953.

Although Hawthorne was primarily a romanticist in mood, his matter was realistic.

2276   Stovall, Floyd, ed. THE DEVELOPMENT OF AMERICAN LITERARY
       CRITICISM. Chapel Hill, N. C.: North Carolina U. P.,
       1955.

2277 Stovall, Floyd, ed. EIGHT AMERICAN AUTHORS: A REVIEW OF
      RESEARCH AND CRITICISM. New York: Modern Lang. Assn.
      of Amer., 1956; 1963, pp. 100-52.

2278   Strandberg, Victor. "The Artist's Black Veil," NEQ, 41
       (1968), 567-74.

       The black veil produces the extreme isolation in which
       Hawthorne places the worst of his unpardonable sinners.
       Hooper's wilful life of isolation may be seen as a
       sacrifice not in pride but in service of truth.

2279   Stratman, Carl J. C., S. V. "Unpublished Dissertations in
       the History and Theory of Tragedy, 1889-1957." BB,
       (1958).

2280   Strauch, Carl F., ed. Critical Symposium on American
       Romanticism, ESQ, 35 (1964), 2-60.

2281 Strauch, Carl F. "Emerson and the Doctrine of Sympathy,"
      SIR, 6 (1967), 152-74.

      P. 152, n. 1. Says that the province of sympathy for
      Emerson is radically different from that established
      for Hawthorne in Roy Male's "Hawthorne and the Concept
      of Sympathy," PMLA, 68 (1953). 138-49.

2282   Strauch, Carl F. "The Problem of Time and the Romantic
       Mode in Hawthorne, Melville, and Emerson," in Critical
       Symposium on American Romanticism, ESQ, 35 (1964), 50-60.

2283   Strauch, Carl F., ed. Symposium on Nathaniel Hawthorne,
       ESQ, 25 (1961), 2-36.

2284 Streeter, Gilbert L. "Some Historic Streets and Colonial
      Houses of Salem," EIHC, 36 (1900), 13-213.

      Contains description of Alice Pyncheon's portrait.

2285 Streeter, Robert E. "Hawthorne's Misfit Politician and
      Edward Everett," AL, 16 (1944), 26-28.

      Edward Everett a possible figure in Hawthorne's
      gallery of satirical portraits in "Mosses."

2286 Stroller, L. "American Radicals and Literary Works of the Mid-Nineteenth Century: An Analogy," in MID-AMERICAN CONFERENCE ON LITERATURE, HISTORY, POPULAR CULTURE AND FOLKLORE. Purdue Univ. (New Voices in American Studies), Ray B. Browne, Donald Winkleman, and Allen Hayman, eds. Purdue Univ. Studies, 1966, pp. 13-20.

2287 Strout, Cushing. THE AMERICAN IMAGE OF THE OLD WORLD. New York: Harper & Row, 1963.

Rev. by Allen Guttmann, AQ, 15 (1963), 595-96.

2288 Strout, Cushing, ed. HAWTHORNE IN ENGLAND: SELECTIONS FROM "OUR OLD HOME" AND "THE ENGLISH NOTE-BOOKS." Ithaca, New York: Cornell U. P., 1965.

2289 Strout, Cushing. "Hawthorne's International Novel," NCF, 24 (1969), 169-81.

2290 Stubbs, John C. "Hawthorne's THE SCARLET LETTER: The Theory of the Romance and the Use of the New England Situation," PMLA, 83 (1968), 1439-47.

Hawthorne drew on mid-19th century theories of prose romance and the central situation of New England romance.

2290.1 Stubbs, John C. "The Ideal in the Literature and Art of the American Renaissance," ESQ, 55 (1969), 55-63.

2291 Stubbs, John C. "A Note on the Source of Hawthorne's Heraldic Device in THE SCARLET LETTER," N&Q, 15 (1968), 175-76.

2291.1 Stubbs, John C. THE PURSUIT OF FORM: A STUDY OF HAWTHORNE AND THE ROMANCE. Urbana: Illinois U. P., 1970.

Hawthorne uses "the quality of artifice basic to the romance form to focus attention on his probing for meaning."

2292 Stubbs, John C. "The Theory of the Prose Romance: A Study in the Background of Hawthorne's Literary Theory," DA, 25 (Princeton: 1965), 4709.

2293 Suh, In-jae. "Hawthorne's Attitude Toward New England Religious Doctrine," ELL, 14 (1963), 78-105.

2294 Sullivan, Barbara W. "A Gallery of Grotesques: The Alienation Theme in the Works of Hawthorne, Anderson, Faulkner, and Wolfe," DA, 30 (Ga.: 1969), 698A-99A.

2295 Suzuki, Jukichi. "Hawthorne as Symbolic Romancer," HSELL, 9 (1963), 2-10.

2296 Swanson, Donald R. "On Building THE HOUSE OF THE SEVEN GABLES," BSUF, 10, 1 (1969), 43-50.

2297 Swift, Lindsay. BROOK FARM, ITS MEMBERS, SCHOLARS, AND VISITORS. New York: The Macmillan Co., 1900.

2298 Symonds, Joseph W. "Address," (Hawthorne Centenary), EIHC, 41 (1905), 23-29.

2299 Symons, Arthur. "Hawthorne," Lamp, 28 (1904), 102-07.

2300 Takuwa, Shinji. "Hawthorne, James, and Soseki: The Sense of Sin," SELL, 12 (1962), 13-28.

2301 Takuwa, Shinji. "Theme in THE SCARLET LETTER," KAL, 6 (1963), 35-40.

2302 Tanner, Bernard R. "Tone as an Approach to THE SCARLET LETTER," EJ, 53 (1964), 528-30.

2303 Tanner, Tony. "Introduction and Notes," HAWTHORNE by Henry James. London: Macmillan, 1967; New York: St. Martin's Press, 1967.

2304 Tanselle, G. Thomas. "A Note on the Structure of THE SCARLET LETTER," NCF, 17 (1962), 283-85.

Suggests revision of John C. Gerber's article, NEQ, 17 (1944), 25-55.

2305 Tapley, Harriet Sylvester. "Hawthorne's 'Pot-8-o Club' at Bowdoin College," EIHC, 67 (1931), 225-32.

2306 Tashjian, Nouvart, and Dwight Echerman. NATHANIEL HAWTHORNE: AN ANNOTATED BIBLIOGRAPHY. New York: 1948.

2307 Tate, Allen. "Emily Dickinson," in THE MAN OF LETTERS
IN THE MODERN WORLD: SELECTED ESSAYS, 1928-1955.
New York: Meridian Books, 1955, 1967.

Repr. in LITERATURE IN AMERICA, Philip Rahv, ed.
Cleveland and New York: World Pub. Co., 1957.

2308 Tate, Allen. "Emily Dickinson," ON THE LIMITS OF POETRY:
SELECTED ESSAYS, 1928-1948. New York: Swallow Press
& William Morrow, 1948, p. 200.

Hawthorne alone in his time kept pure the primitive
vision; he brings the Puritan tragedy to its climax.

2309 Taylor, John Golden. HAWTHORNE'S AMBIVALENCE TOWARD PURITANISM.
Logan, Utah: Utah St. U. P., 1965.

2310 Taylor, John Golden. "Hawthorne's Transmutations of
Puritanism," DA, 19 (Utah: 1959), 2605.

2311 Taylor, Marion A. "Nathaniel Hawthorne and the Curse of
the Pyncheons, The Story behind THE HOUSE OF THE SEVEN
GABLES," [Play], Plays, 19 (1960), 84-96.

2312 Taylor, Walter Fuller. A HISTORY OF AMERICAN LETTERS. New
York: American Book Co., 1936.

Rev. by Henry A. Pochmann, AL, 8 (1936-37), 332-34.

2313 Taylor, Walter Fuller. "Nathaniel Hawthorne (1804-1864),"
THE STORY OF AMERICAN LETTERS. Chicago: Henry Regnery
Co., 1956.

2314 Tennant, F. R. THE ORIGIN AND PROPAGATION OF SIN, BEING
THE HULSEAN LECTURES DELIVERED BEFORE THE UNIVERSITY
OF CAMBRIDGE IN 1902. Cambridge: Cambridge U. P., 1902,
p. 65. . . . .

2315 Terrell, Horace Clifford. THE HAWTHORNE PROBLEM: ANOTHER
VIEW. Diss. (Seattle, Wash.: 1939.

2316 Tharp, Louise Hall. ADVENTUROUS ALLIANCE: THE STORY OF THE
AGASSIZ FAMILY OF BOSTON: Boston, Toronto; Little
Brown & Co., 1959.

2317 Tharp, Louise Hall. THE PEABODY SISTERS OF SALEM. Boston: Little, Brown & Co., 1950.

Rev. by Louis Filler, NEQ, 23 (1950), 410; Henry A. Pochmann, AL, 22 (1951), 367-68; Madeleine B. Stern, "Three Lives in a New England Tapestry," SatRL, 33 (1950), 8-9.

2318 Tharp, Louise Hall. UNTIL VICTORY, HORACE MANN AND MARY PEABODY. Boston: Little, Brown & Co., 1953.

Elizabeth Peabody recommended Hawthorne as a writer of children's books.

2319 Tharpe, Jac. NATHANIEL HAWTHORNE: IDENTITY AND KNOWLEDGE. Preface by Harry T. Moore. Carbondale: So. Ill. U. P., 1967.

Rev. by Roy R. Male, AL, 40 (1968), 239-40; Richard Lehan, NCF, 23 (1968), 117-18.

2320 Tharpe, Jac. SIBYL AND SPHINX: THEMES OF IDENTITY AND KNOWLEDGE IN HAWTHORNE'S WORK. Diss. Harvard: 1965.

2321 Thayer, William Roscoe. Letter from - July 15, 1904 - on occasion of Hawthorne Centenary, EIHC, 41 (1905), 74-75.

2322 Thomas, Edith M. "The Eyes of Hawthorne," (poem), CentM, 68 (1904), 350-51.

2323 Thomas, Henry, and Dana Lee Thomas. "Nathaniel Hawthorne, 1804-1864," LIVING BIOGRAPHIES OF FAMOUS NOVELISTS. Garden City, New York: Garden City Books, 1943, 1959, pp. 165-77.

2324 Thomas, Wright, and Stuart G. Brown, eds. READING PROSE: AN INTRODUCTION TO CRITICAL THOUGHT. New York: Oxford U. P., 1952.

2325 Thompson, Lawrance Roger. MELVILLE"S QUARREL WITH GOD. Princeton, N. J.: Princeton U.P., 1952.

2326 Thompson, Ralph. AMERICAN LITERARY ANNUALS AND GIFT BOOKS, 1825-1865. New York: H. W. Wilson & Co., 1936.

It was no mean service to American literature to provide "the young Hawthorne" with an outlet for his early stories.

Rev. by Frank Luther Mott, AL, 9 (1938-39), 256.

2327 Thompson, W. R. "Aminadab in Hawthorne's 'The Birthmark,'" MLN, 70 (1955), 413-15.

2328 Thompson, W. R. "The Biblical Sources of Hawthorne's 'Roger Malvin's Burial.'" PMLA, 77 (1962), 92-96.

2329 Thompson, W. R. "Patterns of Biblical Allusions in Hawthorne's 'The Gentle Boy.'" SCB, 22 (1962), 3-10.

2330 Thompson, W. R. "Theme and Method in Hawthorne's 'The Great Carbuncle.'" SCB, 21 (1961), 3-10.

2331 Thorner, Horace E. "Hawthorne, Poe, and a Literary Ghost," NEQ, 7 (1934), 146-54.

Motif of "Howe's Masquerade" and Poe's "William Wilson" were possibly derived from legend of Luis Enius which was frequently told, even by Washington Irving in "An Unwritten Drama of Lord Byron."

2332 Thorp, Willard. "American Writers as Critics of Nineteenth-Century Society," THE AMERICAN WRITER AND THE EUROPEAN TRADITION. Minneapolis: Minnesota U. P., 1950, pp. 90-105.

2333 Thorp, Willard. "Did Melville Review THE SCARLET LETTER?" AL, 14 (1942), 302-05.

See R. E. Watters, "Melville's 'Isolatoes,'" PMLA, 60 (1945), 1138n. Declares that Thorp "thoroughly refuted" the "legend."

2334 Thorp, Willard, ed. HERMAN MELVILLE: REPRESENTATIVE SELECTIONS. New York: American Book Co., 1938, p. 338.

2335 Thorp, Willard. "Introduction," THE SCARLET LETTER. New York: Collier Books, 1962.

2336 Thorp, Willard. "THE SCARLET LETTER by Nathaniel Hawthorne," NEQ, 36 (1963), 405-07.

A review of the Centenary Edition of THE WORKS OF NATHANIEL HAWTHORNE, Vol. I, Columbus, Ohio: Ohio St. U. P., 1962.

2337 Thorp, Willard, Merle Curti and Carlos Baker, eds. "Nathaniel Hawthorne, 1804-1864," AMERICAN ISSUES: THE SOCIAL RECORD. Chicago: J. B. Lippincott Co., 1941, pp. 484-93.

2338 Thorp, Willard, et al, eds. "Nathaniel Hawthorne, 1804-1864,"
      THE AMERICAN LITERARY RECORD. Chicago: J. B. Lippincott
      Co., 1961, pp. 377-431.

2339 Thorpe, Dwayne. "'My Kinsman, Major Molineux': The Identity
      of the Kinsman," Topic, 18 (1969), 53-63.

2340 Thorpe, James. "The Ideal of Textual Criticism," THE TASK OF
      AN EDITOR: PAPERS READ AT A CLARK LIBRARY SEMINAR,
      February 8, 1969. Los Angeles: Wm. Andrews Clark Mem.
      Lib., U. C. L. A., pp. 3-32.

2341 Thorpe, James, and Claude M. Simpson, Jr. THE TASK OF AN
      EDITOR: PAPERS READ AT A CLARK LIBRARY SEMINAR,
      February 8, 1969. Foreword Vinton A. Dearing. Los
      Angeles: Wm. Andrews Clark Mem. Lib., U. C. L. A.
      /James Thorpe, "The Ideal of Textual Criticism,"
      pp. 3-32; Claude M. Simpson, Jr., "The Practice of
      Textual Criticism," pp. 35-52./

2342 Thorslev, Peter L., Jr. "Hawthorne's Determinism: An
      Analysis," NCF, 19 (1964), 141-57.

2343 Thurston, Jarvis, and O. B. Emerson, Carl Hartman, Elizabeth
      V. Wright. SHORT FICTION CRITICISM: A CHECKLIST OF
      INTERPRETATION SINCE 1925 OF STORIES AND NOVELETTES
      (AMERICAN, BRITISH, CONTINENTAL) 1800-1958. Denver:
      Alan Swallow, 1960, pp. 70-81.

2344 Ticknor, Caroline. "Hawthorne and His Friend," GLIMPSES
      OF AUTHORS. Boston and New York: Houghton, Mifflin
      Co., 1922, pp. 31-42.

2345 Ticknor, Caroline. HAWTHORNE AND HIS PUBLISHER. Boston and
      New York: Houghton Mifflin Co., 1913; Repr. Port Washington,
      New York: Kennikat P., 1969.

      Hawthorne's letters to elder partner of his publishers
      show "the man of affairs."

      Rev., DIAL, 56 (1914), 13-16; Brief Mention, AL, 42

2346 Ticknor, Caroline. "Records of a Happy Friendship,"
      Dial, 56 (1914), 13-16.

      Discussion of Hawthorne and his publisher.

      See also: "Hawthorne's Opinions," Bookman, 38 (1913),
      217.

2347 Ticknor, Howard M. "Hawthorne as Seen by His Publisher,"
      Critic, 45 (1904), 51-55.

2348 Ticknor, W. D. "Letters of Hawthorne to W. D. Ticknor."
    Newark: Carteret Book Club, 1910.

2349 Timpe, Eugene Frank. "Hawthorne in Germany," Symposium,
    19 (1965), 171-79.

2350 Timpe, Eugene Frank. "The Reception of American Literature
    in Germany, 1861-1871," DA, 21 (So. Calif.: 1961), 3452.

2351 THE TOKEN: A CHRISTMAS AND NEW YEAR'S PRESENT.
    S. G. Goodrich, ed. Boston: Carter and Herndee, 1830;
    Gray and Bowen, 1831, 1832.

2352 THE TOKEN AND ATLANTIC SOUVENIR. A CHRISTMAS AND NEW YEAR'S
    PRESENT. S. G. Goodrich, ed. Boston: Gray and Bowen,
    1833.

    The Seven Vagabonds (Collected in TWICE-TOLD TALES, 1842)
    Sir William Pepperell (Collected in FANSHAWE, 1876)
    The Canterbury Pilgrims (Collected in THE SNOW-IMAGE,
                  1852)

2353 THE TOKEN AND ATLANTIC SOUVENIR. A CHRISTMAS AND NEW YEAR'S
    PRESENT. S. G. Goodrich, ed. Boston: Charles Bowen,
    1835.

    The Haunted Mind (Collected in TWICE-TOLD TALES, 1842)
    Alice Doane's Appeal (Collected in TALES, SKETCHES...,
      1883)
    The Mermaid: a Reverie (Collected in TWICE-TOLD TALES,
      1842, as The Village Uncle.

2354 THE TOKEN AND ATLANTIC SOUVENIR, A CHRISTMAS AND NEW YEAR'S
    PRESENT. S. G. Goodrich, ed. Boston: American
    Stationers' Company, 1838.

    Sylph Etherege (Collected in THE SNOW-IMAGE, 1852)

    The following stories in TWICE-TOLD TALES, 1842:

    Peter Goldthwait's Treasure
    Endicott and the Red Cross
    Night Sketches, beneath an Umbrella
    The Shaker Bridal.

2355 Torrey, Rita F. "'The Great Stone Face': A Lesson Plan
    Designed for Character Building," GrT, 58 (1941), 48, 67.

2356 Trask, Georgianne Sampson, and Charles Burkhart, eds.
    STORYTELLERS AND THEIR ART. New York: Doubleday,
    1963, pp. 259-78.

2356.1 Travis, Mildred K. "Past vs. Present in THE HOUSE OF THE SEVEN
    GABLES," ESQ, 58 (1970), 109-111.

2356.2 Tremblay, William A. "A Reading of Nathaniel Hawthorne's 'The Gentle Boy,'" MSE, 2 (1970), 80-87.

2357 Trent, William P. "The Romancers, 1830-1850," A BRIEF HISTORY OF AMERICAN LITERATURE. New York: Appleton, 1908, pp. 120-28, passim.

2358 Trent, William P., and John Erskine. "Nathaniel Hawthorne," GREAT AMERICAN WRITERS. New York: Henry Holt & Co., 1912, pp. 57-84.

2359 Trent, William P., John Erskine, Stuart P. Sherman, and Carl Van Doren, eds. THE CAMBRIDGE HISTORY OF AMERICAN LITERATURE. New York: Macmillan, 1946, 3 Vols.

"Hawthorne," Vol. II, pp. 16-31.

2360 Trilling, Lionel. BEYOND CULTURE: ESSAYS ON LITERATURE AND LEARNING. New York: Viking, 1965.

Rev. by Richard Lehan, NCF, 23 (1968), 368-69.

2361 Trilling, Lionel. "Our Hawthorne," in HAWTHORNE CENTENARY ESSAYS. Roy Harvey Pearce, ed. Columbus, Ohio: Ohio St. U. P., 1964, pp. 429-58. Revised and repr. in his BEYOND CULTURE: ESSAYS ON LITERATURE AND LEARNING. New York: Viking Press, 1965, pp. 179-208.

2362 Trilling, Lionel. "Our Hawthorne," PR, 31 (1964), 329-51.

2363 Trollope, Anthony. "The Genius of Nathaniel Hawthorne," NAR, 129 (1879), 209-13.

Repr. NAR, 201 (1915), 313-17.

2364 Troughton, Marion. "Americans in Britain," ContempR, 192 (1957), 338-42.

2365 Tryon, Warren S. PARNASSUS CORNER: A LIFE OF JAMES T. FIELDS. Boston: Houghton Mifflin Co., 1963.

2366 Tryon, Warren S., and William Charvat, eds. THE COST BOOKS OF TICKNOR AND FIELDS AND THEIR PREDECESSORS: 1832-1858. New York: Bibliographical Society of America, 1949.

2367 Tucker, Martin, gen. ed. THE CRITICAL TEMPER: A SURVEY OF MODERN CRITICISM ON ENGLISH AND AMERICAN LITERATURE FROM THE BEGINNINGS TO THE TWENTIETH CENTURY. New York: Frederick Ungar, 1969, III, 313-24.

2368 Turcu, Eva. DER PURITANISCHE GEIST BEI NATHANIEL HAWTHORNE. Diss. Vienna: 1951.

2369 Turner, Arlin. "Autobiographical Elements in Hawthorne's THE BLITHEDALE ROMANCE," UTSE, 3526 (1935), 39-62.

2370 Turner, Arlin. "Hawthorne and Reform," NEQ, 15 (1942), 700-14.

2371 Turner, Arlin, ed. HAWTHORNE AS EDITOR: SELECTIONS FROM HIS WRITINGS IN THE AMERICAN MAGAZINE OF USEFUL AND ENTERTAINING KNOWLEDGE. Baton Rouge: La. St. U. P., 1941.

Revs. by Henry Steele Commager, AHR, 47 (1942), 258-59; Norman Holmes Pearson, SatRL, 24 (1941), 18; Stanley T. Williams, AL, 13 (1941-42), 271-72.

2372 Turner, Arlin. "Hawthorne as Self-Critic," SAQ, 37 (1938), 132-38.

Hawthorne's attitude toward the gloom of his stories, the prevalence of allegory, and vagueness of his characters and setting.

2373 Turner, Arlin. "Hawthorne at Martha's Vineyard," NEQ, 11 (1938), 394-400.

An 1836 article reprinted for the first time.

2374 Turner, Arlin. "Hawthorne's Literary Borrowings," PMLA, 51 (1936), 543-62.

Hawthorne's debt to historical or semi-historical sources and to American, English, and continental authors.

2375 Turner, Arlin. "Hawthorne's Methods of Using His Source Materials," in STUDIES FOR WILLIAM A. READ. A. N. Caffee and T. A. Kirby, eds. Baton Rouge: La. U. P., 1940, pp. 301-12.

2376 Turner, Arlin. "Introduction," THE BLITHEDALE ROMANCE. Arlin Turner, ed. New York: Norton, 1958, pp. 5-23.

2376.1 Turner, Arlin, comp. THE MERRILL STUDIES IN THE SCARLET LETTER. Columbus, Ohio: Charles E. Merrill Studies, 1970.

2377 Turner, Arlin. "Mrs. Hawthorne as Censor," SR, 50 (1942), 275-77.

Art.-Rev., of THE ENGLISH NOTEBOOKS BY NATHANIEL HAWTHORNE, Randall Stewart, ed. New York: MLA., 1941.

2378 Turner, Arlin. "Nathaniel Hawthorne in American Studies," CE, 26 (1964), 133-39.

2379 Turner, Arlin. NATHANIEL HAWTHORNE: AN INTRODUCTION AND INTERPRETATION. New York: Barnes and Noble, 1961.

Revs., B. R. McElderry, Jr., AL, 33 (1961), 382; James Schroeder, CE, 23 (1961), 242; TLS, (1961), 330; WR, (1961), 12.

2380 Turner, Arlin. "A Note on Hawthorne's Revisions," MLN, 51 (1936), 426-29.

Mrs. Hawthorne's influence on Hawthorne.

2381 Turner, Arlin. "Recent Scholarship on Hawthorne and Melville," in THE TEACHER AND AMERICAN LITERATURE: PAPERS PRESENTED AT THE 1964 CONVENTION OF THE NATIONAL COUNCIL OF TEACHERS OF ENGLISH. Lewis Leary, ed. Champaign: NCTE, 1965, pp. 95-109.

2382 Turner, Arlin. "Review of Millicent Bell's HAWTHORNE'S VIEW OF THE ARTIST," NCF, 17 (1963), 399.

2383 Turner, Arlin. A STUDY OF HAWTHORNE'S ORIGINS. Diss. Texas: 1934.

2384 Turner, Frederick W., III. "Hawthorne and the Myth of Paradise," Serif, 3 (1966), 9-12.

2385 Turner, Frederick W., III. "Hawthorne's Black Veil," SSF, 5 (1967), 186-87.
Like Ethan Brand and Goodman Brown, Mr. Hooper cannot discover how much of himself and the universe is composed of evil. His veil is a symbol of his inability to answer the most crucial question of his life.

2386 Tuttiett, M. G. "Hawthorne the Mystic," NineC, 87 (1920), 118-25.
Same article in CurOp, 68 (1920), 391-92.

2387 "Twenty Pictures of Hawthorne," ESQ, 39 (1965), 2-12.

2388 Tykessen, Elizabeth. "Fran bokhyllan," BLM, 15 (1947), 497-99.

2389 Tyler, Moses Coit. A HISTORY OF AMERICAN LITERATURE, 1607-1765. Foreword by Perry Miller. New York: Collier Books Ed., 1962, pp. 118, 119.

2389.1 Tyson, Barbara K. "Father and Son: Julian Hawthorne as Heir and Interpreter," CEA, 33 (1971), 19.

Rev. art., of Maurice Basson's HAWTHORNE'S SON. Columbus, Ohio: Ohio St. U. P., 1970.

2390 Tytell, John. "Henry James and the Romance," MarkR, 5 (1969), 1-2.

An early story, "De Grey: A Romance," indicates James's attempt to imitate romanticism as practised by Poe and Hawthorne.

2391 Underwood, Francis H. "Recollections of American Authors," GoodWds, 28 (1887), 664-671.

2392 "The 'Unknown Quantity' in Hawthorne's Personality," CrtL, 42 (1907), 517-18.

2392.1 Vahanian, Gabriel. "Nathaniel Hawthorne: The Obsolescence of God," in his WAIT WITHOUT IDOLS. New York: George Braziller, 1964, pp. 49-71.

2393 Valency, Maurice Jacques. "Feathertop; after a story by Nathaniel Hawthorne." /New York/ Dramatist Play Service /c1963/. (A play in one act.)

2394 Van Der Beets, Richard, and Paul Wetherington. "My Kinsman, Brockden Brown: Robin Molineux and Arthur Mervyn," ATQ, 1 (1969), 13-15.

2395 Van Der Krolf, J. M. "Zen and the American Experience," VBQ, 25 (1959), 122-32.

2396 Van Deusen, Marshall. "Narrative Tone in 'The Custom House' and THE SCARLET LETTER," NCF, 21 (1966), 61-71.

2397 Van Doren, Carl. "Flower of Puritanism: Hawthorne's SCARLET LETTER," Nation, 3 (1920), 649-50.

2398 Van Doren, Carl. "Nathaniel Hawthorne," THE AMERICAN NOVEL. New York: 1921; Rev. ed., Macmillan, 1940.

2399 Van Doren, Charles. "Letters to Mother," Channel, (1959), 323-25.

2400 Van Doren, Mark. "Introduction," THE BEST OF HAWTHORNE.
      Mark Van Doren, ed. New York: Ronald Press, 1951,
      pp. 3-31.

2401 Van Doren, Mark. NATHANIEL HAWTHORNE. New York: William
      Sloane Associates, 1949, 1957.

      Rev. by Edward H. Davidson, AL, 21 (1949-50), 359-60.

2402 Van Nostrand, Albert D., ed. LITERARY CRITICISM IN AMERICA.
      New York: Liberal Arts Press, American Heritage Series
      No. 16, 1957, pp. 89-90.

2403 Van Pelt, Rachel Elizabeth Stanfield. "Folklore in the
      Tales of Nathaniel Hawthorne," DA, 23 (Ill.: 1962),
      627.

2403.1 Van Winkle, Edward S. "Aminadab, the Unwitting 'Bad Anima,'"
        AN&Q, 8 (1970), 131-33.

        "The Birthmark"

2404 Vance, Marguerite. ON WINGS OF FIRE: THE STORY OF NATHANIEL
      HAWTHORNE'S DAUGHTER, ROSE (MOTHER ALPHONSA).
      New York: Dutton, 1955.

2405 Vance, William L. "The Comic Element in Hawthorne's Sketches,"
      SIR, 3 (1964), 144-60.

      Comic detachment and irony are Hawthorne's
      favorite devices.

2406 Vance, William L. "The Comic in the Works of Hawthorne,"
      DA, 23 (Mich.: 1963), 3389.

2407 Vanderbilt, Kermit. "The Unity of Hawthorne's 'Ethan Brand,'"
      CE, 24 (1963), 453-56.

      Transcendentalism played on Hawthorne's imagination,
      "both as a catalyst and irritant."

2408 Veen, Wilhelm. DIE ERZÄHLUNGSTECHNIK IN DEN KURZERZÄHLUNGEN
      NATHANIEL HAWTHORNE. Diss. Münster: 1938.

2409 Vickery, John B. "The Golden Bough at Merry Mount," NCF,
      12 (1957), 203-14.

      Hawthorne a "ritual anthropologist" tracing religious
      evolution.

      See D. G. Hoffman, FORM AND FABLE IN AMERICAN FICTION,
      New York: Oxford U. P., 1961, pp. 126-48.

2410 Vincent, Howard P., ed. COLLECTED POEMS OF HERMAN MELVILLE.
Chicago: Packard and Company, Henricks House, 1949.

Contains poem "Monody" on Hawthorne's passing.

2411 Vincent, Howard P., ed. MELVILLE AND HAWTHORNE IN THE
BERKSHIRES: A SYMPOSIUM. Kent, Ohio: Kent St. U. P.,
1968.

Rev. by Harry Hayden Clark. AL, 41 (1969), 284-85.

2412 Vincent, Howard P. THE TRYING-OUT OF MOBY-DICK. Boston:
Houghton, Mifflin Co., 1949.

2413 Vincent, Leon H. "Nathaniel Hawthorne," AMERICAN LITERARY
MASTERS. Boston and New York: Houghton, Mifflin Co.,
1906, pp. 287-317.

2414 Virtanen, Reino. "Émile Montégut as a Critic of American
Literature," PMLA, 63 (1948), 1265-1275.

Montégut's treatment of Hawthorne.

2415 Vittorini, Elio. DIARIO IN PUBBLICO. Milan: Bompiani, 1957,
pp. 114-15.

2416 Vittorini, Elio. "An Outline of American Literature:
Nathaniel Hawthorne," SR, 68 (1960), 423-37.

2417 Vogel, Dan. "Roger Chillingworth: The Satanic Paradox in
THE SCARLET LETTER," Criticism, 5 (1963), 272-80.

2418 Vogel, Stanley M. GERMAN LITERARY INFLUENCES ON THE
AMERICAN TRANSCENDENTALISTS. New Haven: Yale U. P.,
1955.

Hawthorne's study of German and his allusions to
German thought.

2419 Voight, Gilbert P. "Hawthorne and the Roman Catholic
Church," NEQ, 19 (1946), 394-97.

2420 Voight, Gilbert P. "The Meaning of 'The Minister's Black Veil,'"
CE, 13 (1952), 337-38.

2421 Voight, Gilbert P. "Nathaniel Hawthorne, Author for
Preachers," LuthCQ, 16 (1943), 82-86.

2422 Volpe, Edmund L. "The Reception of DAISY MILLER," BPLQ, 10 (1958), 55-59.

Tradition has confused the favorable reception of DAISY MILLER with the unfavorable treatment given James's biography of Hawthorne.

2423 Von Abele, Rudolph. "Baby and Butterfly," KR, 15 (1953), 280-92.

The climactic scene at the close of "The Artist of the Beautiful" is a symbolic meeting between art and life.

2424 Von Abele, Rudolph. THE DEATH OF THE ARTIST: A STUDY OF HAWTHORNE'S DISINTEGRATION. The Hague: Nijhoff, 1955.

Hawthorne saw reality around him but fled because of shame into the privacy of a masquerade.

Revs. by Edward H. Davidson, AL, 27 (1956), 596-98; Gordon Milne, BA, 30 (1956), 88; TLS (1955), 508.

2425 Von Abele, Rudolph. "THE SCARLET LETTER: A Reading," Accent, 11 (1951), 211-27.

2426 von Hibler, Leo. "Hawthorne in England," NS, 4 (1955), 145-53.

2427 Wagenknecht, Edward Charles. "Mrs. Hawthorne on Dickens," BPLQ, 12 (1960), 120-21.

2428 Wagenknecht, Edward Charles. NATHANIEL HAWTHORNE: MAN AND WRITER. New York: Oxford U. P., 1961.

Rev. by D. B. Bagg, SprR, (March 5, 1961); Booklist, 57 (April 15, 1961), 518; DeLancey Ferguson, NYTBR (1961), 28; Richard Harter Fogle, NCF, 16 (1961), 90-91; Raymond D. Gozzi, MR, 3 (1961), 207-10; Walter Harding, CST (1961), 2; S. J. Haselton, Thought, 37 (1962), 294, 296; Granville Hicks, SatR, 44 (1961), 20; Edward M. Holmes, NEQ, (1961), 404-05; Richard W. Lid, SFC (1961), 25; Kenneth S. Lynn, Reporter, 24 (1961), 54-55; Perry Miller, CSM (February 23, 1961), 7; Randall Stewart, AL, 33 (1961), 380-81; TLS (September 29, 1961), 637-38; James H. Wheatley, JEGP, 61 (1962), 445-56; John R. Willingham, LJ, 86 (1961), 1001-02.

2429 Wagenknecht, Edward Charles. "The Soul's Romance: Hawthorne," CAVALCADE OF THE AMERICAN NOVEL: FROM THE BIRTH OF THE NATION TO THE MIDDLE OF THE TWENTIETH CENTURY. New York: 1952, pp. 38-57.

Rev. Herbert Brown, AL, 25 (1953), 243-45.

2430 Wager, Willis. AMERICAN LITERATURE: A WORLD VIEW. London: Univ. of London Press, 1968; New York: New York, U. P., 1968, pp. 93-97.

The "principal stress" in Hawthorne's work is on recognition that the essentially human condition will fall short of the perfect, the ideal, or the abstract.

2431 Waggoner, Hyatt Howe. "American Literature Re-Examined, Nathaniel Hawthorne: The Cemetery, the Prison and the Rose," UKCR, 14 (1948), 175-90.

2432 Waggoner, Hyatt Howe. "Art and Belief," HAWTHORNE CENTENARY ESSAYS, Roy Harvey Pearce, ed. Columbus, Ohio: Ohio St. U. P., 1964, pp. 167-95.

2433 Waggoner, Hyatt Howe. "'Grace' in the Thought of Emerson, Thoreau, and Hawthorne," ESQ, 54 (1969), 68-72.

2434 Waggoner, Hyatt Howe. "Hawthorne," in AMERICAN LITERARY SCHOLARSHIP: AN ANNUAL, 1963. James Woodress, ed. Durham, N. C.: Duke U. P., 1965, pp. 17-28.

2435 Waggoner, Hyatt Howe. "Hawthorne," in AMERICAN LITERARY SCHOLARSHIP: AN ANNUAL, 1964. James Woodress, ed. Durham, N. C.: Duke U. P., 1966, pp. 16-31.

2436 Waggoner, Hyatt Howe. "Hawthorne," in AMERICAN LITERARY SCHOLARSHIP: AN ANNUAL, 1966. James Woodress, ed. Durham, N. C.: Duke U. P., 1968, pp. 13-24.

2437 Waggoner, Hyatt Howe. "Hawthorne," in AMERICAN LITERARY SCHOLARSHIP: AN ANNUAL, 1967. James Woodress, ed. Durham, N. C.: 1969, pp. 17-28.

2438　Waggoner, Hyatt Howe. HAWTHORNE: A CRITICAL STUDY.
　　　　Cambridge: The Belknap Press of Harvard U. P., and
　　　　London: Cumberlege, 1955. Rev. ed., 1963.
　　　　Revs. Richard P. Adams, JEGP, 55 (1956), 341-44;
　　　　Marius Bewley, SR, 64 (1956), 152-61;
　　　　Walter Blair, AL, 28 (1957), 526-30;
　　　　C. Cestre, EA, 9 (1956), 280-81;
　　　　Davidson, Edward H. VQR, 11 (1955), 490-93;
　　　　DeLancey, Ferguson, NYHTBR (1955), 6;
　　　　Richard H. Fogle, AL, 36 (1964), 370-71; Expl, 15
　　　　　　(1956), Item 1;
　　　　Leon Howard, NCF, 10 (1956), 321-22;
　　　　J. C. Levenson, NEQ, 28 (1955), 404-06;
　　　　B. R. McElderry, Person, 37 (1956), 316-18;
　　　　Nation (May 28, 1955), 468;
　　　　Randall Stewart, UKCR, 22 (1955), 44-46;
　　　　Thought, 30 (1955-56), 618; TLS (Dec. 23, 1955), 773;
　　　　Arthur Voss, BA, 30 (1956), 225;
　　　　Earle Walbridge, LJ, 80, 559-60;
　　　　Charles C. Walcutt, ArQ, 12 (1956), 176-78;
　　　　USQBR (September, 1955), 347.

2439　Waggoner, Hyatt Howe. HAWTHORNE: A CRITICAL STUDY.
　　　　Cambridge: The Belknap Press of Harvard U. P., 1963.

　　　　Some material added to the 1955 edition, some omitted.
　　　　An "entirely new" chapter on THE MARBLE FAUN.

　　　　Revs., Richard Harter Fogle, AL, 36 (1964), 370-71;
　　　　C. Keeler, MASJ, 4 (1963), 80.

2439.1　Waggoner, Hyatt Howe. "Hawthorne and Melville Acquaint the
　　　　Reader with Their Abodes," SNNTS, 2 (1970), 420-24.

2440　Waggoner, Hyatt Howe. "Hawthorne's Beginning: 'Alice
　　　　Doane's Appeal,'" UKCR, 16 (1950), 254-60.

2441　Waggoner, Hyatt Howe. "Hawthorne's 'Canterbury Pilgrims':
　　　　Theme and Structure," NEQ, 22 (1949), 373-87.

2442　Waggoner, Hyatt Howe. "Introduction," THE HOUSE OF THE SEVEN
　　　　GABLES. Hyatt Howe Waggoner, ed. Boston: Houghton,
　　　　Mifflin Co., 1964, pp. v-xxii.

2443　Waggoner, Hyatt Howe. "Introduction," NATHANIEL HAWTHORNE:
　　　　SELECTED TALES AND SKETCHES. Hyatt Howe Waggoner, ed.
　　　　New York: Rinehart, 1956, 1962, pp. v-xxiii.

2443.1　Waggoner, Hyatt Howe. "Introduction," NATHANIEL HAWTHORNE:
　　　　SELECTED TALES AND SKETCHES. New York: Holt, Rinehart
　　　　and Winston, 1970.

2444 Waggoner, Hyatt Howe. "THE MARBLE FAUN" in HAWTHORNE:
A COLLECTION OF CRITICAL ESSAYS. A. N. Kaul, ed.
Englewood Cliffs, N. J.: Prentice-Hall, Inc., 1966,
pp. 164-76.

2445 Waggoner, Hyatt Howe. "Nathaniel Hawthorne," in AMERICAN
LITERARY MASTERS. Charles R. Anderson, gen. ed.
New York: Holt, Rinehart and Winston, 1965, I, 149-315.

2446 Waggoner, Hyatt Howe. "Nathaniel Hawthorne," EngR, 8 (1959),
416.

2447 Waggoner, Hyatt Howe. "Nathaniel Hawthorne," in SIX AMERICAN
NOVELISTS OF THE NINETEENTH CENTURY: AN INTRODUCTION.
Richard Foster, ed. Minneapolis: Minn. U. P., 1968,
pp. 45-81.

2448 Waggoner, Hyatt Howe. "Nathaniel Hawthorne," UMPAL, 23 (1962),
Minneapolis: Minn. U. P., 1962.

2449 Waggoner, Hyatt Howe, and George Monteriro. "Introduction,"
THE SCARLET LETTER. San Francisco: Chandler, 1968,
pp. xiii-lii.

2450 Wagner, Linda W. "Embryonic Characterization in 'The
Custom House,'" EngR, 16 (1966), 32-35.

2451 THE STEPHEN H. WAKEMAN COLLECTION OF BOOKS OF NINETEENTH CENTURY
AMERICAN WRITERS. New York: American Art Association,
April 28-29, 1904. Items 261-439. Sale catalogue.

2452 Walcutt, Charles Child. "The Idle Inquiry: Nathaniel
Hawthorne's 'Young Goodman Brown,'" in MAN'S CHANGING
MASK: MODES AND METHODS OF CHARACTERIZATION IN FICTION.
Minneapolis: Minnesota U. P., 1966, pp. 124-30.

2453 Walcutt, Charles Child. "THE SCARLET LETTER and Its Modern
Critics," NCF, 7 (1953), 251-64.

2454 Waldron, John. "Il fauno di marmo, storia di un innocente,"
FLe, 23 (1951), 4-5.

2454.1 Walker, Kenneth E. SIMPLIFIED APPROACH TO THE HOUSE OF THE
SEVEN GABLES. Woodbury, New York: Barron's Educational
Series, Inc., 1971.

Biography of Hawthorne, setting, theme, symbolism and
characters of the novel, other novels, study questions.

2455 Walker, Warren S. TWENTIETH-CENTURY SHORT STORY EXPLICATION: INTERPRETATIONS, 1900-1960, INCLUSIVE, OF SHORT FICTION SINCE 1800. Hamden, Conn.: Shoe String P., 1951, Supplement I, 1961-1963, pub., 1963; Supplement II, 1963-1964, pub. 1965.

2456 Walker, William E., and Robert L. Welker, eds. REALITY AND MYTH: ESSAYS IN AMERICAN LITERATURE IN MEMORY OF RICHARD CROOM BEATTY. Nashville, Tenn.: Vanderbilt U. P., 1964.

Rev. by Robert Walker, AL, 36 (1964), 392.

2457 Wallace, Archer. "Religious Faith of Great Authors," in RELIGIOUS FAITH OF GREAT MEN. New York: Round Table Press, 1934, pp. 30-55.

2458 Walsh, Thomas F., Jr. "The Bedeviling of Young Goodman Brown," MLQ, 19 (1958), 331-36.

2459 Walsh, Thomas F., Jr. "Character Complexity in Hawthorne's 'The Birthmark,'" ESQ, 23 (1961), 12-15.

2460 Walsh, Thomas F., Jr. "The Devils of Hawthorne and Flannery O'Connor," XUS, 5 (1966), 117-22.

2461 Walsh, Thomas F., Jr. "Dimmesdale's Election Sermon," ESQ, 44 (1966), 64-66.

2462 Walsh, Thomas F., Jr. "Hawthorne: Mr. Hooper's 'Affable Weakness,'" MLN, 74 (1959), 404-06.

2463 Walsh, Thomas F., Jr. "Hawthorne's Handling of Point of View in His Tales and Sketches," DA, 17 (Wis.: 1957), 623.

2464 Walsh, Thomas F., Jr. "Hawthorne's Satire in 'Old Esther Dudley,'" ESQ, 22 (1961), 31-39.

2465 Walsh, Thomas F., Jr. "Howells' A MODERN INSTANCE," Expl, 23 (1965), Item 59.

2465 Walsh, Thomas F., Jr. "Rappaccini's Literary Gardens," ESQ, 19 (1960), 9-13.

2467 Walsh, Thomas F., Jr. "'Wakefield' and Hawthorne's Illustrated Ideas: A Study in Form," in Carl F. Strauch, et al., Symposium on Nathaniel Hawthorne. ESQ, 25 (1961), 29-35.

2468 Walter, Erich Albert, ed. "Old Manse," TOWARD TODAY:
A COLLECTION OF ENGLISH AND AMERICAN ESSAYS PRESENTING
THE EARLIER DEVELOPMENT OF IDEAS FUNDAMENTAL IN MODERN
LIFE AND LITERATURE. Scott, 1938, pp. 391-400.

2469 Wann, Louis, ed. CENTURY READINGS IN THE ENGLISH ESSAY.
New York: Appleton-Century, 1926.

"View of Concord," pp. 388-89; "Walk near Concord,"
pp. 389-390.

2470 Waples, Dorothy. "Suggestions for Interpreting THE MARBLE
FAUN," AL, 13 (1941), 224-39.

Five Freudian ideas similar to the ideas in THE
MARBLE FAUN.

2471 Ward, A. C. AMERICAN LITERATURE, 1880-1930. New York: The
Dial Press, 1932, pp. 5, 6-7.

Comparisons of Hawthorne and George Eliot, Hawthorne
and Charles Lamb.

2472 Ward, A. C. ASPECTS OF THE MODERN SHORT STORY: ENGLISH
AND AMERICAN. New York: Dial, 1925.

2473 Ward, Mrs. Elizabeth Stuart Phelps. Letter from - on
occasion of Hawthorne centenary, EIHC, 41 (1905), 76.

2474 Ward, Mrs. Humphrey. Letter from - to Mr. Choate, June 8,
1904, on occasion of Hawthorne centenary, EIHC, 41
(1905), 49-54.

2475 Ward, Mary A. "Nathaniel Hawthorne," Cornhill, 90, Ser. 3,
17 (1904), 167-71.

A letter from Mrs. Humphrey Ward to the American
Ambassador on the occasion of the Hawthorne Centenary.

2476 Ward, W. S. "Nathaniel Hawthorne and Brook Farm," Letters, 4
(1931), 6-14.

2477 Warfel, Harry R. "Metaphysical Ideas in THE SCARLET LETTER,"
CE, 24 (1963), 421-25.

2478 Warfel, Harry R., et al, eds. "Nathaniel Hawthorne," THE
AMERICAN MIND. New York: American Book Co., 1937, 1947,
pp. 597-630.

2479 Warren, Austin. "The Concord School of Philosophy," NEQ, 2 (1929), 199-233.

2480 Warren, Austin. "Hawthorne, Margaret Fuller, and 'Nemesis,'" PMLA, 54 (1939), 615-18.

See Oscar Cargill, "Nemesis and Nathaniel Hawthorne," PMLA, 52 (1937), 848-62; William Peirce Randel, "Hawthorne, Channing, and Margaret Fuller," AL, 10 (1939), 472-76.

2481 Warren, Austin. "Hawthorne's Reading," NEQ, 8 (1935), 480-97.

Hawthorne not a bookish author but one who read widely in older literatures and contemporary publications.

2482 Warren, Austin. "Introduction," NATHANIEL HAWTHORNE: REPRESENTATIVE SELECTIONS, WITH INTRODUCTION, BIBLIOGRAPHY, AND NOTES. New York: American Book Co., 1934.

Repr., in part in Maurice Beebe. LITERARY SYMBOLISM. San Francisco: Wadsworth, 1960, pp. 101-102; and in Robert W. Stallman, and Arthur Waldhorn, eds. AMERICAN LITERATURE: READINGS AND CRITIQUES. New York: Putnam, 1961, pp. 286-87.

Rev. by Mark Van Doren, NEQ, 24 (1951), 101-02.

2483 Warren, Austin. "Introduction," THE SCARLET LETTER. New York: Holt, Rinehart and Winston, 1947, 1963, pp. v-xi.

2484 Warren, Austin. "Nathaniel Hawthorne," in THE NEW ENGLAND CONSCIENCE. Ann Arbor: Mich. U. P., 1966, 1968, pp. 132-42.

2485 Warren, Austin. "Nathaniel Hawthorne," RAGE FOR ORDER: ESSAYS IN CRITICISM. Chicago: Chicago U. P., 1948, pp. 84-103.

2485.1 Warren, Austin. "The Scarlet Letter," CONNECTIONS. East Lansing, Michigan: Michigan U. P., 1970, pp. 45-69.

2486 Warren, Austin. "THE SCARLET LETTER: A Literary Exercise in Moral Theology," SoR, 1 (1965), 22-45.

2487 Warren, Robert Penn. "Hawthorne, Anderson, and Frost," NR, 54 (1928), 399-401.

2487.1 Wasserstrom, William. HEIRESS OF ALL THE AGES: SEX AND SENTIMENT IN THE GENTEEL TRADITION. Minnesota U. P., 1959, pp. 77-78.

2488 Wasserstrom, William. "The Spirit of Myrrha," AI, 13 (1956), 455-72.

2489 Waterman, Arthur E. "Dramatic Structure in THE HOUSE OF THE SEVEN GABLES," SLitI, 2, i (1969), 13-19.

Hawthorne employs five-act structure. Result is discrepancy in resolution of themes, conclusion of plot, and blurring of reality by gothic elements.

2490 Watters, R. E. "Melville's 'Isolatoes,'" PMLA, 60 (1945), 1138-48.

Cf., Willard Thorp, "Did Melville Review THE SCARLET LETTER?" AL, 14 (1942), 302-05.

2491 Weaver, Raymond M. HERMAN MELVILLE: MARINER AND MYSTIC. Introduction by Mark Van Doren. New York: Pageant Books, Inc., 1961.

2492 Weaver, Raymond M. "Melville," AMERICAN WRITERS ON AMERICAN LITERATURE. John Albert Macy, ed. New York: 1931, p. 104.

2493 Webber, Everett. "Equity, Fourier, Brook Farm, and the Phalanxes," in ESCAPE TO UTOPIA: THE COMMUNIAL MOVEMENT IN AMERICA. New York: Hastings House Publishers, 1959, pp. 165-99.

A chronicle of Hawthorne's Brook Farm experience.

2494 Weber, Alfred. "Der Autor von 'David Whicher' und das Geheimnis der grünen Brille," JA, 10 (1965), 106-25.

2495 Weber, Alfred. "Hawthornes Briefe über THE OLD MANSE," in FESTSCHRIFT FÜR WALTER HÜBNER. Dieter Riesner and Helmut Gneuss, eds. Berlin: Schmidt, 1964, pp. 234-38.

2496 Weber, Carl J. "A Hawthorne Centenary," ColbM, 7 (1942), 97-102.

2497 Weber, Carl J. "Lowell's 'Dead Rat in the Wall,'" NEQ, 9 (1936), 468-72.

See George Knox, "The Hawthorne-Lowell Affair," NEQ, 29 (1956), 493-502; and Evan Charteris, THE LIFE AND LETTERS OF SIR EDMUND GOSS. New York: 1931, p. 200.

2497.1 Weber, Carl J. "More About Lowell's 'Dead Rat,'" NEQ, 9
          (1936), 686-88.

2498
     Wecter, Dixon. THE HERO IN AMERICA: A CHRONICLE OF HERO-
          WORSHIP. New York: Charles Scribner's Sons, 1941.

2499 Wegelin, Christof. "Europe in Hawthorne's Fiction," ELH, 14
          (1947), 219-45.

2500 Wegelin, Christof. "The Rise of the International Novel,"
          PMLA, 77 (1962), 305-10.

2501 Wegelin, Oscar. EARLY AMERICAN FICTION. Boston: 1900.

2502 Weiffenbach, Rose E. A TECHNICAL ANALYSIS OF HAWTHORNE'S
          STYLE. Diss. Boston: 1939.

2503 Wellborn, Grace Pleasant. "The Golden Thread in THE SCARLET
          LETTER," SFQ, 29 (1965), 169-78.

2504 Wellborn, Grace Pleasant. "The Mystic Seven in THE SCARLET
          LETTER," SCB, 21 (1961), 23-31.

2505 Wellborn, Grace Pleasant. "Plant Lore and THE SCARLET LETTER."
          SFQ, 27 (1963), 160-67.

2506 Wellborn, Grace Pleasant. "The Symbolic Three in THE SCARLET
          LETTER," SCB, 23 (1963), 10-17.

2507 Wellek, René, and Austin Warren. THEORY OF LITERATURE, 3rd ed.
          New York: Harcourt, Brace & World, Inc., 1956.

2508 Wendell, Barrett. "Nathaniel Hawthorne," A LITERARY HISTORY
          OF AMERICA. New York: Scribner's, 1901.

2509 Wentersdorf, Karl P. "The Genesis of Hawthorne's 'The
          Birthmark,'" JA, 8 (1963), 171-86.

2510 Werner, William L. "The First Edition of Hawthorne's THE
          SCARLET LETTER," AL, 5 (1934), 559-64.

2511 West, Ray B. THE SHORT STORY IN AMERICA. New York: Gateway Editions, Inc., 1952.

It is to Hawthorne, Poe and Melville that we must look for the beginnings of the short story in America.

2512 West, Ray B., and Robert Wooster Stallman, eds. THE ART OF MODERN FICTION. New York: Rinehart, 1949, pp. 28-33.

Contains an analysis of "Rappaccini's Daughter."

2513 Westbrook, Perry D. "Celia Thaxter: Seeker of the Unattainable," ColLQ, 12 (1964), 499-512.

2514 Wheeler, Otis B. "Hawthorne and the Fiction of Sensibility," NCF, Hawthorne Centenary Issue, 19 (1964), 159-70.

2514.1 Whelan, Robert Emmet, Jr. "THE BLITHEDALE ROMANCE: The Holy War in Hawthorne's Mansoul," TSLL, 13 (1971), 91-110.

2514.2 Whelan, Robert Emmet, Jr. "Hawthorne Interprets 'Young Goodman Brown,'" ESQ, 62 (1971), 2-4.

2515 Whelan, Robert Emmet, Jr. "Hester Prynne's Little Pearl: Sacred and Profane Love," AL, 39 (1968), 488-505.

Pearl, representing allegorically the love of Hester and Dimmesdale, originates in sinful love, but becomes a symbol of holy love that is the salvation of both her parents.

2516 Whelan, Robert Emmet, Jr. "The Invisible World of THE SCARLET LETTER," DA, 21 (Mich.: 1961), 3793-94.

2516.1 Whelan, Robert Emmet, Jr. "'Rappaccini's Daughter' and Zenobia's Legend," RS, 39 (1971), 47-52.

2516.2 Whelan, Robert Emmet, Jr. "Roger Chillingworth's Whole Business is Reflection," RS, 37 (1969), 298-312.

2517 Whelan, Robert Emmet, Jr. "'Roger Malvin's Burial': The Burial of Reuben Bourne's Cowardice," RS, 37 (1969), 112-21.

2518 Whibley, Charles. "Two Centenaries," BwM, 176 (1904), 255-62.

Centenaries of Hawthorne and George Sand.

2519 Whipple, Edwin P. "Nathaniel Hawthorne," /Atl, 1860/ in his
CHARACTER AND CHARACTERISTIC MEN. Boston: Ticknor and
Fields, 1866, pp. 218-42. Repr. in HAWTHORNE AMONG HIS
CONTEMPORARIES. Kenneth Walter Cameron, ed. Hartford:
Transcendental Books, 1968, 70-83; and in THE RECOGNITION
OF NATHANIEL HAWTHORNE. B. Bernard Cohen, ed. Ann Arbor:
Michigan U. P., 1969, pp. 78-90.

2520 White, Morton Gabriel, and Lucia White. "Bad Dreams of the
City: Melville, Hawthorne, and Poe," in THE INTELLECTUAL
VERSUS THE CITY: FROM THOMAS JEFFERSON TO FRANK L.
WRIGHT. Cambridge: Harvard U. P., 1962, pp. 36-54.

2520.1 White, Robert L. "'Rappaccini's Daughter,' The Cenci, and the
Cenci Legend," SA, 14 (1968), 63-86.

2521 White, Robert L. "Washington Allston: Banditti in Arcadia,"
AQ, 13 (1961), 387-401.

The landscapes of Allston established for later
painters Italy's romantic charm, whereas his Gothic
MONALDI, A TALE set a precedent for writers, such
as Hawthorne, of depiction of fundamental corruption
under Italy's superficial beauty.

2521.1 White, Sidney Howard. SIMPLIFIED APPROACH TO THE SCARLET
LETTER. Woodbury, New York: Barron's Educational
Series, Inc., 1971.

Chapter-by-chapter summary, evaluations of the major
characters and of the novel, selected criticism, topics
for discussion.

2522 White, William M. "Hawthorne's Eighteen-Year Cycle: Ethan
Brand and Reuben Bourne," SSF, 6 (1969), 215-18.

2523 White, William M. THE PERSONALITY OF NATHANIEL HAWTHORNE.
Diss. Fla.: 1953.

2524 Whitford, Kathryn. "'On a Field, Sable, the Letter "A,"
Gules,'" LHR, 10 (1968), 33-38.

2525 Willauer, George Jacob, Jr. "Incongruity in Selected Works
of Nathaniel Hawthorne," DA, 26 (Pa.: 1966), 3931.

2526 Willett, Maurita. "The Letter A, Gules, and the Black Bubble,"
in MELVILLE AND HAWTHORNE IN THE BERKSHIRES: A SYMPOSIUM.
Howard P. Vincent, ed. Kent, Ohio: Kent State U. P.,
1968, pp. 70-78.

2527 Williams, Cecil B. "Hawthorne of Salem," [a sonnet], CE, 23 (1962), 401.

2528 Williams, Mentor L. "On Teaching Our Democratic Heritage," CE, 8 (1947), 186-92.

Our democratic heritage includes THE SCARLET LETTER.

2529 Williams, Philip Eugene. "The Biblical View of History: Hawthorne, Mark Twain, Faulkner, and Eliot," DA, 25 (Penn: 1965), 4159-60.

2530 Williams, Philip Eugene. "THE SCARLET LETTER and Hope for History," ESELL, 47 (1965), 31-64.

2531 Williams, Stanley T. AMERICAN LITERATURE. Philadelphia: Lippincott, 1933.

2532 Williams, Stanley T. "Cosmopolitanism in American Literature Before 1880," THE AMERICAN WRITER AND THE EUROPEAN TRADITION. Minneapolis: Minnesota U.P., published for the University of Rochester, 1950, pp. 49-52.

Cosmopolitanism of Hawthorne.

2533 Williamson, G. M. "Bibliography of the Writings of Nathaniel Hawthorne," BookB, 15 (1897), 218-20, 326-27.

2534 Wilson, Carroll A. THIRTEEN AUTHOR COLLECTIONS OF THE NINETEENTH CENTURY. David A. Randall and Jean C. S. Wilson, eds. New York: Scribner's, 1950, I, 119-54.

2535 Wilson, Edmund, ed. SHOCK OF RECOGNITION: (THE DEVELOPMENT OF LITERATURE IN THE UNITED STATES RECORDED BY THE MEN WHO MADE IT). Garden City, New York: Doubleday, 1947; Farrar, Straus, 1955.

2536 Wilson, J. B. "The Antecedents of Brook Farm," NEQ, 15 (1942), 320-31.

2537 Wilson, William D. "The Contemporaneous Critical Response to Hawthorne's Use of Allegory. (Parts One and Two.)" DA, 27 (Columbia: 1967), 4232A-33A.

2538 Wimsatt, William K., Jr., and Cleanth Brooks. LITERARY CRITICISM: A SHORT HISTORY. New York: Alfred A. Knopf, 1959, pp. 679-80, passim.

2539 Winkelman, Donald A. "Goodman Brown, Tom Sawyer, and Oral Tradition." KFQ, 10 (1965), 43-48.

2540 Winslow, David J. "Hawthorne's Folklore and the Folklorist's Hawthorne: A Re-Examination," SFQ, 39 (1970), 34-52.

2541 Winterich, John T. "Good Second-Hand Condition," PubW, 121 (1932), 2423-24.

Bibliographical details in regard to Hawthorne's LIFE OF FRANKLIN PIERCE (1852).

2542 Winterich, John Tracy. "Nathaniel Hawthorne and THE SCARLET LETTER," BOOKS AND THE MAN. New York: Greenberg, 1929, pp. 212-29.

2543 Winters, Yvor. "Henry James and the Relation of Morals to Manners," AmR, 9 (1937), 482-503.

Comparison of James and Hawthorne.

2544 Winters, Yvor. "Herman Melville and the Problems of Moral Navigation" in MAULE'S CURSE. Norfolk, Conn.: New Directions, 1938, 53-89. Repr. in his IN DEFENSE OF REASON, New York: Swallow, 1947, 200-33.

2545 Winters, Yvor. "Maule's Curse: Hawthorne and the Problem of Allegory," AmR, 9 (1937), 339-61.

Also: MAULE'S CURSE, OR HAWTHORNE AND THE PROBLEM OF ALLEGORY: SEVEN STUDIES IN THE HISTORY OF AMERICAN OBSCURANTISM. Norfolk, Conn.: 1938, pp. 3-22.

Repr. in H. L. Beaver, ed. AMERICAN CRITICAL ESSAYS: TWENTIETH CENTURY. London: Oxford U. P., 1959; Marius Bewley. THE ECCENTRIC DESIGN. New York: 1947; and Irving C. Howe, ed. MODERN LITERARY CRITICISM. New York: Beacon P., 1958.

2546 Witham, W. Tasker. PANORAMA OF AMERICAN LITERATURE. Daye, 1947, pp. 90-95.

2547 Wood, Clifford A. "Teaching Hawthorne's 'The Celestial Railroad,'" EJ, 54 (1965), 601-05.

2548 Wood, James Playsted. MAGAZINES IN THE UNITED STATES. New York: Ronald P., 1949, 2nd ed., 1956, 66-67, passim.

2548.1 Wood, James Playsted. THE UNPARDONABLE SIN: A LIFE OF NATHANIEL HAWTHORNE. New York: Pantheon Books, 1970.

2549 Woodberry, George Edward. AMERICA IN LITERATURE. London and New York: Harper & Bros., 1903, pp. 102-07.

2550 Woodberry, George Edward. THE APPRECIATION OF LITERATURE. New York: Baker and Taylor Co., 1909, 125-26, passim.

2551 Woodberry, George Edward. "Conway's HAWTHORNE." Nation, 51 (1890), 216.

2552 Woodberry, George Edward. "Hawthorne," LITERARY MEMOIRS OF THE NINETEENTH CENTURY. New York: Harcourt, Brace & Co., 1921, pp. 201-14.

2553 Woodberry, George Edward. "Hawthorne and Everett," Nation, 75 (1902), 283.

Two stories, "My Wife's Novel," (1832) and "The Modern Job," (1834) have been attributed to Hawthorne, but according to William Everett they were written by the latter's father.

2554 Woodberry, George Edward. "Influence of Puritanism on Hawthorne." Harpers, 106 (1903), 428-29.

2555 Woodberry, George Edward. "The Literary Age of Boston," HarpMM, 106 (1903), 424-30.

Influence of Puritanism on Hawthorne.

2556 Woodberry, George Edward. /Nathaniel Hawthorne/ BookN, 21 (1903), 131.

2557 Woodberry, George Edward. NATHANIEL HAWTHORNE. Boston and New York: Houghton, Mifflin Co., Riverside Press, Cambridge, 1902.

Revs: Atl, 90 (1902), 563-7; Bookman, 17 (1902), 336-8; Dial, 34 (1903), 147; Forum, 34 (1903), 394-7; W. H. Johnson, Critic, 41 (1902), 510-11; Nation, 75 (1902), 464-5; Outlook, 72 (1902), 850; A. S. Van Westrum, BookB, 25 (1902), 330-1.

2558 Woodberry, George Edward. NATHANIEL HAWTHORNE, HOW TO KNOW HIM. Indianapolis: Bobbs-Merrill Co., 1918, p. 90..

2559 Woodbridge, Benjamin Mather. "The Supernatural in Hawthorne and Poe," CCPLS, 2 (1911), 135-54.

2560 Woodress, James, ed. AMERICAN LITERARY SCHOLARSHIP.
Durham, North Carolina: Duke U. P.

2561 Woodress, James. DISSERTATIONS IN AMERICAN LITERATURE,
1891-1955, WITH SUPPLEMENT, 1956-1961. Durham, N. C.:
1962, pp. 21-23, 92-93.

2562 Woodson, Thomas. "Robert Lowell's 'Hawthorne,' Yvor Winters,
and the American Literary Tradition." AQ, 19 (1967),
575-82.

2563 Woodward, Robert H. "Automata in Hawthorne's 'Artist of the
Beautiful' and Taylor's 'Meditation 56,'" ESQ, 31
(1963), 63-66.

Hawthorne and Edward Taylor draw examples from
marvels such as Albertus Magnus's man of brass,
Friar Bacon's Brazen Head, a little coach and horses
that may be set in motion by a spring, and a mechanical
insect.

2564 Wright, Austin. BIBLIOGRAPHIES OF STUDIES IN VICTORIAN
LITERATURE for 1945-1954. Urbana, Illinois U. P., 1956.

2565 Wright, Elizabeth V. "Nathaniel Hawthorne: A Supplementary
Checklist: American Short Fiction Explications,"
CE, 18 (1956), 161-64.

2565.1 Wright, Lyle H. AMERICAN FICTION, 1774-1850: A CONTRIBUTION
TOWARD A BIBLIOGRAPHY. San Marino, Calif.: Huntington
Lib., 1969. (Revision of 1948 edition).

2565.2 Wright, Lyle H. AMERICAN FICTION, 1851-1875: A CONTRIBUTION
TOWARD A BIBLIOGRAPHY. San Marino, Calif.: Huntington
Library, 1957.

2565.3 Wright, Lyle H. AMERICAN FICTION, 1876-1900: A CONTRIBUTION
TOWARD A BIBLIOGRAPHY. San Marino, Calif.: Huntington
Library, 1966.

2566 Wright, Nathalia. "Hawthorne and the Praslin Murder,"
NEQ, 15 (1942), 5-14.

2567 Wright, Nathalia. "The Influence of Italy on THE MARBLE
FAUN," TSL, Special Number (1961), 141-49.

2568 Wright, Nathalia. "The Language of Art: Hawthorne," in
AMERICAN NOVELISTS IN ITALY: THE DISCOVERERS: ALLSTON
TO JAMES. Philadelphia: Penn. U. P., 1965, pp. 138-67.

Rev. by James Woodress, AL, 37 (1966), 495-97.

2569 Wright, Nathalia. MELVILLE'S USE OF THE BIBLE. Durham, N. C.:
1949, p. 7.

Compared to Melville, Hawthorne made slight and
straightforward use of Scripture.

2570 Wright, Nathalia. "MOSSES FROM AN OLD MANSE and MOBY DICK:
The Shock of Discovery," MLN, 67 (1952), 387-92.
Repr. in MELVILLE AND HAWTHORNE IN THE BERKSHIRES:
A SYMPOSIUM. Howard P. Vincent, ed., 1968.

Hawthorne as an influence on fire imagery in MOBY DICK.

2571 Wycherly, H. Alan. "Hawthorne's 'The Minister's Black
Veil,'" Expl, 23 (1964), Item 11.

2572 Wyld, Lionel D. "Technology and Human Values," Vectors, 4
(1969), 21-23.

2573 Yagyu, Nozomu. "Hawthorne's Concept of Original Sin as
Seen in 'The Birthmark,'" EiT, 1 (1962), 1-6.

2574 Yamaya, Saburo. "Poe, Hawthorne, and Melville's 'Benito
Cereno,'" SELit, 4 (1961), 21-32.

2575 Yates, Norris. "An Instance of Parallel Imagery in
Hawthorne, Melville, and Frost," PQ, 36 (1957),
276-80.

The image of the woodpile in all three authors.

2576 Yates, Norris. "Ritual and Reality, Mask and Dance Motifs
in Hawthorne's Fiction," PQ, 34 (1955), 56-70.

2577 Yoder, R. A. "Hawthorne and His Artist," SIR, 7 (1968),
193-206.

2578 Yokozawa, Shiro. "Hawthorne's Use of Pearl in THE SCARLET
LETTER," LAR, 5 (1960), 16-26.

2579 Young, Marguerite. "Marguerite Young on Anais Nin,"
          Voyages, 1 (1967), 63-65.

          Artistry in Miss Nin's works ranks her with
          Hawthorne and others.

2580 Young, Philip. "Hawthorne and 100 Years: A Report from the
          Academy," KR, 27 (1965), 215-32.

2581 Young, Philip. "Introduction," THE HOUSE OF THE SEVEN GABLES.
          New York: Holt, Rinehart and Winston, 1957, pp. v-xvii.

2582 Zabel, Morton Dauwen. "Introduction," LITERARY OPINION IN
          AMERICA. Morton Dauwen Zabel, ed. New York: Harper &
          Bros., 1937, 1951, p. 3.

2583 Zaitchik, Joseph Abraham. "Hawthorne as Truth-Teller: An
          Analysis of Moralistic Techniques in the Tales and
          Sketches," DA, 26 (Boston Univ.: 1965), 2734-35.

2584 Zangwill, O. L. "A Case of Paramnesia in Nathaniel
          Hawthorne," C&P, 13 (1945), 246-60.

          A psychological analysis of Hawthorne's experience
          at Stanton Harcourt.

2585 Zardoya, Concha. HISTORIA DE LA LITERATURA NORTEAMERICANA.
          Barcelona: Editorial Labor, S. A., 1956.

          Rev. by Edd Winfield Parks, AL, 29 (1957), 111-12.

2586 Zauli-Naldi, Camilla. "La fortuna di Hawthorne in Italia:
          Nota bibliografica," SA, 6 (1960), 183-201.

          Bibliography of Italian editions, translations and
          criticism.

2587 Ziff, Larzer. "The Artist and Puritanism," in HAWTHORNE
          CENTENARY ESSAYS. Roy Harvey Pearce, ed. Columbus:
          Ohio St. U. P., 1964, pp. 245-69.

2588 Ziff, Larzer. "The Ethical Dimension of 'The Custom House,'"
          MLN, 73 (1958), 338-44.

2589 Ziff, Larzer. "Introduction," THE SCARLET LETTER. Larzer
          Ziff, ed. Indianapolis: Bobbs-Merrill, 1963, pp. vii-
          xvii.

2590 Zimmerman, Melvin. "Baudelaire, Poe and Hawthorne,"
RLC, 39 (1965), 448-51.

2591 Zipes, Jack David. "Studies of the Romantic Hero in
German and American Literature," DA, 27 (Columbia:
1966), 191A.

2592 Zivkovic, Peter D. "The Evil in the Isolated Intellect:
Hilda, in THE MARBLE FAUN," Person, 43 (1962), 202-13.

2593 Zivley, Sherry. "Hawthorne's 'The Artist of the Beautiful'
and Spenser's 'Muiopotmos,'" PQ, 48 (1969), 134-37.

2594 Zolla, Elémire. "Un alchimista bostoniano et l'immaginazione
orgánica," RdE, 13 (1968), 46-52.

2595 Zolla, Elémire. "Septimus Felton et la letteratura alchemica
inglese e americana," RdE, 11 (1966), 17-55.

2596 Zunder, T. A. "Walt Whitman and Hawthorne," MLN, 47 (1932),
314-16.

Whitman's appreciation of Hawthorne is shown in two
editorials for THE BROOKLYN DAILY EAGLE written
April 6, 1846, and July 10, 1846.

Subject Index

SUBJECT-INDEX

Each number following an index category refers to
the entry number in the master bibliographic list, not
to the page number.

Because many of the biographies are, in fact,
critical biographies, persons seeking information on
specific works by Hawthorne should consult the biographies
in addition to the critical material listed in the Index.

"Ambitious Guest, The," 24.1, 91, 321, 322, 424, 440, 462, 517, 592, 604, 720, 1221, 1470, 1647, 1727, 2080, 2312, 2313

America, Hawthorne's Attitude Toward, 724.1

American Magazine of Useful and Entertaining Knowledge, 940, 1085, 2371

American Notebooks, (See Notebooks, American)

Aminidab, 1656, 2403.1

Analogues, 54, 166, 272

Anarchy, 1255

"Ancestral Footstep, The," 29, 85.1, 87, 256, 413, 530, 1005, 1086, 1470, 1605, 1618, 2180, 2181, 2183, 2212, 2319, 2379, 2398, 2401, 2438, 2439, 2499

Anima, 1348, 2403.1

Annuals and Gift Books, 2326, 2351, 2352, 2353, 2354

Anthon, Charles, 1657 Classical Dictionary

AntiChrist, 2211

Anti-hero, 374.1

Antinomianism, 1609

"Antique Ring, The," 658, 690, 714, 1221, 1470, 2131, 2379

"April Fools," 1803

Arcadia, See Utopia

Archetypes, 325

Architectural, 23, 212, 483, 484, 503, 586, 1554, 2011.2

Art (as setting), 115, 201, 1449, 1996, 2521

Art, Hawthorne's literary, 4, 43, 52, 68, 86, 294, 353, 458, 532, 719, 720, 777, 852.1, 1190, 1288, 1337, 1355, 1505, 1541, 1542, 1543, 1618, 1770, 1781, 1957, 2080, 2587

"Battle-Omen, The," 751, 1087, 1093, 1221

Baudelaire, Pierre Charles, 2590

Bayle, Pierre, 155

Bellow, Saul, 2010

Berkshire County, 180, 181, 182, 1688, 2411

Bible, Hawthorne's use of, 417, 1628, 2260, 2261, 2262, 2328, 2329, 2529, 2569

Bibliography, 49, 145.1, 193, 194, 194.1, 194.2, 262, 270.1, 271, 279.1, 295, 343, 368, 402, 403.2, 418, 455, 530, 631, 656, 657, 663, 677, 700, 701, 713, 739, 770, 784, 847.2, 865, 1212, 1311, 1312, 1319, 1320, 1327, 1333, 1529, 1589, 1597, 1605, 1606.1, 1700, 1736, 1753, 1765.1, 1775, 1788, 1804, 1821, 1855, 1872, 1876, 1877, 1982.1, 2122, 2123, 2179, 2181, 2182, 2219, 2279, 2306, 2312, 2319, 2343, 2366, 2434, 2435, 2436, 2437, 2455, 2482, 2533, 2560, 2561, 2564, 2565, 2565.1, 2565.2, 2565.3, 2586

Bibliography, essays on, 40, 47, 415, 499, 1208, 1231, 1560, 1973, 1983, 2277, 2541

Biographical, 19, 20, 21, 24, 28, 32, 39, 40, 62, 65, 94, 95, 102, 109, 128, 129, 131, 132, 146, 147, 180, 181, 182, 188, 212, 214, 214.1, 237, 243, 252, 253, 259, 296, 297, 302, 327, 329, 331.1, 332, 345, 346, 349, 400, 412, 427, 448, 456, 457, 468, 469, 473, 477, 498, 503, 512, 522, 560, 619, 620, 622, 623, 625, 677.1, 678, 752, 753, 760, 775, 788, 799, 826, 911, 912, 915, 917, 919, 921, 923, 926, 929, 931, 933, 935, 937, 938, 941, 942, 943, 1170.1, 1188, 1211, 1260, 1261, 1262, 1263, 1264, 1272, 1306, 1347.1, 1372, 1382, 1410, 1421, 1427.2, 1516.1, 1597,

Biographical, cont.

1627, 1676, 1719, 1763, 1828.1, 1828.2, 1846, 1994, 2046, 2047, 2050, 2050.1, 2051, 2071, 2072, 2140, 2173, 2198, 2239, 2240, 2250, 2264, 2266, 2271, 2274, 2299, 2316, 2317, 2344, 2345, 2346, 2347, 2348, 2358, 2365, 2373, 2389.1, 2391, 2411, 2412, 2428, 2439.1, 2445, 2478, 2484, 2513, 2519, 2523, 2548.1, 2552, 2556

"Biographical Sketch of Jonathan Cilley," 75, 1088

Biographical Stories for Children (edition), 993, 994

Biography, 85, 241, 343, 455, 462, 561, 677, 801, 811, 910, 916, 922, 1174, 1219, 1296, 1297, 1298, 1299, 1300, 1506, 1545, 1605, 1720, 1803, 2202, 2248, 2265, 2401, 2424, 2428, 2454.1, 2557

"Birthmark, The," 85, 85.1, 86, 87, 91, 128.1, 136, 185, 252, 275, 392, 518, 581, 630, 640, 658, 690, 701, 702, 714, 721, 1182, 1221, 1232, 1238, 1366, 1456, 1470, 1530, 1564, 1597, 1618, 1682, 1853, 1893, 1965, 1980, 2011, 2080, 2210, 2222, 2256, 2274, 2325, 2327, 2403.1, 2459, 2463, 2509, 2573

"Blackness," 1217, 1470, 1544, 1564, 1665

Blake, William, 1859 "Urizen"

Carlyle, Thomas, 1243.1

Catholicism, 588, 641, 642, 648, 701, 761, 1197, 2419, 2485

"Celestial Railroad, The," 154, 188, 248, 282, 339, 359, 404, 412, 495, 580, 714, 900, 1090, 1091, 1092, 1156, 1221, 1232, 1314, 1442, 1466.1, 1470, 1564, 1617, 1618, 1665, 1692, 1822, 1853, 2011, 2055, 2130, 2145, 2146, 2194, 2275, 2320, 2438, 2439, 2482

Cenci, The, 892, 2520.1

Cenci, Beatrice, 586.2, 892

Centenary of Hawthorne's birth, 263, 289, 397, 497, 618, 632, 817, 901, 902, 903, 904, 905, 906, 907, 1203, 1301, 1696, 1741, 1804, 1865, 1870, 1907, 1924, 1925, 1951, 2185, 2203, 2298, 2321, 2473, 2474, 2475, 2518

Centenary of Hawthorne's death, 94, 101, 130, 217, 219, 221, 222, 223, 224, 225, 277, 279, 280, 281, 311, 381, 382, 383, 384, 385, 387, 394, 504, 535, 612, 634, 652, 659, 847, 1249, 1336, 1472, 1491, 1513, 1523, 1596, 1758, 1831, 2258, 2361, 2432, 2496, 2514, 2587

"Certain Venerable Personage, A," 1440.1

Cervantes, Don Miguel, 396

Chain of Being, The, 1610, 1857

Channing, William Ellery, 1950

Character, national, 354, 1688, 1997, 2016, 2058, 2172, 2189, 2190

Character, study of, 8, 166, 183, 446, 553, 555, 883, 944, 1350, 1352, 1412, 1530, 1603, 1767, 2030, 2128, 2278, 2327, 2454.1, 2459, 2462, 2521.1

Criticism, general, 14, 23, 145.1, 166.3, 262, 273, 293, 312,
325, 352.1, 388, 403.2, 404, 408, 431.1, 438, 439, 441,
445, 466, 470, 471, 471.1, 487, 489, 500, 512.1, 512.2,
513, 517, 535, 536, 539, 552, 559, 590.1, 598, 615, 616,
618, 619, 653, 654, 660, 670, 684, 690, 693, 700, 700.1,
705, 706, 721, 728, 807.1, 852.1, 889.1, 1201, 1210.1,
1230, 1250, 1269, 1276, 1277, 1313, 1322.1, 1347.1, 1349,
1353, 1357, 1358, 1391, 1392, 1406, 1425, 1426.1, 1427,
1434, 1447, 1466.1, 1538, 1569, 1576, 1604.1, 1620.1,
1673, 1707, 1737.1, 1762, 1769, 1812, 1819, 1828, 1850,

1873, 1908.1, 1919, 1920, 1921, 1949, 1954, 1955, 1956,
1971, 2025, 2043, 2096, 2135.1, 2162, 2163, 2174, 2175,
2176, 2191, 2192, 2249, 2253, 2276, 2283, 2287, 2315,
2337, 2338, 2356.1, 2360, 2361, 2362, 2367, 2388, 2392.1,
2399, 2400, 2402, 2438, 2439, 2446, 2448, 2482, 2507,
2521.1, 2538, 2546, 2549, 2550, 2551, 2558, 2579, 2582

Criticism, textual, 49, 104, 217, 218, 219, 220, 221, 222,
223, 224, 224.1, 225, 278, 279.1, 282, 283, 284, 315,
329, 382, 383, 384, 385, 436, 480, 500, 729.1, 839, 840,
1249, 1649, 1669, 1678, 1813, 2135, 2138, 2204, 2226,
2227, 2228, 2330, 2340, 2341

Crowds, Hawthorne's use of, 52, 550 (villagers), 702, 1192

Curriculum (American literature), 735, 1189, 1316, 2112, 2251,
2378

Curtis, George Wilham, 400, 1549, 1693

"Custom House, The," 98, 126, 127, 596, 596.1, 672, 752,
1407.1, 1440.1, 1507, 1546, 1633, 1725, 2273.1, 2396,
2450, 2588

Custom House position, Hawthorne's, 328, 427, 752, 1306,
1633, 1757

Dante, 337, Scarlet Letter; 1607, Divine Comedy; 1608,
Marble Faun

Dark lady, 1656, 1945

Darkness, 1275

"David Swan," 154, 662, 720, 1470, 1564, 2080, 2319

"David Whicher," 1419, 1977, 2494

Deism, 1377

Democracy, 36, 124, 1255, 1810, 1840, 1881, 2065, 2066, 2068,
2070

Demons, 173

Determinism in American literature, 2269.1; see also
Interpretations, historical and cultural; Moral;
Religious; and Psychological Insights

Development, Hawthorne's literary, 29, 202, 796, 797, 829,
843, 924, 1422, 1650

Devil archetype, 676, 737, 1192, 1535, 2092, 2209, 2210

Devil (Diabolus), 3, 13, 159, 518, 1535, 2097, 2115.1, 2198,
2209, 2210, 2417, 2460

"Devil in Manuscript, The," 154, 170, 658, 743, 1221, 1442,
1597, 1618, 2080, 2379, 2438, 2439

Diaries (editions), 976, 977, 978

Diary, Hawthorne's, 1408, 1879, 1880, 1960, 2415

Dickens, Charles, 42, 394, 1817, 2427; Bleak House, 2268.1

Dickinson, Emily, 2307, 2308; "Further in Summer Than the
Birds," 1497; "I Felt a Funeral in My Brain," 1635

Diction, Hawthorne's, 325, 822, 1285, 1575

Digby, Richard, 750

Digby, Sir Kenelm, 750, 1965

Dimmesdale, Arthur, 5, 74, 490, 528, 544, 564, 806, 855, 1304.1, 1592, 1656, 1767, 1780, 2019, 2263

Dolliver Romance, The, 85.1, 128.1, 185, 247, 462, 530, 701, 1314, 1470, 1597, 1618, 1936, 1945, 2180, 2181, 2183, 2224, 2320, 2379, 2438, 2439

Dolliver Romance, The, (editions), 1003, 1004, 1005

Donatello, 1656, 1823

Dostoievski, Feodor, 96, 1573

Drama (structure), 466, 478, 568, 2489

Dramatization of Hawthorne's works, 632.1, 1524, 1525, 1571, 1572, 1786, 2142, 2311, 2393

Dream, 355, 759, 790, 823, 1822, 1824, 1853, 2011.1, 2186, 2520

"Dr. Grimshawe's Secret," 52, 85.1, 128.1, 167, 185, 247, 529, 530, 531, 720, 743, 770, 1399, 1470, 1490, 1597, 1618, 1656, 2070, 2180, 2181, 2183, 2212, 2319, 2320, 2379, 2429, 2438, 2439, 2500

"Dr. Grimshawe's Secret" (editions), 1001, 1002, 1490

"Dr. Heidegger's Experiment," 52, 167, 185, 370, 460, 640, 776, 854, 896, 1470, 1618, 1624, 2060, 2080, 2379, 2438, 2439

"Drowne's Wooden Image," 43, 170, 404, 465, 658, 714, 720, 1221, 1470, 1618, 1647, 1967, 2080, 2210, 2379, 2557

Dumas, Alexander, 776

The Fall, 90, 91, 117, 177, 528, 628, 715.1, 1490, 1495, 1496, 1656, 1868

Fall, Fortunate (<u>Felix Culpa</u>), 91, 148, 1247, 1656, 1711

<u>Famous Old People</u> (see <u>Grandfather's Chair</u>)

"Fancy's Show Box," 5, 75, 85, 186, 582, 650, 658, 714, 720, 1221, 1470, 1564, 1597, 1686, 1692, 2080, 2131, 2379, 2401, 2438, 2439, 2482, 2557

<u>Fanshawe</u>, 52, 85.1, 128.1, 202, 222, 296, 316, 352, 384, 388, 462, 530, 645, 789, 829, 830, 1360, 1470, 1477.1, 1502, 1508, 1564, 1618, 1656, 1796, 1836, 2109, 2180, 2181, 2183, 2209, 2210, 2319, 2429, 2438, 2439

<u>Fanshawe</u> (editions), 1000, 1004, 1005, 1006, 1007

"Fated Family," 1097

Faulkner, William. <u>Absalom, Absalom</u>! 1998.1; <u>As I Lay Dying</u>, 242, 446; "The Bear," 1223; <u>The Sound and the Fury</u>, 778; 27, 123, 462, 583, 1778, 1840, 1909, 2234

Faust (See Devil Archetype)

"Feathertop," 17, 87, 154, 256, 340, 412, 530, 591, 592, 630, 658, 689, 714, 720, 756, 1221, 1226, 1316, 1342, 1368, 1369, 1470, 1547, 1561, 1597, 1656, 1883, 1884, 1934, 1967, 2080, 2223, 2313, 2319, 2320, 2374, 2379, 2393

<u>Federalist Papers</u>, 1255

Feminism, 578, 1242, 1243, 1534.1, 2172.1

Fiction in America, See Literary history

Fields, James T., 102, 386, 596, 605, 1588, 2228, 2237, 2239, 2245, 2246, 2250, 2252, 2254, 2365

"Great Stone Face, The," 85, 87, 110, 154, 252, 404, 592, 630, 707, 714, 720, 881, 1183, 1442, 1453, 1470, 1479, 1503, 1536, 1561, 1597, 1653, 1682, 1745, 1871, 2011, 2080, 2159, 2276, 2319, 2379, 2439.

Green, Julien, 1360 Le Voyageur sur la Terre

Greenough, Horatio, 286

Greenough, Richard, 286

Grotesque, 867, 1778, 2294

Guilt, 5, 97, 476, 488, 541, 673, 722, 1355, 1507, 1562, 1586, 1823, 1936, 1998.1

H., J. B., 1520, "Indian Troubles at Dunstable"

Haggard, Rider, 1348 She

"Hall of Fantasy, The," 128.1, 404, 460, 537, 580, 592, 658, 701, 714, 720, 1221, 1322, 1470, 1564, 1597, 1618, 1680, 2379, 2412

Hamilton, Gail, 2250

Hammett, Dashiell, 192

Hardy, Thomas, 1237

Harris, Joel Chandler, 882

Hartley, L. P., 1662

Hate, 1244

Hathorne, Justice John, 20, 1464, 1646, 1994.

Hathorne, Major William, 20, 1994

Hauff, Wilhelm. Das Kalte Herz, 1880.2

"Haunted Mind, The," 52, 417, 742, 744, 896, 1470, 1594, 1597, 1618, 1686, 2080, 2131, 2186.1, 2209, 2210, 2320, 2438, 2439

"Haunted Quack...The," 1111, 1481

Hawthorne, Elizabeth M. (sister), 130, 930, 940, 2252

Hawthorne, Elizabeth Manning, Mrs. (mother), 943

Hawthorne, Julian (son), 128.1, 130, 131, 380.1, 1313, 1394, 1395, 1700, 1704, 2497

Hawthorne, Maria Louisa (sister), 939

Hawthorne, Capt. Nathaniel (father), 1213

Hawthorne, Rose (daughter), 299, 300, 909, 913, 1407, 1625, 1626, 1801, 2117, 2404

Hawthorne, Sophia, 129, 212, 237, 462, 926, 1169, 1170, 1170.1, 1410, 1784, 1848, 1903, 1926, 1987, 2218, 2228, 2237, 2239, 2242, 2245, 2246, 2254, 2317, 2377, 2380, 2427

Hawthorne's Historical Tales for Youth (See Grandfather's Chair)

Hay, William, 1191, 1193

Head and Heart, 114.1, 138, 419, 462, 633, 855, 1423, 1915, 1980, 2070.1 (See also Imagery)

Heans, Sir William (character), 1191, 1193

Heart (See Head and Heart and Imagery)

Heredity, 203, 1936

Heresy, 357

Hero, (American), 92, 137.1; (tragic), 806; 1304, 1945, 2115.1, 2199, 2498, 2591

Heroines, Hawthorne's, 183, 340, 358, 462, 676, 764, 850, 1185, 1242, 1243, 1267, 1268, 1431, 1432, 1612, 1690, 1912, 1945, 2195, 2199, 2269

Heroism, 842, 847.2

Hester (Prynne), 6, 79, 99, 206, 215, 242, 319, 357, 490, 578, 676, 1205, 1242, 1267, 1268, 1304, 1352, 1359, 1629, 1677, 1945, 2269, 2515

Hilda, 162, 164, 183, 1267, 1268, 2592

"Hints to Young Ambition," 1113

History, Hawthorne's concept and use of, 7, 23, 31, 36, 43.1, 143, 143.1, 354, 405, 462, 533, 547, 551, 576, 715.1, 719, 749, 836, 838, 878, 1326, 1387, 1451, 1507.1, 1792, 1793, 1839, 2057, 2261

Hoffman, E. T. A., 1307, "Weird Tales"

Holgrave, 137.1, 1243.1, 1388.1, 1583, 1656

"Hollow of Three Hills, The," 24.1, 52, 168, 169, 170, 185, 294, 526, 581, 592, 714, 896, 1221, 1470, 1506, 1596, 1597, 1618, 1635, 1794, 2080, 2210, 2313, 2379, 2438, 2439

Holmes, Oliver Wendell, 203,

Mr. Hooper, 493, 1656, 2462

House of the Seven Gables, The, cont.

2442, 2454.1, 2485, 2489, 2525, 2544, 2545, 2576, 2580, 2581

House of the Seven Gables, The (editions), 1008, 1009, 1010,
1011, 1012, 1013, 1014, 1015, 1016, 1017, 1018, 1019,
1020, 1021, 1022, 1023, 1024, 1025, 1025.1

"Howe's Masquerade," 43, 52, 574, 701, 1114, 1316, 1470, 1597,
2080, 2331, 2438, 2439

Howells, William Dean, 203, 291.1, 310, 380.1, 1179, 1611,
1612, 1862, 2171; 2465, A Modern Instance

Hudson, Henry Norman, 2189

Humanism, moral, 137, 589, 1965

Humor, 178, 237, 336, 350, 351, 594, 1304.1, 1354.1, 1539,
2016, 2405, 2406

Hypocrisy, 100

Idealism, 1289, 1436, 1637, 2275, 2290.1

Identity, 333.2, (see also Initiation)

Imagery, 2067; brand, 1647.1; cave, 820; Cenci, Beatrice, 586.2;
circle, 1361; color, 191; cosmic, 690; cross, 1656; Eden,
1656; fall, the, 1656; father, 1458, 1825, 2005, 2019;
fire, 2570; flower, 1389; forest, 458.1; fountain, 1210,
1389; hand, 1238; heart, 818, 1238, 2059, 2131; hellfire,
138; light and dark, 67, 191, 358, 363, 701, 702, 703,
764; Madonna, 1527; Maule's well, 1656; mermaid, 1485;
mirror, 467, 1424, 1485; nature, 290; oaktree, 184;
Puritan, 1648; rose, 337; scaffold, 2059, scarlet bean
flowers, 362; serpent, 304.1, 372; value, 854; world of,
1477.1

Imagery - medical, 152, 232

Interpretations, moral, 11, 12, 17, 91, 99, 144, 199, 226, 233, 238, 245, 319, 357, 398, 409, 422, 474, 480, 485, 507, 510, 511, 515, 518, 544, 564, 578, 644, 649, 650, 699, 782, 837, 838, 1256, 1279, 1548, 1558, 1737, 1936, 2187, 2485, 2486, 2544

Interpretations, psychological, (see <u>Psychological Insights</u>)

Interpretations, religious, 199, 226, 287, 319, 357, 378, 526, 588, 666, 667, 668, 686, 729, 809, 815, 1232, 1315, 1363, 2009, 2023, 2089, 2116, 2152, 2222, 2421, 2457, 2559

"Interrupted Nuptials," 1115

Inversion, 1583.1

<u>Invisible Man, The</u>, Ralph Ellison, 655.1

Irony, 336, 357, 508, 518, 564, 592, 711, 1323, 1581, 1582, 1583.1, 1771, 1941, 2193, 2259, 2396, 2405, 2406

Irving, Washington, 416; <u>Bracebridge Hall</u>, 1590; 2331

Isolation, theme of, 17, 97, 136, 216, 421, 462, 518, 579, 1259, 1615, 1620, 1682, 1686, 1750, 1811, 2278

Italy, Hawthorne in, 72, 83, 109, 251, 258, 304, 761, 884, 1287, 1398, 1913, 1914, 1946, 2521, 2568, 2586

Ives, Charles, 724

Lincoln, Abraham, 861

"Lincoln in War Time" (see "Chiefly about War Matters")

Literary History, 57, 60, 76, 156, 228, 247, 249, 250, 252,
      256, 262, 274, 275, 290, 295, 301, 306, 312, 316, 339,
      347, 355, 389, 399, 407, 449, 462, 464, 465, 481, 482,
      496, 505, 509, 533, 555, 558, 602, 603, 614, 615, 629,
      630, 637, 654, 657, 658, 694, 696, 771, 866, 872, 890,
      1202, 1204, 1231, 1239, 1253, 1328, 1329, 1330, 1407.1,
      1532, 1547, 1593, 1818, 1820, 1863, 1864, 1890, 1913,
      1916, 1918, 1919, 1934, 1944, 1972.1, 1974, 2173, 2178,
      2180, 2181, 2183, 2312, 2357, 2359, 2389, 2501, 2508,
      2535, 2585

Literary history, pictorial, 261, 332, 554, 574, 1186, 1917,
      2062

Literary theory, Hawthorne's. See critical views, Hawthorne's

Literature, children's, 1219; critical history, 1660; 2077,
      2318

"Little Annie's Ramble," 1121, 1122, 1123, 1165, 1597, 2379

"Little Pansie," 1124, 1138

Liverpool, Hawthorne in, 291, 477

Lockhart, John Gibson, Adam Blair, 1592

Lockridge, Ross, Jr., Raintree County, 1503

Longfellow, Henry Wadsworth, Evangeline, 403; 891, 932, 935,
      945, 1218, 1515, 2238

Love, romantic, 494, 1244, 1474, 2052, 2515

Lovewell's Fight, 174, 1520

Lowell, James Russell, 380.1, 1395, 2497

"Maypole of Merry Mount, The," 24.1, 30, 44, 52, 91, 152.1,
154, 191, 312, 377, 491, 547, 574, 701, 702, 714, 742,
1128, 1178, 1180, 1221, 1404, 1442, 1451, 1470, 1550,
1564, 1596, 1597, 1618, 1692, 1724, 1792, 1793, 1888,
1980, 2069, 2080, 2118, 2210, 2282, 2313, 2320, 2379,
2409, 2438, 2439

McCarthy, Mary, <u>The Oasis</u>, 803

"McLuhanism," 190

Melville, Herman, 155, 180, 259, 264, 308, 339, 462, 549, 616,
675, 764, 833, 908, 1174, 1175, 1177, 1193, 1195, 1207,
1217, 1251, 1371, 1377, 1441, 1470, 1477, 1480, 1489,
1494, 1598, 1618, 1624, 1637, 1674, 1681, 1682, 1683,
1688, 1717, 1726, 1739, 1740, 1766, 1811, 1856, 2009,
2101, 2102, 2107, 2189, 2190, 2222, 2238, 2243, 2256,
2282, 2325, 2333, 2334, 2410, 2411, 2412, 2439.1, 2490,
2491, 2492, 2544, 2575; Ahab, 1826; "Bartleby," 1478,
1723; <u>Benito Cereno</u>, 860, 2574; <u>Clarel</u>, 2272; <u>Confidence</u>
<u>Man, The</u>, 1417, 2130; <u>Encantadas</u>, 1324; <u>Letters</u>, 546;

<u>Mardi</u>, 358; <u>Moby Dick</u>, Hawthorne's influence on, 443, 733,
734, 1183, 1668, 2570; <u>Pierre</u>, 237, 358, 525, 1209, 1381,
1531, 1638; <u>Redburn</u>, 2078; <u>Typee</u>, 140, 2100

Mesmerism, 108, 462, 2221, 2267

Metaphor, 1647.1 (see also Imagery)

Methods, Hawthorne's literary, 1427.1

Miller, Arthur, <u>The Crucible</u>, 166, 166.1

Milton, John, <u>Paradise Lost</u>, 437, 536, 1389; 1496

Mimesis, 2268

"Minister's Black Veil, The," 41, 42, 52, 91, 97, 128.1, 154,
169, 170, 275, 334, 353, 370, 377, 422, 462, 491, 493,
506, 607, 658, 699, 701, 702, 720, 791, 1178, 1354,
1388, 1418, 1442, 1470, 1561, 1564, 1597, 1703, 1884,
2055.1, 2080, 2131, 2210, 2211, 2259, 2278, 2319, 2379,
2385, 2400, 2412, 2416, 2420, 2430, 2438, 2439, 2462,
2463, 2485, 2571

Miriam, 163, 164, 850, 1267, 1268, 1945

"Monsieur du Miroir," 154, 592, 658, 1470, 1561, 1597, 1618,
2080, 2210, 2379, 2438, 2439

Montégut, Emile, 268, 2143.1, 2414

Monuments to Hawthorne, 149, 150, 731, 1173, 1910, 1911

Moral critic, Hawthorne as, 96, 97,

More, Paul Elmer, 589

Mosses from an Old Manse, 28, 85.1, 185, 210, 262, 275, 339,
379, 530, 537, 538, 580, 701, 707, 801, 1221, 1260,
1296, 1442, 1470, 1564, 1597, 1617, 1618, 1665, 1688,
1853, 2101, 2107, 2180, 2181, 2183, 2285, 2313, 2334,
2379, 2412, 2438, 2439, 2570

Mosses from an Old Manse (editions), 1036, 1037, 1038, 1039,
1040

Mother Alphonsa, O. S. D., 299, 300

Motif, dance, 2576; folklore, 272; general, 325, 1508;
mysterious stranger, 1566; Theseus, 2006; Wandering
Jew, 53, 462, 581, 1192; witchcraft, 581

Motif - Journey, 233, 245, 567, 1476, 2063

Motive (motivation), 1352, 2042

"Rappaccini's Daughter," 24, 24.1, 29, 43, 45.1, 54, 56, 85,
85.1, 91, 96, 136, 138, 154, 185, 193, 204, 236, 251,
252, 275, 312, 379, 409, 462, 486, 518, 526, 530, 536,
545, 565.1, 581, 628, 630, 634, 635, 640, 658, 662, 676,
690, 701, 714, 720, 726, 748, 855, 1221, 1232, 1234,
1244, 1315, 1348, 1354, 1366, 1388, 1389, 1418, 1423,
1442, 1450, 1470, 1496, 1530, 1541, 1558, 1561, 1564,
1586, 1590, 1597, 1618, 1631, 1656, 1682, 1730, 1853,
1867, 1884, 1888, 1891, 1912, 1915, 1945, 1950, 1952,
1953, 1980, 2007, 2011, 2014.1, 2015, 2036, 2049, 2055,

Rapp, Father George, 565.1

Radcliffe, Anne, The Mysteries of Udolpho, 42

Queen Christina, 158

Quakerism, 734, 827

Pyncheon, Phoebe, 1656

Pyncheon, Judge, 1530, 1851

Pyncheon, House of, 144, 1344.1

Pyncheon, Hepzibah, 1656

Pyncheon, Clifford, 441, 1293

Puritanism, 23, 36, 44, 46, 71, 84, 85.1, 100, 124, 135, 153,
160, 186, 199, 248, 305, 312, 339, 357, 358, 398, 442,
450, 462, 485, 544, 570, 588, 608, 666, 686, 817, 866,
1178, 1239, 1258, 1354, 1363, 1377, 1452, 1618, 1622,
1623, 1672, 1687, 1692, 1738, 1749, 1793, 1809, 1875,
1881, 1931, 1936, 1940, 1957, 2069, 2091, 2121, 2209,
2210, 2214, 2290, 2309, 2310, 2368, 2397, 2485, 2554,
2555, 2587

"Rappaccini's Daughter," cont.

2080, 2093, 2131, 2156, 2209, 2210, 2222, 2223, 2224, 2274, 2313, 2319, 2379, 2400, 2430, 2438, 2439, 2443, 2466, 2488, 2512, 2516.1, 2520.1, 2572

Read, Herbert, 1190

Reader, Hawthorne's, 852

Reading, Hawthorne's, 211, 314, 331, 433.1, 520, 918, 1373, 1374, 1409, 1839.1, 1976.1, 2481

Realism, Hawthorne's inclination to, 339, 509, 654, 665, 823, 837, 1256, 1853, 2040

"Recollections of a Gifted Woman," 1142

Redemption, 545, 1315, 1562, 1754, 2234, 2433

Reed, Sampson, 331

Reform and reformers, 510, 576, 1178, 1583, 2054, 2055, 2370

Regionalism, Hawthorne's, 462

Relevance, Hawthorne's, 63, 85.1, 89, 363, 441, 616, 640, 687, 1340, 1471, 1939

Relics, Hawthorne, 1166

Religion, Hawthorne's concept and use of, 24.1, 320, 667, 668, 2293, 2325, 2409

Renaissance, American, 26, 31, 1618

Reputation, Hawthorne's literary, 22, 31, 121, 146, 147, 188, 302, 311, 323, 324, 339, 393, 403.1, 656, 687, 693, 729.1, 763, 812, 847, 873, 886, 1167, 1172, 1266, 1271, 1322.1, 1355, 1390, 1413, 1667, 1713, 1872, 1886.1, 2075, 2231, 2258

Reputation, Hawthorne's literary (English), 33, 64, 157, 656, 783, 785, 787, 816, 1488, 1537, 1570, 2020, 2021, 2363, 2430

Reputation, Hawthorne's literary, European, 2430; French, 268; German, 662, 1196, 1765.2, 2349, 2350; Italian, 317, 1890; Spanish, 663, 1892

Research, trends in, 50, 193, 1208, 1438, 1439, 1882, 1973, 2251, 2277, 2381, 2434, 2435, 2436, 2437, 2560, 2561

Reverie, Hawthorne's use of, 479

Reviews during Hawthorne's lifetime, 403.1, 1665, 1872, 1885, 1886, 1886.1, 1887, 2333, 2596

Revisions, Hawthorne's, 839, 1680, 2380

"Rill from the Town Pump, A," 185, 339, 630, 701, 1143, 1144, 1221, 1470, 1597, 1618, 1686, 2080, 2557

Ritual, 24.1, 1221, 1224, 2210

"RLR," 1226, 1368, 1369, 2154

"Roger Malvin's Burial," 24.1, 30, 174, 184, 377, 462, 488, 568, 581, 630, 742, 1178, 1232, 1296, 1466.1, 1470, 1520, 1564, 1597, 1639, 1682, 1797, 1829, 1838, 1989, 2002, 2011, 2039, 2080, 2223, 2261, 2262, 2320, 2328, 2379, 2400, 2401, 2438, 2439, 2517, 2557

Rogers, Richard S. (See "RLR")

Romance, 71, 152.1, 176, 185, 291.1, 391, 392, 396.1, 404, 686, 868, 1222, 1309, 1321, 1380, 1493, 1499, 1507, 1800, 1830, 1839, 1862, 1893, 1931, 1993, 2038, 2147, 2166, 2290, 2291.1, 2292, 2295, 2357, 2372, 2390

The Romance of Monte Beni. See Marble Faun

Romantic Individualism, 6, 252, 494,

Romanticism, 26, 31, 53, 114.1, 117, 200, 205, 227, 249, 262, 333.1, 339, 509, 570, 709, 821, 1198, 1232, 1234, 1247, 1342, 1351, 1370, 1561, 1581, 1582, 1645, 1745, 1785, 1795, 1816, 1856.1, 1857, 1912, 1993, 2040, 2084, 2219, 2275, 2280, 2514

Rome, Hawthorne in, 258, 761, 1345, 1398, 1914, 1946

Ruskin, John, 1504, 2207

Salem, 106, 132, 253, 307, 760, 792, 793, 923.2, 925.1, 1274, 1441.1, 1464, 1646, 1756, 1994, 2026, 2032, 2079, 2115, 2284; transcendentalism in, 2004.1

Sand, George, 817, 2518

Sargent, Epes, 2045

Satire, 77, 100, 374.1, 580, 1584, 1679, 2121, 2285, 2464

Scarlet Letter, The, 3, 5, 6, 7, 8, 9, 9.1, 11, 16, 17, 23, 24, 29, 30, 44, 51, 52, 54.1, 56, 63, 74, 75.1, 78, 79, 80, 84, 87, 88, 96, 98, 99, 100, 106, 111, 118, 125, 126, 127, 128.1, 135, 138, 139, 141, 152, 152.1, 157, 166, 166.1, 166.3, 168, 169, 176, 183, 186, 187, 191, 192, 195, 199, 203, 206, 207, 210, 215, 216, 219, 225, 226, 228, 230, 235, 236, 242, 246, 248, 275, 278, 283, 288, 307, 309, 312, 316, 319, 335, 336, 337, 339, 340, 347, 355, 356, 357, 359, 363, 364, 371, 373, 374, 377, 382, 388, 390, 391, 392, 401, 403.1, 404, 407, 409, 413, 419, 436, 452.1, 461, 462, 465,

Scarlet Letter, The, cont.

466, 467, 472, 474, 490, 491, 518, 523, 526, 527, 528, 529,
530, 534, 544, 553, 555, 562, 564, 570, 574, 576, 578, 583,
585, 588, 596, 597, 603, 608, 626, 628, 633, 645, 650, 654,
657, 659, 662, 667, 668, 672, 673, 676, 686, 701, 703, 714,
715.1, 720, 727, 729, 736, 756, 759, 767, 768, 769, 771,
777, 781, 804, 805, 806, 807, 837, 842, 843, 844, 851,
857.1, 862, 863, 866, 869, 870, 872, 874, 887, 895, 898,
920, 925, 944, 1065.1, 1178, 1185, 1198, 1220, 1232, 1234,
1242, 1243, 1256, 1270, 1279, 1299, 1304.1, 1314, 1315,
1334, 1347, 1350, 1352, 1354, 1361, 1362, 1385, 1391,

1400, 1412, 1423, 1424, 1431, 1432, 1441.1, 1441.2, 1442,
1451, 1454, 1459, 1463, 1465, 1468, 1469, 1470, 1483, 1490,
1507, 1516, 1527, 1530, 1544, 1546, 1551, 1559, 1561, 1562,
1564, 1570.1, 1571, 1572, 1578, 1580, 1586, 1592, 1597,
1600, 1603, 1610, 1614, 1617, 1618, 1619, 1622, 1624, 1632,
1643, 1644, 1647, 1654, 1656, 1658, 1672, 1674, 1677, 1682,
1690, 1692, 1698, 1716, 1738, 1742, 1749, 1754, 1767, 1772,
1780, 1783, 1790, 1793, 1794, 1795, 1802, 1807, 1830, 1834,
1854, 1860, 1874, 1884, 1888, 1893, 1919, 1922, 1934, 1936,
1938, 1939, 1940, 1942, 1944, 1945, 1964, 1966, 1968, 1969,

1970, 1980, 2003, 2004, 2012, 2016, 2017, 2018, 2019, 2021,
2024, 2033, 2035, 2037, 2039, 2042, 2044, 2052, 2055, 2059,
2064, 2069, 2080, 2085, 2088, 2091, 2092, 2102, 2103, 2108,
2110, 2113, 2116.1, 2123, 2124, 2131, 2132, 2135.1, 2142,
2143, 2148, 2149, 2170, 2177, 2180, 2181, 2183, 2193, 2194,
2194.1, 2195, 2196, 2199, 2204, 2209, 2210, 2214, 2216.1,
2220, 2222, 2224, 2263, 2268.1, 2269, 2273.1, 2274, 2275,

Teaching Aids..., cont.

"Celestial Railroad, The," 1466.1, 2547; "Custom House,
The," 672; "Dr. Heidegger's Experiment," 1999; "Feathertop,"
1290; "Ethan Brand," 122; "Gray Champion, The," 1774;
"Great Stone Face, The," 627, 730, 810, 881, 894, 1227,
1697, 2141, 2355; House of the Seven Gables, The, 61, 90,
441, 611, 766, 1021, 1384, 1670, 1684, 1984, 2454.1;
"Lady Eleanor's Mantle," 2139; "Minister's Black Veil,
The," 1393; "Mr. Higginbotham's Catastrophe," 2125;
"My Kinsman, Major Molineux, 365.1, 858, 1292.1, 1455,
2192, 2213; "Pine Tree Shillings, The," 1291; Scarlet
Letter, The, 141, 515, 1339, 1932, 1979, 2022, 2169,
2521.1, 2528; "Rappaccini's Daughter," 661, 1366;
Twice-Told Tales, 1383; "Wakefield," 754; "Young Goodman
Brown," 452, 744, 1494.1, 1552, 1978, 2136, 2142.1, 2215

Techniques, 192, 294, 298, 313, 425, 461, 524, 636, 845, 1362,
1596, 1597, 1631, 1644, 1787, 2082, 2408, 2467, 2583

Technology (see Machine)

Thaxter, Celia, 2513

Themes, Hawthorne's, 24.1, 86, 100, 148, 166, 192, 197, 216,
248, 274, 294, 301, 305, 325, 364, 462, 491, 508, 547,
550, 565, 578, 582, 586.1, 633, 692, 755, 944, 1305, 1346,
1375.1, 1402, 1411, 1526, 1597, 1630, 1686, 1723, 1729,
1798, 1912, 1933, 1934, 1937, 1980, 2039, 2073, 2150,
2301, 2319, 2320, 2330, 2441, 2454.1

Theocracy, 651, 1377

"Thomas Green Fessenden," 1149

"Twenty Days with Julian and Little Bunny," (American Notebooks,
   also reprinted separately, New York, 1904), 128.1

Twice-Told Tales, 58, 85.1, 256, 272, 275, 339, 340, 404, 499,
   500, 530, 662, 701, 720, 759, 771, 1178, 1221, 1364, 1442,
   1470, 1515.1, 1564, 1617, 1618, 1647, 1709, 1789, 1837,
   1884, 1885, 1886, 1886.1, 1887, 1893, 1919, 2057, 2069,
   2094, 2180, 2181, 2183, 2313, 2379, 2438, 2439

Twice-Told Tales (editions), 1076, 1077, 1078, 1079, 1080,
   1081, 1082, 1083

Typesetting, 387

Typology, 160, 287, 446, 550

Tyranny, American women, 137.2

Ukraiъa, Lesya, In the Wilderness, 1574

Unitarianism, 1377

Unity, Hawthorne's, 703.1

Upham, Thomas C., 1423

Utilitarianism, 1628, 1849

Utopia, 137, 140, 251, 257, 258, 380, 512, 697, 786, 803,
   871, 877, 936, 1246, 1255, 1289, 1323, 1354, 1814, 1923,
   2493

Vanzetti, Bartolomeo, 847.3

Very, Jones, 77

"Village Uncle, The," 52, 183, 406, 412, 571, 585, 1221,
   1296, 1485, 1597, 1618, 2313, 2379

Villains, Hawthorne's, 125, 1530

"Virtuoso's Collection, A," 43, 52, 53, 154, 185, 537, 581, 592, 701, 792, 793, 1221, 1314, 1470, 1564, 1597, 1618, 2080, 2210, 2379

"Vision of the Fountain, The," 52, 154, 840, 1597, 2080, 2319, 2379

"Visit to the Celestial City, The," 1156

"Visit to the Clerk of the Weather, A," 1157

"Visit to an Old English Abbey, A," 1158

Voltaire, Francois Marie Arouet de, 540

"Wakefield," 24.1, 95, 97, 128.1, 154, 167, 198, 252, 312, 630, 650, 658, 701, 702, 1221, 1354, 1470, 1597, 1618, 1821, 1884, 2063, 2080, 2313, 2319, 2379, 2398, 2438, 2439, 2467, 2485

Wayside, The, 105, 484, 773, 1517, 1518, 2237

"Weal-Reaf,....." 1159

Webber, Charles Wilkins, 2255

"Wedding Knell, The," 24.1, 701, 714, 896, 1221, 1233, 1470, 1597, 2080, 2379

"White Old Maid, The," 52, 185, 339, 340, 896, 1178, 1470, 1597, 1686, 2080, 2313, 2379, 2401

Whitman, Walt, 246, 259, 2596

Whittier, J. G., 2255

Will, 1423, 2088

Wilson, Edmund, 2010

Witchcraft trials, 1464, 1994

Table of Abbreviations
and Publications

TABLE OF ABBREVIATIONS AND PUBLICATIONS

ABC	American Book Collector
Accent	
AHR	American Historical Review
AI	American Imago
AIUO-SG	Annali Instituto Universitario Orientale, Napoli, Sezione Germanica.
AJGE	Aoyama Journal of General Education (Tokyo)
AL	American Literature
AmC	American College
Americana	
AMH	Annals of Medical History
AmH	American Heritage
AmM	American Mercury
AmMag	American Magazine
AmMMag	American Monthly Magazine
AmN	American Neptune
AmNor	American Norvegica
AmR	American Review
AmRR	American Monthly Review of Reviews
AmSp	American Spectator
AmSR	American Scandinavian Review

<u>Anglia</u>	
AN&Q	American Notes & Queries (New Haven, Conn.)
AQ	American Quarterly
<u>Archiv</u>	Archiv fur das Studium der neueren Sprachen und Literaturen
ArcHQ	Archaeological and Historical Quarterly, Ohio State University
<u>Arena</u>	
ArQ	Arizona Quarterly
AS	American Speech
ASch	American Scholar
ASocR	American Sociological Review
<u>Athenaeum</u> (London)	
Atl	Atlantic
AtlM	Atlantic Monthly
ATQ	American Transcendental Quarterly
AuCJ	Autograph Collector's Journal
AUMLA	Journal of the Australasian Universities Language and Literature Association
BA	Books Abroad
BardR	Bard Review
BB	Bulletin of Bibliography
BBPL	Bulletin of Boston Public Library
BGM	Boys' and Girls' Magazine

BKAA	Kieler Beiträge zur Anglistik und Amerikanistik
BLM	Bonniers Litterära Magasin (Stockholm)
BM	Boston Miscellany of Literature and Fashion
BNYPL	Bulletin New York Public Library
BookB	Book Buyer
BookC	Book Collector
Booklist	
Bookman	
Bookmark	
BookN	Book News
BowQ	Bowdoin Quill
BPLQ	Boston Public Library Quarterly
BRMMLA	Bulletin of the Rocky Mountain Modern Language Association
BSTCF	Ball State Teachers College Forum
BSUF	Ball State University Forum
BungR	Bungaku Ronshu (Konan Univ.)
BuR	Bucknell Review
BW	Book Week
BUSE	Boston University Studies in English

BwM	Blackwoods Magazine
BYUS	Brigham Young University Studies
CaiSE	Cairo Studies in English
CamR	Cambridge Review
CathHR	Catholic Historical Review
CathSJ	Catholic School Journal
CathW	Catholic World
CC	Christian Century
CCPLS	Colorado College Publication, Language Series
CE	College English
CEA	CEA Critic
CEAAN	Center for Editions of American Authors Newsletter (MLA)
CentM	Century Magazine
CentR	The Centennial Review (Michigan State)
Century	
CF	The Child's Friend
Channel	
Chautauquan	
ChesL	Cheshire Life

ChilM	Chilmark Miscellany
Choice	
CHR	Catholic Historical Review
ChR	Church Review
ChS	Christian Scholar
Cithara	
CL	Comparative Literature
CLAJ	College Language Association Journal (Morgan State Coll., Baltimore)
ClareQ	Claremont Quarterly (Claremont, Calif.)
CLS	Comparative Literature Studies (Univ. of Ill.)
ClW	The Classical Weekly
CM	Carleton Miscellany
CoLA	Country Life in America
ColbM	Colby Mercury
Colliers	
ColLQ	Colby Library Quarterly
Colophon	
ConnR	Connecticut Review
Conrad	Conradiana

ContempR	Contemporary Review
Cornhill	
Coronet	
C&P	Character and Personality
Critic	
Criticism	(Wayne State)
CritQ	Critical Quarterly
CrtL	Current Literature
CS	Christian Scholar
CSMM	Christian Science Monitor Magazine
CST	Chicago Sunday Tribune (Magazine of Books)
CurH	Current History
CurOp	Current Opinion
Cw	Commonweal
DAI	Dissertation Abstracts International (Supersedes DA)
DemR	The United States Magazine and Democratic Review
DenQ	Denver Quarterly
Descant	
Dial	

Diameter	
DickR	Dickenson Review
DiS	Dickens Studies (Emerson College)
Discourse	(Concordia College)
Discussion	
DM	The Dollar Magazine
DR	Dalhousie Review
EA	Études Anglaises
EALN	Early American Literature Newsletter
EclM	Eclectic Magazine
EdinbR	Edinburgh Review
Educ	Educator
EducR	Education Review
EIE	English Institute Essays
EigoS	Eigo Seinen (The Rising Generation) Tokyo
EIHC	Essex Institute Historical Collections
EiK	Eibungakukai-Kaiho (English Literary Society of Nihon University)
EiT	Eibungaku Tenbo (Meiji Gakuin Univ.)
EJ	English Journal

ELeaf	English Leaflet
ElER	Elementary English Review
ELH	Journal of English Literary History
ELL	English Language and Literature (English Literary Society of Korea)
ELN	English Language Notes (Univ. of Colorado)
EM	English Miscellany
EngR	English Review
EngRec	English Record
EngS	Englische Studien
Erasmus	
ES	English Studies
E&S	Essays and Studies by Members of the English Association
EsCr	Essays in Criticism
ESELL	Essays and Studies in English Language and Literature (Sendai, Japan)
ESQ	Emerson Society Quarterly
EUQ	Emory University Quarterly
Europe	
Expl	Explicator

FAGAAS	Frankfurter Arbeiten aus dem Bebiete der Anglistik und der Amerika-Studien
FLe	La Fiera Letteraria (Italy)
FMLS	Forum for Modern Language Studies (Univ. of St. Andrews, Scotland)
FMod	Filologia Moderna (Madrid)
FnR	Fortnightly Review
ForumH	Forum (Houston)
FR	French Review
Freeman	
FreieG	Freie Gesellschaft
FSF	Fantasy and Science Fiction
FSUS	Florida State University Studies
FUB	Furman University Bulletin
FurmS	Furman Studies (Furman University, Greenville, S. C.)
Genre	Genre (University of Illinois at Chicago Circle)
Gak	Gakuen (Showa Women's University)
GaR	Georgia Review
GentM	Gentlemen's Magazine
GM	Graham's Magazine

GMLB	Godey's Magazine and Lady's Book
GoldB	Golden Book
GoodWds	Good Words
GrT	Grade Teacher
HarpB	Harper's Bazaar
Harpers	
HarpMM	Harper's Monthly Magazine
HarpNMM	Harper's New Monthly Magazine
HEDC	Historiographer of the Episcopal Diocese of Conn.
H&H	Hound and Horn
HJ	Hibbert Journal
HLQ	Huntington Library Quarterly
Hobbies	
HoosF	Hoosier Folklore
Horizon	
HSELL	Hiroshima Studies in English Language and Literature (Hiroshima, Japan)
HSL	Hartford Studies in Literature
HudR	Hudson Review
Humanist	

IIENB	Institute of International Education News Bulletin
IJAS	Indian Journal of American Studies
IMM	International Monthly Magazine
Indep	Independent
InfD	Informations et Documents
Instr	Instructor
InternM	International Magazine
InternS	International Studio
INUFS	Indiana University Folklore Series
Italica	
IUF	Indiana University Folio
JA	Jahrbuch für Amerikastudien
JAAC	Journal of Aesthetics and Art Criticism
JAamS	Journal of American Studies
JAF	Journal of American Folklore
JASPsy	Journal of Abnormal and Social Psychology
JEGP	Journal of English and Germanic Philology
JHI	Journal of the History of Ideas

Jimb	Jimbungaku
JOrg	Journal of Orgonomy
JSKK	Jinbun-Shizen Kagaku Kenkyu (Hitotsubashi University)
Jubilee	
KAL	Kyushu American Literature (Fukuoka, Japan)
Kam	Kamereon (Kamereon Society)
KBAA	Kieler Beiträge zur Anglistik und Amerikanistik
KbM	Knickerbocker Magazine
KFQ	Keystone Folklore Quarterly
KM	Kansas Magazine
KN	Kwartalnik Neofilologeczny (Warsaw)
KR	Kenyon Review
LaHJ	Ladies Home Journal
Lamp	
LangQ	Language Quarterly (University of Southern Florida)
LanM	Les Langues Modernes
LAR	Liberal Arts Review
LC	Literary Criterion (University of Mysore)
LetM	Letterature Moderne

LetN	Lettres Nouvelles
Letters	
Letture	
LHR	Lock Haven Review (Lock Haven State College, Pa.)
Lib	Library
Lif&L	Life and Letters Today
Lipp	Lippincott's
List	Listener
L'It	L'Italia (Rome) Eng. ed.
Lit	Literature
LitC	Literary Collector
LitD	Literary Digest
LitD-IBR	Literary Digest International Book Review
LitHY	Literary Half-Yearly
LitR	Literature Review (Fairleigh Dickinson University, Teaneck, N. Y.)
LittLA	Littell's Living Age
LittleR	Little Review
LitW	Literary World
LivA	Living Age

LJ	Library Journal
L&P	Literature and Psychology (University of Hartford)
LuthCQ	Lutheran Church Quarterly
MAlQ	Michigan Alumnus Quarterly
Mandrake	
MarkR	Markham Review
MASJ	Midcontinent American Studies Journal (University of Kansas, Lawrence)
MassR	Massachusetts Review
Mentor	
MethR	Methodist Review
MF	Midwest Folklore
MFS	Modern Fiction Studies
MichA	Michigan Academician
MissQ	Mississippi Quarterly
MLN	Modern Language Notes
MLQ	Modern Language Quarterly
MLR	Modern Language Review
More Books	
MP	Modern Philology

MQ	Midwest Quarterly (Pittsburg, Kans.)
MR	Monthly Review
MRR	Mad River Review (Dayton, Ohio)
MS	Medieval Studies (Toronto)
MSE	Massachusetts Studies in English
MunM	Munsey's Magazine
MwJ	Midwest Journal
NA	Nuova Antologia (Roma)
Names	
NAR	North American Review
Nation	
NatlR	National Review
NBR	North British Review
NC&A	Nineteenth Century and After
NCF	Nineteenth Century Fiction
NChr	New Church Review
NCRev	New Century Review
NE	National Era
NEG	New England Galaxy

NEM	New England Magazine
Neophil	Neophilologus (Groningen)
NEQ	New England Quarterly
NewL	New Leader
Newsweek	
NineC	Nineteenth Century
NL	Nouvelles Littéraires
NMQ	New Mexico Quarterly
N&Q	Notes and Queries
NR	New Republic
NS	Die Neueren Sprachen
NS&N	New Statesman and Nation
NSt	New Student
NStm	New Statesman
NY	New Yorker
NYFQ	New York Folklore Quarterly
NYHTBR	New York Herald Tribune Book Review
NYR	New York Review
NYRB	New York Review of Books

NYT	New York Times
NYTBR	New York Times Book Review
NYTSR	New York Times Saturday Review
Outlook	
Overland	
Paunch	(Buffalo, New York)
PBSA	Papers of the Bibliographical Society of America
PCP	Pacific Coast Philology
Person	Personalist
Phylon	
Pioneer	Pioneer Magazine
Plays	
PLL	Papers on Language and Literature (Southern Illinois University)
PMASAL	Papers of the Michigan Academy of Science, Arts, and Letters
PMLA	Publications of the Modern Language Association of America
Poetry	
PQ	Philological Quarterly
PR	Partisan Review
Preuves	

PS	Pacific Spectator
PSQ	Political Science Quarterly
PsyR	Psychoanalytic Review
PubW	Publisher's Weekly
QH	Quaker History
QJS	Quarterly Journal of Speech
QQ	Queen's Quarterly
Ramparts	
RdE	Rivista di Estetica (University di Padova)
ReadD	Reader's Digest
Reader	
REL	Review of English Literature (Leeds)
Ren	Renascence
RevR	Review of Reviews
RHM	Revista hispánica moderna
RikR	Rikkyo Review
RL	Revista de Literatura
RLC	Revue de Littérature Comparée
RLMC	Rivista di Letterature Moderne e Comparate (Firenze)

RLV	Revue des Langues Vivantes (Burssels)
RLz	Radjans'ke Literaturoznavstvo (Kiev)
RPsyP	Revue de Psychologie et Peuples (France)
RS	Research Studies (Washington State University)
RUO	Revue de l'Université d'Ottawa
SA	Studi Americani (Roma)
SAQ	South Atlantic Quarterly
SarNMM	Sargent's New Monthly Magazine
SatR	Saturday Review
SatRL	Saturday Review of Literature
SB	Studies in Bibliography: Papers of the Bibliographical Society of the University of Virginia
SCB	South Central Bulletin (Studies by Members of South Central Modern Language Association, Tulsa, Okla.
ScbM	Scribner's Monthly
SchRv	School Review
SCN	Seventeenth-Century Notes
Scrutiny	
SCSML	Smith College Studies in Modern Languages
ScSt	Scandinavian Studies

SDR	South Dakota Review
SEL	Studies in English Literature, 1500-1900
SELit	Studies in English Literature (English Literary Society of Japan, University of Tokyo)
SELL	Studies in English Literature and Language (Kyushu University, Fukuoka, Japan)
Serif	The Serif (Kent, Ohio)
SFC	San Francisco Chronicle
SFQ	Southern Folklore Quarterly
SG	Salem Gazette
SH	Studies in Humanities (Doshisha University, Japan)
SHR	Southern Humanities Review
Shur	Shuryu (Doshisha University)
SierEN	Sierra Education News
SIR	Studies in Romanticism
SlavonR	Slavonic Review
SLitI	Studies in the Literary Imagination (Georgia State College)
SmCS	Smith College Studies
SNNTS	Studies in the Novel (North Texas State University)

SophiaT	Sophia: Studies in Western Civilization and the Cultural Interaction of East and West (Tokyo)
SoR	Southern Review (Louisiana State University)
SoRose	Southern Rose
SoUB	Southern University Bulletin
Southerly	(Sydney)
SP	Studies in Philology
SR	Sewanee Review
SSF	Studies in Short Fiction
StELLit	Studies in English Language and Literature (Seinan Gakuin University)
StH	Studies in Humanities (Osaka City University, Japan)
Style	(University of Arkansas)
SWR	Southwest Review
Sylvan	
Symposium	
TCL	Twentieth Century Literature
Thoth	Department of English, Syracuse Univ.
Thought	
Time	

USQBR	United States Quarterly Book Review
UR	University Review (Kansas City)
UNCSGLL	University of North Carolina Studies in Germanic Languages and Literatures
UnCh	University Chronicle
UMPAL	University of Minnesota Pamphlets of American Writers
ULR	University of Leeds Review
UKCR	University of Kansas City Review
UKCK	University of Kansas City, Kansas
UCQ	University College Quarterly
TWA	Transactions of the Wisconsin Academy of Sciences, Arts, and Letters
TSLL	Texas Studies in Literature and Language
TSL	Tennessee Studies in Literature
TSE	Tulane Studies in English
TSB	Thoreau Society Bulletin
TPWk	T. P.'s Weekly
Topic	
TokenAS	The Token. Boston: American Stationers' Company
Token	The Token. Boston: Gray and Bowen
TLS	Times Literary Supplement (London)

UTQ	University of Toronto Quarterly
UTSE	University of Texas Studies in English
VBQ	Visva-Bharati Quarterly (Santiniketan, India)
Vectors	Astme Vectors
VN	Victorian Newsletter
Voyages	
VQR	Virginia Quarterly Review
WayneER	Wayne English Remembrancer
Western	
WHR	Western Humanities Review
WisSL	Wisconsin Studies in Literature
WPQ	Western Political Quarterly (University of Utah)
WR	Weekly Review (London)
XUS	Xavier University Studies
YK	Youth's Keepsake
YouthC	Youth's Companion
YR	Yale Review
YSE	Yale Studies in English
YULG	Yale University Library Gazette